Deans of Women and the Feminist Movement

HISTORICAL STUDIES IN EDUCATION

Edited by William J. Reese and John L. Rury

William J. Reese, Carl F. Kaestle WARF Professor of Educational Policy Studies and History, the University of Wisconsin-Madison

John L. Rury, Professor of Education and (by courtesy) History, the University of Kansas

This series features new scholarship on the historical development of education, defined broadly, in the United States and elsewhere. Interdisciplinary in orientation and comprehensive in scope, it spans methodological boundaries and interpretive traditions. Imaginative and thoughtful history can contribute to the global conversation about educational change. Inspired history lends itself to continued hope for reform, and to realizing the potential for progress in all educational experiences.

Published by Palgrave Macmillan:

Democracy and Schooling in California: The Legacy of Helen Heffernan and Corinne Seeds
   By Kathleen Weiler

The Global University: Past, Present, and Future Perspectives
   Edited by Adam R. Nelson and Ian P. Wei

Catholic Teaching Brothers: Their Life in the English-Speaking World, 1891–1965
   By Tom O'Donoghue

Science Education and Citizenship: Fairs, Clubs, and Talent Searches for American Youth, 1918–1958
   By Sevan G. Terzian

The Founding Fathers, Education, and "The Great Contest": The American Philosophical Society Prize of 1797
   Edited by Benjamin Justice

Education and the State in Modern Peru: Primary Education in Lima, 1821–c. 1921
   By G. Antonio Espinoza

Desegregating Chicago's Public Schools: Policy Implementation, Politics and Protest, 1965–1985
   By Dionne Danns

A Social History of Student Volunteering: Britain and Beyond, 1880–1980
   By Georgina Brewis

Deans of Women and the Feminist Movement: Emily Taylor's Activism
   By Kelly C. Sartorius

Deans of Women and the Feminist Movement

Emily Taylor's Activism

Kelly C. Sartorius

DEANS OF WOMEN AND THE FEMINIST MOVEMENT
Copyright © Kelly C. Sartorius, 2014.

All rights reserved.

First published in 2014 by
PALGRAVE MACMILLAN®
in the United States—a division of St. Martin's Press LLC,
175 Fifth Avenue, New York, NY 10010.

Where this book is distributed in the UK, Europe and the rest of the world, this is by Palgrave Macmillan, a division of Macmillan Publishers Limited, registered in England, company number 785998, of Houndmills, Basingstoke, Hampshire RG21 6XS.

Palgrave Macmillan is the global academic imprint of the above companies and has companies and representatives throughout the world.

Palgrave® and Macmillan® are registered trademarks in the United States, the United Kingdom, Europe and other countries.

ISBN: 978–1–137–34325–3

Library of Congress Cataloging-in-Publication Data is available from the Library of Congress.

A catalogue record of the book is available from the British Library.

Design by Newgen Knowledge Works (P) Ltd., Chennai, India.

First edition: December 2014

10 9 8 7 6 5 4 3 2 1

Transferred to Digital Printing in 2015

*For my mother,
Mary Christine Wonneman Levi
who always inspired me to revel in the next challenge,
and for my grandmother, Virginia Kellerhals Wonneman,
the daughter of a teacher, a teacher herself,
and a mother determined that her daughter would have
a higher education*

Contents

List of Illustrations — ix
Series Editors' Preface — xi
Preface — xiii
Acknowledgments — xxi
List of Abbreviations — xxv

Introduction — 1
1. Visions of Economic Citizenship — 19
2. Practicing Political Citizenship — 43
3. Unlocking Women's Autonomy — 59
4. A World without Parietals — 87
5. The Dean of Women in the Age of Protest — 119
6. From Quiet Activism to Radical Tactics — 145
7. From Deans to Presidents — 169

Notes — 187
Archival Records — 235
Index — 237

Illustrations

I.1	Emily Taylor at her home during an interview with the author	2
3.1	Emily Taylor as a new dean of women, University of Kansas, 1950s	62
4.1	Emily Taylor at her desk, Strong Hall, University of Kansas, 1960s	105
5.1	Students work and research in Taylor's office library	133
5.2	Taylor with a gift from her students, a poster entitled "Emily Taylor's School of Feminism"	138
6.1	Emily Taylor leading a group discussion, 1970s	153
6.2	February Sister Sarah Scott as a University of Kansas student and an Associated Women Students leader	165
7.1	Kala Stroup, Emily Taylor, and Donna Shavlik attend an American Council on Education National Identification Program event	179

Series Editors' Preface

As this book makes abundantly clear, Emily Taylor was a most remarkable woman, educator and leader, and Kelly Sartorius tells her story by setting it in the rich historical context that it warrants. Starting with the vibrant national network of collegiate deans of women in the early twentieth century and extending to the tumultuous days of campus upheaval and change during the 1960s and 1970s, the narrative arc of this biographical study illuminates a process of transformation that reshaped American higher education. Taylor was more than a witness to this. Determined to free women from the tightly circumscribed roles that defined their status as "coeds," she pushed and prodded young women at the University of Kansas to take charge of their lives and responsibility for their behavior. This was not an easy task, and Sartorius perceptively describes the balance that Taylor struck in promoting a feminist agenda at a public institution in the traditionalist Midwest. Eventually she shows how Taylor helped to guide women at the university through the unsettled years of the student protest era, a time of unparalleled change in collegiate life, to achieve their goals for institutional reform.

Emily Taylor closed her career at the American Council on Education where she created a system that facilitated the doubling of women in higher education presidencies, a fitting capstone for a life's work dedicated to opening doors for them. Sartorius conveys the significance of her many accomplishments by carefully recounting the social and cultural tenor of the times, particularly with regard to gender roles and institutional resistance to change. This book is a welcome reminder of the distance that the nation's colleges and universities have traveled on these questions, and the critical role that a relatively select number of individuals can play in contributing to a very large-scale process of transformation.

Preface

In June of 1956, a staffer in the Office of the Dean of Women opened mail on the second floor of Strong Hall, the imposing administration building at the University of Kansas (KU). A letter in the stack bore the imprint of Ohio's Miami University. She unsealed the envelope, likely thinking it a letter from Emily Taylor who would arrive shortly from Miami to take the dean of women's post. Instead, she unfolded the crisp letterhead to find: "You have heard the old adage 'the bark is worse than the bite'? Well, in a way this applies to Miss Taylor. At first her natural tendency to make sarcastic remarks may mislead you, but you will soon find that they are all in fun and to be taken with a grain of salt!"[1] Taylor's two staffers at Miami had decided that Taylor needed a letter of introduction, and sent "a few pointers we have picked up," advising the KU women that "if perhaps you don't see their value now, save this letter and read it again in a few months!"[2] They provided a primer on Taylor's personality and tips for a successful working relationship, titled "How to Keep the Dean Happy":

> Her birthday is April 13, and she will make it known to you that this occasion will be celebrated starting one month before the big day! She loves coffee; cream is a necessity, sugar is out. She smokes Tareyton Filter-tip, and it is handy to have an extra pack around the office in case she runs out. Also, have several books of matches stored in convenient places. Hope you're good spellers or handy with the dictionary—also with telephone numbers and the directory.[3]

Clearly, the women enjoyed Taylor but worried that the KU staff might take an immediate dislike to her brusque manner. They closed by advising the KU staff: "It may look like we're painting a dark picture, but we are sure you will find that Miss Taylor is really a grand person with whom to work. If you feel blue, she'll pick you up; and she will always have humor to add to your daily routine."[4] The mix between caring, humor, impatience, rigor, and intellect meant Taylor matched few of society's prescriptions for women in the 1950s. She was not meek, rarely asked permission to undertake an effort, liked to be waited upon, and was free with her criticisms when encountering irrational thinking. Perhaps the only things conventional about her were her impeccable dress and her reliance on authority as a tool for her work.

While this book is not a traditional biography, it uses Taylor's life and work as a prism through which to understand the relationship between deans of women, feminism, and women's leadership in academia—particularly in academic administration and women's student governance. As such, it is organized by themes, roughly analyzing the phases of her career in relation to the history of deans of women in American higher education. To understand these core themes and Taylor's feminist activism, it is essential to gain insight into the woman herself. This preface provides a chronological view of Taylor's life, briefly tracing her career path, the distinctions she earned in the field of student affairs, and her involvement in the women's movement. Most importantly, though, it provides a picture of Taylor's personal style—one that was so distinctive and out of the norm that the Miami of Ohio women felt compelled to share it with the KU assistants in advance of Taylor's arrival on the KU campus.

A Brief Biography

Mary Emily Taylor was born on April 13, 1915, in Columbia, Alabama, to Lee Roy Taylor and Laura Rollins Taylor. Shortly thereafter, her family moved to De Graff, Ohio. Her father would have liked to have pursued law. Instead, he sold farm equipment and pursued various jobs outside the professional realm. The second of three daughters, Taylor recalled her mother's strength of carriage as a role model for her own demeanor. As a child, she often elicited chuckles by announcing she planned to be an attorney when she grew up—undoubtedly influenced by her father's unrequited ambitions. A born organizer, Taylor often created clubs among friends and she and her sister were active in church youth activities. By today's definitions, Taylor was a profoundly intellectually gifted child, leaving her outside the prevalent social norms for girls and women of the era. One of two individuals to attend college out of her 1933 high school class, Taylor graduated as valedictorian in De Graff and attended a two-year school, Urbana Junior College, where she earned an associate's degree in 1935.

Despite Depression-era financial challenges, Taylor completed a bachelor's of science degree in 1937 at Ohio State University (OSU). While an undergraduate, she lived in a residence hall and became involved in student activities run by the OSU dean of women's office. Taylor never married—her most serious boyfriend having died in a tragic accident during World War II. From that point on, while she did date on occasion, she became increasingly focused on her own education, then singularly devoted to her career and the students whose lives she touched. As a student, Taylor resented the tight rules and regulations administered by OSU Dean of Women Esther Allen Gaw and disagreed with Gaw's approach to advising women students. In particular, Taylor objected to Gaw's emphasis on marriage. "I even heard her say one time that people really had a choice between whether they'd go on for a doctorate, or go for a 'M R S.' And the 'M R S.' was every bit as good."[5] Even as an undergraduate, Taylor recalled disliking how Gaw framed women's education as a choice between marriage or degree advancement.

After graduating from OSU, Taylor taught at her former high school in De Graff for one year before a family friend recommended her to Deer Park

High School just north of Cincinnati, Ohio. At Deer Park, Taylor counseled students and taught English, American Literature, and a theater course. Her feminist impulses appeared early. As a drama teacher, Taylor often assigned women to play male parts to help them consider options outside of traditional roles for women in US society. She frequently referred women students to college and remembered writing to the president of Urbana Junior College to help secure her students scholarships and jobs. She must have been beloved, as the Deer Park students invited her to their reunions in the 1990s. While teaching, Taylor continued to attend OSU, completing a master's degree in counseling and guidance in 1944. Upon completing her MA, Taylor accepted a position as resident counselor in the dean of women's office at Indiana University (IU) in 1944.[6]

At IU, Taylor supervised Forest Hall, which housed junior and senior undergraduate women. She also found her lifelong mentor in Kate Hevner Mueller, IU's dean of women. During her time in Forrest Hall, she and a colleague conducted a study of women's friendships to determine which students were involved in cliques and which remained outsiders. Mueller asked Taylor—always a polished speaker—to present the results of the study to an audience that included Hilda Threlkeld, the president of the National Association of Deans of Women (NADW).[7]

Taylor's speech caught Threlkeld's attention. The NADW president needed a summer interim dean of women at the University of Louisville in order to handle the extra duties of this elected office. She hired Taylor as her replacement. During her second summer at Louisville, Taylor received dean of women employment offers from various schools. To sort through the options, she considered how each campus structured the rules and regulations governing female students' activities. She chose locations she believed provided latitude for women students—and the dean of women who guided them. When the president of Northern Montana College offered Taylor twice her IU salary to become dean of women at that institution in Havre, Montana, she accepted her first administrative post. Like her mentors, Taylor continued her memberships in women's groups, becoming president of the Montana American Association of University Women, and continuing her NADW connections. She served the school until 1951, when the college president resigned. She then chose to return to IU in 1952 to earn her doctorate with Mueller as her advisor. While still pursuing her EdD, she accepted the position of associate dean of women at Miami University in Ohio in 1953, planning to assume the deanship upon the impending retirement of Dean of Women Helen Page. Taylor finished her doctorate in 1955, and when Page decided to remain in her post, Taylor accepted the position of dean of women at KU in 1956.[8]

At KU, Taylor developed the dean of women's office from a two-person professional staff to a varied program including ten professional employees and numerous graduate assistants. There, as dean of women—and long before the emergence of an organized women's movement in the United States—Taylor's feminism was evident in her advocacy of greater independence for her female students via the end of parietal restrictions.

In 1958, she founded the first university Commission on the Status of Women in the United States, and produced and moderated a radio program, "A Feminist Perspective," which aired weekly from 1969 to 1973. A multi-decade member of NADW, Taylor served as NADW liaison to the Intercollegiate Association of Women Students (IAWS) in 1970, among other roles. She also served as president of the Kansas Association of Deans of Women and the Kansas Association of Student Personnel Administrators. Upon her retirement from KU in 1974, the Kansas Board of Regents renamed the Women's Resource and Career Planning Center she established in the dean of women's office as the Emily Taylor Women's Resource Center. Today it is the Emily Taylor Center for Women and Gender Equity.[9]

In 1975, Taylor left KU to accept a position with the American Council on Education (ACE) as the director of the Office of Women in Higher Education (OWHE). Her feminism drove her goal to secure more women at the administrative helm of the nation's colleges and universities. There, she would again work with former KU dean of women's staff member Donna Shavlik, who had once served as the executive secretary for the IAWS. Located at the ACE headquarters in Washington, DC, the OWHE office secured a Carnegie Corporation grant to develop the National Identification Program for the Advancement of Women in Higher Education (NIP). Today known as the ACE Network, NIP identified, promoted, and supported women in academia who were ready to accept the challenges of the presidency of an academic institution. This tactic addressed the regular stance universities took when searching for a president—as their search committees claimed they could find no qualified women to interview. The OWHE achieved success. Its programs helped facilitate the growing number of women in higher education presidencies as the nation saw women move from holding 5 percent of the top university posts in 1975 to 10 percent in 1984, just two years after Taylor retired. In addition, during Taylor's time at ACE, she and Shavlik wrote a guide for evaluating institutional compliance with the newly adopted Title IX regulations. The model they recommended became an accepted and institutionalized practice to evaluate gender equity. In addition, they worked with ACE's office of minorities to develop a similar model that could be used to audit compliance with Title VI of the Civil Rights Act.[10]

During her career, Taylor served a number of nationally significant groups, always using her post to promote gender equality. While at KU, she joined Women's Equity Action League (WEAL) activist Bernice Sandler's efforts to open higher education careers more broadly to women. Joining the national WEAL board in 1974, Taylor worked with Sandler to convince the US Health, Education and Welfare Department to enforce affirmative action requirements in higher education.[11] Taylor was also significantly involved with the state commissions that flowed out of the 1961 President's Commission on the Status of Women. She served on the Kansas Commission on the Status of Women from 1969 until 1975 and on the Maryland Commission on the Status of Women beginning in 1975, both by gubernatorial appointment. She supported the effort to create an umbrella organization for all state commissions on the status of women, and edited the newsletter, *Breakthrough,* for the newly founded National Association of Commissions for Women (NACW).[12] From 1975 to 1977, she served as NACW national president. Out of this network, she chaired the Maryland State Coordinating Committee for the International Women's Year (IWY) conference, and both she and Bernice Sandler served as Maryland's delegates for the IWY in Houston in 1977.

In 1978, the Women's Institute, housed at the American University, named her president until the early 1980s when she became chair of the board. The advisory council for the Women's Institute included, among others, Marguerite Rawalt, the first legal counsel for the National Organization for Women; Sandler, often called the "god-mother of Title IX"; and Sheila Tobias, a founder of the women's studies discipline and author of the influential *Overcoming Math Anxiety*. In fact, while Tobias' name has become synonymous with the advent of women's studies, she credits Taylor with her sudden rise. "She turned my book into a national best seller by framing three conferences around the concept, and recommending me as a speaker across the country. She saw the significance of the book before I did for the network of women already interested in women's education," said Tobias.[13] Through the Women's Institute and her longtime network within NADW, Taylor fostered the National Conference for College Women Student Leaders (NCCWSL) as a leadership training environment for women college students. Co-sponsored by the Women's Institute, AAUW, NADW's successor organization—the National Association of Women Educators (NAWE), and the Association of American Colleges. NCCWSL took the place of the 75-year-old IAWS, a women-only student government group fashioned by early deans of women. The NCCWSL continues today as a partnership between the AAUW and the National Association of Student Personnel Administrators (NASPA), which absorbed NAWE in 2000.[14]

Taylor's career awards are too many to list, though a truncated version reveals her influence on student affairs and higher education. NASPA bestowed on Taylor the eighth Outstanding Contribution to Higher Education Award and named Taylor a Pillar of the Profession in its first class of recipients; NAWE honored her with the Esther Lloyd-Jones Award for Distinguished Service; and the American College Personnel Association (ACPA) deemed her a Diamond Honoree.

After retiring from ACE in 1982, Taylor became an OWHE Senior Associate and returned to Lawrence, Kansas in 1986. In retirement she remained active as a consultant on women's issues, education, and, later, health care and hospice. A longtime Republican, Kansas governors appointed her to the State Advisory Council on Aging, and to the Kansas Board of Healing Arts, where she served for eight years. In the final five years of her life, after being diagnosed with leukemia, Taylor became interested in pain management through her service on the Board of Healing Arts. She founded the Lawrence Caring Communities Council to focus on end-of-life issues, and advocated for patients to die with dignity and in comfort. She worked to establish laws in Kansas that allowed doctors to prescribe pain medicine at the end of life without fear of legal retribution, and she served on the Kansas LIFE Project board until her death. Taylor died at the age of 89 in Lawrence, Kansas, on May 1, 2004.

Taylor's Personal Style

One distinction absent in Taylor's long list of career achievements is president of the National Association of Deans of Women. Though her name was often nominated, she never made the ballot.[15] Her style likely prevented election to this post. Taylor's no-nonsense, take-charge style appeared to some as brusque, especially in an age of narrowly defined feminine comportment. She had little patience for women administrators who approached "deaning" without a feminist slant, and her willingness to (and enjoyment in) debate ran contrary to the norms of politeness that many deans of women considered critical. Sandler, who adored Taylor, recalled that not everyone found her strong personality comfortable.[16] Taylor had a towering carriage that both enabled her success and sometimes limited it. Like many intellectually gifted individuals, she lacked patience, and did not feel compelled to smile politely just for decorum's sake. Instead, she blazed trails, willingly intimidating people along the way. She always cultivated important relationships she needed to achieve her goals, though some recoiled from her approach. Over and over, people recall Taylor's presence, saying: "I had never met a woman like her."

Politically savvy regarding working in a power structure at KU, Taylor anticipated decisions and "was always there first [often in front of the Dean of Men] so she would speak for [both of] them."[17] Staff members and fellow administrators understood that changing Taylor's mind took significant planning, a thorough understanding of the relevant data, and preparation with ready answers to meet her interrogation of the subject.

Taylor's own accounts of testifying at the state capitol reveal her imperious style, her disdain for unreasoned thinking, and her dedication to women's equity. As Title VII of the Civil Rights Act of 1964 called into question the legality of state labor laws across the nation, Taylor frequented the Kansas statehouse. When a woman testified to a legislative committee that her position was to work only on the blatantly discriminatory employment laws, Taylor remembers that when she took her turn at the podium she responded:

> "Excuse me, I don't know who 'we' is, but I'm not included in it. I don't agree." And I opened a book and my eye hit upon the perfect example...it talked about the governor's secretary and the governor's assistant and when it referred to the secretary it said "she" and when it referred to the assistant it said "he." And I read them this and I said, "Does that seem nondiscriminatory to you? Obviously someone has decided that secretaries are women and governor's assistants are men." And there was absolute silence for a few minutes.[18]

Within KU, Taylor and Registrar James Hitt often engaged in shouting matches, even though the two colleagues were friends.[19] Taylor readily admitted that some disliked her manner. Her tough-as-nails approach extended to her student advising. In fact, Taylor told women who wanted counseling about boyfriends that she had nontraditional ideas:

> I warned them that my advice would be very unconventional and that I had no sympathy for many things...[One] young woman said she wanted to talk about...this awful story about this fellow that she was dating [who] was treating her so badly and [she] just went on and on...I just listened. And then she said, "What do you think I should do?" And I said, "Well, I think you should get yourself another man."[20]

Former KU Assistant to the Dean of Women Donna Shavlik summarized Taylor's blunt approach and motivations:

> I think that's really where Emily was—every woman student should have an opportunity to be the best that she could be...every action that she took was designed to do that even though she challenged and chided people and made people cry, and she was very hard on a lot of people...She was very forceful, always, then and now. I can see that people both respected that and feared that.[21]

The result was that Taylor had strong, loyal supporters, just as she had others who disliked both her style as well as her controversial programming. She recalled being quite aware that "there were parents who would have liked to have had me drawn and quartered," and some faculty and other administrators also protested her approach.[22] The censure extended to at least one member of the Kansas Board of Regents, the governing body of the State of Kansas higher education system. When Taylor retired from ACE and returned to Lawrence in the 1980s, she met a woman who told Taylor that she was the reason the woman had not attended KU. Her father, who served on the Kansas Board of Regents, had refused to allow her to enroll at KU because he disagreed so stridently with Taylor's approach.

While Taylor's style was demanding and imperious, women often wrote to thank her later in life. The letters she kept encompass those from women who chose traditional routes to those who opted for careers. Several recounted stories like this one from former student Susan Comer:

> I had planned to enter the school of Social Welfare for my junior year...I casually mentioned that I had considered going into medicine, but I had several reasons why that could not be possible at that time. You got on the phone and in short order wiped away these reasons. You proposed that I major in French, as I had considerable credits in French already, and would thus have more time for the premed courses. If I still wanted to be a social worker at the time of graduation, you said I could get into graduate school in Social Welfare with a French degree. Within months of starting the premedical curriculum, I knew

that that was where I wanted to be...and am very grateful that I am not a social worker!...You changed my life.²³

Taylor's style could be abrasive, but her willingness to help women clear the bureaucratic hurdles of the university meant that many women suddenly found themselves re-routed into career trajectories commensurate with their abilities. Taylor's commanding presence made it difficult for students to say "no" to her recommended changes. In fact, many likely questioned the changes initially, but ultimately followed due to Taylor's firm manner.

As a result, her supporters were extremely loyal, recognizing how Taylor helped them mature. In fact, M. Kay Harris described Taylor's peremptory approach as a part of teaching Harris about her competencies:

> I think of you as someone who took me seriously at an age and stage when few did. [This] was one of the most valuable aspects of our association for me because I began to take myself much more seriously...I found myself working hard to merit your time and attention...You gave meaning to some of my favorite quotes about a woman's duty—"to face the world with a go-to-hell look in your eye," and "to speak and act in defiance of convention," and showed me how such obligations can be carried-off with grace, leaving strong and positive impressions after you. I learned from you that "being tough" and "caring" can go together well, a mixture that I had been taught to regard as impossible.²⁴

Clearly, Taylor's style jettisoned the quiet, complacent femininity associated with gender roles for women, providing a different model of womanhood for students to contemplate. KU alumna Carole Suzanne Atkins told Taylor, "You were the first woman I ever knew who had a 'real' job, where you were in charge, and who not only didn't have a husband and children, but who didn't seem at all fazed by this personal state of affairs. Meeting someone like you opened up new worlds of possibilities in my mind."²⁵

Taylor's hard-nosed, challenging style pushed students to consider what they might accomplish—even when they doubted their own abilities to do so. This book details Taylor's own brand of feminism—but more importantly, how she brought the streak of feminism that had always existed within the dean of women's profession to change the academy, working with her counterparts at other schools and ACE to permanently change women's stature in higher education.

Acknowledgments

This book began 17 years ago because Phyllis Brownlee, a 1940s alumna of Kansas State University, insisted on me meeting Emily Taylor. Mom Brownlee, as we called our housemother in college, did not insist often—so I agreed. For her foresight, I will always be grateful. The research for this book has been an odyssey that I undertook by serendipity, and for almost half my life I have enjoyed the lessons it has taught me. While my housemother introduced me to Emily Taylor, Susan Zschoche introduced me to women's history, American culture studies, and feminist theory as a 19-year-old. It has been a great pleasure to learn from her—few are as gifted in the classroom—and she embraced my growing interest in women deans as did professors Louise Breen, Angela Hubler, and Lou Falkner Williams, along with Albert Hamscher who never let me forget the importance of the craft of writing.

The greatest thanks goes to Emily Taylor and her sister Genevieve McMahon who shared their home and their stories with me as I visited often. After Taylor's death, McMahon has been generous with her memory whenever I have needed clarification, and both Donna Shavlik and Kala Stroup have repeatedly leant their recollections and interpretations for me to consider, as has Frank Shavlik. I thank all Taylor's former staff and students interviewed for this project—this is more their story than it is mine—especially Janet Sears Robinson who hosted me in her home and helped me trace key people, and also Ann Peterson Hyde who allowed me to use the photograph of her as KU AWS president on the cover of this book. Taylor's colleagues Mary Emily Kitterman, Bernice Sandler, Sheila Tobias, and Judy Touchton have all offered their memories or assistance in important ways.

I am not a traditional academic. My work has happened on weekends, early mornings, and when my family would disappear for activities. Archival research under those circumstances can be a challenge. I worked with several terrific archivists who made research possible despite my "weekends only, please" mantra including Becky Schulte at the University of Kansas (KU), Carrie Schwier at Indiana University, and Lindy Smith at Ohio State University—and most especially Ann Bowers of Bowling Green State University and Letha Johnson at KU who both went to extraordinary lengths to assist me.

After years of gathering material for this book, several helped me chart a path through writing the monograph. First, I thank Bill Tuttle who had faith in my topic and research, as did John Rury and William Reese. Mary Ann Dzuback, Elizabeth Childs, Andrea Friedman, Marie Griffith, Linda Nicholson, Carolyn Sargent, Leigh Schmidt, and Kit Wellman of Washington University in St. Louis all provided helpful advice about the writing process. Mark Jordan, I thank you for your sage advice on how to let theory define a project without overrunning it. To Jean O'Barr, I am grateful for both your interest in my work, as well as your very good (and effective) suggestion about how to finish. Sarah Nathan, Mara Berkoff, and Rachel Taenzler at Palgrave Macmillan, thank you for guiding this author through her first book. And, to Debra Michals, I appreciate your sage advice and development editing at the last stages when it became difficult to see the forest (or for that matter, the trees).

There are a number of people who have made this project possible. In my professional career, I thank especially John English, Kent Glasscock, Steven Rosenblum, Liz Townsend Bird, and Kim Schrier for their support and interest. For the nine years I worked among engineers, several cheered on this historian, particularly Noel Schulz, Don Lenhert, and Richard Gallagher. My author next-door neighbor, Mary Jo Colagiovanni, always shared great advice, Beth Shook read the manuscript when it most needed it, Stephanie Konradi engaged my son as the writing grew more complex, and Sonny Sagar twice rescued my research from dying computers. Research assistants Kelly Collingwood—and particularly Melissa Zissman—helped me create a final manuscript. Without Melissa's indefatigable efforts, the project would truly have taken another six months to finish. Perhaps most fitting for this book, I thank my long-time college friend, Amy Johnson Casey, whom I met on my first day as a first year college student, and who has helped me balance my life ever since. The friendship of my sister, Stacy Watson, has been a rock of support as well.

To my father, Donald R. Levi, I owe my love of research and writing. I am proud to follow in my father's footsteps by publishing a monograph (and I believe my son will have memories of me writing a manuscript longhand on a yellow legal tablet just as I hold a child's memory of my father doing the same on family vacations). Dad, thank you for coaching me through the writing process. I know you and mom read many more drafts of this project than you probably cared to! My mother, Christine Wonneman Levi, not only helped countless times as I tried to balance work, motherhood and writing (not always so gracefully)—she is also responsible for modeling strong, capable womanhood. A former physical education teacher trained at Stephens College and the University of Missouri, mother came from a family of women educators and is herself the product of the student government leadership structure that this book is about. My mother taught me I could tackle any project I wanted (as long as it did not involve cooking!), and both of my parents are educators at heart. I am grateful they instilled in me an appreciation for critical thinking and higher education. Mom and Dad, thank you.

Finally, this book would not have been possible without the patience and support of my husband, Erik Sartorius, and my eight-year-old son, Jonathan Carter Sartorius (also known as "little Jack"). They have both made innumerable sacrifices so that I would have time to write. Particularly over last five years, Erik has done so much more than his half in order to see this project to completion. It is impossible to thank him enough. Erik, your support has been unwavering and I will always be grateful that you made it possible to turn Emily's story into a book. Thank you for your patience, partnership, and your sense of humor. They are daily gifts in my life.

Abbreviations

AAUP	American Association of University Professors
AAUW	American Association of University Women
ACE	American Council on Education
ACPA	American College Personnel Association
ADWAGNS	Association of Deans of Women and Advisers to Girls in Negro Schools
AKA	Alpha Kappa Alpha
ALI	American Law Institute
AMA	American Medical Association
APGA	American Personnel and Guidance Association
ASC	All Student Council
ATO	Alpha Tau Omega
AWS	Associated Women Students
BGSUCAC	Center for Archival Collections, National Student Affairs Archives, Bowling Green, OH
BPW	National Federation of Business and Professional Women's Clubs
BSU	Black Student Union
CEW	Commission on the Education of Women
CGPA	Council of Guidance and Personnel Associations
CORE	Congress of Racial Equality
COSA	Council on Student Affairs
CPGA	American Council of Personnel and Guidance Associations
CRC	Civil Rights Council
EEOC	Equal Employment Opportunity Commission
ERA	Equal Rights Amendment
FBI	Federal Bureau of Investigation
FMWA	Focus on Minority Women's Advancement
GLF	Gay Liberation Front
HEW	Department of Health, Education and Welfare
IAWS	Intercollegiate Association of Women Students
IU	Indiana University
IWPR	Institute of Women's Professional Relations
KU	University of Kansas
KU-Y	University of Kansas YWCA and YMCA
KUCA	KU Committee for Alternatives
KUCC	KU Coordinating Committee
LWV	League of Women Voters

NAACP	National Association for the Advancement of Colored People
NAAS	National Association of Appointment Secretaries
NAWE	National Association for Women in Education (previously NADW, NAWDC, and NAWDAC)
NACW	National Association of Commissions for Women
NADAM	National Association of Deans and Advisors of Men (previously NADM)
NADM	National Association of Deans of Men
NADW	National Association of Deans of Women (later NAWDC, NAWDAC, and NAWE)
NASPA	National Association of Student Personnel Administrators (previously NADM and NADAM)
NAWDAC	National Association of Women Deans, Administrators, and Counselors (previously NADW and NAWDC, and later NAWE)
NAWDC	National Association of Women Deans and Counselors (previously NADW, later NAWDAC and NAWE)
NCCWSL	National Conference for College Women Student Leaders (successor to IAWS)
NIP	National Identification Program for the Advancement of Women in Higher Education Administration
NLWV	National League of Women Voters (also known as LWV)
NOW	National Organization for Women
NVGA	National Vocational Guidance Association
NWP	National Woman's Party
OADW	Ohio Association of Deans of Women
OSU	Ohio State University
OWHE	Office of Women in Higher Education
PCSW	President's Commission on the Status of Women
ROTC	Reserve Officers' Training Corps
RVSS	Rape Victim Support Service
SDS	Students for a Democratic Society
SIECUS	Sexuality Information and Education Council of the United States
SPU	Student Peace Union
STEM	Science, technology, engineering, and math
UC	University of California
UHRC	University Human Relations Council
WC	Women's Coalition
WEAL	Women's Equity Action League
WEIU	Women's Educational and Industrial Union
WFH	Women's Foundation for Health
WIS	Woman in Industry Service
WLF	Women's Liberation Front
WSGA	Women's Self-Government Association
YMCA	Young Men's Christian Association
YWCA	Young Women's Christian Association
ZPG	Zero Population Growth

Introduction

On an April afternoon in 1997, I nervously tugged at my blazer as I stood on the porch waiting for 83-year-old Dr. Emily Taylor to answer the door. My college housemother had arranged for us to meet, although I truly did not know what we had in common—this was before social media and the current ease of perusing someone's biography. I had completed master's work in American and women's studies, but I did not know that Taylor once led the Office of Women in Higher Education (OWHE) at the American Council on Education (ACE), or what that meant. At that time, women's studies rarely discussed the institutionalization of feminism in offices such as the OWHE. Nor did I understand what a dean of women was. The position had disappeared in the late 1970s after Title IX became law, well before I enrolled in college in 1989. Sixty years my senior, Taylor later confided that she met me only as a courtesy—but there we were in her living room in Lawrence, Kansas. She sat in a tall wingback chair by the fireplace, an imposing figure in a black dress, her left hand atop a silver-headed cane, her hair snow white. I felt small and unsure perched on the edge of a velvet settee. We began with pleasantries and I hesitatingly asked what it was like to be dean of women at the University of Kansas (KU).

That is when I discovered Taylor's gift for storytelling. She talked about her women students—Deanelle Reece Tacha, who went on to be chief judge in the Tenth Circuit Court of Appeals and dean of the Pepperdine University School of Law; Kala Mays Stroup, who became president of Murray State University and Southeast Missouri State University, and served as Missouri Commissioner of Higher Education; Mary Mitchelson, Deputy Inspector General at the US Department of Education; Janice K. Mendenhall, senior executive at the US General Services Administration; Sara Paretsky who redefined the image of women in crime novels by introducing a female protagonist; and Kathryn Vratil, senior judge of the US District Court for the District of Kansas, who, Taylor chuckled, likened being Taylor's mentee to being a post under a pile driver. How, I asked, had she found the potential in these women students as undergraduates? "The Associated Women Students," she responded. I had never heard of it. So I asked, "Was it a KU activity?" She laughed. "AWS was nationwide—it was our student government group for women. We used it to train our leaders."

And the stories began: AWS students arranging for a rape-crisis center; AWS students working with New Left radical feminists who occupied the East Asian Studies building, demanding university-provided childcare and

Figure I.1 Emily Taylor at her home during an interview with the author

free gynecological exams; AWS posting an organization chart of the university on Taylor's door just 200 feet from the chancellor's office. The chart listed all the KU administrative positions, and replaced the names of the employees with the sex of the office holder. It went: Governor—male; Board of Regents—male, male, male, male, male, male, male, male; Chancellor—male; and on through the ranks. Taylor, as dean of women, was the only female listed in the KU hierarchy.

I was hooked. How did a dean of women from 1956 to 1974 advocate for women's issues and equality from inside a university administration—especially when she did not have tenure? Why were her stories about sorority women, and not the New Left student radicals that historian Sara Evans catalogued as carrying feminism into the academy in the late 1960s and early 1970s?[1] Why had I never heard of the AWS? When I impulsively asked if she would be interested in me writing an oral history of her life, she declined. She did ask to read a copy of a project I had recently written. I sent it, and two weeks later, she called announcing she was ready to discuss the project I had mailed to her. Anyone who knew Taylor will understand when I say this was not a question of whether I wanted to meet with her, but a directive. I drove the 45 minutes back to her home, wondering why she found the project so interesting. Instead, I found that Taylor had reconsidered my invitation for an oral history—and we began formal interviews. The project continued for seven years until her death in 2004. No longer a student, I drove to her home after work once a week where we discussed AWS, feminist strategy, organizational politics, coeducation, the deans' profession, and the impact of the Equal Employment Opportunity Commission and Title IX on women's education.

Charting Taylor's career, I found links between deans of women, the Women's Bureau at the US Department of Labor, the Women's Equity Action League (WEAL), the National Association of Commissions for Women (NACW) spawned by John F. Kennedy's presidential commission, and advocacy for the Equal Rights Amendment (ERA). Taylor participated in the National Organization for Women (NOW) with her AWS student leaders, and her circle included "god-mother of Title IX" Bernice Sandler, attorney Catherine East, and NOW Vice President Kay Clarenbach; Women's Bureau directors Elizabeth Koontz, Mary Keyserling, Esther Peterson, and Alice Leopold; Jewish women's activist Olya Margolin; and even women's studies leaders like Jean O'Barr and Sheila Tobias. Through all of this, Taylor told a story of feminist activism in higher education. She talked of pay equity, opening careers to women, deconstructing gender roles, and women controlling pregnancy so they could plan families and careers. Yet, her starting point for these concepts stretched before the rise of the New Left, before Betty Friedan's *The Feminine Mystique*, and before President Kennedy's Commission on the Status of Women. None of this fit the "dual waves" theory of the US feminist movement that still reigned in 1997, and her stories clearly did not fit the "doldrums" I had learned about between suffrage and women's liberation of the late 1960s.[2] Nor did it escape my notice that Taylor was a lifelong Republican whose work occurred in Kansas, a traditionally Republican state today known for its social conservatism.

How did a dean of women foster feminism during the height of the Cold War when the ethic of domesticity and the marriage rate soared to produce the baby boom? How could a dean of women use the office in charge of women's discipline to teach young women autonomy, and about the possibilities outside of wifehood and motherhood? The answers lie both in the story of Taylor's career, and in the history of the position of the dean of women. This book explores both, revealing a streak of feminism in the profession of women's "deaning" that supported women's economic and political citizenship since the turn of the twentieth century.

The feminism inherent in the dean of women's role originated with the position in the late 1800s, when higher education in the Midwest and West opened its doors to women students, and presidents hired academically-trained women to supervise them. By tracing the training and career of Emily Taylor, this book illuminates the world of deaning from the position's inception through its dissolution in the 1970s. Taylor's life history provides a window onto the trajectory of feminism within American twentieth-century higher education, deans' efforts to move women into vocations outside the home, deans' role in the dissolution of parietal rules, the development of Women's Studies as a field of study, and even women's entry into the presidencies of coeducational institutions. Although deans of men would eventually co-opt the student affairs field by the middle of the twentieth century, deans of women crafted the premise that still largely undergirds the student personnel profession—the commitment to helping students fulfill their potential as full citizens of the nation.[3] While female deans reproduced white cultural norms and sometimes displayed racism and classism, the premise of full citizenship pushed the profession toward support of other marginalized students in addition to women. Just in Taylor's time at KU alone, she and her staff worked with students advocating on behalf of civil rights, the New Left, radical feminists, and gay and lesbian students.

Taylor's career stood on the platform of knowledge and philosophy developed by early deans. She had garnered her feminist philosophy and strategies from women in the deans' offices at Ohio State and Indiana universities, where she earned her degrees. On those campuses, she met her two scholar mentors, economist Grace S. M. Zorbaugh and psychologist Kate Hevner Mueller, both active in the National Association of Deans of Women (NADW) and with the AWS governments on their campuses in the 1930s and 1940s. Both women adhered to the professional conventions originally established by midwestern and western deans, drawing from the tradition of Progressivism.

Other deans also promoted principles of women's equality through their offices during the hyper-domesticity of the 1950s and early 1960s. Some entered the profession a generation before Taylor, like Althea Kratz Hottel at the University of Pennsylvania, Lucy Diggs Slowe of Howard University, and Eunice Hilton of Syracuse University. Others, like Dorothy Truex, Laurine Fitzgerald, Hilda Davis, and Sarah Healy came to their roles as Taylor's contemporaries. All of these deans of women carried feminist activism in higher education between the so-called two "waves" of the women's movement—suffrage and women's liberation—on some of the nation's largest campuses. Using student government to encourage young women to build leadership skills and individual autonomy, deans built roads for young women, especially intellectually gifted ones, to craft lives that would fulfill broad interests and capabilities. These women administrators created scholarships and financial loans for women, pushed for academic rigor, and guided young women to consider careers. They quietly brought sex education and information about reproduction into women's education, allowing them to learn to plan their families and control their bodies.

At the core, deans of women developed a system that helped women students shift from seeing themselves as contingent citizens, as primarily future wives and mothers, to full citizens exercising all the options available to white men. Theirs was a feminist project developed in an effort to open the world of professional work to women. Because they focused on college women, their tactics benefited women whose families could afford college or which did not depend on a daughter's labor. Largely, then, college women were white, like the vast majority of deans. While deans developed their strategies and tactics to serve the concerns of middle- and upper-class women who felt bound by the strictures of domesticity, some deans recognized the racism and classism prevalent in the white community and worked to address it. Many others did not and neither NADW nor their partner, the

American Association of University Women (AAUW), presented a welcoming environment for women of color before the 1960s. However, black deans of women found the same methods useful for deaning and adopted them for their students at historically black colleges. And, from the beginning of the profession, women deans linked with the labor feminists at the Women's Bureau which Dorothy Sue Cobble has identified as a coalition of diverse women from varying socioeconomic and racial backgrounds.[4]

There was a reason for the overlap between women deans, labor feminism, and the Women's Bureau. The first deans, and their practices, were born in the social housekeeping, labor organizing, and suffrage reform efforts of the early twentieth century. With the profession led by Marion Talbot at the University of Chicago, she and her assistant dean, Sophonisba Breckinridge, worked closely with Jane Addams and the Hull House. The Progressive philosophies and social feminism emanating from the Hull House underpinned their approach to deaning as they employed both Addams' methods and John Dewey's educational philosophy. This included support for woman suffrage, working-class labor issues, and civil rights. Breckinridge herself was involved with the National American Woman's Suffrage Association as vice president, the Women's Trade Union League, and the National Association for the Advancement of Colored People. Together with AAUW, these early deans produced knowledge about women, work, and citizenship from the fabric of Progressivism. Imperfect as their approaches may have been, they adopted the call for all women to earn equal pay and a living wage, whether as college graduates or as laborers. This laid a foundation for feminist activism in the profession of deans.

Historians of education have investigated deans of women, tracing how they developed the student affairs profession, and identified a quiet, careful mid-century feminism in NADW. These scholars explored the activities of the earliest deans from the Midwest and their later counterparts in the South.[5] This book's consideration of Emily Taylor's career in the context of the history of deaning is possible because of their scholarship. Even in these explorations, though, there has been little consideration of the Intercollegiate Association of Women Students (IAWS) and the AWS system of student governance. And, while education scholars have noticed these female administrators, historians of US feminism and of the New Left have paid little, if any, attention to the dean of women as a part of the production of US feminism. Deans are missing from the research on the women's movement, labor feminism, and campus protests. Many of the historians who defined the historiography of these topics were involved with the New Left themselves and viewed university administrators as conservative obstacles to civil rights, Vietnam War protest, and removal of the parietal rules that treated students as children under the parental authority of the university. In many cases, administrators did act as barriers to social change. However, as Christine Stansell has reminded gender historians, "there was a longer, quieter route to the new feminism, one that is overlooked when historians are too quick to fasten on to the combustion of the late 1960s."[6] Because historians of women and student protest have often focused on 1960s as the genesis of the late twentieth-century women's movement and the New Left, deans of women are missing from the predominant narrative of US feminism and student activism on higher education campuses.

Stereotypes have much to do with the forgotten deans of women. The prevailing images of these female administrators have clouded historical memory regarding both the profession and how these women administrators interacted with their students. The world they occupied bears little resemblance to today's college experience, which makes it more challenging to understand deans within their historical context. Until the late 1960s and early 1970s, women students lived only in university-sanctioned housing under *in loco parentis* rules that mirrored parental control. Without keys to their dormitories and sororities, women came and went from residences based on closing hours, returning by curfew when the housemother or residence hall director locked the doors. Anyone arriving late faced a disciplinary punishment—or she relied on a friend to help her sneak in through a window. In contrast, men lacked curfews, and held keys to their housing and to their freedom to come and go as they pleased.[7] Women's safety provided the official rationale for differential rules for female students. However, the primary effect of the codes was to limit unsupervised time between male and female students in order to enforce society's norms against premarital sex.[8] The dean of women oversaw this regulatory world and youth often viewed her as repressing fun, while parents considered her the watchful authority over their daughters. Rarely understood as scholars or as an integral part of a higher education institution, deans of women appeared at best as a figurative parent responsible for protecting young women's virtue from rambunctious college men. At worst, she was characterized as an unattractive old maid, overzealously disciplining students for minor infractions.

The reality of the deans' supervision of women strengthened the power of the stereotype. When universities first hired deans, propriety dictated that a chaperone oversee women students admitted onto campuses away from their homes and parents. Since supervision by a male faculty member or administrator ranked as inappropriate, women scholars found their first jobs as faculty on coeducational campuses *because* of their gender. These deans lived with the students, supervising them in a literal sense. At the time, neither society nor faculties completely endorsed women's participation in higher education institutions serving men. The well-educated deans of women who fought prevailing attitudes to achieve their own college training worried that poor behavioral choices by less serious women might shut the doors opening to women in higher education. To allay these fears, deans created strict rules of conduct to ensure proper behavior.

Rapidly growing women's enrollments in the early 1900s overwhelmed deans with the sheer volume of housing and behavioral guidance needs. Deans of women borrowed the eastern women's college cottage system of student government to organize students.[9] Beginning in the Midwest in 1913, the various campuses joined together in a national consortium of women's student government groups, which became the Intercollegiate Association of Women Students (IAWS). On coeducational campuses, AWS broadly influenced the daily lives of women students through both regulations and women's programming. By 1939, 84 coeducational schools registered women's student government groups with the national organization, and by the 1960s, over 300 universities and colleges housed an AWS chapter, including almost all of the large, public campuses.[10] Over time, it became common practice for women to vote on their regulations, though the dean retained her right to veto student decisions. The women's student government operated like Congress, with each residence sending delegates to vote on student matters. With this structure mirroring the US government, it is easy to see why early deans saw this arrangement as preparing young women for suffrage and full citizenship, teaching women the machinery of democracy.

From the beginning, deans overlaid this residential government with the concept of self-governance—an idea that would continue until parietals disappeared on campuses in the 1970s. Self-governance—not a simple synonym for student government—involved each individual student learning to govern herself according to the customs of the society and school. In many ways, this tied to John Dewey's theory that students could learn self-control by participating in peer groups which had adopted positive behavioral norms. Early deans of women invested in this concept, encouraging each woman to discipline her own behavior according to the campus expectations as set out by the student government of each residence. The earliest deans focused women's governance on feminist ends, teaching young women to make their own decisions through voting, extending their understanding of both autonomy and citizenship.

Throughout the first half of the twentieth century, many women deans used the AWS governance structure to help young women consider careers outside the home. Here, deans of women exposed students to hearty discussion about how to blend marriage and motherhood with work. Activist deans utilized AWS to teach women how to be autonomous individuals and ensured that women learned about heterosexuality and family planning in order to have a measure of control over their bodies and health, teaching young women to understand themselves as more than contingent citizens bound for the private sphere.

At the same time that deans implemented their philosophy of women's education, deaning began to professionalize. Universities tapped deans of men to manage male students and the forces of professionalization began to codify and normalize the deans' practices into the mainstream of university life. While deans of women remained in the margin of higher education because women were considered secondary to men as students in coeducational institutions, their methods moved into the mainstream of administrative practice for guidance and counseling.[11] These normalizing forces gained strength by the middle of the century and the feminist roots of deaning took a backseat in the developing field as it became increasingly performed by male deans of students.¹² As the field shifted, fewer deans of women reported to the president, and AWS rules grew more rigid at some schools.

If one considers this professionalized system using Michel Foucault's theory of discipline, the dean of women functioned as the university's panopticon over a separate sphere of women students, monitoring their behavior for the institution.¹³ The flow of power relegated women's participation in higher education to the margins of the university by segregating women students through housing, regulations, and guidance. Through self-governance, young women disciplined their own behavior into expected norms—many of which revolved around socio-economic class expectations for middle-class white women. Using Foucault's theory, a picture emerges of young women using student government to produce the gender restrictions that limited white, middle-class women's lives. In other words, student government taught women students to psychologically adopt behavioral expectations as a part of their personal identities. In this version of the narrative, we see how deans of women garnered their stereotype as dower disciplinarians controlling student behavior. The larger society, and likely many university presidents and their trustees, saw women deans in this light.

The history of deans of women is complicated by a bifurcation between society's prescription for deaning, and the feminist activism some deans of women pursued. Deans of women did not enter the academy on equal footing with other administrators. They existed because society considered young women as fundamentally different from male students, as ancillary learners to the larger project of academia. The fact that the word "coed" means a female student—not any student—serves as a reminder that coeducation originated and centered on male students with women added as secondary members of the campus. The institutions, administered by white men for white male students, hollowed out a small space for women to attend college. Deans of women oversaw this sphere of activity in the margins of higher education. Their advocacy was limited by several factors: a dean's own sensibility about women's potential role outside the family, the opinions of the president and governing board of the institution on coeducation, and the political milieu of the locale of the university. For public institutions, prevailing social norms acted as a further factor regarding which activities received sanction. Deans of women captained their sphere by navigating the political eddies of the administrative, faculty, local, and parental expectations. A successful dean of women charted a direction all agreed upon *and* used self-governance to encourage young women to follow. Feminist deans took the role a step further, balancing the competing priorities, and using AWS to foster non-normative beliefs about women's leadership, careers, and citizenship. The fact that institutions relegated women's sphere to the margins of the university meant that the deans *who could avoid public controversy* had broad latitude to foster their own programs.

What caused controversy varied across the twentieth century as behavioral norms for youth changed over time. In the early 1900s, it was a woman attending an off-campus party or drinking wine.¹⁴ By the 1950s, it was an unmarried couple registering at a hotel. Deans who wanted to foster feminism had to advocate change while maintaining student conduct that fit within the larger expectations of the community. Whether the AWS self-governance system produced conventionality or feminism depended upon the kinds of behavioral norms endorsed by the dean. Deans like Taylor took advantage of the fact that higher education treated women as "incidental students" and used women's marginality to foster a college within a college, a scholarly community of students where women could fulfill their personal potential.[15] These deans used gender segregation as a platform to organize an effort to break down certain gender expectations rather than to enforce them.

However, within every stereotype there lies perhaps a grain of truth. Unquestionably, some deans of women would embrace the AWS structure as a process for discipline in service to traditional norms for women. Some later mid-century deans of women, no longer scholars like the earliest women administrators, adopted the role of disciplinarian and panopticon. Instead of using the AWS to help young white women learn self-governance in preparation for full public citizenship and for leadership positions beginning to open for women, they adhered to middle-class norms and used AWS to foster young women ready for the traditional roles of women. These deans pushed college women to adopt the parietal rules and regulations as a prescription for socially acceptable behavior, embracing the gender role norms as a part of their personal identities. This was the path of normalization.

Not all deans of women abandoned the feminist roots of the profession, though. Taylor adhered to the feminist roots of the early deans, as did the deans of women at Purdue, Wisconsin, Minnesota, Alabama, Oklahoma, Syracuse, and Pennsylvania. The feminism of early deans created a radical foundation in the student affairs profession that still exists today—one that supported each student reaching her full citizenship in the society. This basis for the premise of social justice, still visible in student affairs offices today, arose not from the disciplinary function, but from the early women deans' insistence on student government and self-governance to build young women's leadership, decision-making, and citizenship skills.

Taylor, a strong activist dean of women who became a torchbearer of feminist practice in the academy, was one of the many deans who bridged the first and second waves of feminism within higher education. Though some deans would accept the hyper-domesticity of the 1950s and the subordination of the dean of women role in student affairs offices, Taylor—and other colleagues such as Dorothy Truex—would marry the liberal feminist tradition to women's liberation within their offices. She and her colleagues provided vocational guidance and self-governance to foster feminism in the 1950s until the wheels of the New Left carried the feminist movement into the radical politics of the late 1960s.

This study is about the time between the first and last deans of women, the story of how these deans used their socially sanctioned role in higher education to pry open new spaces for women in US colleges and universities. As Taylor always reminded the women around her, "There is no substitute for a seat at the table." Deans received their seat because society saw women as fundamentally different. As society shifted to Title IX and sex equity, deans of women disappeared. However, women in academia today still walk in the path they tread, with the feminism they developed now institutionalized in student affairs, career services, leadership and sexual assault prevention initiatives, women's studies departments, and fair employment practices. This book recovers a part of the history of feminism between the two waves of the women's movement and reveals the footprints deans of women left in today's higher education world.

Notes on the Word "Feminism"

This book chronicles a portion of how US women created and acted upon the ideology today widely termed as feminism. Writing about the production of an ideology and the activism it engendered creates a challenge of semantics. The word "feminism" has no easy, single definition. Over the course of time, the word has meant different things to different coalitions of people based on historical context. Taylor and other deans of women decided upon activist approaches that meet today's definition of feminism, though they did not use the phrase themselves before the end of the 1960s. Years later when talking about feminism among deans of women, Taylor described her colleagues as feminists "before we used the word feminist."

A brief history of the word "feminism" and the way historians have catalogued feminist activism provides a helpful context for understanding the work of deans of women like Taylor. The passage of woman's suffrage in 1920 occurred due to a coalition who believed women should vote—some supporters called themselves feminist, though most did not, and many advocated for suffrage for reasons other than equity between men and women. After suffrage became law, this coalition split up, and the word feminism linked with the efforts of Alice Paul and the National Woman's Party (NWP) to pass the Equal Rights Amendment (ERA). The labor-oriented activists in the US Women's Bureau fought Paul's group, concerned that the federally based ERA would gut women's protective legislation, which had been implemented in a patchwork of state laws across the nation. As the NWP locked horns with the Women's Bureau, popular understandings of the word "feminism" became negative, associated with the inflexibility of the NWP, and the abandonment of women's domestic responsibilities.

In the 1950s, the McCarthy era's drive to weed out "subversive" influences meant the word "feminism" became associated with communism, and organizations like AAUW and NADW steered clear of the term. In fact, when Ruth Barry and Beverly Wolf accused NADW of "feministic" aims in 1957, the organization responded by creating a committee to study the criticism, ultimately asserting the organization's purpose lay in supporting women as a separate group, though avoiding the word "feminism" and its negative connotations. By the late 1960s, however, the word was in frequent use, mixing its meaning with both employment equity and the more radical ideas of women's liberation. By the 1980s and 1990s, the feminist initiatives of the 1960s had become well integrated into our society's laws and institutions. However, the rise of the Christian right to political prominence again generated negative connotations of the word. Radio commentator Rush Limbaugh popularized the phrase "femi-nazi," suggesting that feminists hated men and desired the dissolution of domesticity and the elimination of families.[16]

Today, the word "feminism" in the United States largely refers to an activist doctrine that advocates for social justice and that all women and men should experience the same opportunities in the public world of work and governance, without women bearing an inequitable share of domestic or childcare responsibilities. It also calls upon society to understand women as full human beings and as more than sexual figures or future mothers, and focuses on eliminating violence against women, fostering healthy female body images, and other social justice efforts. Yet conservative circles within political feminism continue to carry a negative connotation of feminism as a rejection of motherhood and wifehood or marriage in a traditional sense. In other ways, though, feminist practices and policies have become common enough that some high school and college women see the word "feminism" as representing a historical phenomenon of sexism that has been largely eradicated.

The way historians have written the account of feminism has also shifted over time. Using a metaphor of waves to describe US feminist activity in the nineteenth and twentieth centuries, historians once identified two distinct periods when women's issues and advocacy held wide support—surging forward for suffrage, then receding until the next swell of broad-based activism in the late 1960s. Chronicling the period between the two waves as "the dark ages," the waves metaphor may have provided a useful way to consider the periods of expansive support for women's issues.[17] However, the metaphor eclipsed the quiet activism more recent scholars have identified between the suffrage in 1920 and the 1960s. And, as Linda Nicholson has argued, the waves metaphor suggested only one story of feminist activism, leaving out the stories and political motivations of non-white and poor women who never had the luxury of staying out of the public sphere of work. This left scholars in the 1990s and 2000s looking for a "third wave" that did not seem to exist, and made the gender activism during the times between the waves difficult to explain.[18]

Today, most scholars of feminism find that the waves metaphor shadows more than it reveals, believing it failed to capture the complexity and diversity of how issues of gender coalesced to both limit and enable women of various races, ethnicities, classes, and backgrounds. It also focused historians on two types of feminist philosophy—liberal and radical—and defined women's activism using those philosophies as measuring sticks for how feminism developed. The result has been that scholars of the "second wave" have generalized the philosophies of liberal feminism as belonging to older professional women, and radical feminist ideals as coordinating with younger women associated with Women's Liberation and the New Left.[19]

The split between liberal and radical feminism by generation obscures not only racial and class diversity, but also political and ideological similarities—*as well as* the purposeful exchange of feminist ideas between younger and mature women.[20] Taylor and like-minded deans of women used their feminist systems to foster the intergenerational exchange of feminist philosophies, deliberately mixing liberal and radical, younger and older, interweaving ideologies across generations to share ideas about women's role in society. Perhaps not surprisingly, in deans of women's work, elements associated with radical feminism also turned up in the 1930s, 1940s, and 1950s. These were always a part of the ideology, if often missing from the liberal strategies of implementing change in women's roles.

The majority of Taylor's career existed before the so-called second wave crested in the late 1960s and early 1970s. She exhibited a quieter feminism during the period between the waves, a part of the labor feminist coalition that Dorothy Sue Cobble identified as a diverse coalition of women across race and class divides working together with the Women's Bureau, advocating for women's employment. Though Cobble does not discuss deans of women, the feminist ones constituted a part of this coalition since the Women's Bureau's founding. Accordingly, many deans of women pushed for women's expansion into the public sphere, while supporting the Women's Bureau position against the ERA. Taylor recalled deans largely supported the anti-ERA position until the late 1960s, when Title VII of the Civil Rights Act and the following executive orders for employment equity changed the conversation regarding women's access to fair and equal wages. The careers of Taylor and her activist counterparts operated across these changes in the use of the word "feminism." Their stories tell us how our modern concept of feminism began, grew, and shifted inside higher education.[21]

That some women deans forged a part of the prevailing feminist doctrine from within the ivory tower comes as little surprise. When the dean of women's role was born at the turn of the twentieth century, the act of educating a female within a university or college, by definition, meant a woman student stepped outside the normative expectations for her gender. NADW and the deaning profession grew out of this history, and Taylor's counterpart, Dorothy Truex, once called NADW a "feminist organization with a ladylike emphasis."[22] Deans always advocated for a liberal arts education for women, and worked to ensure female students did not become limited to domesticated forms of education. These deans wanted women to access "[t]he essence of a liberal education...learning to think for oneself," as Barbara Solomon has called it.[23] Though not all educated women embraced advocacy for women, many deans like Taylor chose their profession in order to inspire young women to become autonomous adults. They pursued deaning to help college women negotiate the gaps between society's prescription for women and the fulfillment of personal potential. From today's vantage point, this activism looks like feminism. Just as Taylor frequently used the word "feminism" to describe her work—earlier and later in her career—so this book also uses the term to describe the activities she pursued on behalf of women's equality. At the same time, Taylor would have been the first to point out that different types of feminist thought and activism existed at different times in her career, and that specificity determined what was—and was not—possible to achieve during the various historical contexts of the twentieth century.[24]

Notes on Oral History, Biography, and Ethnography

Most of the history catalogued here would have remained invisible without in-depth oral history and the ethnographic approach. Anthropologists have long argued for the benefit of participant observation, for immersing oneself in a different culture for a substantial amount of time so that scholars build trust with those they observe as well as an appreciation of the cultural values of those they study. This, of course, is impossible for a historian. We cannot go back in time. However, historians can extend oral history past short, focused interviews to build trust between those being interviewed and the historian. My interviews with Taylor, occurring over seven years, allowed me to understand the world of deaning and enabled Taylor to build confidence in my ability to represent her.

Our interviews went through phases, beginning with formal interviews in her living room, often with dinner to follow at the dining room table where we were joined by Taylor's sister, Genevieve McMahon. Over time, they welcomed me in their home with less formality, and I began to carry beechwood trays with our dinner back to Taylor's bedroom, where she spent most of her time. Usually I arrived with a topic, which we explored for one or two interviews. For instance, how did her communication style play a role in building influence at KU? Why did she establish the national identification program at the ACE? On some occasions, Taylor brought out her own materials—letters, most often—to discuss. Sometimes, I brought a text—like Cynthia Harrison's *On Account of Sex* or Beth Bailey's *Sex in the Heartland*—to examine specific developments and interpretations of women's history.[25] Often, we talked over current events rather than interviewing, and for a short period after Taylor was diagnosed with leukemia, I spent a large amount of time helping her navigate the Internet so that she could read as much as possible about the disease. It was clearest to me then that Taylor handled a challenge by learning all she could about the topic.

Eventually, Taylor decided to let me into her world behind the public persona, greeting me at the front door in her housecoat rather than the businesslike dresses she had always worn. Still, it was not until the end of Taylor's life that she discussed the most radical parts of her work—counseling women with unplanned pregnancies, dealing with rapes, addressing back-alley abortions, and her involvement with the February Sisters' takeover of the East Asian building at KU. I attribute her willingness to discuss these activities at the end of her life both to the relationship we developed over time, and to her knowledge that the more radical parts of her work would remain outside the historical record if she did not disclose them.

When we began the project, she smirked when I told her of my plans to visit the KU archives to review the dean of women's files. Only when I talked with then university archivist Ned Kehde did I understand her wry grin. The dean of women's records were comprised mainly of form letters, news clippings, and publications by her office. When I asked Taylor about the lack of material, she said she shredded the vast majority of her files, and kept few records in the first place. This habit began in the early 1950s at Miami of Ohio, when the Federal Bureau of Investigation (FBI) conducted a major review of a student because the woman's file revealed she had participated in a conversation on communism during her freshman year. Taylor thought the FBI action overblown. Later, at KU, another incident confirmed her commitment to working with as few records as possible. There, a prospective student made an appointment with Taylor to discuss enrollment at KU. The need for the appointment puzzled Taylor as enrollment did not require her permission. However, the student explained that she had been dismissed from an eastern school for suspected lesbian activity, and that each time she applied at another institution, she was denied admission once her file was transferred. To shortcut the process, she asked Taylor directly whether she would be admitted. KU accepted the student and Taylor instituted a policy with her staff that they would not record sexual activity information in the office files.[26] Taylor's interest in protecting the privacy of students, however, meant she did little to foster her own historical footprint.

If Taylor's case is representative, part of the reason deans of women's offices are missing in the history of feminism lies in the fact that it is difficult to discern their work from the archival materials alone. Stacks of AWS rule books do little to represent the incremental feminist activity that went on within deans of women's offices, only reifying stereotypes of deans as strict disciplinarians. Activities seen as controversial at the time were least likely to be recorded, and only oral history can fill in the areas where the written record lacked substance. However, interviews also present the challenge of the fallibility of an individual's memory, and the fact that individuals perceive events differently and have various agendas that overlay their interpretations of events. Because of these obvious issues, I have relied upon archival materials to supplement and confirm the interview data which I amassed from Taylor and others. Without their memories as a roadmap, though, the archival research would not have been possible. In fact, the existing histories of KU lack a full understanding of the role Taylor's office played on the campus because the full set of activities are difficult to trace without Taylor's memory as a guide. At KU, the documentary evidence was scattered throughout the dean of women's records, the chancellor's papers, the AWS minutes, the Emily Taylor Women's Resource Center records, and the dean of students' and the dean of men's files. (The KU dean of men clearly took the opposite approach from Taylor as his records were stuffed with police reports and personal conduct reviews filed among more routine administrative reports.) Overall, the history this book explores depended upon my years of oral history with Taylor. I used them to map my journey through the archival records at KU, Ohio State University, Indiana University, the National Student Affairs Archives at Bowling Green State University, Women's Bureau records at the National Archives and Records Administration, and the IAWS records housed in the Schlesinger Library on the History of Women.

This biography, then, is part cultural history, part ethnography, and not simply a chronicle of one woman's life. Traditional biography, after all, has a debatable role in the historical discipline. Its reliance on one person worries scholars that the genre will fall short of helping the discipline to understand the pattern and context of a historical period and phenomenon. When biography is accepted, it is often because the individual ranked of such import to society that understanding his or her life becomes inordinately important—as in the case of Thomas Jefferson, Abraham Lincoln, or Elizabeth Cady Stanton. Emily Taylor is not one of these individuals. She worked in a marginalized field, with students seen as "incidental" to the project of higher education. She was an activist, much more likely to pick up the phone and organize an effort than to publish her ideas in refereed journals. The knowledge she produced ended up catalogued in lists of best practices for the IAWS, in status reports on women at the University of Kansas, and in the processes universities still use today for conducting fair searches for new faculty members and administrators.

Historian Leigh Schmidt, a biographer of marginal figures in history, notes that biography developed in the seventeenth century to catalog the lives of "worthy" individuals of significant social stature, and that the conventions of the genre push historians to find customary reasons an individual "counted" as significant to his or her society.[27] As an author, I have felt those pressures, looking for why Taylor's story matters to the larger society based on traditional measures. Taylor ranks as a significant player among women in higher education advocating for equity on college campuses. She served as president of NACW, as a WEAL board member, and worked closely with Bernice Sandler among others. Her work at ACE identified and prepared women for presidencies, pushing universities to change their selection processes for new leaders so women would be considered for the posts.

Even with these reasons to document Taylor's influence, the problem with a biography of a marginalized figure is that an outsider's life rarely reaches the conventional measures of worthiness. By definition, Taylor was outside of the mainstream story of higher education. The field of student affairs sits on the border of academia—an EdD less respected than the PhD—and many scholars look down on the field of guidance and counseling as mere support functions. Her presence inside an administration concealed her feminist advocacy in bureaucracy, behind student activities and within pragmatic choices between imperfect options. In addition, many historians who traced the women's movement in higher education participated in the New Left as students, which made them vulnerable to discounting older women's advocacy. The phrase "never trust anyone over thirty" percolated into the epistemology behind the histories of women's liberation. These factors left Taylor and her feminist counterparts rarely remembered in the scholarly record of feminism.

Outside of higher education, Taylor participated in many of the significant second wave events, though often just outside the main cast of characters so often recited in the history of US feminism. She attended the 1966 Women's Bureau convention for the state commissions on the status of women where the National Organization for Women was founded. However, she was not among the small group who met in Betty Friedan's hotel room to craft the plan for NOW. Instead, she joined the organizing group the next day through her good friend Kay Clarenbach. She took KU AWS leaders to the first NOW conference, brought Gloria Steinem to the IAWS meetings, and identified and promoted Sheila Tobias as a speaker on what was then called "sex equity." Maryland sent her as a delegate to the International Women's Year Convention, and her protégé, former IAWS Executive Secretary Donna Shavlik, took the reins of the OWHE when Taylor retired. Hundreds of women credit Taylor with setting them on a career path with ready skills for leadership. Still, only vestiges of Taylor's influence remain in historical lists of organizations, of student affairs career awards, and at KU in the name of the Emily Taylor Center for Women and Gender Equity. By these measures, Taylor worked in the eddies of the mainstream US women's movement; her story a minor plotline in the overall push to change women's status in US society. But, as Schmidt contends, the cultural historian can use the anthropologist's vision to turn "the mundane, particular, and negligible from miniature to panorama."[28] Implicit in biography turned cultural history is that the marginal world becomes central—commenting both on the mainstream, and on how those with non-normative views experienced and dealt with exclusion.

While Taylor displayed a distinct personality, she was not unique in her role. At first, I thought she predated and anticipated the women's movement of the 1970s. However, the more I reviewed the historical records of her mentors, the more it became clear that she followed in a line of feminist deans. This book traces the early work of deans so their legacy is visible not only in Taylor's career, but in today's universities. Instead of being a "first," Taylor's significance lies in the fact that she was one of the last strong deans of women still reporting to the chancellor and wielding considerable influence over women students and her campus despite the pressures for consolidation under a male dean of students. As one of the last deans of women, her story reveals the various types of feminism deans fostered through their offices. When Taylor reached the ACE, this meant she brought the philosophy and knowledge accumulated by almost a century of deans of women to bear on opening coeducational presidencies to women.

This book centers Taylor's life at the heart of the narrative because her story reveals the terrain of women's advocacy in the margins of higher education. Taylor's work illustrates how deans fostered feminism before "consciousness raising" found a name among radical feminists. Organized by themes rather than as a traditional biography, this book argues that the marginalized figure of the dean of women—often minimized by stereotypes of stern disciplinarians—is a "worthy" figure to understand. The themes of this book deconstruct the stereotypical image of the dean of women as a trivialized, dour administrator of rules. Rather than functioning as a figurative parent, Taylor and her staff acted as professional role models counseling women for career advancement. Instead of strict disciplinarians, activist deans taught young women to make their own decisions as autonomous individuals. And, despite the caricature of protector of female virtue, Taylor and others educated women students on responsible sexuality, providing information on contraception, counseling those with unplanned pregnancies, and supporting lesbian and gay students. Rather than dilettante bureaucrats, deans clearly produced new knowledge about women and work, as well as about the status of women in higher education, which ultimately created a bedrock for the field of women's studies. Taylor's recruits, though, were sorority women, former beauty queens, and the intellectually gifted women living in scholarship halls, all of whom she cultivated through their participation in AWS.

This book is a part of the effort to recover the history of higher education activism on behalf of women that occurred between suffrage and women's liberation—a time scholars used to consider "the doldrums" or "the dark ages." Since Taylor's 1950s feminism stands on the shoulders of the first deans of women, chapter 1 traces how her training arose from the thinking of early deans of women interested in moving women into careers. Taylor absorbed their philosophy regarding women's work, equal pay, and unemployment equity shortly after deaning professionalized. A network of women developed across several associations and the Women's Bureau to form a hub for women's career placement expertise, which the deans took back to their respective campuses. Taylor trained at two of these universities—Ohio State and Indiana—eventually becoming a part of the network of these midwestern deans of women. Chapter 2 also begins with early deans, outlining the development of student government and how it linked with parietals and self-governance. This governance structure became the IAWS and undergirded all of the dean's work. Though historians have overlooked its place in deaning, women's self-governance contained important elements of citizenship, which provided a basis for the feminism Taylor fostered at KU. Chapter 3 outlines how Taylor sidestepped pressures limiting deans of women so that she could implement these early systems of vocational guidance and student governance on the KU campus in the 1950s. This chapter investigates the ties between career development, student government and women's adoption of autonomy and citizenship. Here, Taylor pushed students to shed parietal rules in favor of what she termed personal responsibility. The fourth chapter considers how Taylor replaced parietal rules with a counseling system for sex education that included advice regarding contraception, unplanned pregnancies, and sexual assault prevention. Like her predecessors, Taylor believed women should be prepared to make personal decisions about dating, marriage, and planning children around a career. Chapter 5 considers how her activism on behalf of women overlapped with civil rights and the New Left, as she involved her office directly in the interests of these student protests. Next, chapter 6 illustrates how the various feminist theories and coalitions overlapped in her office, creating an intergenerational flow of feminist ideas between students, staff, and Taylor. During this time, the AWS transitioned to a fully political effort on behalf of women's equity both at KU and other schools. Chapter 7, then, considers how Taylor brought the legacy of deans of women to the ACE to open coeducational presidencies to women leaders, completing the project University of Chicago Dean of Women Marion Talbot and her highly educated counterparts began at the turn of the twentieth century.

Overall, Taylor's story shows the inner workings of a feminist activist effort cloaked in smartly dressed fashion and well-coifed hairstyles, which made feminism socially acceptable enough that many young women could see themselves as a part of it. Deans like Taylor bridged community and campus expectations, sustaining a precarious balance between change and controversy, quietly moving young women to see the inequality inherent in traditional gender roles. Taylor employed incremental techniques, often recalling, "You couldn't get too far out in front of the students," and her example shows that students did not always instigate parietal change. Rather than students prodding Taylor, this biography demonstrates that Taylor pulled young women along toward more freedoms and expanded opportunities. This trajectory flies in the face of the historiography of campus social protest, which places New Left students like those involved in Students for a Democratic Society as the anti-parietal agitators in the mid-to-late-1960s. While student-driven protest may have been primarily true for mainstream male college students, parietal rule elimination occurred very differently for the women students at KU. Taylor pushed sorority and residence hall women to adopt less university oversight *against* their wishes, insisting that women see themselves as autonomous adults able to make their own decisions. This is how women's social change was wrought from within KU. Viewing this history from the margins, the world of deans of women enables us to uncover their deep-seated feminist approach that today remains cloaked by stereotypes.

The story of Taylor's career shows that the divisions between liberal and radical feminists and between professional and activist feminists were not so separate on college campuses. Instead, her work was purposely intergenerational, linking young and old, liberal and radical, professional and the New Left. She implemented organizational change by mentoring AWS leaders and harnessing the AWS to produce calls for removal of parietal rules, access to contraceptives, unplanned pregnancy counseling, and rape awareness. These efforts extended nationally through the IAWS and NADW. Not all deans and AWS chapters adopted them, but many did. And while the structures born of gender segregation ultimately faded from campuses after Title IX, many of the deans' initiatives remain woven into the fabric of higher education. The way feminist deans used their offices exposes the democratic motive of what seemed a simple authoritarian control of women students. Taylor's story alludes to the broad reach of the many deans of women among the vast majority of college women, helping to explain why so many women supported the changes in society accomplished by the second wave of the women's movement. Taylor's narrative is the story of the legacy of deans of women.

CHAPTER 1

Visions of Economic Citizenship

Twenty-two-year-old Emily Taylor sat quietly in a corner of the dean of women's office suite at Ohio State University (OSU). Unsure about pursuing a career in the field of guidance and counseling, Taylor had asked Associate Dean of Women Grace S. M. Zorbaugh if she could shadow her to learn more about the profession of "deaning." On that summer day in 1937, she glanced down at a document on the table, hoping the student meeting with Zorbaugh would not notice Taylor's presence as she listened intently to the conversation on the other side of the room. She typically found the stories she heard interesting. This one, however, disturbed her.

The young woman who sat across the wide desk from Zorbaugh in Pomerene Hall differed from most of the students who came to the dean of women's office for advice. This woman was older, in her mid-to-late twenties, and a mother of two young children. During her sophomore year of college, she had married a smart young man with aspirations for an academic career. She then dropped out of the university herself and waitressed to finance her husband's graduate schooling. To celebrate the completion of his PhD, the couple took their children on vacation—where he drowned. As the woman recounted the story to Zorbaugh, Taylor realized that this woman, responsible for two children, had invested all of her earnings into her husband's education, and was now left with no means to support the family, and no qualifications other than waiting tables. Taylor, who had just completed her bachelor's degree at Ohio State that year, found herself questioning one of the most normative expectations for white, middle-class womanhood: that a young woman should secure her financial future through marriage to a well-positioned man. For this young woman, the choice had gone horribly wrong. Zorbaugh often reminded her graduate students that all college women should be prepared for a career—and now Taylor understood why.

The young widow's story produced an epiphany for Taylor. It clarified why a college education mattered for women, and fed a latent feminism inside her—one that had been growing since her high school days. Taylor had experienced her own disappointments in a society that favored male accomplishment and relegated women to second-class status. First, there was the secondary school oratory contest that she had clearly won, but the judges awarded first place to a boy because they felt he should not lose to a girl.

Then, she learned that her high school principal recommended the male salutatorian of her high school class to OSU as if he were the valedictorian, despite the fact that Taylor actually earned the top title. Her discontent with society's unequal treatment of men and women would continue to grow. Soon, as a part-time graduate student and full-time high school teacher, she discovered that she earned significantly less income than a male counterpart of equal experience. When she asked the principal about the inequity, he dismissively replied that the man had a family to support. In that moment, Taylor became an equal-pay advocate. Disgruntled over the principal's logic, especially since she was paying for both her own graduate education and her younger sister's undergraduate degree, these inequities sparked in her an advocacy for women's fair and equal wages that would never cease during her many decades as a dean of women.[1]

However, in 1937, Taylor did not have a word to label her feelings—no one she knew used the word "feminism." Instead, Taylor was simply following the path she thought would provide her with much-needed income. Like most college women of the 1930s who planned to work, she trained to be a teacher, an acceptable and welcoming profession for women. She dated a young man she met at Urbana College—he was intellectually her equal, and the two considered marriage—though Taylor had a difficult time imagining herself in the supporting position that gender roles prescribed for wives. As she questioned how education, career, and her personal life might fit together for her, she worked her way through college during the Depression. She felt lucky to secure a part-time job for Ohio State students at a local government agency. The position paid a wage near what she might make as a teacher, and when she graduated with her Bachelor of Science degree, her manager suggested she enroll in graduate school so she would continue to have income until she found employment as a teacher.

> I thought that was a wonderful idea...I went over to register and since I'd just graduated, my record was right there. No difficulty in getting admitted...There was a young man, probably a graduate assistant, and he said, "What field?" And all of a sudden I said, "Gee, I don't know." "You don't know? What do you want to be when you grow up?" And I said, "Well, I think I'd like to be the dean of women." And he said, "Oh, that's guidance and counseling."[2]

Although a bit haphazard, Taylor made a pragmatic decision to enroll in guidance and counseling—abandoning her deeper hope to study law. She knew that she needed an income, and most advised her that employment as an attorney would be impossible as a woman. Perhaps, she thought, as a dean of women she might help other young women move into the field of law. Zorbaugh, she knew, spent hours preparing women for work, and studying how to open occupations to women.

Taylor possessed an unusually clear picture of the work of deans of women. As an undergraduate, Taylor first glimpsed the world of deaning when she stopped by Zorbaugh's office for advice as a transfer student from Urbana

College. Waiting to speak with someone, Taylor thumbed through the only reading material in the waiting room. Zorbaugh walked in, saw Taylor reading an article on consumption economics, "and said 'Oh, you are interested in consumer cooperatives. I just got back from Sweden where I've been studying them.'"[3] Zorbaugh promptly invited Taylor to do a radio show on consumer cooperatives with her, and though Taylor had little interest in economics, she began volunteering with the associate dean regularly, attracted to the opportunity to learn outside the classroom. Zorbaugh drew Taylor into the inner organization of the office, involving her in the campus Associated Women Students (AWS) chapter, and during Taylor's senior year, appointing her as the formal assistant to the AWS Vocational Information Committee.[4] Once involved in Zorbaugh's occupational counseling efforts, Taylor gained access to the national stage of deans of women and their feminist organizing to move women into careers outside the home. At Zorbaugh's vocational conferences, Taylor heard professional women, other Ohio deans, and the US Department of Labor Women's Bureau Director Mary Anderson discuss opening male-dominated lines of work and creating career options outside marriage and motherhood.[5]

Without realizing it, by attending OSU Taylor had chosen a university in the heart of the network of midwestern deans of women—the group that largely defined both US student affairs and the dean of women's role in coeducational institutions. At OSU, Taylor's counseling education stood on the cumulative efforts of the earliest deans of women, and her training covered the methods they developed to prepare college-educated women to access gainful employment. Through Zorbaugh, Taylor absorbed the feminist philosophy of women's coeducation that early deans involved in Progressivism and social housekeeping incubated into deaning.

A direct descendant of this legacy, Zorbaugh taught Taylor guidance techniques crafted out of an economic theory of women's financial independence which early deans developed. An economist herself, Zorbaugh developed a counseling strategy to help each female student determine how she planned to obtain basic needs such as food, shelter, and clothing. For the many young women who answered that they expected their husbands to provide these, Zorbaugh steered them to think about contingency planning. How, she asked, did young women intend to support themselves and their children if their husband died or became disabled?

After hearing the widow of the drowned husband recount her desperate situation, Zorbaugh's lesson stuck with Taylor. In fact, much further into her career, more than one of Taylor's students recalled elatedly announcing engagement plans to Taylor, who then promptly asked the student how she planned to support herself if her fiancé died. Taylor's stark question arose from decades of knowledge produced by deans of women. While other deans may have delivered the message more subtly than Taylor, "contingency planning" permeated their philosophy and practices, providing a socially acceptable means to advocate for women's professional employment and economic citizenship.[6]

Taylor's formative experiences of injustice—her frustrations during her young life that society valued her contributions less than those of men around her—crystallized into a feminist agenda for women's access to careers, equal pay, and professional advancement on the same terms as white men.[7] She would combine this consciousness with an activist approach as she donned the mantle of a dean of women. Her advocacy for women's education—and particularly, vocations for women—grew out of her awareness that the economic dependency of women limited not only their independence, but their ability to care for their families if they became single parents. These concerns became the hallmark of her early forays into college administration of women, and would define her brand of feminism. Through her mentors and the knowledge produced by early deans of women rooted in the Midwest and its coeducational institutions, Taylor became one of the most progressive deans of women; insisting all women prepare for economic citizenship—the right to earn a living and be paid equitably—and make their own decisions for themselves.

A College within a College

One of the nation's last deans of women, Taylor's story of feminist deaning began when middle-class and elite white women first entered male higher education. In the nineteenth century, these women stepped out of the private sphere of domesticity and into the public world, which historically belonged to white men of means. The "problem" of coeducation, as it was so often called, was a problem of overlapping private and public spheres and the gender roles that accompanied them. When a woman matriculated into a college or a university, she signed up for participation in public life, and American society had few blueprints for that in the late 1800s. While women of color and working-class women had always labored in the public world through low-paying service jobs, the spheres had long stood as separate for white men and women of means. This divide left little basis for determining the curricula that women should study. As Northwestern University acting president Oliver Marcy said in 1877, "We are now very sure the public opinion was, and still is, not just clear as to the kind of education most young women would seek if all the institutions of the country were open to them and they comprehended the character of the course of instruction given in them."[8]

Some who supported women's education advocated the same liberal arts curriculum prescribed for men. Most, however, called to train women for domestic roles in the private sphere of home and family—with one exception—teaching. Collegiate alumnae planning to work found employment in the nation's schoolhouses due to a long tradition of educating women to prepare the next generation of male citizens. The concept of Republican Motherhood, educating women in order for them to teach their own sons, meant society had long accepted teaching as an occupation for women. However, only single or widowed women taught, making the profession a bridge between women's education and their assumed eventual marriage.[9]

Others argued that women were unsuitable for higher education altogether. By the late nineteenth century, opponents frequently referenced

Dr. Edward Clarke's 1873 book *Sex in Education*, which asserted that higher education for women would tax women's brains, cause their bodies to weaken, and their reproductive organs to atrophy. While this thesis sounds ridiculous today, the book went through 16 printings and garnered significant attention in its time. Clark's argument summarized the prevailing opinion regarding women's education: "Educate a man for manhood, a woman for womanhood, both for humanity."[10] It is not surprising, then, that some of the earliest women scholars applied their knowledge to curricular programs that dealt with domesticity, including household sanitation and hygiene.[11]

Higher education responded to women's pursuit of postsecondary study in several ways. The established schools of the Northeast and South rarely admitted women, so women's colleges in these regions filled the gap by educating women separately from men. However, the younger institutions in the Midwest and West often offered coeducation. Oberlin Collegiate Institute first admitted young women alongside male students in 1833 as part of a religious project to train women as Christian teachers and missionaries. Most of these schools, though, admitted women because they faced a stark challenge to find the funds needed to construct campuses and hire faculty. With a limited number of families able to afford higher education, enrolling daughters alongside sons provided a significant increase in needed tuition dollars. While elite schools of the Northeast often receive the most historical attention, these midwestern and western schools are where most early college women received their training. By 1915, the Midwest and West's coeducational institutions housed 75 percent of all women students. This influx of women propelled presidents to create a means to manage women students, particularly in the Midwest, where females had reached close to 50 percent of some schools' student bodies by the early 1900s.[12]

As the numbers of women students grew, late nineteenth-century coeducational university presidents found themselves on new ground. Saddled with lingering Victorian social conventions, presidents could not simply mix young men and women on campuses and expect parents' or society's approval. At the time, middle- and upper-class white women depended upon their sexual purity to remain marriageable, and parents expected social conventions that ensured young women had a constant chaperone when with men. Most university presidents came to the same conclusion that William Rainey Harper of the University of Chicago reached in 1892—he needed a scholarly woman to take charge of women students' academics and guard their virtue. In appointing the first formally titled dean of women, Harper recreated society's separate spheres on the Chicago campus. Other coeducational presidents and trustees followed suit with a dean of women to head the women's arena—sometimes in formally separate "women's colleges"—though most often dividing women from the core institution through housing, advising, and campus regulations. This "college within a college" approach replicated within the institution the normative organization of society, and provided a structure to regulate women's conduct, control interactions between male and female students, and enforce the supervision and chaperoning parents expected. For presidents, the arrangement satisfied public expectations, and freed male faculty from advising women. For deans of women and their students, it fashioned a realm within the public sphere for their own advancement. Early women deans, some of whom remembered isolation during their own coeducational experiences, prized this socially sanctioned space. It provided both a community for women students, and a platform for organizing women's educational pursuits.[13]

At the University of Chicago, Harper recruited the respected scholar and former president of Wellesley, Alice Freeman Palmer, to define women's education on the new Chicago campus. The nation's first to bear the title "dean of women," Palmer had graduated from the University of Michigan in 1876, and served as president of Wellesley College until 1887. Palmer accepted Harper's offer in 1892, though she spent only twelve weeks a year in Illinois because of her recent marriage to Harvard University's George Herbert Palmer. She brought with her to Chicago a protégé, Marion Talbot, a Boston University and Massachusetts Institute of Technology graduate who specialized in sanitary science (the application of chemistry toward safe housekeeping). Talbot functioned as the dean of women in Palmer's absence, and both women actively worked with the Association of Collegiate Alumnae (ACA), which was founded by Talbot's mother and other college women of her generation and later became the American Association of University Women (AAUW). Together, Palmer and Talbot would link the Northeastern women's college network to the coeducational institutions of the Midwest in new ways, especially when Talbot formally assumed the title of dean of women in 1899, after Palmer resigned.[14]

With her promotion, Talbot hired a new partner in the dean of women's office, Wellesley alumna Sophonisba Breckinridge. An attorney from a politically active Kentucky family, Breckinridge took the position as Talbot's secretary because she found it difficult to establish a law practice as a woman. Breckinridge earned her PhD in political science and economics at Chicago in 1901, and would become a cofounder of the University of Chicago's School of Social Service Administration. Breckinridge also spent summers at Jane Addams' Hull House, and involved herself in the Chicago Women's Trade Union League, where she worked with labor organizers, including Mary Anderson, who, in turn, would become the first director of the Women's Bureau in the US Department of Labor in 1920. Like Talbot, Breckinridge lived on the University of Chicago's campus in the women's residence hall, where the two scholars supervised women students for most of their careers. Talbot and Breckinridge blended the social service and labor politics of Hull House, reflective of the era's Progressive political spirit, with their approach to women's education, creating a tributary for social feminist activism to flow into women's higher education.[15]

Faced with growing numbers of women students and little infrastructure for managing their participation on campus, Talbot quickly saw a need to collaborate with other women deans to share practices. Just as her mother had initiated the AAUW, from her new post in Chicago Talbot began to organize a group of mostly midwestern deans of women. At the first official meeting of the Conference of Deans of Women of the Middle West in 1903, deans of women (or "advisers to women," as they were sometimes called) attended from the universities of Wisconsin, Kansas, Michigan, Illinois, Iowa, Colorado, and Ohio, along with Ohio State, Indiana, and Northwestern universities; the colleges of Illinois, Lawrence, Ripon, Oberlin, and Beloit; and, a lone easterner, Barnard. By the third meeting in 1907, the universities of Missouri, Nebraska, North Dakota, and Minnesota had joined, along with Wyoming and California, and a few schools from the East and South. Among the women who met for the conferences were Martha Foote Crow (Northwestern), a former AAUW president; Ada Comstock (Minnesota), future president of both AAUW and Radcliffe; Laura Drake Gill (Barnard) also future AAUW president; and educational reformer Lucy Sprague (UC Berkeley).[16]

Like Talbot and Breckinridge, most of the deans were scholars. With PhDs in hand, they found themselves largely locked out of the male professoriate. By accepting the position of dean of women, they achieved assistant and associate professorships along with the responsibility for managing women students. The new role of dean of women cracked open a fissure into the all-male academy, and together the deans Talbot assembled charted the early course for coeducation of women. Fundamental questions lay beneath their conversations: Why educate women? What could women graduates do with their educations? Were they, like men, preparing for work in the public realm? If so, which employers would hire women? Few deans thought the curriculum should prepare women solely for the domestic sphere, but none were sure about the options for college alumnae other than teaching.[17]

By 1910, both the AAUW and the Deans of Women of the Middle West supported women studying the same traditional liberal arts curriculum men studied, plus additional courses that would provide vocational preparation for women in teaching, social work, and other newly emerging fields that would accept women.[18] But as a small percentage of academic leaders, women deans expressed this minority opinion in an academy where men either called for women to gain education aimed toward domesticity, or they eschewed courses enabling career preparation as the "bacteria of vocation" that irreparably damaged the traditional liberal arts degree. By supporting a hybrid position, these women deans asserted the primacy of a liberal arts education and also claimed that women should be prepared for employment and public sphere participation, albeit in a feminized realm. However, despite women deans' insistence on vocational preparation, the only vocational path available to collegiate women at the turn of the twentieth century was teaching—largely in primary or secondary schools. Since few jobs existed for college-educated women outside a classroom—the growing numbers of collegiate alumnae flooded the teaching market. When Lucy Sprague (Mitchell) arrived in Berkeley at the University of California (UC) as dean of women in

1903, she noted, "The more I saw of these vigorous western girls, the more preposterous it seemed that they should have no choice except to become teachers... For what other professions could the University prepare them? To find an answer to that question became an obsession."[19] It was an obsession that found few easy answers. Clearly, the academy and the commercial world had thought little about what educated women could do for gainful employment in the public sphere.[20]

Feeling the same compunction as Sprague, deans of women, the AAUW, and women's college faculty began a series of approaches between 1900 and 1915 that would result in the creation of new knowledge about women and work. First, as with any research project, these academic women started with a review of the existing literature. University of Chicago professor (and future Northwestern Dean of Women) Martha Foote Crow published a bibliography on women's higher education that included a section on "Occupations and Opportunities for College-bred Women," in the 1897 AAUW journal. This led the deans to consider occupations in social service where white, middle-class women already interacted as volunteers in poor communities through "social housekeeping." Talbot, involved with the social housekeepers at Hull House, began to consider how women might find employment by bringing women's nurturing, legitimately domestic work, into the public realm to care for children, run orphanages, or work with the poor. The deans of women in Chicago were among the first to see social service as a possible employment option thanks to the local partnership between Talbot, Crow, Breckinridge, Edith Abbott, and Julia Lathrop with Hull House founder, Jane Addams. Lathrop (future US Children's Bureau director) called for educated women's increased involvement in public service at the 1903 AAUW annual meeting. In response, Talbot and the Chicago AAUW branch conducted a citywide survey of the employment options in social service in 1903 and 1904. Breckinridge, then AAUW national secretary, sent their findings to the nation's AAUW members in a report, "Public and Social Service as Vocations for College Women." These efforts began the modern social work profession, with Breckinridge, Edith Abbott and her sister, Grace Abbott, eventually founding the University of Chicago School of Social Service Administration which remains one of the strongest social work schools in the nation.[21]

Between the AAUW, the Deans of Women of the Middle West, and women's college faculty members, these vocational efforts spread quickly. At Chicago, Talbot and Breckinridge found that few women students realized any vocational options existed outside teaching, and began offering electives and vocational conferences to prepare their students for field-specific work. As much as possible, Talbot and early deans featured women professionals as role models, especially well-known Chicago social workers. By 1909, deans of women had determined women could find employment in professions such as dairy and poultry industries, journalism, philanthropy, and library and business management. Deans of women at public institutions asked their schools to offer classes in corresponding areas.[22]

The deans, now meeting annually as a caucus within the AAUW, formalized these efforts with Susan Kingsbury, herself the daughter of the dean of women at College of the Pacific. An economist who studied the incomes of college women graduates, Kingsbury directed research at the Women's Educational and Industrial Union (WEIU) of Boston, where she created an economic model for increasing college women's salaries. Arguing that the glut of women in teaching kept teacher salaries low, Kingsbury called for moving some women out of teaching as a strategy to increase wages for all women in trained occupations. By reducing the number of women looking for teaching positions, she hoped to increase competition and wages as women entered other fields. AAUW responded to Kingsbury's economic theory by establishing a committee to move college graduates into new employment lines. They appointed as chairwoman chemist Ellen Richards, founder of the home economics discipline, Talbot's mentor, and an initial founder of the AAUW who believed in achieving a living wage for women. The committee recruited an impressive roster: Breckinridge; Kingsbury, who would later found the Summer Institute for Women Workers at Bryn Mawr and conduct the 1930s AAUW and Women's Bureau survey *The Economic Status of University Women in the U.S.A.*; Mary Coes, who would soon become dean at Radcliffe; Edith Abbott (future coauthor of the 1935 Social Security Act) and AAUW First Vice President May Cheney. Cheney, an 1883 UC alumna, had established a women's employment bureau on Berkeley's campus—originally for teachers—and become a close colleague of Dean of Women Lucy Sprague (Mitchell) as they worked together to find employment options for UC graduates. Likely the first woman in the United States to formally place college graduates into jobs, Cheney would later preside over the first National Association of Appointment Secretaries (NAAS) meeting, the organization which would become the American College Personnel Association (ACPA) and a steadfast partner with deans of women.[23]

This new AAUW effort, the Committee on Economic Efficiency, formed the backbone of the collaboration between the AAUW, women's college administrators, and the Deans of Women of the Middle West on a project to broaden career options for women. Drawing on the University of Chicago and UC Berkeley's efforts, as well as successful employment placement practices from women's colleges, this coalition clearly understood it would be impossible to chart a path for women to gain employment outside of teaching without understanding which fields would admit them. They undertook a project to identify employers who would hire alumnae in nonteaching positions, locating the effort at the WEIU in Boston, home to both Richards and Kingsbury. AAUW president Laura Gill (the same Barnard dean of women who traveled to Talbot's initial 1903 deans of women meeting in Chicago) moved to Boston for 18 months to direct this new effort, the WEIU Business Vocational Guidance Bureau. The AAUW asked Gill to discover facts about new occupations women might pursue.[24] Gill and a fieldworker collected information on nonteaching options and compiled occupational bulletins that they sent to deans of women across the country for use in advising students. By 1913, appointment bureaus like those of Cheney and the WEIU multiplied as Chicago, New York, and Philadelphia all now housed offices to help college women find nonteaching employment alternatives. In addition, the AAUW reported the appointment bureaus' successful practices in *News Notes*, a newsletter mailed across the country.[25]

The practices established by the AAUW, deans of women, and the employment placement centers included individual counseling sessions linking graduating students with employed alumni, which had proved successful at Wellesley, Smith, and Radcliffe. This exposed students to career women as role models. They also advocated both part-time and summer work in a chosen field to gain experience before graduation and to "try-out" an occupation. These practices, used today for all students in higher education career offices, were developed by women for women. Since male college graduates often found employment via family or faculty connections, male administrators had little need to produce a method for men to find jobs. Women, however, had no such connections and needed a network of campuses, cities, alumnae, and employers because few pathways existed into the public world for female graduates. Once they defined the model, deans replicated the practices using vocational conferences such as those Marion Talbot created at the University of Chicago to educate women about the possibilities outside teaching, aiming to match women with employers through employment bureaus.[26]

This vocational network expanded, spreading the practices across the country as AAUW branches coordinated with the Boston's WEIU, Chicago Collegiate Bureau of Occupation, the New York-based Intercollegiate Bureau of Occupations, and the Philadelphia Bureau of Occupations for Trained Women. Outside of these major cities, the AAUW branches often collaborated with a local university and its dean of women in areas such as Bloomington, Indiana; Columbus, Ohio; Lawrence, Kansas; Lincoln, Nebraska; Columbia, Missouri; Ann Arbor, Michigan; and Madison, Wisconsin. The women fashioning these approaches included leaders Taylor would encounter through Zorbaugh and the AAUW-deans network: women like Mary van Kleeck, Florence Jackson, and Helen Bennett all of the employment bureaus. Not surprisingly, the decade of work by midwestern and western deans in coeducational institutions outpaced the eastern schools, and the AAUW Vocational Committee offered the University of Chicago and Cheney's operations as prototypes for all to emulate.[27]

By the mid-1910s, a deaning model had emerged for vocational preparation, loosely based on Marion Talbot's early efforts. Ohio-based Oberlin exemplified the practice as Dean of Women Florence Fitch hired an appointment secretary to advise women on vocations, and hosted speakers from the WEIU bureau and the New York Intercollegiate Bureau of Occupations, holding annual conferences to connect students with professional role models. Wisconsin Dean of Women and AAUW President Lois Kimball Mathews Rosenberry promoted this strategy as well in her 1915 book, *The Dean of Women*, the primary text on the practice of women's guidance for a number of years. Rosenberry steered deans of women to refer graduates who preferred not to teach to the bureaus of occupations in New York City, Philadelphia, and Chicago, and recommended campus vocational conferences to educate women regarding employment options. To complement these efforts, Rosenberry recommended Ada Comstock's practice of developing a part-time job placement service in the dean's office to help students acquire work experiences that would prepare them for a particular field.[28] Rosenberry also adopted Kingsbury's economic model, which she used herself to leverage support for elective courses on her own campus. There, she told the University of Wisconsin president:

> The teaching profession for women is so "overstocked" that salaries are kept down to a mere living wage... The opportunities for women in business, welfare work, in play-ground work, in charities and correction associations, and in all lines opened up by household economics and its allied subjects are almost numberless and as yet there are not enough trained women to fill them.[29]

Rosenberry's argument for the University of Wisconsin to offer vocational coursework to women rested upon Kingsbury's economic analysis. The idea of building employment options outside teaching became a part of the philosophy of deans of women as Rosenberry's book—and her stature among deans and AAUW members—influenced the widespread adoption of the vocational guidance model through elective classes, vocational conferences, and role model lectures.

Early deans of women utilized the "college within a college" to actively advise women students on how to prepare for and to enter the world of paid employment. They played a key role in producing new knowledge about how to ready women for work, developing and implementing career services practices that still exist today: networking, summer internships, and employment fairs. As deans participated in these efforts, they fused their philosophy on women's education with practical tactics to help young women work toward economic citizenship. They developed a new rubric, asserting that college should prepare *all* women for work, and that employed college-educated women should earn living wages and equal pay by entering occupations in addition to teaching. Like Rosenberry, deans adopted Kingsbury's economic argument to convince university presidents to increase vocational course offerings as a means to bolster enrollments and university coffers. This recipe for women's coeducation fused influences from the Progressive movement's social housekeeping with practical techniques to guide women graduates into the public sphere, allowing females to prepare for work and retain the full traditional liberal arts education in the same classrooms as men.

Deans developed these practices at the same time that the professionalization of work spread across the United States, resulting in a flurry of new associations where practitioners met to define and disseminate their particular brand of "expertise." For deans of women, the proliferation of vocational associations provided an avenue to share and improve guidance practices for women. They took advantage of this by affiliating with multiple associations, and they used the combined architecture of these professional groups to build support for women's vocational guidance. At the same time that deans of women built structures to prepare women for new vocations, they also created the profession of deaning, thereby opening yet another field to women—this one in college administration.[30]

Careers and Contingency Planning

As deaning professionalized, leading deans recommended all women prepare for an occupation in case she might one day need to support herself and her family. Ada Comstock at Minnesota even went so far as to suggest women could successfully combine work and marriage, a concept that few considered at the turn of the twentieth century. Deans of women, who coordinated with the Women's Bureau from its inception in 1920, were integrally connected with the National Vocational Guidance Association (NVGA), the American Council of Personnel and Guidance Associations (CPGA), and the National Association of Appointment Secretaries (NAAS) which later became the American College Personnel Association (ACPA). These associations either have histories that overlooked deans of women as a professional group within them, or their histories have disappeared as new alliances refashioned old organizations into new ones. These ever-changing association connections have obscured how deans of women influenced vocational guidance and worked with the labor feminists of the Women's Bureau. A brief overview of the connections between associations provides an important context for understanding how the feminist practice of deaning operated through these overlapping organizations. Within this network of women developing ways to move women into careers, Taylor trained and adopted the philosophy that the early deans developed.[31]

The earliest connections began between the NVGA and the AAUW-deans network. Both Boston's WEIU and the Hull House worked with child labor advocates who developed the NVGA to prepare working-class youth—usually males—for trade employment after high school. Inaugurated by Bostonians Frank Parsons and Meyer Bloomfield in 1913, the NVGA focused on practices to guide young people into work, helping them identify a vocation. From the beginning, the NVGA involved women from the AAUW-deans network, including Hull House founder Jane Addams herself. Taylor's Ohio State mentor, Zorbaugh, also worked with Bloomfield early in her career and was a long-time NVGA member. The overlap between women deans and the NVGA was so strong that when the organization faltered during World War I, it was University of Minnesota Dean of Women Katherine Ball who initiated its rescue.

With the NVGA in place, deans of women and deans of students from women's colleges decided they needed a professional association themselves, rather than just the hybrid coordination between the AAUW and Talbot's midwestern meetings. Nebraska State Normal School Dean of Women Kathryn Sisson (Phillips) established the National Association of Deans of

Women (NADW) in 1916, which eventually enveloped the Deans of Women of the Middle West. The NADW absorbed the early deans' philosophy and vocational strategies, featuring familiar partners including the New York bureau's Mary van Kleeck and the Chicago bureau's Helen Bennett. The AAUW-deans coalition thrived in the NADW, with the organization calling the AAUW, Cheney's employment bureau group (NAAS), and the NVGA three of their most important organizational alliances. In fact, Cheney and other appointment secretaries attended NADW meetings regularly, even after they created the NAAS in 1924.[32]

This cooperative network linked with the Women's Bureau. As an outgrowth of the World War I Woman in Industry Service (WIS) agency, the Women's Bureau should have been led by WIS director Mary van Kleeck, who resigned to care for an aging mother. Van Kleeck, of the New York Intercollegiate Bureau of Occupations, was a well-known participant in the AAUW-deans-occupational bureau network. She attended AAUW Vocational Committee meetings, knew many deans of women, and spoke at campus vocational conferences. Since van Kleeck could not direct WIS, she tapped close friend Mary Anderson to take the director position, making Anderson the first Women's Bureau leader when WIS converted to the bureau in 1920. A Chicago Women's Trade Union activist, Anderson knew Breckinridge through the thriving Chicago Hull House community. Anderson participated in NADW and NVGA national meetings in the 1920s and collaborated with deans of women, naming NADW as one of the most important organizations with which she worked. Later, at the agency's fortieth anniversary, the Women's Bureau listed NADW among the key associations in its history.[33]

In the early 1920s, NADW locked arms with the newly established Women's Bureau, promoting trade union membership for collegiate alumnae in order to allow women to bargain for fair pay, and to support the women's protective legislation that was the hallmark of the early twentieth-century women's movement. Anderson called for deans of women to support equal pay initiatives, and NADW founder Phillips agreed, reminding her colleagues that they must teach students to recognize that taking a job below fair market salary rates reduced all working women's incomes. To build support for fair wages, deans of women reached the same conclusion that labor organizers did—similar workers needed a group consciousness to advocate collectively for their interests as a group. Phillips asked college-educated women to recognize the "oneness of all aspects of the women's movement" and to reject the "snobbish[ness]" common among middle-class white women in order to develop a group consciousness across all women workers.[34] Phillips believed women would achieve better wages for all females if they formed a coalition across socio-economic classes. This approach wedded the deans to a concept of universal womanhood that became a cardinal—albeit at times contested—principle of twentieth-century feminism. However, as late-twentieth-century feminists would show, collapsing all women's experiences into one category of "womanhood" proved problematic as white women of means often assumed working class women and women of color experienced discrimination that mirrored their own. Many times over, educated white women exhibited racism and classism in their efforts to secure opportunities for women. Despite this elitism, deans of women heralded the premises of pay equity, a living wage, and universal womanhood on behalf of "organized working women." This created a platform for feminist activism within their profession upon which stood Taylor's career and approach.[35]

As deans adopted the concept of labor solidarity, they needed more information on placing college women in professional employment outside of teaching. In 1929, AAUW added to the deans' network by working with Catherine Filene Dodd (later Shouse), whose department-store family had participated in the establishment of the NVGA. Dodd financed a new effort, the Institute of Women's Professional Relations (IWPR), to synthesize research on women and work, and to produce new knowledge and publications about occupations open to college-educated women. An outgrowth of AAUW's concern over women's wages, the IWPR involved a number of women from the original AAUW-deans network in its leadership, including Comstock, Iva L. Peters (Syracuse), Alice Baldwin (Duke), and Helen Bennett (Chicago Collegiate Bureau of Occupations). Directed by Professor Chase Going Woodhouse, a University of Chicago economics PhD, the Institute expanded what former Barnard Dean of Women Laura Gill began at WEIU, producing updated bulletins on occupational fields. IWPR avoided the term "feminist," considering the word too controversial, and drew on the notion that higher education should prepare women to move in and out of the workforce based on the phases of motherhood, a concept which Gill suggested through AAUW.[36]

The agendas of the Women's Bureau, NADW, NVGA, NAAS, and IWPR overlapped substantially, causing the NADW to initiate a 1934 collaboration, which would ultimately be called the American Council of Personnel and Guidance Associations (CPGA). A concept birthed by NADW, this umbrella organization housed almost every vocational guidance association, including NADW, NVGA, ACPA, Personnel Research Federation, the Teachers College Personnel Association, the Southern Women's Educational Alliance, the National Bureau of Occupations, and the National Occupations Conference. Members of the Women's Bureau staff attended meetings regularly as well. However, the National Association of Deans of Men (NADM) was noticeably absent, preferring an informal approach rather than the research-based efforts of NADW, which was now exploring student personnel and the application of psychological methods within vocational placement and deaning. Interested in collaboration for the betterment of college women's employment avenues, the women deans had no intention of abandoning either their NADW organization or their AAUW-deans philosophical roots by creating the CGPA. However, ironically, the CGPA eventually adopted the student personnel model that would ultimately demote deans of women to work for male deans of students.[37]

Despite what would come in the future, for almost two decades the CGPA fused the deans of women's practice with the larger vocational guidance and placement network. In this nexus, the partnership between the deans of women and the Women's Bureau blossomed—institutionalizing the vocational guidance model early deans had created. A part of this partnership happened to be at OSU, where Zorbaugh served as the appointment secretary in the dean of women's office. Bringing her NVGA background to OSU, Zorbaugh arrived as a seasoned advocate for women and fostered one of the most advanced vocational programs for women in the country. Taylor engaged in this milieu as Zorbaugh introduced her to the vocational machinery in action—a manifestation of the knowledge produced by the nation's earliest deans of women. At OSU, Taylor began to absorb the philosophy and knowledge that Marion Talbot and the early deans worked so hard to produce.[38]

Forging a National Model

When Taylor arrived at OSU in 1935, Zorbaugh had established one of the strongest women's vocational guidance operations in the nation, involving the key players from the growing coalition on women and work. Through Zorbaugh, Taylor was exposed to the entire network from the IWPR and Women's Bureau, to the NVGA, AAUW, and NADW. At OSU, Taylor heard Women's Bureau Director Mary Anderson and IWPR leader Chase Woodhouse speak on women's employment, she absorbed the labor feminist position supporting fair wages, and read books from the now regularly maintained bibliographies that early deans developed on women's roles and occupations. She observed the successful mentoring of college women through OSU vocational conferences, and by volunteering with Zorbaugh, she witnessed the ways volunteering enlightened students' own thinking on opportunities for women in general. These lessons formed the backbone for her own future deaning, with Zorbaugh a model Taylor sought to emulate.

Already in her fifties, Zorbaugh arrived at the OSU dean of women's office in 1929 as an experienced product of midwestern coeducation. She followed in the line of women scholars who found a faculty position through employment in a dean of women's office. A Wisconsin PhD who studied with John R. Commons, Zorbaugh had adopted Commons' Progressivism and pursued her own pioneering work on consumption and consumer economics—an effort that answered Kingsbury's call for training more women in personal finance. With a faculty appointment as an associate professor of economics, Zorbaugh actively participated in the academic and professional communities that early college-educated women created. She belonged to the AAUW, NADW, NVGA, National Federation of Business and Professional Women's Clubs (BPW), Young Women's Christian Association (YWCA), and the National League of Women Voters (NLWV), formerly the National American Woman Suffrage Association. At both NLWV and NADW, she served as national chairman of the research committee. Her philosophy of vocational guidance drew on these affiliations, as well as her work with NVGA cofounder Meyer Bloomfield.[39]

OSU Dean of Women Esther Allen Gaw hired Zorbaugh to reinvigorate the vocational aspect of her office. OSU's first formal dean of women,

Caroline Breyfogle, was a suffragist and student of Talbot's who graduated from the University of Chicago with an A.B. in 1896 and with her PhD in 1912. Arriving at OSU soon after, Breyfogle instituted vocational guidance, partnering with state and municipal employment bureaus so successfully that the AAUW promoted her model through their national Vocational Committee. However, after Breyfogle left OSU in 1918, the program withered and was handed off to a student-led group within the YWCA. When Zorbaugh arrived, all that remained were small, hour-long vocational sessions adjoining the AWS meetings for three evenings in the fall, of which she remarked: "Attendance, to say the least, was discouraging and quite out of proportion to the arduous efforts on the part of the small program committee…The mass of women students were practically untouched, including many of the twenty-five per cent who had made no vocational choice."[40]

Zorbaugh renewed OSU occupational guidance by utilizing the early deans' best practices. First, she began meeting individually with students for vocational advising, and she followed Ada Comstock's technique at Minnesota of helping young women find part-time work to finance their college educations. By the time Taylor arrived at OSU during the Depression, student financial advising was an integral part of Zorbaugh's efforts. Forty percent of the women students funded their OSU educations through employment, and eight percent covered all their expenses with their earnings. Seventy percent of these women working their way through college sought out the dean of women's office for advice or leads on part-time work. The OSU dean's office also helped young women finance college by administering loans, a tradition Talbot began in the 1880s. Across the country, through deans of women's offices, loans originated with AAUW branches, alumnae associations, and AWS chapters, to be paid back directly to those groups. At OSU, women's student loans came from the Columbus Pan-Hellenic organization, the AWS, the Columbus Scholarship Society, and the alumnae associations of Detroit, Pittsburgh, New York, and Springfield, Ohio, among others.[41]

In addition to helping students fund college through loans and part-time work, Zorbaugh established vocational conferences according to the NADW model. She saw this as a means to "combat the well known tendency of women students to drift into gainful occupations on the strength of temporary advantages rather than to make well considered long-run choices."[42] Zorbaugh drew on the base left by Breyfogle, and acquired funding to increase the reach of the small informational meetings so women could better plan their job futures after college. At first, Zorbaugh, Gaw, and other nonstudent organizers paid for expenses and, when the Depression allowed it, Gaw allocated some of her budget to the conferences. The AWS chapter provided some funding, and eventually the OSU administration supported her conferences as well. Zorbaugh carefully tracked statistics to provide justification for university funding, and those detailed reports provide a window into OSU vocational advising and the world in which Taylor trained.[43]

Following Marion Talbot's turn of the century tradition, Zorbaugh organized a fall conference and spring meetings covering summer employment, as well as "intimate fireside conferences" between students and well-known women often employed in social service. When Taylor arrived at OSU in 1935, the fall conferences attracted between five hundred and nine hundred women students. When she left in 1944 with her master's degree, the conferences had grown to over two thousand student participants and at times rose to 45 percent of the female student body. Zorbaugh's results eclipsed national figures for the late 1930s, when only 5.3 percent of women students reported contacts with the dean of women's office, 35 percent of which were vocational in nature. By 1939, Zorbaugh placed almost one in every four participants in jobs. Given that 75 percent of all women students would marry shortly after college, she produced excellent results.[44]

No small effort, Zorbaugh's fall conferences stretched from between 9 a.m. and 10 p.m. for three consecutive days. The sessions informed coed students about career options in over 50 occupational fields, featured career women as role models from various industries, taught students how to apply for a job, and matched them with employers for interviews. Zorbaugh used the students involved in the AWS chapter and the YWCA to organize the conference. It took 8 committees, 60 students, and 50 adult advisors to organize the fall effort alone, with another 150 freshman volunteers during the conference proceedings. These students built their organizational and leadership skills as they ushered attendees, tracked attendance, sold lunch and dinner tickets, served as secretaries and chairwomen of each industry panel, hosted guests, and learned to work in and run committees as well as to manage budgets. Though already working a part-time job as an undergraduate student, Taylor joined the activity when she could. By her senior year, she formally assisted Zorbaugh with the AWS University Vocational Information Committee for Women Students.[45]

Each fall conference began with a keynote speaker chosen to inspire young women to think about their vocational and avocational interests. Zorbaugh consistently emphasized avocation in order to attract to the conferences the many women who expected to marry. She wanted these women to be exposed to the deans' vocational philosophy and adopt the "contingency planning" approach to prepare to earn a living if necessary. As Zorbaugh told the press, "Women now are waking up to the fact that prospect of marriage should be a stimulus, not a deterrent, to vocational preparation."[46] Once the students attended, they learned that marriage and career were not mutually exclusive, an idea gaining ground in the 1930s. Zorbaugh had solid data to report on the trend. By 1930, 20 percent of female office workers were married and Zorbaugh consistently featured this topic.[47]

In 1935, Taylor's first undergraduate semester at OSU, the topic of marriage, motherhood, and work undergirded the entire fall conference when Zorbaugh chose as keynote speaker Gelene Bowman, past national president of the BPW, and a successful married businesswoman with twin children. Women like Bowman illustrated to OSU students that women could straddle both the public and private spheres and be successful mothers. That year, Ohio newspapers covering the conference publicized Zorbaugh's philosophy that "children have greater respect for parents who do things," and featured women's vocational preparation as a "contingency planning" model that provided options for a woman who might face financial emergencies later in her married life.[48] Zorbaugh specifically argued against the prevalent presumption that college-educated women wasted parents' money, often stating that women's education served "as a type of insurance investment—protection against emergencies which may force the wife and mother to find work to keep her family together."[49] Still, prescriptions against married women working intensified during the Great Depression, even as families faced extreme financial hardship. Eighty-two percent of those responding to a 1936 Harris poll said that wives should not work when husbands had jobs.[50] Within this context, the contingency-planning rationale provided a socially acceptable reason to promote occupational training for college women, as so many families struggled financially. The prevailing culture, though, mediated Zorbaugh's message. Not surprisingly for the era, some OSU conference speakers specifically advised young white women not to mix a career and homemaking, and the overall middle-class culture still called for women to serve society from the home.[51]

Zorbaugh's conferences brought the AAUW-deans network into the lives of OSU young women. She featured the Women's Bureau, hosting bureau head Mary Anderson and Louise Stitt, director of the division of minimum wage, on topics including "Professions Other Than Education in Government Service." Other visitors from the network included such key organizers as Florence Jackson, the former chairman of the AAUW Committee on Vocational Opportunities and the former director of the WEIU, where Kingsbury conducted her research; Chase Woodhouse, director of the IWPR; Helen Voorhees, director of the Mount Holyoke College Employment Bureau; and speakers from the Chicago Collegiate Bureau of Occupations and Columbus Counseling Bureau, to name a few.[52]

Zorbaugh continued the AAUW-deans' practice of producing a bibliography to disseminate the growing knowledge regarding women and work. She involved students in its production, which familiarized them with the resources on women and work. The bibliography circulated widely and Zorbaugh often received more requests for it than could be fulfilled. By 1937, the 29-page bibliography catalogued over 50 fields including engineering, insurance, archaeology, chemistry, pharmacy and medicine, quietly showing women the vast array of options for them outside of teaching, secretarial work, and nursing. Zorbaugh's listing of publications catalogued the work of the Bureau of Occupations in New York, and the IWPR, relying heavily on the periodical *Independent Woman* published by BPW. At the same time, the bibliography also compiled a general reference section that continued to draw on the thinking of the early deans and AAUW, citing the AAUW and Women's Bureau study of the economic status of women written by Kingsbury, Breckinridge's *Women in the Twentieth Century*, and the vocational series by the University of Chicago board of vocational guidance and placement. She referenced the research of deans of women like Hilda

Threlkeld (Louisville) and Adah Pierce (Hiram College), while also tucking into the bibliography references specifically for black and Jewish women, and for women contemplating combining marriage and career.[53]

The occupational information spread through Ohio, as did Zorbaugh's philosophy. Zorbaugh estimated 5,800 secondary school girls benefited from the OSU fall vocational conference, and the project engaged deans and vocational bureaus across the region, including those from Ohio Wesleyan, the University of Cincinnati, Antioch College, Purdue University, and Hiram College. Zorbaugh published and spoke on women's occupational counseling, sharing her vocational counseling tactics with NADW, NVGA, and the Ohio Association of Deans of Women (OADW). As NADW's Research Committee Chair, Zorbaugh continued the early deans' practice of collecting new research to be published in a NADW bibliography which eventually became the NADW *Guide to Guidance*. From this national post, she advocated against the emerging trend of combining men and women's vocational advising. She frequently noted that the university—by its organization into colleges and departments—provided expanded vocational counseling to male students who frequently received it from faculty. While faculty in the home economics, education, and social work disciplines advised women on careers, only the dean of women's office provided women guidance on nonnormative professions like law, science or medicine.[54]

Zorbaugh's vocational conferences quietly advocated that young college women consider alternative ways to live their lives, and chipped away at attitudes that treated gender roles as natural laws. Zorbaugh prodded women to think of themselves as working in public realms outside of teaching, just as the early deans and the AAUW had advocated. By now, Kingsbury's economic argument that women needed to look outside teaching to increase college women's wages had become a standard assumption among deans promoting vocational training. And Zorbaugh called for women to raise their salaries by entering nonteaching professions, noting that in the Depression, "girls who prepared for work in the less crowded fields have had better luck in holding their jobs."[55]

Zorbaugh chose a subtle approach on the OSU campus, weaving occupational opportunity into conversations among women planning to marry. While the subtlety was necessary for both young women and the OSU administration, Zorbaugh shared her forthright contentions among her peers at Ohio deans meetings. There, Zorbaugh asked her colleagues to continue the long and strategic "pull" to "consolidate the gains made in the last century." Although she did not term it "feminism," Zorbaugh clearly intended to engender such a consciousness in young college women:

> We have won the right to cut our hair and show our legs, and also to select our occupations...We must develop a "will-to-power" among young women. They must be made dissatisfied with "piffling successes." If even a handful of our young people learn to spot piffle, bunk, we shall not have labored in vain.[56]

Zorbaugh called for deans to help young women cultivate objectivity, accountability, and loyalty to other women, building a consciousness of the commonalities in women's interests. This, she argued, would enable young women to participate in the public sphere of work and open the largely closed arena of politics to women's participation as elected members of government. Both labor and feminist philosophy underlay Zorbaugh's approach, and though not all deans subscribed to the premises of this project, Taylor was among Zorbaugh's converts.[57]

A Path toward Economic Citizenship

Taylor's desire to become a dean of women was born in the midst of this vocational organizing as she watched Zorbaugh mentor students and organize a quiet feminist effort for young women to consider employment in addition to marriage and motherhood. Taylor learned that vocational guidance was inextricable from the educational process for women, that women would need to guide themselves in life as adults, and that a dean's job was to provide students with broad, quality information about occupations so women could make informed choices about how they would employ their time. Zorbaugh showed Taylor that AWS committees provided an experiential learning environment for women to build leadership and organizational skills while also allowing a dean to subtly expose students to alternative roles for women. Zorbaugh's feminism—steeped in the knowledge the early AAUW-deans' network created—indelibly shaped Taylor's thinking and approach. This associate dean not only introduced Taylor to the network of deans and women's vocational advocates, but she also set Taylor on a path to become a dean of women with a feminist agenda.[58]

Though Taylor moved on to Indiana University for her first job in a dean of women's office, the OSU vocational world in which she trained became the national model endorsed by the Women's Bureau. The bureau staff institutionalized the knowledge and practices Zorbaugh refined, legitimizing the early AAUW deans' approach and disseminating it as a government-recommended technique throughout the vocational network of the CGPA by 1947. Zorbaugh knew Washington DC staffers Louise Stitt and Marguerite Zapoleon well from their attendance at the national vocational conferences. These two Ohio natives recognized the value of Zorbaugh's vocational machinery, and worked to promulgate it after Zorbaugh's retirement. They also encouraged Zorbaugh to publish a "how to" article on the OSU vocational conference, and continued their collaboration with the OSU conferences, seeking ways to replicate it nationally.[59]

In 1947, the Women's Bureau piloted a new pamphlet for use at the OSU vocational information conference, with the intention of distributing it across the United States. The leaflet, "Your Job Future After College," closely resembled the philosophy developed by the AAUW-deans network, and reflected Zorbaugh's approach. It recommended that students conduct an individual conference with an advisor, referred women students to employment bureaus, and suggested they study the publications listed in growing bibliographies, meet role models working in a proposed field, and find summer or part-time work as "try-out experiences." Perhaps most importantly, the pamphlet proclaimed the possibility of marriage and career in the "contingency-planning" model. The first phrase emblazoned on the inside of the pamphlet read: "DON'T Try to Choose Between Marriage OR Career, but Get Ready for BOTH Home AND Job." The publication specifically reflected Zorbaugh's contention that young women "drifted" into jobs based on short-term needs, not long-term desires, and recommended that women consciously decide a vocation. While emphasizing that women would find more opportunities in established professions that accepted women—such as teaching, social work, nursing, and librarianship—the 1947 leaflet still included nontraditional fields for women such as pharmacy, medicine, the professoriate, psychology, and law as options.[60]

To prepare the leaflet, Marguerite Zapoleon shared the new OSU document with the AAUW-deans network for their comments, including Taylor's next two mentors, Kate Hevner Mueller (Indiana University and future *NADW Journal* editor), and Hilda Threlkeld (University of Louisville and NADW president, 1945 to 1947), as well as Elsie May Smithies (Occidental and NADW president, 1943 to 1945; CGPA president, 1946 to 1947), Dorothy Gebauer (University of Texas and incoming NADW president, 1947 to 1949), and Eunice Hilton (Syracuse University, and NADW president 1955 to 1957). Zapoleon also consulted with Mount Holyoke's Helen Voorhees and Wellesley's Joan Bishop, both employment bureau directors, and AAUW women. The Women's Bureau distributed the finished pamphlet to the national network of deans of women's offices, university vocational guidance centers, women's colleges and congressional offices.[61]

The leaflet proved so popular that secondary educators and the YWCA requested a new version specifically for girls in high school. The "Job Future" publications were widely used on college campuses, and also by the National Association of College Women and the Urban League which used the brochures to educate young black women. Popularizing the approach, *Mademoiselle* published the availability of the booklet in their 1947 August "Job News" section. At the same time, the Women's Bureau recommended NADW's *Guide to Guidance* as a key publication regarding college women's employment, further endorsing the philosophy and practice early deans of women collected and created on women and work. Rooted in the bibliographies Zorbaugh, NADW and AAUW established to advance women's employment, the *Guide to Guidance* featured IWPR, BPW, and Women's Bureau publications. With the IWPR phasing out by the mid-1940s, the bureau took over producing informational bulletins on various employment fields. Zapoleon published an exhaustive series, *Outlook for Women*, delineating women's employment options in medicine, dentistry, architecture, engineering, occupational therapy, physical therapy, nursing, social work, general science, biological sciences, psychology, psychiatry, X-ray technology, chemistry, and medical librarianship. The series also addressed employment options for African American women in the sciences, noting statistics on black women with PhD degrees, and the more pronounced problem of educational access to graduate science programs for women of color. Deans of women used these publications extensively in their counseling.

The pamphlet and *Outlook for Women* marked the institutionalization of the AAUW-deans' thinking and practice. Ultimately, the completion of these two publications solidified the vocational vision of Talbot and other early deans into a government-recommended method. Here, the fledgling turn-of-the-century knowledge about women and work resulted in a "how-to" primer and series on vocational options for college women to enter the public sphere as an approved practice endorsed by the federal government.[62]

As women steadily moved into employment after World War II, the Women's Bureau, NVGA, and deans of women began a series of studies to determine the pay and career paths of collegiate alumnae. Conceived by Wisconsin's Emily Chervenik, a placement advisor who worked in the dean of women's office in Madison, Wisconsin, the Women's Bureau oversaw surveys in 1954, 1955, 1956, and 1957 under the leadership of NADW members Eunice C. Roberts (Indiana), and Margaret B. Fisher (Mills College). From this collaboration, the bureau updated the Kingsbury-AAUW salary survey to produce "College Women Go to Work" and a companion leaflet "Young Women of the Year," which outlined earnings, job placement by profession, and new information about patterns of employment. Clearly stating that college women worked in phases around the responsibility of home and young children, in 1958 the Women's Bureau disseminated the salary survey results to 1,200 deans of women across the country.[63]

This vocational partnership between deans and the Women's Bureau flourished into the 1970s when Title IX finally eliminated the dean of women position in favor of a gender-neutral approach to student affairs. The bureau included deans of women in their inner circle of advisors, with three deans among the 25 individuals it gathered in 1950 for its thirtieth anniversary discussion of the future of women and work. There, these deans reminded the bureau that 90 percent of college women expected to work at some point in their lives, and that post-World War II college women wanted to achieve a triad of experiences: meaningful work, family life, and motherhood. The cooperation between the groups was strong. When the CGPA began to move toward "student personnel" and away from sex segregation in guidance, letters show bureau staff following up with male association members when they omitted deans of women and NADW from their deliberations.[64]

When, in 1951, NADW chose not to join the newly established American Personnel and Guidance Association (APGA) which absorbed the CGPA—and the ACPA and NVGA with it—the Women's Bureau continued its coordination with NADW by sending representatives to both NADW and APGA meetings to reach the same audience of women deans they had at the CGPA.[65] APGA and the renamed deans of men's organization, NASPA, marked the change in tide in the 1950s as deans of students rose to lead student personnel offices, beginning to replace the sex-segregated deans of men and deans of women. And, as the trend to subsume deans of women in offices of deans of students grew, so did the combination of male and female vocational guidance into one streamlined operation. The Women's Bureau and deans of women worked against this current, trying to protect the specialized vocational guidance available to women through dean's offices. As Zorbaugh feared in the 1930s, when men and women students were combined into one vocational guidance service, colleges tended to prioritize male needs. To combat the loss of specialized vocational guidance for women, the Women's Bureau developed a "kit" that provided easy-to-use materials so that women students advised outside a dean's office might still receive the benefit of the broad range of information that the network had assembled over the first half of the century.[66]

The strategy the early deans of women, the AAUW, and employment bureaus developed at the turn of the century resulted in a productive, collaborative project with the Women's Bureau, bringing the knowledge and practices created by early deans of women and their colleagues into a government-sanctioned process. With the University of Chicago at the helm of developing the practices that deans later institutionalized, the Progressive principles from Chicago's Hull House network filtered into the profession, bringing into the deans' philosophy support for a living wage and equal pay. This activity, coupled with the political science and economic academic training many deans possessed, led early deans of women to prepare their students for full economic citizenship, and to reject the notion of paying a woman based on her "needs" as a part of a larger household headed by a male earner.[67]

By preparing women to advocate for equal and adequate pay in the public sphere, deans directly opposed gender expectations for white women of means to marry and remain in the domestic sphere. They also provided working class, black and rural women able to work their way through college with a means for changing their socio-economic conditions. When World War II arrived, the conflict abroad swung wide the doors of employment venues conventionally closed to women, but most shut again with the return of the war's veterans. As a result, the reality of increasing domesticity in post–World War II America tempered the labor feminist agenda that historian Dorothy Sue Cobble details in *The Others Women's Movement*, creating a quieter message of arranging work around women's home and motherhood responsibilities. Nevertheless, the deans, with the AAUW's and Women's Bureau's help, had produced a system that was distributed nationwide to advise college women how to enter the public sphere. The methods they developed—individual counseling, summer work experiences, meeting with employed alumnae, part-time student positions to "try out" a field, and listening to career role models—remain as bedrocks in today's career services offices in universities across the country.

The methods and knowledge of deans of women influenced a wide array of female students, especially since most women attended large public universities where deans of women oversaw their educations. By 1950, the strategy had played a role in 1.75 million women entering professional or semiprofessional work. However, the vast majority of women still worked in teaching, with nursing (now requiring college preparation) following closely behind. Nevertheless, as the early coalition had hoped, women had successfully pushed into other realms outside teaching. In 1870, nine-tenths of all employed professional women worked in teaching. By 1940, the number dropped to just over half of employed professional women. Women's participation in social work had risen by 1950 to almost 70,000 women in that field. Despite the growth, the most lucrative professional work remained out of reach for most women, and the post-World War II influx of returning servicemen further restricted women's access to graduate and professional schools. In general, the closer a job fell to society's prescription for women to be caregivers and homemakers, the more likely women were to fill the position's ranks. Clearly, women remained limited in their access to the public sphere. However, the vocational guidance and counseling deans of women pursued across the nation's coeducational institutions played a significant role in opening women's understanding of the possibilities for work after college and to combine work with marriage.

Through Zorbaugh, Taylor became invested in the emerging labor feminism of the Women's Bureau, seeing a vision for college women to achieve complete economic citizenship. Taylor would stay connected to this vocational network at Indiana University. There, her second mentor, Kate Hevner Mueller, taught her how an adept dean of women undergirded her commitment to women's economic stability by allowing young women to practice as political citizens through a well-run AWS.[68]

CHAPTER 2

Practicing Political Citizenship

In the summer of 1944, Indiana University (IU) Dean of Women Kate Hevner Mueller and her husband, Associate Professor of Sociology John Mueller, took a much-needed vacation, both hoping to enjoy a break from IU business. Still, some work arrived by post from her Assistant Dean of Women Margaret Wilson, who managed the office while the dean was away. With war-time jobs offering women high salaries, Mueller found it difficult to maintain head residents in Indiana's women's residence halls. She lacked enough supervisors to round out the women's staff, and Emily Taylor, recently finished with her master's work, hoped to land one of these positions. Mueller, though, preferred a woman with collegiate dormitory experience, and Taylor had none. Perhaps more important, Mueller did not hold Ohio State's dean of women, Ester Allen Gaw, in high esteem. Despite Associate Dean Grace S. M. Zorbaugh's economic and vocational expertise, Mueller found Gaw's thinking too conventional and hesitated to hire a woman from Gaw's program over women trained at places such as Syracuse University or Columbia University's Teachers College. Although deans of women as a group supported women's liberal arts education and preparation for employment, each dean's degree of feminist thinking and desire to change women's roles varied according to many factors—the campus locale and political climate, the university administration, and the dean's own opinions, to name a few. Mueller and Gaw were at opposite ends of the spectrum. Mueller, a psychologist educated at Columbia and the University of Chicago, had a marked feminist streak and a strong research record before becoming a dean of women. Despite Mueller's doubts about Taylor, when the field of applicants unexpectedly narrowed, Mueller hired her, placing Taylor in charge of junior and senior women in Forest Hall, one of the four dormitories on the IU women's quadrangle.[1]

The appointment began a lifelong friendship between the two women, with Taylor recalling years later the IU dean's office as the first place she ever felt truly at home, enjoying a peer group of like-minded women. "Everyone in the dean of women's office at Indiana was a feminist" before the term was widely used, recalled Taylor.[2] In Mueller, Taylor found an administrator who directed women's student life through the local chapter of the national Intercollegiate Association of Women Students (IAWS), crafting an intergenerational mentorship program between students and staff that pervaded all living arrangements, women's activities, and counseling. Mueller taught Taylor to link the dean of women's office and Associated Women Students (AWS) to every aspect of women's student life, using statistical studies and research methods to investigate any challenges the women's community met on campus. Taylor also benefitted from Mueller's involvement with the national networks of the American Association of University Women (AAUW), and the National Association of Deans of Women (NADW), as well as the Women's Bureau of the US Department of Labor. Most importantly, Mueller's thinking on women's education provided a framework for the feminist principles Taylor held. Mueller's ideas presaged what feminists would say much more loudly and directly about women's self-determination in the 1970s women's movement. She also provided Taylor with both a feminist philosophy and a feminist praxis that relied on the AWS group and self-governance to develop women's full citizenship and autonomy.

For Emily Taylor, the theory and practice of both self-governance and student government that she learned from Mueller became the cornerstone of her approach to "deaning" and to advocating for women's advancement and opportunity. She relied on the local AWS chapter and the IAWS network to carry her feminist philosophy into the lives of women students, firmly believing that practicing leadership through student government taught women how to act as full citizens, capable of making decisions for themselves as adults. Through AWS and the national IAWS meetings, deans like Mueller—and Taylor after her—identified women leaders out of their student bodies, personally mentoring these women in student government meetings, elected office, and volunteer roles. Just as Zorbaugh had mentored Taylor as an undergraduate, Taylor now saw the AWS and IAWS as a system for mentorship and crafting women's leadership.

Mueller was not the first to combine these goals in an AWS chapter. Student governance had long permeated deaning. In fact, AAUW president, former suffragist and Vassar faculty member Eva Perry Moore reminded the AAUW in 1907 that "'self government' is no name to conjure with. It represents at best another channel into which to pour the best of [a university officer's] mind and heart, and another script on which to write large the principles for which she stands."[3]

Often, historians of women's education interchange the phrases "student government" and "self-government" as synonyms. If identical, then Moore described deans pouring their hearts into Robert's Rules of Order, the procedures of government, and voting on campus rules. Perhaps as a pure disciplinarian, a dean of women might thrive on such a system. It seems unlikely that early deans of women—strong academics working to move women into careers—would focus their life's work into student government on those terms. So, what did deans mean by self-government? Why was it so central to their work? And, how did it link with student government?

A Brief History of Women's Governance

While early deans worked to find professional options for their students after college, their day-to-day duties revolved around housing and advising the significant numbers of women streaming onto coeducational campuses at the turn of the twentieth century. In addition to housing shortages, each school year deans faced a wave of new women, many of them from the rural Midwest and West, who were unaccustomed to living away from parents. As Talbot recalled: "At the time the University was organized, women were just beginning to feel the shackles loosen which had been fettering them…the situation was confusing. No formulation of the principles which should guide the new freedom had been worked out to take the place of the old restrictions and taboos."[4] Deans of women needed both to define behavioral guides for women's conduct in the public sphere and to create methods to help young women adjust to these campus expectations.

Rejecting what Berkeley's Lucy Sprague disdainfully called being the "warden of women," deans adopted student government to organize women's residence halls.[5] In the early twentieth century, deans such as Palmer, Ada Comstock, and Wisconsin's Anne Crosby Emery quickly reconstructed the cottage living arrangements they experienced at women's colleges in order to manage the growing numbers of women enrolling at their universities. At all-women's schools such as Bryn Mawr, Vassar, and Wellesley, students in each hall ran the residence with their own student government. The cottage system usually placed a faculty woman in charge of the dormitory, and she advised house leaders who had been elected by their resident peers. Loosely replicating the US system of government, the elected representatives voted on living arrangements, house rules and activities, creating regulations around the consensus of opinion regarding when women should sleep, what counted as too noisy, and times and locations for studying.[6]

The deans of women at coeducational institutions implemented this basic student government system in each of their residence halls to help coordinate students. By 1903, at Talbot's first Deans of Women of the Middle West meeting, these administrators agreed that residential student government should underlie women's student life as much as "practicable."[7] They believed the system would acclimate women to college life and provide a way for deans to easily communicate information to students. More importantly, it put decision-making in the female students' hands, which the deans hoped would make women more invested in house rules and expectations. Indiana's Mary Bidwell Breed, a leader on the topic as it affected public institutions, encouraged the establishment of sororities because the houses had internal student government that lent itself to setting scholarship and behavioral standards for their members. She found this distinctly helpful in settling students into college expectations. Other deans of women established student government in residence halls, concerned that sororities were not within reach of more financially strapped women.[8]

When the deans borrowed cottage governance from eastern women's colleges, they also adopted the system's underlying premise—that student government prepared women for participation in a democratic society. In fact, some women's college faculty believed using the electoral process in cottages primed women students for the potentiality of suffrage. While most deans of women found public endorsement of suffrage too controversial in light of their positions, the democratic structure of residential government nevertheless taught students how electoral machinery operated, preparing them for the vote and for participation as citizens of the nation.[9]

Though deans may not have advocated publically for suffrage, many seemed to regard it as inevitable and as compatible with women's future in American society. NADW founder Kathryn Sisson Phillips recalled that early deans typically supported suffrage, noting she and her colleagues were "determined to affirm the essential role of the woman as wife, mother, homemaker, but we were just as determined that she should not be restricted to these functions and horizons."[10] In fact, the tie between student government and suffrage was close enough that, under Lois Kimball Mathews Rosenberry's leadership, the University of Wisconsin Women's Self-Government Association (an AWS chapter) formed an Equal Suffrage League in 1912. This involved over 500 students, and by 1916, they actively petitioned Wisconsin congressmen regarding women's right to vote.[11]

While deans used student government to teach women about democracy, the electoral process, and responsibility to society, they did not necessarily envision women's public participation as exactly the same as men's. Minnesota's Comstock and Wisconsin's Rosenberry envisioned women's duty to society as "social efficiency"—improving society—rather than as "citizenship," which they aligned with men's role in society. In practice, women's student government blended democratic methods with campus legislation, and by the late 1910s, deans of women adopted the word "citizenship" for women as well. The concept of student government as preparation for participatory democracy stretched from women's colleges to public coeducational institutions and into black colleges as well. By the 1920s, Lucy Diggs Slowe, the first dean of women at Howard University and a graduate of the premiere deans training institution, Teachers College at Columbia, promoted women's government as citizenship preparation for young African American women.[12]

Using residential student government as a tool to coordinate students, turn-of-the-century deans tackled how to guide what were largely upper- and middle-class white women into the public world of education. It was a precarious balancing act. As Talbot noted, society had no prescription for young women mixing with men at a residential university. More concerning to deans of women, higher education had not yet unconditionally accepted women students. Deans feared either poor scholarship or unseemly behavior by women would result in ending coeducation, taking with it women's access to the same faculty and courses as men. In this climate, women students' behavioral choices held high stakes, so expectations were strictly enforced.

Rules, however, never achieved total compliance. As Talbot once noted about student government, it was "futile to pass much general legislation to regulate procedure, since there seems no limit to human ingenuity in evolving social problems."[13] In short, students found loopholes in the rules, and even NADW founder Phillips later recalled her undergraduate college days of helping her friends sneak into the dormitory after curfew. With the future of coeducation riding on women's conduct, though, deans of women invested in the concept of student government as a way to encourage each female student to adopt campus behavioral norms.[14]

Early deans fused student government with a concept called self-governance, which M. Carey Thomas instituted at Bryn Mawr when she was dean of the college in 1891. Deeming it one of her highest achievements that her students learned to "bind themselves to take charge of all matters of conduct and behavior," Thomas believed self-governance meant each student developed the self-discipline and ethics to adhere to peer-defined campus standards of conduct.[15] She felt this prepared women for autonomous decision-making in adulthood, readying women to independently determine their own behavior within the structure of US society's laws and social norms. By 1903, deans of women affiliated with Talbot's Middle West group fostered these combined notions of self-governance and personal self-control, the latter of which reflected the thinking of Progressive educational reformer John Dewey. A University of Chicago professor active in the Hull House when he developed his main tenets on education, Dewey promoted self-discipline as a key precept in American education. Believing that a democratic society needed an education system that taught students how to govern themselves, Dewey proposed that the road to "freedom is in turn identical with self-control."[16] For Dewey, an individual's personal freedom arose from learning to think, to reflect upon one's situation, and to make choices about one's actions through personal self-control. His approach centered on an individual's desire to belong to a group, as Dewey believed students would self-discipline their behavior into the customs of a student community in order to gain peer acceptance. M. Carey Thomas, before him, had discovered this as well, and deans of women unified these ideas in self-governance. As Talbot stated succinctly, "true freedom comes through self-control."[17]

Like Thomas and Dewey, then, deans believed each woman would develop self-control in service to the norms of the residence hall or sorority because she desired to belong to the community of women there. Early deans taught each young woman that her personal freedom arose from her ability to make her own choices using group expectations as her guide. Unquestionably, social norms circumscribed the entire system, limiting women's sphere of activity. Nonetheless, this system taught women self-determination.

For most early deans, self-governance meant teaching a young woman to think for herself and to make choices that aligned with campus expectations; student government, on the other hand, referred to the mechanics of voting as a student body. While deans of women agreed that self-governance should occur through residential student government, they did not all implement the dyad in the same way. Many coached their residential governments to adopt codes of specific rules for women's behavior through legislation. Talbot refused this trend toward rigid rules and supervision, believing that organizing student government around disciplinary matters produced a triad of undesirable results: students governed only trivial matters, the faculty or supervisors often manipulated student choices, and the time invested in rule setting encroached on women's academic work. Since she thought it improper for women students to discipline each other, she embraced instead a system of personal advising. Instead of codified rules, Talbot believed in one-on-one conferences regarding behavioral issues and choices. As she once noted, "This was, of course, a long-drawn-out process; but I doubt if it consumed more time or effort than would have been necessary to enforce a body of minute rules."[18] In the 1920s, Howard University's Slowe similarly disliked rigid rules for her African American students. Like Talbot, Slowe avoided pushing parietal rules—regulations regarding women's behavior and housing—believing this would only lessen her students' adoption of independence and self-guidance. Though early deans chose to emulate Talbot in many ways, most were not like Slowe, and felt Talbot's rules were too few and gave more "freedom" than necessary. Despite these differences in how various deans combined residential government with self-governance, deans of women regularly used the combination of the two to craft a balance between behavioral standards, student freedom, and citizenship preparation.[19]

Clearly, deaning intertwined with organized student government and self-governance from the very beginning of coeducation. As campuses grew beyond a single women's dormitory, deans extended this governance dyad across multiple women's residences. At UC Berkeley, their first dean of women, Mary Bennett Ritter, established an overarching student government that linked all women's housing, from dormitories to sororities in 1894. One of the first groups named as the AWS, this alliance connected all women students on campus regardless of socio-economic background. Membership was not optional; upon enrollment, all female students automatically became members. Each residence elected representatives to serve on an executive committee that voted on women's concerns for the entire women's student body. Berkeley's structure would become the national model as colleges and universities either named their organizations AWS or the Women's Self-Government Association (WSGA). Aside from teaching young women citizenship skills, deans also supported strong AWS chapters because they increased the political clout of women students. When the entire women's student body called for a change or action together, administrators listened more readily. Berkeley began this tradition with its early AWS and used the group to provide marginalized women students with a base of power to push for "equality and integration."[20]

In 1907, just five years after Talbot gathered the deans for the first midwestern meetings, deans of women began to explore connecting each campus's student government into an intercollegiate network. The impetus for a midwestern alliance of women's governance organizations came from Wisconsin's

Rosenberry. In 1912, she sent two Wisconsin WSGA student leaders to observe a meeting of the four-year-old partnership between the eastern women's college student government chapters, called the Women's Intercollegiate Association for Student Government. When the Wisconsin students reported that challenges on coeducational campuses differed substantially from those that the women's schools discussed at the conference, Mathews organized a 1913 conference of women's governance associations from midwestern coeducational universities. Of the attending schools, only three had a formal campus-wide student government, though the others wanted to establish one. Not surprisingly, the schools hosted by Wisconsin's WSGA chapter in 1913 mirrored those in the original deans of women network, including the universities of Indiana, Iowa, Kansas, Minnesota, Missouri, Nebraska, North Dakota, Northwestern, and Ohio. The glaring exception was the University of Chicago, where Talbot refused to mix behavioral codes with student government, preferring personal consultation instead.[21]

Deans of women played a significant role in institutionalizing student government cooperation across campuses. Shortly after the Mathews' alliance began as the Middle Western IAWS, small women's colleges in the South created the Southern Intercollegiate Association of Student Government. Next, western states organized the Pacific Coast Conference. After a decade, deans began to consider consolidating all the intercollegiate AWS groups. At a 1923 meeting, on the Ohio State campus, the Middle Western IAWS changed its name to the Intercollegiate Association of Women Students (IAWS), merging its 45 chapters with the Pacific Coast Conference, which included UC Berkeley's active AWS organization.[22]

Later in 1939, NADW engineered the 22 women's colleges in the Women's Intercollegiate Association for Student Government to join the 84 IAWS chapters under the IAWS name in order to create a national umbrella for women's student government. Any institution which accepted at least 50 female students in the first-year class could join the IAWS. Most large coeducational institutions that had powerful deans of women established AWS chapters and joined the intercollegiate group. This stretched the reach of IAWS through the institutions that educated the largest percentage of women students, with chapters encompassing almost all large midwestern and western state schools. NADW formally oversaw this expanded IAWS with a new post, the IAWS National Advisor, elected from the NADW membership roster.[23]

The IAWS cleaved to the dyad of student government and self-governance, adopting Dewey's theory that seniors would influence younger students to accept the behavioral standards on college campuses. And, as the University of Ohio's dean noted in 1939 when the IAWS became a national group, deans of women sought to leave responsibilities "upon the students themselves" and "avoid methods...which might be construed as dominating."[24] Nationally elected IAWS officers routinely attended national AAUW meetings, and the two organizations built each other's membership rosters as AAUW asked university campuses to formally establish AWS chapters, and deans offered seniors AAUW membership information. By the mid-1930s, the deans of women regularly wove the IAWS into the AAUW-deans-Women's Bureau network as AWS chapters hosted career programs like the one at Ohio State. Across the nation, Women's Bureau staffers spoke to the AWS vocational conferences that dean's offices organized. And, just as Women's Bureau Director Mary Anderson traveled to Ohio State for Zorbaugh's programs, bureau employees like Marguerite Zapoleon and Louise Stitt spoke at schools throughout the 1930s and 1940s. By the 1950s, new bureau director Alice Leopold visited IAWS meetings, and the organization established what was for students an ambitious schedule of biennial national meetings, with regional meetings in the off years.[25]

The national meetings mirrored political conventions, with campus delegations sitting together next to their respective school signs on a convention floor, ready to vote on resolutions and bylaws that the college women prepared themselves. Practicing for political citizenship underpinned the entire organization in the 1940s and 1950s. In 1953, IAWS called on AWS chapters to prepare young women for "effective citizenship," recommending women take courses in economics and political science in addition to classes on family life and the arts. The association encouraged chapters to build women's leadership skills through mock political conventions, and efficient campus elections. Deans of women also suggested IAWS strengthen the membership of the League of Women Voters (LWV) by acquainting women students with local LWV clubs in order to facilitate college women's political participation after graduation.[26]

This broad IAWS system outpaced male student government. In fact, a 1930s national study found women students more organized than men, with two-thirds of the colleges saying the men on their campuses did not have student governance at all. Just as deans of women led male student affairs professionals in developing and organizing the student personnel field, they also led the development of student government ahead of male administrators and male students. Women students reported that 40 percent of their contacts with deans of women occurred through student government. However, deans of women remained bifurcated in their approach—some fostering minute rules, and others using student government to teach women decision-making skills. With the trend in the 1920s away from Talbot's approach and toward students voting on behavioral rules, only 4.2 percent thought their dean "had progressive ideas" about student governance and activities. Students with more conservative rule-bound deans like Esther Allen Gaw at OSU expressed a desire to have a more authentic voice in regulations than they were allowed.

By the 1930s, coeducational institutions no longer questioned women's right to attend college. However, the strict behavioral codes deans developed to protect women's position in higher education remained. And during the active professionalization of deaning in the 1930s, Marion Talbot's approach became a minority viewpoint. Women influenced by Talbot, like Mueller, avoided the most stringent rules produced by AWS through legislation. Taylor, though, would always recall resenting the rules that Esther

Allen Gaw enforced at OSU, and, like Marion Talbot, Taylor never lost her own distaste for the more conservative approach to parietals.[27]

INDIANA UNIVERSITY AS LEARNING LABORATORY

When IU appointed Kate Hevner Mueller as dean of women in 1938, she inherited an expansive AWS that extended through sororities and residence halls. However, it linked tightly with the governance of rules and a disciplinary board of faculty women who strictly oversaw behavioral infractions. Mueller's own experiences as a student at Wilson College, Columbia University, and the University of Chicago provided her with other models of women's student governance. As a doctoral student, she had lived in Chicago's Green Hall where Sophonisba Breckinridge was in residence supervising undergraduate women. There, as a graduate student, Mueller had no regulations at all. And, at Columbia, she studied with John Dewey. These experiences prompted her to loosen the women faculty's hold on student conduct at IU, moving decision-making into the women's student body by implementing a student-led board of standards which worked with students to improve behavioral choices rather than simply adjudicate rules.

As dean of women at Indiana, Mueller cultivated an advising strategy that linked head residents with the interests of students, noting that hall residents "should feel that the Head Resident was always on her side."[28] Mueller left most discipline to be implemented by the residential staff member unless a student rejected rules repeatedly. As head resident of Forest Hall, Taylor advised the dormitory's student government and handled all the counseling needs of these juniors and seniors. At Mueller's request, Taylor and her colleagues from other halls met weekly with the dean to address the regular problems of student administration. Each of Mueller's staff members oversaw a living group ranging from dormitories to sororities, so that all women's residences connected to the dean's office through the AWS. They also advised women's organizations like the YWCA, bringing every extracurricular women's activity under the dean of women's counseling umbrella as well. Ultimately, Mueller saw a strong dean of women's office as the means to "focus and indeed control the Panhellenic, the AWS, YWCA, loans, scholarships, landladies, and all the Halls to say nothing of the many honorary societies for women scattered through the many departments...[and the] activities off campus with women's groups in the state."[29]

When systemic challenges arose, Mueller (an accomplished statistician who had studied with L. L. Thurstone) crafted research studies to gather data in order to analyze situations. She used this tactic on everything from noise complaints that reached the IU president to changing the campus policy on dances. Other administrators pushing for conventional choices often found it difficult to argue with the data Mueller collected, and this made it easier for her to craft the women's programs she preferred. To conduct these studies, Mueller often involved AWS students. This practice taught undergraduates research skills, and provided the dean's office with volunteers to accomplish large analyses.³⁰ Taylor became a part of this effort when she began studying how to connect women through community and friendships. Taylor and a colleague conducted a study of women's friendships in Forest Hall, mapping out who had befriended whom, and where friendships and cliques overlapped. This provided her with a map of the women who, as outliers, risked school failure by not connecting well with a peer group. Taylor then counseled popular women to help link outsiders into the community.

Outside of work, Taylor and Mueller spent hours discussing the nature of women's education and how democratic governance prepared women for citizenship. "We talked about women having the opportunity to make as many decisions for themselves as much as possible," said Taylor.³¹ Mueller believed that "good citizenship would recognize no sex differences," arguing that men and women should receive the same education to prepare them both as future voters in American society.³² Drawing on the early deans' platform of knowledge, Mueller envisioned women's education as "citizenship training" that coupled studying economics, history, and sociology with learning electoral mechanics through the AWS.³³ A "good campus government" had to "furnish a working model of good government, able to deal fairly and quickly with all problems which concern students." It also had to "have a self-conscious awareness of the specific functions assigned to it...and must take care that it speaks for the entire student body."³⁴ In Mueller's view, women's citizenship education provided students with the opportunity to learn democratic values and skills, and to be conscious of the rights of others. In the governance dyad, Mueller believed young women learned self-discipline and self-control, and the ability to choose their own path within the parameters of the parietal rules and social conventions of the time. In addition, she believed AWS provided women with the means to respond collectively to social and political events on and off campus, ranging from World War II to developments in popular culture's gender norms.

Like all deans trying to foster young women's autonomy in a society with narrow behavioral expectations for unmarried women, Mueller wrestled with balancing the need to protect women from the double standard that punished them for sexual experimentation with her goal of freedom through self-government. In an era not ready to reject *in loco parentis* (the university acting in place of parents), Mueller recommended a system that helped women develop "appropriate standards" in a student-governed learning environment where older students could guide younger—and more immature—ones:

> The current mores and codes of conduct are no longer authoritative and fixed, but relative, flexible, and self-determined...there is danger when the standards of behavior are to be evolved from the group out of its own traditions and needs that a youth's lack of perspective will make him endorse experimental standards unacceptable to society. The student is after all still legally a minor, still a learner; he does not feel the restraints imposed by responsibilities of family, occupation, financial investments, or business pressures...Paradoxically, therefore, the campus must provide the forces which make him choose the

right actions "of his own free will!" Ideally, these forces should emanate from those students who have gained the maturity and the right to speak for the student group.[35]

Mueller balanced self-governance and student government by placing the leadership of AWS in senior women's hands, using their maturity to temper the immaturity of first year students. Since all women automatically belonged to AWS, Mueller cultivated a conscious awareness among AWS leaders that they must make choices for the entire women's student body. When conducting change, she suggested "short, compromising" steps that moved forward slowly to bring all women students into agreement and compliance with new AWS decisions.

Taylor adopted these concepts from Mueller. They formed the basis for her approach to student governance and would reappear in her work to create social change as a dean at the University of Kansas (KU). But before she could hope to lead women at a large university, Taylor needed to gain experience under Mueller and via positions at smaller colleges. In this, Mueller's tight connection with the NADW leadership launched Taylor as a dean in her own right only two years after she arrived at IU. To help Taylor advance, Mueller invited her to speak about her friendship study to an audience that included NADW President Hilda Threlkeld. From that, Taylor landed a position as Threlkeld's summer interim at the University of Louisville for both 1945 and 1946. Taylor recognized this temporary role as a path to her own deanship, and by 1946, she received employment offers from small schools. After reviewing the structure of each school's AWS and their women's regulations, Taylor settled on the dean of women's position at Northern Montana College where the AWS provided her latitude to lead, and the president offered her twice her salary to join the remote school.

Threlkeld sent Taylor off with sage advice on deaning that aligned with Mueller's insistence on slow, incremental steps for creating change: "The one word of wisdom I would give you is not to attempt anything revolutionary too soon. Win the confidence and friendship of the faculty and students, study the situation, psychology of the community, and traditions of the campus. Skillfully plant suggestions for changes among your student leaders and let them come apparently from them."[36]

As Threlkeld suggested, seasoned deans quietly steered AWS leaders, teaching women citizenship, autonomy, and responsibility to society through AWS itself. Taylor embraced this strategy, shepherding the Northern Montana women until 1951. When the college's president left, Taylor decided to return to IU for her doctorate in education with Mueller as her advisor.

FACING CHALLENGES IN POSTWAR AMERICA

During Taylor's time in Montana, the world of deaning shifted beneath her feet. The student affairs landscape permanently endorsed the male-dominated dean of students structure. NADW leader Esther Lloyd-Jones originally advocated for the shift to the "student personnel point of view," believing the streamlined system would retain women's stature. Later, after the Council of Guidance and Personnel Associations (CGPA) disintegrated and the consolidated system pushed women administrators out of leadership roles, she apologized to deans for not foreseeing how the move would dismantle women's position in the profession. Under the new streamlined system, deans of men renamed their organization the National Association of Student Personnel Administrators (NASPA), claiming to represent all of student affairs. However, NASPA rarely welcomed women deans who often reported a chilly climate when they participated in meetings during the 1950s.

Some deans of women found themselves losing their jobs or being "reorganized" out of a position that reported directly to the president into one that ranked lower in the administrative hierarchy. However, few demotions of a dean of women shocked the NADW more than Indiana's removal of Mueller in March of 1946. Six months before Taylor left for her first dean of women's post at Northern Montana College, Mueller received a day's notice to move out of the dean's suite of offices. IU's newly appointed Dean of Students Colonel Raymond Shoemaker, a military officer with no student personnel experience, sent Mueller packing without even speaking to her personally. He sent a young male assistant dean to tell Mueller she would move into a small office with two file drawers and a promise for a single bookcase. She read in the newspaper that her demotion to "senior counselor" ranked as a small part of Shoemaker's efforts to streamline student services in the new "student personnel" fashion. Mueller never understood her dismissal; ironically, of the entire IU counseling operation, only she held any formal counseling certification. Although some suggested Mueller a poor administrator, much of the NADW leadership—and Taylor—believed her demotion was an outgrowth of the dismissive attitudes about women's role on campus, especially as male veterans returned from World War II.[37]

Nationally, many deans of women lost their footing as the Servicemen's Readjustment Act of 1944 brought large numbers of men to coeducational campuses, decreasing the women students from close to 50 percent to a third of the student body by the mid-1950s. The influx of veterans who received tuition assistance under the GI Bill meant universities wrestled with inadequate classroom space and limited student housing. University presidents frequently displaced women, whom they saw as "incidental students," even moving them out of housing or classes in order to meet returning GI needs.[38] In fact, while Taylor served as acting dean of women at the University of Louisville, President Einar Jacobsen called her to his office at the end of World War II, pounded on his desk and ordered: "Get the women out of the men's residence halls...I don't care if you put them six in a room!"[39] The flood of male students, the adoption of the "student personnel point of view," and the demotion of women like Mueller sounded an alarm to deans of women. Both NADW and AAUW considered formal protests over the removal of Mueller, and eventually NADW established the Commission on the Education of Women (CEW) with the American Council on Education (ACE) to try to stem the minimization of women's higher education in post-World War II America.[40]

Such efforts faced a strong, popular countercurrent. While the nation widely discussed educating men for science and engineering as a critical component of national defense, the question of educated women's role in the nation's democracy became a footnote. Postwar culture reinvigorated the assertion that higher education should prepare women for domestic roles, and a new hyperdomesticity in the late 1940s and 1950s promoted the nuclear family as a key to capitalism, making gender roles a part of the nation's defense against communism. Proponents of a new popular psychology embraced and promoted Sigmund Freud's notion that "anatomy is destiny," claiming that biology destined women for marriage and motherhood. Books like Robert Foster's and Pauline Park Wilson's *Women after College* argued that the traditional liberal arts curriculum inadequately prepared women for marriage, and promoted the idea of women's education for the "average girl," which left intellectually gifted women out of the picture. Lynn White, president of Mills College, led the call for the "domestication" of women's higher education in his 1950 book, *Educating Our Daughters*, which criticized a liberal arts curriculum for preparing women to be men.

With the nation's media and experts like White calling for the country to tailor women's educational curriculum to domestic life, the policy debate revolved around whether and when married women should work. These trends significantly changed enrollment patterns for women. By 1956, one quarter of all white college women married while attending college in part because it was increasingly difficult for women to find professional positions, and their chances to marry decreased the longer they waited. Once married, many of these women left the university.[41]

To contest this growing consensus, women's advocates organized a response. AAUW took a strong stance against pro-veteran graduate school acceptance policies that limited women's entry, and the sociologist of women, Mirra Komarovsky, responded to White's book with *Women in the Modern World*, defending a liberal arts education as *the* basis for all human potential. Mueller followed with her 1954 book, *Educating Women for a Changing World*, which reasserted the AAUW-deans approach that a woman's education should prepare her for work whether or not she was married.[42]

CEW, borrowing on the prestige of ACE, brought attention to NADW's contention that a liberal arts curriculum should remain the basis for women's education. With national higher education policy ignoring women, CEW took an activist stance to fill the void, enjoying the backing of ACE President Arthur Adams for almost a decade until he retired. Adams lent his support to CEW, though he balked at anything that might seem to be feminist critique. This allowed CEW to blossom until the next ACE president, Logan Wilson, dismantled CEW in 1962. During its tenure, CEW published *How Fare American Women?*, a 1955 report by CEW Director Althea K. Hottel, on leave from her University of Pennsylvania post as dean of women. This booklet advanced three main points: college preparation for women did not align with the recent changes in American society; research suggested women should widen their career choices and options; and women could organize their desire to work around their responsibility to marriage and motherhood. Like NADW, however, CEW deferred to popular convention that motherhood should be women's primary role, though they were careful to report that no evidence illustrated a biological difference between women's and men's ability to earn a higher education degree.[43]

Not only did CEW's philosophy echo the vocational work by early deans, the commission reconsolidated the AAUW-deans-Women's Bureau partnership. Women's Bureau Director Alice Leopold lent CEW her support, and, together in 1957, the CEW steering committee and a select group of thinkers convened in Rye, New York. The conference attendees included current or former deans of women, Kate Hevner Mueller, Anna Rose Hawkes (George Washington University), Esther Lloyd-Jones (Northwestern), Kathryn Sisson Phillips (Ohio Wesleyan), Margaret Habein (KU), Althea Hottel (University of Pennsylvania), Eunice Hilton (Syracuse University), and AAUW general secretary Helen Bragdon (University of Rochester) along with Women's Bureau occupational expert Marguerite Zapoleon. Mueller worked closely with CEW as the Rye group published *The Education of Women* and further recommended liberal arts and the concept of life-phases which grew into the basis for continuing education.[44]

The CEW publications spread this philosophy nationally. The AAUW adopted *How Fare American Women?* as its program guide for local chapters and thousands of its members studied the publication. Taylor kept a well-read copy of the report at her desk, even saving it in her papers after she retired. The deans brought the CEW findings into IAWS as well, and students read and discussed the CEW newsletters and reports. At the 1953 IAWS national convention, women leaders from 97 universities or colleges listened to CEW director Althea Hottel, Maryland's Dean Adele Stamp, and the Women's Bureau's Marguerite Zapoleon report on CEW activities. NADW guided the IAWS to establish a repository of resources on women's education reflecting CEW's views which further cemented the connection with college women leaders.[45]

ACE invited IAWS as one of two student groups on its council membership in 1955. This recognized IAWS as *the* national voice of American college women. IAWS student leaders served on the CEW steering committee, ACE's Commission on Student Personnel, ACE's Commission on the College Student, and attended ACE annual meetings as well as NADW national conventions. Clearly, by the late 1950s, NADW had aligned IAWS with AAUW and CEW to address the minimization of women's education. They did so with a quiet feminism, accepting the popular opinion that the primary role of women was motherhood, and then arguing for a liberal arts background to prepare women for vocation and home, relying on the contingency planning arguments outlined in the previous chapter.[46]

Beyond "Quiet" Feminism; beyond CEW and NADW

Mueller's involvement with CEW and the national AAUW Education Committee took some of the bite out of her intense embarrassment over her almost complete dismissal from IU student affairs. She stayed at the university as an associate professor of education because she and her husband felt it would be very difficult for them to both find academic positions elsewhere. To escape the campus gossip, her disappointment, and the boredom of a "senior counselor" job with few tasks, she spent the years after the war writing her book, *Educating Women for a Changing World*, and immersing herself in CEW and AAUW activities. Her book's success brought frequent invitations to lecture across the country as well.[47]

When Taylor returned to IU for her doctoral work, she and Mueller spent hours discussing women's education and how to encourage women to make their own decisions as much as possible through AWS. In her book, Mueller outlined a vision for women's education that surpassed the quiet activism of CEW and NADW and offered a more radical goal—educating women for social change. Synthesizing the work of early deans of women on vocation, fair wages, government, and citizenship, Mueller's *Educating Women* advocated feminist positions that would resurface again in the late 1960s and 1970s. Rather than assuming that a philosophy of women's education must start with women's presumed domestic role as mother, Mueller dismissed biology altogether. Instead, she argued that both women and men needed family and called for education to prepare for the inevitability of college-educated women and men both working in professional positions and having a family.

Mueller foresaw the social changes required to support such a future, and asked the major thinkers in women's education to recognize that men had a role to play in the solution to sex inequality. She once told Women's Bureau director Alice Leopold that the bureau should place

> emphasis on what *men* should be thinking and doing. Why not solve that mother's problem of getting her daughter into the kitchen...by getting the fathers and brothers into it too? Let us not talk about how to care for children so that *mothers* can work, but so *fathers* can work. Of course, we are a long way from this, but somebody should start it. Many of the younger generation are thinking this way.[48]

Or, at the Rye conference, Mueller noted that women are "both pushed and pulled into the labor force: pushed by need for more money to maintain higher standards of living, and by the emptiness of a home life with too many gadgets and too little responsibility."[49] These ideas filled Taylor and Mueller's talks as they built new theories on how women's education could prepare women for this future of dual-career couples. In their discussions, the two considered what mainstream feminists would later label as Betty Friedan's bored, educated housewife, Pat Mainardi's *Politics of Housework*, and feminist calls for affordable, accessible daycare.

Despite predicting the future expansion of women's work and dual-career marriages, Mueller's mid-century feminist expressions of women's equal citizenship did not avoid the class and race bias that characterized the mainstream women's movement. Throughout her memoirs, scholarly work, and correspondence, Mueller considered working-class values as something for students to overcome. She believed higher education served as a means to assimilate working class youth into the norms of middle- and upper-class society. For women, Mueller considered AWS as a place to practice white, middle-class propriety—skills she thought all women would need to access the financial prosperity of professional work. In this approach, Mueller also called on black women to adopt middle-class norms of white culture as the pathway to economic opportunity, without recognizing the racism within such an assumption. Mueller, like many white feminists, held racial and socioeconomic biases that overlooked the ways race and income inequality further discriminated against poor women and women of color. Taylor, too, struggled with class bias, wanting to put the economic limitations of her childhood behind her. Only later in her career did she begin to understand the discrimination inherent in asking black women to assimilate into white culture. Instead, in the 1940s and 1950s, both Mueller and Taylor saw white middle-class norms as the route to economic prosperity and encouraged poor women and women of color to adopt these customs in order to find entry into the professional workplace.

Despite these biases, women's governance provided deans of women with a means to teach all women full citizenship. While some deans would apply the dyad of women's student government and self-governance in restrictive ways that invested in parietals, others would use it to foster women's autonomous thinking about how to make one's own decisions, albeit within the confines of a community's expectations. In support of women's political citizenship, deans developed a national, intercollegiate alliance for women students to give them a voice in campus and national venues, building support for women's liberal arts education among college women themselves. NADW used CEW and the power of ACE to try and stem the marginalization of women on coeducational campuses, and reconsolidated the AAUW-deans-Women's Bureau coalition to do so—linking it with the IAWS in an effort to forestall the domestication of women' education. Mueller, however, took the quiet individualistic feminism of NADW a step further, calling for higher education to prepare young women for a future world where gender equity existed. She borrowed many of her premises from early deans, and fused them with AWS practice. Out of these feminist underpinnings Taylor fashioned a philosophy of women's citizenship, autonomy and self-determination in order to educate women for the future. Always Mueller's student, Taylor put her mentor's vision for feminist change into practice at KU.

CHAPTER 3

Unlocking Women's Autonomy

In the spring of 1956, Emily Taylor answered a telephone call in her office at Miami University in Oxford, Ohio. On the line was Laurence C. Woodruff, dean of students at the University of Kansas (KU), asking to interview her for their dean of women position. The outgoing KU dean of women, Martha Peterson, had landed one of the nation's most prestigious dean of women's positions at the University of Wisconsin, and Taylor's name had been recommended to Woodruff as a possible replacement. Taylor welcomed the call. She had recently enlisted Kate Hevner Mueller's help to begin culling their shared professional network for a new post. When she accepted the associate dean of women role at Miami in 1953, they promised her the deanship on the impending retirement of the present dean. However, Helen Page had decided not to retire. And, while Taylor's family lived in Ohio, KU appealed to her. The position held prestige. Peterson, the National Association of Deans of Women (NADW) advisor to the Intercollegiate Associated Women Students (IAWS), had just hosted the 1955 national IAWS convention at KU. More important to Taylor, the women's organizations at KU operated solely through the dean of women's office, which would give her significantly more freedom to craft her programs. She saw the opposite at Miami where all the policy decisions regarding the female students required faculty senate approval. Miami's slow process limited the dean of women's ability to respond to female students' needs and to implement change.[1]

During her interview at KU, Taylor found a Kansas campus that reflected national trends regarding gender in academia. Male enrollments increased dramatically in the decade after World War II, as the Servicemen's Readjustment Act (GI Bill) made it possible for large numbers of veterans to attend college. At KU, the number of male students nearly doubled, from 6,300 in 1945–1946 to over 11,700 in 1959–1960. While KU welcomed the expansion, the veteran influx exacerbated mainstream attitudes that female students should use campus as a dating market rather than as an arena for intellectual pursuit. KU Chancellor Deane W. Malott agreed, noting in 1946 that he thought the presence of the veterans pleased the women students and that the men would "in turn attract more girls [to KU]."[2]

The KU faculty gender composition reflected broader national trends as well. The women who attended KU in the 1950s sat in lecture halls led largely by male faculty. One of the few female faculty members, art historian Marilyn Stokstad, recalled that when she arrived at KU in 1958 there was no "community" of women faculty members, nor were there any formal connections between female faculty and the dean of women's office.[3] KU enforced an anti-nepotism rule that stated that when a husband and wife both taught in the classroom, only one could advance through promotions—typically the husband. At colleges across America, female faculty appointments in the mid-twentieth century peaked in the early 1940s at 27.7 percent, dropping to 24.5 percent in 1950 and to 22 percent in 1960. Nationally, the number of women faculty varied greatly based on the size and prestige of an institution. In 1955, women totaled only 13 percent of faculty in private institutions, and 16 percent in public universities. Teacher's colleges fared better, with women constituting over 35 percent of the faculty, and small private colleges trailed just behind with 30 percent women.[4]

Within areas of specialization, though, women's faculty representation concentrated in categories associated with traditional gender roles. For instance, 96 percent of home economics professors and 71 percent of library scientists were women. Conversely, 0.5 percent of engineering faculty and 1.7 percent of law faculty were women. In larger, more prestigious institutions, women faculty resided almost exclusively in home economics. Not surprisingly, the dean of women was the only ranking female in most university administrative organizational charts, except for those with strong home economics schools where women often served as academic deans.[5]

Despite similarities between KU and other universities, the new KU chancellor, Franklin Murphy, chose not to follow national trends in one seemingly minor way. He did not collapse the dean of men's and dean of women's positions into one role—dean of students, as had been happening at other colleges since the 1930s—especially as the student personnel point of view gained prominence. Murphy did streamline his student personnel staff in 1953, "in a move to enlarge and coordinate personnel services for students" by promoting then Dean of Men Laurence Woodruff to the newly created position of dean of students. But he did not demote Martha Peterson.[6] Although the organizational chart showed the dean of women as subordinate to Woodruff, Murphy nevertheless maintained Peterson's autonomy. As Murphy noted, this "in no way affects the right of direct access to the chancellor's office possessed by the dean of women...she retains the primary responsibility for women's activities."[7] Peterson escaped the fate Mueller and other deans of women met in the "student personnel" approach that realigned female students under a male dean of students.

Taylor's interview at KU cemented her interest in the job. She particularly liked Murphy, a young chancellor who assumed leadership of KU at age 35. Taylor judged his thinking progressive regarding students' involvement in their own governance, and she liked his desire for a student personnel operation that fostered student achievement, leadership, and personal growth. Murphy clearly preferred Taylor too, and offered her the position shortly after she returned to Ohio. However, the structure of the position had already been changed. Once Martha Peterson announced her departure in

1956, Woodruff made a power play, lobbying Murphy to subsume the dean of women's role under him as dean of students, asserting: "Such a change of course is not at all acceptable to the militant suffragette but is the plan currently being followed by most of the institutions, which we might like to emulate."[8] It is not clear if Woodruff thought Peterson a "militant suffragette" who successfully fought for the dean of women's role to continue at KU, or if he meant any supporter of political citizenship for women. Either way, he convinced Murphy to acquiesce.[9]

Under these new terms, Taylor refused Murphy's offer of employment. Well-acquainted with the results of realignment at Indiana University where Mueller had lost her direct report to the president, Taylor resolved to continue looking for positions. If Murphy wanted to hire Taylor, he had a choice to make—did women students' concerns deserve a direct line to the top administrative officer?

Despite Woodruff's preference, Murphy agreed to maintain the dean of women's direct report to him, and Taylor accepted the job. Salary data shows that Murphy honored his commitment to a strong dean of women's role. In the 1957–1958 school year, he paid Taylor a salary of $8,000 ($1,600 more than Peterson's outgoing salary), while Dean of Men Donald Alderson (the former assistant dean of men who still reported to Woodruff) received only $6,700. These salaries illustrate the operation of KU's student personnel administration. Instead of a dean of men and a dean of women, KU maintained a dean of students and a dean of women, both reporting to the chancellor. As dean of students, Woodruff (paid $10,500) functioned as the dean of men with Alderson operating as his assistant, overseeing male student discipline. Taylor remained responsible to the chancellor, and she eventually delegated discipline activities to an assistant as well. At KU, reorganizing student affairs did not result in the dean of women losing her influence as it did at many other colleges where this demotion sheared women deans of their political influence as they lost their seats on key policy-making committees with a direct impact on women students. Instead, Murphy solidified women students' voices in the KU administrative structure—a factor that would provide women faculty, staff and students with a platform for organizing social change once the upheaval of "the sixties" arrived. More importantly to Taylor, by gaining sole responsibility for women's housing, student activities, and governance, Murphy provided her with the authority to craft women's student life at KU.[10]

Taylor would prove to be an activist dean of women in a nonactivist age, bringing with her the commitment to women's equality she developed in her own academic coming of age a generation earlier. During her years as KU's dean of women, Taylor bucked prevailing notions of rules, control over women, and domesticity. In doing so, she not only brought an inspired feminism to campus that predated the women's movement, she also challenged young women's adherence to and acceptance of the 1950s restrictive gender roles and notions of female respectability. In the process, she revolutionized women's presence on the KU campus—and the freedoms they enjoyed—blazing a trail with future national implications.

62 ❖ DEANS OF WOMEN AND THE FEMINIST MOVEMENT

Figure 3.1 Emily Taylor as a new dean of women, University of Kansas, 1950s

An Activist Dean of Women at the University of Kansas

Taylor arrived in Lawrence, Kansas, for the fall 1956 semester to a second-floor office near the chancellor's in Strong Hall. Across the corridor stood the doors for the offices of the dean of students and dean of men. The passageway divided men's and women's student affairs—a silent metaphor for the sex segregation that permeated student life in the 1950s. At KU, *in loco parentis* operated through a dual system of student conduct rules, which applied differently to males and females. One set, governed by Woodruff and Alderson, applied to all students, including women. The other set, overseen by the dean of women, regulated women's daily activities. Both sets of rules were peer-reviewed—or "student-governed"—through the All Student Council (ASC) and the campus AWS chapter, respectively. In both cases, administrators retained their right to "veto" student initiatives, and students—particularly women—viewed the administration as the ultimate authority.[11]

Like other coeducational schools, KU's application of *in loco parentis* policed the campus life of students through the control of women. Rules permeated KU women students' lives. Unlike male students, women on campus lived with daily closing hours (curfews) in the housing units and observed set times when men could call on them at their residences. Women's calling hours at men's living quarters were even more narrowly defined. Women sometimes stayed out after curfew for a special occasion, though only with the dean of women or her staff's approval of a "late permission." The AWS enforced the regulations in a heavily codified manner, employing a disciplinary board to review infractions that, by today's standards, seem quite trivial—such as arriving one to five minutes late for curfew on several occasions. Not only did men have no curfews or closing hours, but they—unlike female students—also possessed keys to their dormitories, fraternities, and rooming houses, and came and went as they pleased. Men's rules primarily dictated appropriate and legal consumption of intoxicating beverages and proper behavior at social events like dances. ASC officers, under the direction of the dean of men, also punished infractions with a disciplinary board. However, the rules left men largely free to do as they chose with only the abbreviated regulations outlining the parameters for their behavior. Because women were governed by both AWS and ASC rules, their extracurricular lives were tightly monitored. By controlling women's movements, coeducational schools indirectly hoped to control men, assuming that once the women returned to their housing, men would as well.[12]

Mirroring the national model, the AWS chapter at KU interlocked with almost every aspect of the dean of women's office. All undergraduate women who enrolled at KU belonged to the AWS chapter, and the women's activities included everything from freshman orientation, to women's academic honoraries, to women's athletics. Before she left KU, Peterson had moved KU's self-government group under the IAWS umbrella as an AWS chapter in 1946. A bicameral governing organization, it consisted of a house of representatives comprised of members elected by the women's housing units, and a smaller elected senate that met regularly with the dean of women to act on women's policies. By 1958, the *Lawrence Daily Journal-World* noted that AWS had grown to a significant stature at KU. Just as early deans intended, the KU AWS taught coeds leadership, parliamentary procedure, public speaking, and organizational skills. More importantly, it provided Taylor with a communication and organizational structure to manage women students and their campus life.[13]

Taylor fostered a feminist approach through the AWS, using her prerogative to define women's programming, only needing to justify her choices to the chancellor of the university. Because Murphy and other administrators regarded women as "incidental students," they left Taylor to her own plans as long as the female students and their activities did not generate any untoward publicity. Inspired by both her Ohio State mentor Grace S. M. Zorbaugh and her Indiana University mentor Kate Hevner Mueller, Taylor began to craft the KU AWS to support women's professional employment, to recognize sex discrimination, and to help young women reach their full potential. Out of Peterson's strong basis, Taylor set up programs—including role model speakers—designed to show students possibilities outside and alongside marriage and motherhood, eventually redirecting the focus of AWS from social activities and parietals toward leadership, vocational planning, and intellectual pursuits.

As a first step, Taylor established a resource library to support research on women and work. Zorbaugh had done the same at OSU, collecting books on women's vocations. Taylor brought her own collection of materials to KU, ranging from a report entitled "Reference Data on the Status of Women in America" to Mueller's *Educating Women for a Changing World,* which she required her staff to read. The majority of the materials she assembled came from the Women's Bureau, and were likely the same ones listed in NADW's *Guide to Guidance.* By the end of the 1950s, the books in the collection included Simone de Beauvoir's *The Second Sex,* Morton Hunt's *The Natural History of Love,* Mirra Komarovsky's *Women in the Modern World,* and CEW's publications. The library constantly expanded, with AWS students organizing subject notebooks full of news clippings and other documents ranging from human sexuality to women in religion. By 1973, the library boasted 50 subject notebooks, and KU believed it to be the second largest women's resource center in the United States. In the library, women students could find graduate school catalogs, financial aid materials, handbooks for professional job positions, career planning materials, and letters from KU alumnae pursuing nontraditional careers that described their work experiences. Like early deans of women, Taylor's office included a job placement service that helped students find part-time jobs to assist with their school expenses. She combined the placement service, career planning, and the library to provide comprehensive support to women considering careers and graduate school.[14]

As a second step, Taylor kept the solid infrastructure of AWS committees that Martha Peterson left behind, including groups responsible for IAWS coordination, student-faculty relations, sophomore counseling, hosting a high school leadership day for incoming women students, hosting an "all-women's day" for the university, and orienting first-year students to campus life. She added one new committee, the Commission on the Status of Women, to examine women's economic and political stature in American society. Likely the first campus commission on women's status in the nation, Taylor modeled it on the AAUW committee that had existed since 1926. At the end of her life, Taylor counted the commission among her greatest accomplishments, proud that it predated the presidential effort by John F. Kennedy by at least three years.[15]

In the commission, Taylor involved female students in research on women's status in society and at KU. The idea was controversial and Murphy asked her to rename the group because he thought "commission on the status" too provocative a phrase. She changed the name to the "Roles of Women Committee," though she switched back to her original terminology later. The interim title, however, shows her clear recognition of "gender roles," though they were not yet labeled as such. (Even the term "sex roles" did not appear until the late 1960s.) Taylor invited to the roles committee women who had already made non-traditional choices—like those studying pre-medical or pre-law curricula, or law students themselves. The group conducted research on women's lives and invited speakers to campus to discuss women's career options. Taylor featured the continuing education "life phases" model proposed by Mueller, showing women that motherhood only encompassed a small portion of women's overall lives. College women should prepare for meaningful work even if they planned to have a family, as either a contingency plan, or as an avenue of fulfillment when children were grown. The group worked with CEW publications and collected data regarding KU women. For instance, in 1959, the group investigated the increasing number of female student withdrawals from the university in the previous year. Here, Taylor educated the women on the post-World War II pitfall of women dropping out of college once married. And, in 1960, the year birth control pills went on the market, the committee conducted a survey on campus morals, endeavoring to understand "women's attitudes toward accepted behavior," including sexual activity.[16]

Before the women's movement of the 1960s began, Taylor taught KU women about gender roles and the issues of women's rights. In the 1960–1961 school year, she gathered women to work on a special subcommittee called "The Bright Woman" which Taylor oversaw herself. The call for members asked "Are You a Dedicated, Ambitious, Intelligent Woman?" listing qualifications for committee membership as the ability to do research and an interest in the roles of women. The research project objectives explicitly tied the committee to what Taylor saw as the genesis of the US women's movement and feminist ideals. The committee planned to "trace the progress of woman's rights" since 1776, review "present attitudes and prejudices" regarding intellectual women, and to "suggest corrections, alternatives and possible improvements" to those attitudes. The group also sought to consider "complete and approved freedom to combine marriage, child-raising and cultural advancement" by showing that "a woman's life can end at 40 if she has no outside interests besides her children," and that a woman has "30 to 40 years after her children are gone" when an education will allow her to find personal fulfillment through work. Familiarizing these KU women with the life phases approach "The Bright Woman" committee submitted a composite report to the KU liberal arts and sciences college, the education school, the sociology department, to a faculty member at Michigan State who was collecting national data, and to CEW at ACE.[17]

Centered on the questions that drove women's educational policy at a national level in CEW, the roles committee and "The Bright Woman" used speakers to explore key topics. As she had seen Zorbaugh and Mueller do, Taylor used these speakers to expand students' view of women in the workplace. Taylor and the roles committee selected speakers who illustrated options for women's life choices, often highlighting aspects of the CEW policy debates and encouraging her students to consider employment options. Taylor hosted lecturers on such topics as "The Problem of Women in Political Action" and the "Status of Women" in the United States. Just like Zorbaugh, Taylor chose speakers who provided women students with non-traditional role models, combining marriage and career in their own lives. An early example of this came in her first year, when she brought

Mueller, a married professional, to speak on the Manpower Commission at the "AWS All Women's Day" activities. Mueller called for women to "take their share of leadership," as the nation needed women's participation in the employment market due to the low birthrates of the Depression years.[18]

Cutting-edge speakers became a linchpin in Taylor's programming. "[Emily] was really a genius at...finding the new information or getting the new ideas [out]...or bringing the smart people into contact with the students," said Shavlik. For instance, "[s]he heard Sheila Tobias speak some place, and brought her for Women's Honors Night."[19] From the beginning, Taylor's speakers and topics contrasted starkly with the students' historic KU AWS programming that included a fashion show and a "Best Dressed Girl" contest. While Taylor did not eliminate the social aspects of AWS, she shifted the focus by expanding the program to a more intellectual approach, adding elements such as an annual scholarship dinner to recognize women's academic success, and awarding AWS scholarships to strong academic women whom she knew faced significant financial hardships. She coupled these AWS efforts with women's academic societies—strengthening the Mortar Board program for seniors, the Chimes junior women's honorary, and establishing a chapter of the women's sophomore honorary, the Society of Cwens (today called Lambda Sigma) where she served as the national advisory dean.[20]

Taylor strategically took a subtle approach, much as her mentor Zorbaugh had done. She carefully created her initiatives so that they stretched women students' thinking without being so far from the cultural norms about gender as to cause the women to reject them. Before she even arrived at KU, she was purposely matching the subject matter to the audience's awareness of options beyond traditional gender roles. In a letter to Mueller regarding an upcoming speaking engagement at Miami of Ohio, Taylor had written:

> The title and plan for your talk sounds fine to me. So far as I have been able to observe, our women students have heard little about the possible paths that they might take in the future. As I think I told you once before, we still have many in the marriage or career stage of thinking. *It seems to me that the specifics of educating women for the future are less important*, in comparison to other things that you might say, *than helping to convince them of the various possibilities of personal choice* [emphasis added].[21]

At KU, Taylor took the same approach, providing programming that expanded what women undergraduates understood as their future options. "When I came here [to KU]...The issue was still...whether they should be working at all if they had children, or at what point they should be in the workforce," recalled Taylor.[22] Few students saw marriage or motherhood as a choice. Instead, they considered them women's natural destiny. As such, Taylor purposely chose presentations to reach her audience of young women who were accustomed to domestic convention. In fact, Taylor recalled an incident that crystallized her commitment to this strategy. During an AWS panel presentation, one of the women speaking on the topic of women's equity (whom Taylor had not met before) presented a very negative attitude.

"She was an angry woman and that anger showed in everything that she had to say so that you were listening to her anger rather than to her words."[23] A student later told Taylor that several young women had rejected the concept of women's equality because of the speaker's vitriol. Taylor recalled:

> On the way home that night a whole group of women that came from one house walked home in silence. Then one of them said, "Well, if that's what equality is all about, I don't think I want any of it." And I [Taylor] thought we've just got to kind of cool it. This is not the right approach. This is not going to win any converts. We didn't have any laws, we didn't have any Executive Orders, we didn't have anything actually, except one or two civil rights or civil service regulations that were protective in any way. And I didn't want to see anyone driven off...I remember thinking that we're not going about this right...This is not in trying to explain things to men, this is to young women...After that, we were a lot more careful, I never, never allowed my name to be associated with any program where I was on the program committee and I hadn't either personally heard the woman speak or knew somebody whom I had trusted who had heard him or her speak and could say exactly how their approach would be.[24]

Taylor studiously avoided what would become the stereotype of radical feminism—public presentation of anger—and worked within the AWS chapter to subtly educate young women about women's equity. Reflecting on her time at KU, Taylor said she worked to encourage the students to implement the changes.[25] She also understood, however, that "there was a limit to how far ahead of them you could get."[26]

Taylor purposely used the AWS to reach widest possible number of women students, though she reserved personal mentoring for those who were particularly promising intellectually and as leaders:

> The programs were usually for the majority. But at the same time, there were always small groups of people who were way ahead. There were people who frequented my house, who just came to call. There were people that would be in a class that I'd teach, who'd come to the office to talk about something...that's what we were trying to get them to do was look at themselves and what they wanted, not what was right for the majority of the people.[27]

One set of women on whom Taylor focused her time were the Watkins Scholars. KU awarded these honors students full scholarships for their superior academic achievement in high school, and Taylor mentored them closely. "That was a very important program to Emily and she spent a lot of time with the Watkins Scholars in building support systems and structures for them, and working with those really bright women who may or may not have had anybody else who had cared about them in quite the same way," remembered Shavlik.[28] Taylor held more patience for intellectually gifted women, taking time with them to encourage their personal development.

Taylor mentored by the Socratic method, questioning and encouraging her students and employees to think critically about conventional attitudes about women, and to intellectually engage in questions regarding sex equity. As Taylor noted:

> What I tried to do was to get them to think through this whole situation for themselves, about themselves and not what they read somewhere, or what somebody told them was the appropriate thing to do. What did they personally want to do [regarding work and marriage]?...So, we tried to let everybody talk, and not to respond to every single thing that anybody said, but leave them at least with something to think about.[29]

Borrowing another strategy from Mueller's playbook, she frequently hosted dessert parties, dinners, and overnight retreats at her home, where she could casually address these topics. She used every opportunity to engage in these discussions, including frequently driving student leaders to conferences so she could spend the time in the car addressing equity topics with her captive audience. In one instance, she recalled hosting a sorority pledge class at her home while the sorority actives prepared for initiation. "We got into a big discussion about women working and what their lives should be like," said Taylor.

> Some of them wanted to argue about it...They just weren't at all sure that's the way it ought to be. And then their boyfriends picked them up and they went to Kansas City to a show...and when they came back, I think I'd already gone to bed, and they [returned and] said, "we just want you to know that we understand now what you were talking about." They had gotten into the same discussion with these fellows and these fellows were...espousing the idea of how important it was for the woman to be at home and to help her husband rather than to try to have this ambition for herself. And, all of a sudden, they were on the other side [of the argument].[30]

Taylor closely guided the AWS and personally built relationships with the student leaders in order to help these women consider their futures as a set of choices they could make for themselves, an alternative to relying only on conventional understandings of womanhood.

Taylor challenged her students to question gender roles through both programmatic and individual interactions. She often met with the AWS president at her home on Sundays or in her office on Mondays in preparation for the weekly AWS senate meetings. "She fed me ideas," said Anne Hoopingarner Ridder, president in the 1960–1961 school year. "I knew exactly what I was supposed to do when I ran the meeting...I felt very enabled and knowledgeable. Looking back, I was her disciple."[31] These interpersonal relationships formed the base she needed to foster her programming. Ridder recalled Taylor often relied on the women to "market" her suggestions through their social networks. "She wasn't radical or confrontational; she co-opted us," recalled Ridder, who added that Taylor subtly asked the women broad questions about their role in society, their reasons for attending university, and their plans for their lives after graduation. Ridder remembered, "In her query was...a more forward looking agenda than I was aware."[32]

As Taylor's programming grew, so did her budget and staff. In 1956, Taylor had inherited a dean of women's office with a total budget of $14,801, with $1,225 of that for non-salary expenses. The office included Assistant Dean Mary Hardman and a secretary. By the 1957–1958 school year, Taylor's second year at KU, Murphy agreed to increase Taylor's total budget by $12,000, an 81 percent increase. She hired IAWS Executive Secretary Donna Younger (Shavlik) as first assistant to the dean of women, further strengthening KU's connection with the national organization. The trend continued, with Murphy approving two more assistants to the dean by 1960–1961. By 1962–1963, she added staff positions at Corbin, Gertrude Sellards Pearson, Lewis, and Hashinger halls, and also funded new part-time positions, called "preview assistants," to help orient first year women. Ten years after her arrival at KU, Taylor's budget totaled $50,085 and had grown almost 240 percent over Peterson's last appropriation.[33]

Taylor's Widening Reach

The increasing financial investment KU made in Taylor's office blossomed into a growing network of women that Taylor trained and placed in women's organizations, residence halls, sororities, and academic honoraries across the campus. Taylor replicated Mueller's IU operation and divided the halls across her staff so that each residential group had a person accountable for it. "We tried to arrange it [so] that everybody was involved with some kind of a living group. Either a scholarship hall or as a special advisor...for the out of town or for the commuters...That was something that ran through the whole thing."[34] Taylor often hired the staff from her network within NADW and IAWS, or from recent KU student leaders. For instance, Taylor had met Shavlik at an IAWS conference, and then offered her a job living in Gertrude Sellards Pearson Hall and planning the freshman orientation program with former KU AWS student leader Kala (Mays) Stroup. As with Stroup, Taylor mentored undergraduate students through AWS, encouraged them to enroll in graduate school at KU, and then employed them on a part-time basis in residence halls or in her office. Stroup exemplified this "grow-your-own-staff" pattern, as she had served in the KU AWS senate leadership, attended national IAWS conferences with Taylor, and, after her graduation in 1959, joined Taylor's staff. Eventually, Stroup became associate dean of women and finally dean of women when Taylor left in 1974. Shavlik and Stroup are just two examples of the networked system Taylor developed, which provided professional positions to the young women she mentored.[35]

Taylor's "deaning" operation overlapped with the realities of working in a state-funded institution. As Taylor once noted, the dean of women met a plethora of expectations regarding her role that were "wildly diverse and sometimes totally incompatible."[36] In short, a dean of women dealt with reconciling the opinions of the governor, board of regents, chancellor, parents, both men and women students, the local and alumni public, the faculty, and her staff, not to mention her own. As Taylor recalled, "[T]o me the most important roles were those I chose for myself."[37] Taylor emphatically noted that no dean of women could satisfy all the constituencies all the time—the key was balancing her own agenda with the other viewpoints.

At a state university, all these constituencies ranked as important, and Taylor clearly understood that her responsibilities included keeping the university out of the news due to student behavior problems. To do so, Taylor asked that her staff keep her informed of anything that might become controversial so that she would have an opportunity to resolve it before it became a public relations problem. Taylor always alerted the chancellor to any concerns she felt might come to his attention through another venue. The types of issues that ranked as reportable varied depending upon the period in which they occurred. In the 1950s, a woman spending the night at a hotel with a man would rise to the level of a report to the chancellor. By the late 1960s, drug use ranked within this category.[38]

However, Taylor often refrained from reporting events that would not cause public relations problems. As much as possible, Taylor handled discipline issues within the dean of women's office. "The way I felt about it was that if there was a standard list of 'if you do this, x happens, and if you do that y happens' you don't need a dean of women—you need a book that tells you what to do."[39] Examples abound of Taylor's commitment to help women learn from their mistakes. Once, she convinced the Weaver's department store owner to drop charges against a woman student who had shoplifted merchandise, promising rehabilitation for the student. Taylor's style opposed that of Dean of Men Don Alderson, who frequently involved police and invoked campus disciplinary policies in accordance with formal procedures. In fact, most of the student disciplinary records at KU reside in the dean of men files. Taylor kept few notations. Her discretion built her a strong reputation with students, which meant that many women (and men) came to her office for assistance without fear of reprisals. Rather than seeing her role as disciplinary, Taylor wanted women to learn to self-govern in the same way that Marion Talbot wanted her students to learn autonomy.[40]

Her tightly woven network of employees carried Taylor's philosophy into the day-to-day operations of the living units, women's organizations, and scholarship honoraries. Taylor mentored staff about how to apply feminist philosophy during weekly, often long, staff meetings. "Emily let us work it out," said Stroup, recalling that many of the women affiliated with the dean's office were in different frames of mind regarding the development of their own feminist consciousness. "When someone said, 'Oh, we can't do *that*,'" Stroup noted Taylor would facilitate the group discussion so that the women would think through how convention might be influencing their reasoning.[41]

Much of the individual student counseling occurred at the staff level closest to the student's daily campus life, so that women accessed guidance without needing to make a trip to the dean of women's office. The network functioned at all hours as Taylor, Shavlik, and Stroup all experienced frequent visits from students at night. The counselors kept Taylor abreast of the activities in the various living units, providing her extensive knowledge of women's individual and group activities. Both Taylor and her staff helped KU coeds see that limitations on women were cultural constructions rather than biologically based natural differences between males and females. Later, the women's movement of the 1960s would name this process of deconstructing normative, social expectations in small circles of women as "consciousness-raising."[42]

While the women's liberation movement has claimed the term, the work Taylor did with her office and AWS leaders incorporated the same "consciousness-raising" method. In one activity, Shavlik recalled Taylor culling data from Women's Bureau reports, and drafting "futures" onto slips of paper for each student to adopt in a role play activity. As each young woman pretended to live a fictional future, all the women came to understand that some would be divorced, others widowed, some working, and some staying at home to raise children. This provided them a much clearer picture of the reality of women's lives after college than did the popular media which defined many coeds' outlook. "We were trying to tell women that nine out of ten of them were going to be in the labor force whether they thought they were going to be or not," said Taylor.[43] Taylor combined this "consciousness-raising" strategy with her mentorship, helping young women like AWS president, M. Kay Harris, to understand they could make non-traditional choices.

> Dean Taylor helped me understand the phrase "the personal is political" and made me think through my personal choices. She said: "Well, Kay, you just have to figure out how it seems to you if you never marry. If that's okay with you, then go about your business." I have not ever married and I knew I did not want children. I felt she gave me a form of liberation; she gave me permission to make a choice when everyone thought of marriage as a given.[44]

Taylor used the AWS to help young women understand that marriage and motherhood were choices, not directives. She integrated this core understanding throughout her program wherever she could, raising young women's understanding about women's roles, equality between men and women, and opportunities for professional work.[45]

At KU—years before Betty Friedan published *The Feminine Mystique*—Taylor challenged her students and staff to question the conventional wisdom regarding marriage, career, and self-potential. She did so by implementing the same methods early deans developed: vocational libraries, lectures, and role models, along with data—often from the Women's Bureau—regarding women and work. In the structure of AWS, the programs she offered, her advising style, and the breadth of her office organization, Taylor helped women build self-efficacy and leadership skills. Like Zorbaugh with her volunteer-run conferences, Taylor developed a system at KU to teach them practical skills while also raising their awareness of systemic discrimination against women, and how they might achieve economic opportunity.

> I wanted to encourage women students to challenge the status quo, avoid dumbing-down their ambitions and seek equality with men in every legal,

social and economic arena. I wanted a program through which we could be a guide to all women students, a sponsor for many, and mentor for the leaders we identified among them. I wanted to find ways to promote women on campus, encourage women to accept responsibility, inspire them to dream important dreams. I urged women students every chance I got not to downsize their goals, their intelligence, their ability to change what needed changing. I even taught a few about Irish diplomacy: The ability to tell someone to go to hell in a way that makes him look forward to the trip. I wanted to create an environment in which women would feel comfortable in establishing a vision that goes beyond the conventional. I wanted a program that would help them realize their dreams—an active program to empower women and increase their leadership skills and their desire to lead and to protest inequities wherever they were found.[46]

Taylor's intentions cast a broad footprint across women's student life at KU. However, for many coeds, Taylor's promotion of AWS leadership, vocational advising, and educational equity would square up against the students' own investment in the behavioral gender norms that were reflected in parietal rules. Taylor found that with differential rules in place, women students limited their scope of vision for themselves. Taylor's largest impediment to her agenda would not be administrative pressure or even budget. Instead, the biggest stumbling block was the socially determined attitudes of the women students themselves.

Don't You Trust Your Daughter? Taylor Takes on Parietals

Clearly, Taylor's operation emulated the practices early women's deans crafted—implementing vocational speakers, a library of resources, and guidance toward careers and graduate education. However, by the mid-1950s, many AWS chapters had become Marion Talbot's nightmare—the use of student government in service to petty, trivial behavioral rules. While the AWS chapters met Mary Bidwell Breed's early goal that self-governance would help coeds adopt campus behavioral norms, the early deans' vision had morphed into a myriad of detailed rules governing dating, curfews, study hours, and social arrangements. Young women understood the machinery of democratic governance, but they put their knowledge of parliamentary procedure into service for the production of disciplinary regulations. In addition, the flurry of professionalization and consolidation in student affairs associations and deans of students' offices in the late 1930s through the early 1950s meant that the AWS operated more and more in service to the "student personnel point of view," and less and less in service to the original feminist notions of preparing young women for public sphere participation. With deans of women in the 1950s no longer concerned that women would not be welcome in higher education, the rules that had once protected women's participation in the academy began to serve mainstream ideas about women's domestic roles, reinforcing normative ideas about proper behavior—a reflection of normative, white, middle-class womanhood. Despite the vocational and CEW programming across the country, AWS leaders of the 1950s often spent hours refining the established regulations rather than learning to think for themselves.

In the 1950s, KU's AWS chapter mirrored this trend. In fact, before Taylor's arrival in the fall of 1956, the AWS chapter planned to spend more time on the rules in order to clarify behavioral expectations for women students. The KU AWS leaders invested in the concept of self-discipline, and called for more intense discussion of rules in the hope that young women would internalize them and make appropriate behavior choices. They produced a handbook that set out expectations in what seems today to be ridiculous detail. Curfews varied based on whether it was a "school night" or a date night, and overnight outings had to be approved even for visits to family or friends' homes. Taylor, never a patient woman, found the AWS rule discussions almost painful, an excruciating trip through minutiae. The process particularly annoyed her because it steered student attention away from their studies, her campus commission on women's status, and the vocational work of the AWS.[47]

Taylor purposely laid groundwork to eliminate the special parietal rules for women. Her efforts would make KU the second campus in the country to allow senior women keys to their housing, and one of the first large campuses to allow all women the freedom to come and go as they pleased while in college. Taylor, lucky to have significant support from Chancellor Murphy, received little attention in 1958 when she quietly began to dissolve the regulations. The initiative pushed the boundaries of conventional standards of the era, though, and likely many women deans considered the idea too controversial to implement on their own campuses. "Senior keys," as the students called them, quietly unlocked the door for significant change that would arrive in 1966, when the university eliminated curfews for most KU women. At that point, a thorny debate erupted. Many parents and citizens howled in protest. Letters of opposition poured into Chancellor W. Clarke Wescoe's office. Not surprisingly, Taylor's leadership was scrutinized. Historical studies of KU student life have noted the 1966 furor over eliminating closing hours for women's residences, but little attention has been paid to how the elimination of parietals began.[48] With higher education history often focused on the chaos of the 1960s and the presumption that students pushed administrators to change, few historians have looked for an administrator prodding students to change. Taylor was that administrator.

Taylor saw women's student government as a training ground for leadership and a venue for women to define their own policies. For her, self-governance was about self-determination. Taylor set out to have her students consider why—and for what purpose—they attended a university. She envisioned student governing bodies as a way for students to participate in designing campus procedures in more than name only. Although it was controversial on most campuses to allow any student involvement in disciplinary matters, she advocated that general policies be set by student groups and the implementation of the policies in individual disciplinary cases be handled by administrators in order to protect the privacy of the student.[49]

When reflecting on her career, Taylor recalled over 40 years later that nationally, AWS advisors "kept talking about self-governing as if that's what they were doing, governing somebody." Taylor disagreed. She believed that AWS's role was "devising ways through...programming to help women understand more about the world and be more independent and learn more leadership skills."[50] Taylor wanted to provide women the opportunity to become autonomous and self-governing according to Dewey's and early deans' philosophy. On campus, she felt this started with young women developing personal behavioral standards and the confidence to apply them in their own lives without an authority dictating their personal actions:

> I thought that our job was to help those women grow up and get rid of their adolescent ideas about the relationships of men and women. We wanted to produce leaders...and to look at issues...thinking of what was going on rather than just accepting it. We wanted them to learn how to challenge what was wrong.[51]

At KU, this philosophy underpinned her actions, as she exchanged the conservative understanding of "self-governance" and "self-discipline" for what she termed "personal responsibility."[52]

Soon after her 1956 arrival, she began shifting the discussion of rules out of the AWS senate meetings and into the individual houses in order to free AWS senators to focus on women's activism and scholarly activity. She set up an AWS committee to work with her to rewrite the AWS constitution to allow women's living groups to implement more of the rules themselves. Under this new constitution, student resident leaders could approve curfew exceptions and resolve their own disciplinary infractions unless the behavioral problems were particularly significant. The revisions provided more autonomy and responsibility to the women and distributed some of the dean of women's power to the student-run housing governments. Taylor evangelized that each woman had to take responsibility for her own actions, consistently reminding AWS that student government was not simply a court for behavioral infractions to mete out punishments.[53]

To help with the conceptual transition, Taylor restructured the disciplinary panel of AWS by changing the "judiciary board" to the "board of standards," signifying a move from the punitive toward self-development. She also assigned the board of standards to her assistant dean, Pat Patterson, showing students that the dean of women's job encompassed more than student behavioral rules. Through these changes, Taylor set the stage for a shift in the AWS away from parietals toward intellectual development. She hoped the transition would clear the way for vocational and leadership counseling—so women would accept responsibilities beyond the conventional confines of gender roles. First, though, Taylor needed women to understand that they, as the female student body, set and administered their own rules. She wanted them to stop relying on a parental figure to govern their behavior. College, she believed, prepared young women to become adults, ready for their own self-governance and autonomy. The students, however, currently looked to the dean of women as the rule-setter, thinking little about where the rules originated or who developed them.[54]

Taylor set out to change this in her second year at KU. Inviting the senate to her home for a sleepover retreat, Taylor hosted the AWS leadership to plan the next year's activities. Students—including Kala Mays (Stroup)—arrived with their pillows and pajamas, ready to discuss areas for AWS growth. Taylor put women's status and intellectual pursuits on the agenda. Most importantly, though, she convinced the AWS leadership to try an idea she had begun considering in graduate school at Indiana—a special convention to set new AWS rules and regulations. Taylor suggested a campus-wide women's meeting so that the AWS could refashion the parietals to reflect their thinking on how women should behave. The students agreed to the convention, laying out a plan for each women's housing unit to create its own slate of behavioral expectations. Each residential group, then, would send its slate of ideas to the convention along with a delegation that would vote on a final set of rules for all KU undergraduate women. Taylor intended that the conference would make the women in each house cognizant that they set their own rules as a group. She believed the convention would give the women an opportunity for real student governance.[55]

However, the residence governments—beset by women who "could not forget about the old rules"—generated few new ideas.[56] The house members seemed stumped about the purpose of the project, and the AWS senators frequently asked Taylor for guidance on how to advise their sororities and residence halls to complete their slates of regulations. In an age when women found social acceptance through domestic conformity, the students had trouble imagining themselves as the arbiters of their own behavioral norms. Instead of greater responsibility and freedom, the houses simply revisited existing curfews and male visiting privileges for the convention to consider. Even the AWS officers with whom Taylor met weekly found reconceptualizing the parietals to be difficult. The senate meeting minutes frequently recorded the senators failing to understand they could create peer-defined norms that were arbitrated by the AWS and not the dean. When the February 1959 AWS convention began with Kala Mays (Stroup) chairing the convention, the delegations actually recommended less autonomy for themselves by voting to reverse the new constitution and to reassign approvals for curfew exceptions back to the dean of women. Clearly, the women preferred a parental authority implementing rules—trying to avoid the awkward position of sanctioning a peer.[57]

Despite Taylor's attempt to have women take ownership of their own behavior standards, the convention resulted in only two notable changes to existing rules—extending the curfew during finals week to midnight, and recommending "senior privileges," which would permit senior women to operate outside standard rules in limited situations. Although the history of student protest often assumes students pushed for and welcomed more freedoms, the AWS and its leaders resisted even these two changes. Both needed ratification by the senate, and neither found easy approval despite Taylor's support, reflecting the strength of women students' opposition to eliminating even a small portion of the parietal rule apparatus.[58]

Taylor had to do some wrangling to overcome the women student leaders' objections to even these modest rule changes. AWS Board of Standards Chairman Mays (Stroup) ran the ratification meeting, sitting behind the dean's mammoth wooden desk next to Taylor. The two heard extensive complaints from the student senators against extending curfews to midnight during finals week. The students worried that women would have too much unsupervised time with the library closing at 10 p.m. Taylor nullified that complaint by negotiating with the university administration for the library to remain open during finals week until 11 p.m., and the senate finally agreed to extend the finals week curfew. Taylor structured this one-week change in closing hours as an experiment that, if successful, would lay the groundwork for more expansive curfew changes. Knowing that any enduring parietal adjustments depended upon women behaving reasonably, Taylor often reminded the students that "the whole group is responsible for the action of any individuals."[59] Here, Taylor drew on the early deans' reliance on peer pressure to ensure female students' conformity to expectations as she loosened the strictures on their tightly controlled lives. Certainly, as dean of women at a public institution, Taylor took a risk endorsing student freedoms. However, finals week flew by with no incidents.

Despite the success, senators were not convinced they should approve a permanent midnight curfew for weeknights, which Taylor now recommended. Senate leaders catalogued their concerns, contending that women arriving home late at night would wake others in the residences, and that campus buildings closed too early, leaving women with no sanctioned, public places to frequent late in the evening. What they did not specifically articulate was their fear that this "free time" would mean an extra hour of ungoverned time with men on dates—which might either lead to sexual temptation or to pressure by their dates to engage in sexual activity. Taylor dismissed these arguments by suggesting that the houses increase their quiet hours penalties to prevent disruptions, and insisting that the early curfews restricted women's intellectual growth by limiting study. Despite student concerns, the finals week experiment had convinced Chancellor Murphy that women's closing hours could be permanently extended to midnight. Taylor worked with him to arrange for more campus buildings to remain open later at night for all students to study. Eight months after the convention, a brief note in the September 1959 AWS minutes indicates that the hours had become permanent at the library and other halls. This part of Taylor's "experiment" worked. The women accepted later weeknight hours, taking a small step toward autonomy and Taylor's goal for women to make their own behavioral decisions.[60]

At the same time, Taylor had an opportunity to house upper-class women in a coeducational dormitory. The men's dormitory, Carruth-O'Leary, which housed the football team, was not projected to fill to capacity for the 1959–1960 school year. Structured with two separate wings and a common entrance and recreation room, the building allowed a division in sleeping quarters, with separate areas for socialization. With an overflow of women who were required to live on campus, Taylor worked behind the scenes to arrange for a coeducational dormitory experiment. If that proved successful, she felt administrators would begin to support the dissolution of parietals. Taylor appointed Donna Shavlik as the hall counselor, and the residents moved into Carruth-O'Leary in the fall of 1959. Shavlik fondly recalled standing at the front door, signing in women, and the male residents being quite protective of them. The *Lawrence Journal-World* reported a success, the living arrangements proof that the administration could have "confidence in the maturity of young men and women attending university these days."[61] The men in Carruth-O'Leary earned the campus' highest grades for men, and the women residents earned the second highest grade point averages among women's residential groups. The coeducational programming paved the way for Taylor to begin to eliminate parietals, proving to the administration, community, and students that upper-class students made responsible choices even when living in the same building. For her next step, Taylor planned to implement senior privileges.[62]

The 1959 convention had approved senior privileges, but the AWS senate was reluctant to approve them, and the officers found little consensus on how to structure them. Prior to the convention, Taylor suggested that the AWS senate consider providing senior women with keys to their residences and eliminating senior curfews. Taylor explained, "We were at this meeting and they were talking about these piddly little things, like fifteen minutes here and half an hour there, and I just said, 'Have you considered keys?' It was an electrifying moment." Taylor remembered that the women paused, "It took them a while [and they finally] asked 'to the sorority house?'" as they slowly understood the dean's meaning.[63]

The idea of senior privileges was not entirely new. Since 1941, Florida State College for Women had allowed academically strong seniors to enjoy longer hours, and Taylor knew another dean in Colorado who was also considering keys for seniors. At KU, the senior women inducted into the women's honorary, Mortar Board, already received keys due to their maturity and scholastic accomplishments. Taylor's suggestion simply extended to all senior women the same privileges Mortar Board already enjoyed. The women, however, found the idea of controlling their own hours foreign. Ridder, who was AWS president during the year AWS adopted senior keys, recalled that she resisted the change. Many women welcomed the rules on behavior as a means to protect their reputations, thinking of the school as a parent providing guidance on what was socially acceptable and what was not. While many snuck around the rules, they liked the security of knowing they could turn down a date or a sexual advance by claiming they must follow the regulations. Ridder said Taylor finally convinced her to consider the senior keys by stressing that many women circumvented them.

"I was naïve. I thought everyone followed the rules," said Ridder, remembering how Taylor proved her point. "[Taylor told me] 'you think everyone is in at closing hours. Let's go visit the sororities and scholarship houses, bring treats and have a party and see.'" Ridder recalled driving Taylor around Lawrence one night after closing hours, stopping at each house and announcing that the dean of women was there with refreshments, and inviting everyone down to the lobby. "Half of everyone was gone," said Ridder, remembering that the sign-out sheets recorded them as being in the residence for the night. Ridder said this finally clarified for her that a number of women already avoided the rules when it suited them.[64]

Taylor contended that it would be safer for women if they did not hide their whereabouts by sneaking around rules. This was a real concern as accidents and date rapes happened when students snuck in and out of their halls and sororities.[65] Taylor learned this at another campus when she witnessed an incident where a couple died from carbon monoxide poisoning at a "lover's lane." In that accident, the woman's sorority sisters noticed her missing, but none knew where she was. Using safety as a part of her rationale, Taylor pushed Ridder and her AWS peers to consider keys and for seniors to report their destination rather than sneaking out of the residence.[66] This promoted a wider range of acceptable activities for senior women and claimed for them their ability to make their own responsible decisions about how to behave as an adult.

The women, experiencing college life amid strict 1950s gender role expectations and social norms that held a sexual double standard, saw the rules as something breakable when desired, but also as a convenient tool for politely declining dates. In this, KU women were no different than those at other universities. Nationally, a mid-1960s survey reported college women supported curfews "because they were useful in helping girls leave their dates after local night-spots closed."[67] Taylor recognized this as the crux of the problem. Although few women voluntarily told Taylor why they regularly broke the rules, the fact that Taylor's office oversaw discipline left little question for her as to how and why women manipulated the regulations as disciplinary cases often involved dating and sexual activity. Former assistant Donna Shavlik recalled the issue similarly. "I always hate this extreme language, but I guess it really is true, [there was] such oppression of women that they had bought into it. So women students who did not set their own hours used it [curfew] for excuses [to return to the dorm or sorority while] on dates and it kept them from having to make decisions themselves."[68] Conversely, women who determined to forgo the normative restrictions broke the rules purposely, willing to gamble that they would not be caught sneaking in late at night. In either case, the rules allowed women to avoid accountability for their own behavior as adults.[69]

Despite the 1959 convention approving senior privileges, the AWS senate still resisted senior keys in the fall of 1960. Taylor went back to her strategy of having each house propose a slate of options for an overall vote—this time on how to structure seniors' expanded freedoms. Taylor asked the AWS board of standards to take the lead, setting a deadline for each house to turn in their members' preferences, and asking each group to specifically include keys as an option in their slate. Rather than jumping at the chance to have keys to their residences so the seniors could come and go as they pleased, most housing groups preferred to keep closing hours for senior women. Of the 16 living groups, only six—37 percent—supported some type of key program. Another three living groups offered limited support for one key for occasional use by all senior women, while one residence noted that their senior women had few problems with the current system. The remaining seven rejected keys and asked for later hours with someone maintaining "door duty" to let seniors in at night. In fact, the Sigma Kappa sorority responded that they "also felt the idea of keys for seniors was a little too lenient and a bit dangerous, as well as costly if keys were lost and locks had to be changed."[70] Many sorority leaders likely felt caught between Taylor and their sorority corporation boards run by alumnae. Most alumnae expressed concern over projected increases in liability insurance premiums, and some boards consulted attorneys over the key concept.[71] With over 60 percent of the women's housing groups against keys, the responses illustrate that the undergraduates themselves did not instigate this change to provide women more freedom.

Despite the lack of support, Taylor was not going to give up on her belief in women's autonomy and called on the senate to approve an "experimental" key program in October of 1960 that would be reviewed at the end of the semester. "She pushed the seniors [to have keys]," said Shavlik. "They didn't want them."[72] The AWS senate settled on a plan that required written parental permission to participate. However, it did not actually provide each senior student with a key for her possession at all times. Instead, in yet another example of the women's resistance, the AWS created a knot of rules governing key check-out, insisting this was needed for safety. The women determined that seniors would lock keys in a box kept by the house director during the day and that keys would be checked out only after 5 p.m. and before the house closed for the night. In a revised version of the sign-out sheet, a woman checking out keys recorded her name, the person accompanying her, and her expected time of return, a tacit reminder to seniors that they should only go to appropriate and disclosed locations. A senior counted the hall's keys by 8 a.m. daily to make sure they were all accounted for—and no one younger than a senior could enter the house with a key holder. Any "irregularity" resulted in the loss of senior privileges for the woman and possibly for the entire house. If a woman lost a key, the residence members changed the locks on the same day and all seniors shared in the cost of replacing the lock and keys.

This tangle of regulations arose from women's concern both over sorority insurance costs, and over maintaining their reputations as respectable women, ensuring everyone knew senior women could not disappear for a weekend with a date. Along with answering arguments about safety, these precautions illustrated that keys would be closely supervised, that younger women could not access them, and that the chaste expectations for women would still be maintained.⁷³ Taylor's key program, though, resulted in senior women receiving complete freedom to return to their residences at whatever hour they preferred before 8 a.m. the next morning—so long as they left the residence before closing hours began for the underclassmen. Consistently emphasizing that the program was for seniors and run by them, Taylor placed behavioral decisions squarely in the hands of senior women, whether they wanted that autonomy or not.

Information regarding the reception of the senior key program is sparse. When asked about KU's administrative response to her plan, Taylor replied, "I didn't ask their opinions...They didn't say anything. Well, if they did, it's nothing I remember. They [the administration] certainly didn't oppose it."⁷⁴ The archival files support Taylor's contention. There is nothing to indicate concern either in the chancellor's files or in the dean of students and dean of men's files. In fact, aside from a final report on the senior privilege plan in Murphy's files, it would have been difficult to know from his records that either the 1959 convention or the issuance of keys had occurred. As for parents of seniors, AWS senate minutes note at various points in the process that none had rejected the privilege for their own daughters. Taylor successfully managed to balance this progressive change without causing any public controversy, always a significant factor at a public institution.⁷⁵

Criticism existed, however. Taylor received a strongly worded letter opposing the program. In addition, Taylor recalled sorority advisors, usually off-campus alumnae, as particularly upset:

> I remember one woman [advisor] who invited me to go out to lunch and she said that she wanted to know if I could explain to her why I thought that [a key] was progress. And I said I think this is progress because it requires people to grow up. It requires people to make their own decisions as to when it's time for them to be out and when it's time for them to be in [the sorority house], the same as anything else they do whether they are studying or eating or sleeping or what. Those decisions shouldn't be made by someone else.⁷⁶

Taylor believed educated women should be "grown up" and possess the decision-making skills to act autonomously and determine their own paths, rather than to operate solely by convention or by the dictates of authority.⁷⁷

Despite KU women's resistance to the autonomy the key program provided, it garnered interest by college women nationally. At least eight colleges—or students at them—wrote to Taylor, requesting information on how the senior key system operated so that they might replicate it on their own campus. At the University of Massachusetts, the student newspaper ran an editorial using the KU program as an example of what their campus should consider. In addition, by the mid-1960s, IAWS disseminated the KU senior key plan as a model for other campuses to consider. Nonetheless, Taylor's leadership in this area had outpaced national attitudes. Between 1956 and 1960, the *Journal of the National Association of Deans of Women* published no articles dealing specifically with the subjects of changing closing hours, rules and regulations, or judiciary boards. Although the topic formally arose at least once at a NADW convention, parietals were not regularly visible in the scholarly discussions of student individual responsibility, most likely because they were considered a normative necessity.[78]

What made Taylor's approach so trailblazing is that in regional and national IAWS conferences, Taylor called to limit parietals on the grounds that they interfered with women's studying opportunities, keeping the focus on women's conduct rather than on intellectual conversation and more substantial leadership opportunities. Ridder, who attended the 1958 and 1959 national IAWS conferences with Taylor, recalled that IAWS meeting attendees often found Taylor's suggestions to be shocking. Ridder said she realized that KU was "way ahead" of the norm at these meetings. One KU undergraduate noted that, "[t]here is probably fear in some schools that students would misuse any such power given them. Kansas is known as a liberal school, and one finds at any convention that many problems of other schools have long been solved at KU."[79] Taylor repeatedly reminded IAWS and her own AWS group that parietals—a prescription for women's subordination to authority figures—stood in the way of progress for women.[80]

Nationally, the student personnel field did not begin to consider general issues surrounding student freedoms on campuses until 1960–1961. That year, NASPA, the dean of men's group, circulated a commission report regarding this topic, which IAWS shared with all its AWS chapters. However, NASPA and NADW did not formally suggest that students should have further freedoms with accompanying responsibility until 1967. Only by 1969—11 years after Taylor began KU's senior key discussion—did the trend to issue keys and eliminate closing hours begin to popularize across the nation. In 1969–1970, IAWS, which maintained a "clearinghouse" system for sharing best practices with chapters nationally, noted that requests for information regarding modifying or eliminating women's curfews outpaced all other informational inquiries that year. By that time, KU led the nation's large public institutions in dissolving women's parietals, giving all freshman women the choice of whether they wanted to live under closing hours or not. However, even in the late 1960s, KU AWS President Kay Harris recalled some KU women still resisting the changes.[81]

The closer Taylor moved toward keys for all KU women, the more student resistance she faced. The women in the AWS senate overwhelmingly rejected her 1962 call to provide keys to underclassmen except freshmen, saying that parents would not approve, that it was "idealistic," and that closing hours kept "KU as a respected leader in the Big 8 and the Midwest."[82] The students saw personal freedom (which they thought dangerous to their individual and group reputations) as the antithesis of female responsibility (behaving respectably), and the majority fought to keep the rules for all but senior women. Taylor eventually overcame student objections against eliminating curfews for younger women, though not before Murphy left KU to become chancellor at the University of California, Los Angeles. In March 1966, another AWS Rules Convention, this one with Ann Peterson (Hyde) as AWS president, voted to give keys to second-semester sophomores through seniors, and to eliminate the closing hours and sign-outs for these women altogether.[83]

This news was reported in a national climate that had recently "discovered" the campus organizing of the New Left. In early 1965, the media covered the Free Speech Movement protest at the University of California, Berkeley. By the spring of 1965, *Newsweek, Time,* and *U.S. News & World Report,* as well as the *Nation* and *Saturday Evening Post,* reported on the Berkeley protest, which catapulted the topic of student governance structures into the national conversation. In this atmosphere, the AWS vote in favor of abolishing closing hours for younger KU women made news across Kansas. *The Kansas City Star, The Wichita Eagle, The Topeka Daily Capital,* and *Lawrence Daily Journal-World* all carried the story. In Topeka, a front-page article detailed the entire plan, which still needed approval from the new chancellor, W. Clarke Wescoe.[84]

This time, Taylor would not escape public controversy regarding her efforts for change. The statewide media caught the attention of parents and Kansas citizens who wrote to Wescoe—not one reflecting a positive sentiment. Instead, the correspondents condemned the proposal and encouraged Wescoe to stop it.[85] The letters revealed that many understood that Taylor directed these changes and linked her advocacy to the student protests now occurring sporadically across the nation. For instance, one mother wrote:

> [I]n a more critical vein, may I go on record as being against all the changes proposed by AWS concerning closing hours... We feel that the whole trend is a terrible mistake, as has been pretty well proven wherever this idiocy has been allowed. The first mistake at K.U., in my opinion, was the senior keys. From the beginning the girls seem to have had unusually poor advice.[86]

Direct critiques of Taylor's advising were not always as politely stated, and illustrated some parents' frustration with Taylor's unconventional ideas. Another mother bluntly stated in her letter to Wescoe:

> Come now, Dr. Wescoe, you surely don't think that I am naïve enough to think that the little darlings thought up this whole new world all by themselves. I loved your phrasing "does not of necessity represent the views of the Dean." You see, I feel sure that little suggestions have been dropped at those sweet little fudge or dessert parties at [Taylor's] home that I have been hearing about for years. Surely, the idiotic conception of Senior Keys was hers, as no one is allowed to discuss dropping that idea. In fact, at a Panhel rush meeting last year, she informed the Pi Phi representatives that she felt it was not the Mother's club business to discuss Senior Keys. Ha! [A]nd now they are allowed to vote on having no closing hours. Did Dean Emily anticipate they would vote against? Or is she still using that juvenile homily, "Don't you trust your daughter?"[87]

Letter after letter sent to Wescoe and other administrators expressed sentiments like: "abolition of closing hours...it's like letting the tail wag the dog!

Why not let the parents and/or taxpayers who foot the bill have a voice in this."[88] Or, in one case, a citizen complained that the dissolution of regulations for women would hurt men by distracting them from their studies:

> By nature, girls are usually more aggressive than boys and are prone to monopolize the boy's time. We have heard male students at KU speak out in disapproval of the proposed relaxation of closing hours as they will now have no legitimate excuse to return the girls to their houses and get back to their own for study and duties. Generally, the boys carry a heavier academic load. As far as their health is concerned they don't get enough rest now to do justice to their packed schedules so we don't see how it would be possible for them to do their best work under the circumstances proposed.[89]

Not only did the rules circumscribe women's lives and freedom, the community regarded it as appropriate to use these constraints on women to limit young men's behavior. The subtext of letters like the ones above illustrated concern over unsupervised dating time and opportunity for sexual relations. Amid comments regarding "'rebels' influencing policy," more than one parent complained that this dissolution of parietals would lead to illegitimate births and the need for a campus nursery.[90] One letter began, "Dear Dr. Wescoe, I am enclosing two clippings from the morning paper. Thought the AWS might be interested in planning a nursery for their next project."[91] In addition to parent and citizen protests, Taylor remembered a legislator complaining that she used state resources to encourage "insurgents."[92] Over and over, Wescoe responded that the decision would not be "capricious" and that his action would be taken with "reasonableness for all."[93] He also regularly cited the success of the senior keys and the lack of problems associated with them as evidence that the 1966 plan had merit. As she had hoped, Taylor's strategy of using gradual "experiments" to relax parietals provided the university administration with a measure of proof that the concept would work.

However, in the late spring of 1966, Wescoe succumbed to political pressure and called Taylor into his office after a particularly difficult telephone call from a Pi Beta Phi advisor. He told Taylor expanding the keys to more students and eliminating all closing hours and signing out procedures at the same time was too controversial and indicated he would not support the plan. She remembered responding, "I think you have the wrong dean of women so I'll put in my resignation."[94] Taylor left the Chancellor's office only to receive a hasty invitation from Wescoe for dinner at his home that evening. Cancelling plans in Kansas City, Wescoe capitulated to Taylor's threat of departure, and the two worked out arrangements for accepting the policy changes. In the end, sophomore women remained under closing hours while junior and senior women received key privileges without sign-outs or curfews.[95] Taylor believed that Wescoe did not want her to resign because he "was afraid of a real uprising" if she left. Taylor stated, "I had a great many friends who would have raised trouble," including a strong base of male and female students.[96] "I suppose I should have been concerned [about these changes], but I wasn't. I didn't even ask their [dean of students and the chancellor] opinion. It seemed so reasonable to give the keys...We ended up the only school in the country who had given keys to everyone first."[97]

In the heart of the cultural conformity of the 1950s, Taylor incrementally challenged conventional restrictions on women, facing increasing protests with each step. With Taylor's threat of resignation, she "educated" Wescoe, forcing him to reexamine his understanding of the dean of women's role as a disciplinarian. Taylor pushed KU women students on a path toward autonomy. She built on the AWS foundation left by Martha Peterson, and implemented student government programming that mirrored many of the practices early deans developed. Drawing on her lessons from Zorbaugh and Mueller, Taylor promoted careers, and graduate and professional education; encouraged young women to consider marriage and career; and promoted Women's Bureau and CEW views on women in the workplace. Under her tutelage, women studied the history of US women's rights and the socioeconomic status of women, realizing that most of them would eventually enter the workforce—so they should consider preparing for it.

Despite this comprehensive program to open women's minds to full economic and political citizenship, Taylor found the AWS leaders holding tightly to the levers of rules and regulations, arguing about 15-minute curfew extensions and whether the sorority president or the dean of women should approve a late permission. These young women of the 1950s had adopted the AWS regulations as a part of their identities, using them as the measuring stick for respectability. Just as early deans envisioned, these young women "self-governed," disciplining their own behavior according to campus norms. However, the self-government early deans intended to help young women become full citizens of the public sphere morphed by the postwar decade into a system of self-discipline that taught young women to embrace mainstream social conventions. Taylor, though, reinvigorated the feminist basis early deans established, as she operated the machinery of student government to "de-program" gender normativity. She named gender restrictions as structural arrangements society prescribed, and called on women to rethink their presence at KU—why did they attend college, how would they support themselves and their families, and how would they manage supporting a family alone if they were widowed or divorced? These questions—the same ones Zorbaugh first asked Taylor when she was an undergraduate herself—pushed KU women to question domestic conformity, and to begin to think of themselves as autonomous citizens who could make choices regarding how to spend their own lives.

Taylor's rules conferences blatantly called on KU women to recognize that each had a responsibility for making her own behavioral decisions. Taylor pushed KU coeds into autonomy, whether they wanted it or not, using student government to suggest women each adopt "self-government," not in disciplining themselves to act in accordance with gender expectations, but in full autonomy to make one's own decisions as someone who could be a professional, a wife, a mother, or all three. Taylor's method brought forth the heart of a liberal arts education—teaching women to think for themselves. At KU, she incrementally prodded the women—particularly the AWS leaders—to apply these critical thinking skills to their own lives. She focused them on new inquiries: What did they think of the history of US women's rights? What did the Women's Bureau job statistics suggest their futures would hold? Despite her programming, the parietal structure limited women's thinking, making it difficult for them to imagine taking responsibility for their own behavior. As a result, Taylor pushed through parietal change in the form of keys, extending curfews, and forcing young women to see themselves as full adult citizens able to make their own decisions without relying on a parental authority.

In the atmosphere of Cold War hyperdomesticity, this was a difficult project. Taylor preceded by a decade the popular national conversation on shifting gender roles for educated women. She dispersed the first keys to senior women three months before President John F. Kennedy established the President's Commission on the Status of Women in December of 1961. By January of 1962, Taylor was already suggesting the elimination of closing hours for *all* women except freshmen. This was one year before Betty Friedan published *The Feminine Mystique*, and two years before the President's Commission reported its results and Congress passed the Civil Rights Act providing for women's employment equity. Slowly, her students began to see marriage, motherhood, and careers as choices—and not necessarily mutually exclusive ones. Taylor named women's roles as socially constructed and helped young women to see how they operated. In short, Taylor used the AWS to create consciousness-raising groups—using *Roberts Rules of Order* to guide young women to envision new opportunities for themselves as adults entitled to the same freedoms and accountability as men. Drawing on the institutionalized practices of early deans, Taylor implemented AWS in the feminist spirit of economic and political independence for women.

Certainly, by unlocking the parietals which governed women's lives, Taylor opened the door for college women to face the world of dating autonomously. With the rules gone, women increasingly found themselves facing questions regarding dating and sexuality. Rather than monitoring discipline through strict rules, the dean of women's office and her staff found themselves at the forefront of preparing women to face decisions regarding sexuality and helping them to have the information they needed to make responsible decisions for themselves.

CHAPTER 4

A World without Parietals

One semester after University of Kansas dean of women Emily Taylor's first rules convention with the Associated Women Students (AWS), Delta Tau Delta hosted its 1959 fall party at the fraternity house. Held in the public living areas of the home, members and their dates enjoyed a university-sanctioned evening of socializing. The men's housemother, likely in her quarters on the main floor of the house, chaperoned. In the midst of the evening, one fraternity member and his date disappeared to the third-floor dormitory rooms. Rarely did a coed leave the public areas of men's residences, and several reports quickly reached the dean of women's office. The young woman, a first year student, soon found herself sitting across from the women students serving on the AWS board of standards and Assistant Dean of Women Pat Patterson in a disciplinary hearing. Facing expulsion, the young woman explained she had gone upstairs looking for her date and that she simply "sat on his bed until he was feeling better." The AWS leaders "questioned the validity of her statements as they were contrary to many other reports." AWS placed the woman on social probation and required her to write to her parents confessing that she had accompanied her date to his bedroom.[1]

The young woman undoubtedly wished the whole incident behind her. However, she soon found herself in the midst of a campus scandal. Though never explicitly stated, a furor arose over the potential for this—or any—couple to have sexual relations at a fraternity party. Reporters at the *University Daily Kansan* clamored for details and demanded open disciplinary records. Taylor met with fraternity housemothers to clarify expectations for chaperoning, and the dean of men sanctioned Delta Tau Delta with social probation. Students protested, arguing that the students involved should bear the responsibility rather than the fraternity. The administration and the All Student Council refused to name the individuals involved, trying to protect what was left of the young woman's reputation.[2]

Sexual experimentation—or the hint of sexual activity even if none existed—extracted a high price for young women in the 1950s. Society's double standard shunned unmarried women labeled promiscuous—and what counted as immoral among students depended upon youth culture. Since the 1920s, American youth had created peer-defined courtship norms that mediated heterosexual dating relationships. By the 1950s, these elaborately coded mores determined when various levels of sexual engagement were appropriate. Acceptable intimacy directly corresponded to the seriousness of the couple's relationship, progressing from casual dating, to "going steady," to engagement, and finally, to marriage. Couples who "went steady" could partake in sexual activity, and those planning to be married might engage in sex—as long as it did not result in a pregnancy. Then, a whole other set of standards would apply.

Young women of the 1950s found this terrain fraught with risks. Taylor, like other feminist deans of women, blazed trails on the issues of women's sexuality years before the women's movement came to address these issues publically. As Taylor disassembled KU's parietal rules for women, she quietly led women through the rapidly changing era that has since been dubbed the "sexual revolution." Guiding the AWS to consider heterosexuality, birth control, abortion, women's health, homosexuality and rape, Taylor founded sex education, sexual assault and rape crisis programs that are now standard in colleges and cities across the nation.

While AWS rules of the 1950s reflected the larger taboo against any premarital sex, students frequently broke these regulations and, in the spirit of peer customs, looked the other way. Even Taylor regarded the norms as somewhat flexible. She offered AWS President Anne Hoopingarner her driveway as a parking location so she could have private time with her boyfriend and future husband, Wendell Ridder. As AWS President, Hoopingarner needed to model decorum for other young women, and in Taylor's driveway the couple did not risk being seen. For the Delta Tau Delta incident to cause such a campus uproar, the couple at the fall party was likely dating only casually or had just begun to see each other, placing their activity well outside the norms of both mainstream and youth culture.

The fraternity party incident illustrates how Taylor's brand of guidance and counseling operated at KU as it intersected with post–World War II student sexuality. Taylor, like Mueller, believed young women experimenting with dating and sexuality "learned by rote, by practice, often by trial and error," and as dean of women she endeavored "to make...the errors least damaging."[3] Rather than expel the student over sexual experimentation, Taylor's office gave this 1959 freshman an opportunity to continue her education at KU. In order for this to be a "least damaging" error, Taylor kept the woman's name private so she might recover from the reputation-wrecking mistake. Implementing this approach meant working with student government leaders to think past discipline as an end in itself. Taylor encouraged the young women not to simply judge their peers, but for the board to support each student in developing her own personal standards to apply in decision making.[4]

Taylor frequently applied the "errors least damaging" approach. Before the elimination of closing hours (designed to limit men's time with female students), Taylor often sent young women caught out after curfew to the home of art history faculty member, Marilyn Stokstad, who let them sleep on her couch for the night. Technically, this met the letter of the rules, and the embarrassment of knocking on Professor Stokstad's door late at night likely made the student think twice before breaking curfew again. As Shavlik later noted, Taylor "was pretty well-known for helping people out of problems whatever they were."[5] Sororities particularly appreciated Taylor's discretion, and these groups reported difficulties more readily because of the relationship developed between the dean of women's office and the houses. As Kala Stroup noted, Taylor believed she and her staff "were there to help [students]...not punish them."[6]

However, this did not mean Taylor did not carry out disciplinary guidelines if women's behavior would cause public controversy. One student, a future radical feminist, Caroljean Brune, skipped a required AWS meeting, visited a man's apartment for dinner, helped a friend sneak into the dormitory after curfew, and found herself nearing expulsion with a warning letter mailed to her parents. With no alternative living arrangements allowed for undergraduate women outside of university housing in 1964, Brune still maintains that she married in order to "get away from Emily Taylor" and the structure of the university's student life.[7] When students like Brune continually pushed past the accepted norms that the AWS developed, Taylor enacted disciplinary procedures. She first looked for ways students might learn from infractions to bring their behavior into line with the norms of the community.[8] However, Taylor knew her experiment in removing parietals would only work if the women's behavior did not attract public controversy, and in the early 1960s behavior like Brune's put at risk her larger goal of dissolving parietals.

By eliminating curfews and residence hall sign-outs for senior women in 1960, Taylor told KU upperclasswomen they would be responsible for their own choices, navigating the world of college dating and sexual behavior as adults capable of making their own decisions. As Taylor pressed all women students to accept dormitory keys in the early 1960s, the students resisted losing the parietals which they felt shielded their reputations. To them, parietals embodied female respectability, protected against premarital sex, and helped them navigate toward marriage. Without the regulations, KU women would have to negotiate dating and sexuality on their own—and, as the 1959 freshman at the Delta Tan Delta party discovered, the consequences of failure in post-war America could be steep.

By dismantling parietals, Taylor addressed women's safety and sexuality directly, rather than allowing young women to embrace parietals as a fiction of protection. Always advocating intercourse after marriage, Taylor recognized that there had long been a percentage of women students who engaged in premarital sex—and that this fact was unlikely to change. Because of this, she felt it necessary to build sexual education into her program to aid young women in making informed decisions. Eventually, the introduction of oral contraceptives in 1960 changed youth culture, and her office facilitated an agenda that challenged convention regarding sexuality, women's health, contraception, unplanned pregnancy, access to abortion providers, and sexual assault. While these efforts ran counter to the prevailing post-World War II cultural norms, Taylor was not the only dean of women quietly on this path, as the history of "deaning" included sex education from its inception.

Early Deans of Women and Sex Education

Long before Taylor entered academia, some of the same deans of women who organized vocational preparation, women's housing, and self-governance at the turn of the century also sorted out women's health education—which included human sexuality. In the late nineteenth century Dr. Edward Clarke predicted female students' physical and reproductive decline as a consequence of participation in higher learning, so deans of women supported women's physical education to bolster college women's health. Deans often included "sex hygiene" as an element in the curriculum. As public concern over syphilis rose in the early 1900s, so did social acceptance of sex education, and higher education institutions introduced lectures on how to prevent venereal infection. As a part of this, early deans implemented sexuality education with women students. At the University of California, Berkeley, Dean of Women Lucy Sprague met with small groups of students to provide information about syphilis. She developed this effort in concert with placement bureau director May Cheney and Berkeley's women's physician Dr. Eleanor Bancroft. They instituted lectures for large groups of women on "sex physiology," menstruation, pregnancy, and childbirth as a "sex hygiene" prelude to the sexually transmitted infection information. At Stanford, Dr. Clelia Duel Mosher, the women's medical advisor, worked closely with the Stanford dean of women's office on similar topics. Comparably, at the University of Michigan, Dean of Women Eliza Mosher, an M.D. and professor of hygiene, sanitation, and household economics, taught sex education with models of female reproductive organs fashioned out of silk. These trends flowing through western and midwestern public universities also influenced KU, where all students studied "personal hygiene," and the campus YWCA taught sex education by 1913.[9]

While early deans of women educated coeds regarding the mechanics of sex and human reproduction, the codes for women's conduct remained strict. Michigan's Mosher suspended a student for sitting up all night in her train coach seat rather than retiring to the required sleeper car, and Marion Talbot sent home any young woman at the University of Chicago who engaged herself to be married. In the early 1900s, the academy still questioned whether women belonged on a college campus with men, so women like Talbot sought to ensure no female student's behavior gave male faculty a reason to reject coeducation. At the same time, the Progressive Era brought young men and women from rural to urban environments, and the first sexual revolution began to loosen Victorian customs.

In NADW, deans tried to determine appropriate interactions between male and female students, and fashioned a statement on morality that specifically guided students to avoid exploring their sexuality. In 1918, NADW's "Principles of Social Conduct" called for women and men to refuse "to live chiefly on the plane of physical needs and appetites, or to be controlled by physical impulse." They asked for students to "play fair," suggesting women consider how "by dress or posture, [she] stimulates the physical instincts in a man," and for male students to not take "advantage of the hospitality or confidence or ignorance of a girl in howsoever slight a way."[10] Corresponding with the national "sexual purity" campaigns developed to combat the spread of sexually transmitted infections, "Principles of Social Conduct" called for an end to the double standard where poor women stood in for the sexual appetites of men so that women of means could remain virtuous. Their proposed solution to the double standard, however, centered on ignoring human sexuality and focusing on other pursuits until marriage.[11]

The national concern over syphilis opened the door for broader discussion of women's sexuality among deans of women at the campus, state, and national levels. Deans developed methodology regarding how to teach sexuality, with Antioch's dean of women recommending lectures on the topic, supplementary books in the library, and referring students to talk with a faculty member, advisor, or the health department. NADW took the call for women's health seriously and established the Women's Foundation for Health (WFH) through a partnership with 14 other organizations, including AAUW, American Home Economics Association, Council of Jewish Women, YWCA, and BPW. The organization tied closely with NADW, including deans of women like Gertrude S. Martin (Cornell) as Secretary, and Ada Comstock (formerly Minnesota), among its leaders. Formed in the fall of 1919, the WFH recommended physical education, promoted hygiene during menstrual periods (including the "Mosher Exercise" developed by Stanford's Clelia Mosher to relieve pain associated with menstrual periods), and helped deans of women "intensify" health programming on their campuses. By 1926—at the behest of Indiana's Dean of Women Agnes Wells—NADW promoted the use of WFH's *Handbook on Positive Health*, which included a chapter on sexuality, intercourse, and sexually transmitted infections.[12]

By the early 1930s, NADW adopted "sex hygiene" as an important part of health education in colleges and universities, and professional practices expected deans of women to counsel students in the "sex development" area. At the 1932 NADW annual meeting, deans discussed "training for marriage while in college" and "sex hygiene," both euphemisms for sexuality education. That same year, Ohio State's Esther Allen Gaw published an article in the *AAUW Journal* on educating college women on heterosexuality. Gaw recommended vocabulary for discussing intercourse, and suggested that students learn about the mechanics of human reproduction through reading. She called for libraries to make available texts on the topic. Avoiding any endorsement of premarital sex, she advocated that birth control information be available only to those married or preparing to marry. At the same time, Gaw encouraged extreme modesty among her students on the OSU campus, even advising them to turn their photographs of their boyfriends to face the wall while they dressed.[13]

Gaw's AAUW article was inspired by an Ohio Association of Deans of Women (OADW) project that investigated education for "effective parenthood and family life."[14] That committee, led by Dean Audrey Kenyon

Wilder of Ohio Northern University, developed a bibliography on the topic by surveying how the fields of biology, physical education, psychology, child psychology, and sociology treated the topics. Gaw and Wilder's report borrowed the list of academic fields from an unpublished report of the White House Conference on Child Health and Protection which had a section on "Education for Marriage, Parenthood and Family Life at the College Level."[15] Together, these Ohio deans compiled over 20 pages of recommendations for a "pre-parental" course to educate young women on the physical and psychological aspects of marriage.[16]

By the time Taylor arrived at Ohio State as a junior, Gaw and the male student affairs officers were implementing "education concerning marriage," and building a curriculum for students that avoided "public relations...danger in any frank discussion."[17] In the autumn of 1937, the council initiated weekly Institute for Social Living classes which met in the women's building to cover courtship, love, and facts about sexuality and "sex control." The council created this non-credit course to prepare students for sexuality after marriage, and to help them "resist" the "definite influence working toward promiscuous sex relations."[18] Clearly, deans of women like Gaw were steering students away from premarital sex, believing that women needed preparation for marriage and motherhood.

Although sex education for unmarried youth remained controversial in the 1930s, the Depression significantly liberalized American opinion regarding birth control as many families struggled to feed the children they already had. A Gallup poll indicated that almost two-thirds of Americans favored teaching and practicing contraception, and the American Medical Association endorsed contraception as "normal sexual hygiene in married life" in 1937.[19] By 1940, the Comstock laws prohibiting distribution of contraceptive information disappeared in all states but Massachusetts and Connecticut, leaving many couples to obtain contraceptives such as condoms and diaphragms through the mail, especially from Sears, Roebuck. However, while support for birth control rose, technology and education regarding reliable methods had not yet advanced to produce dependable results. Couples using condoms in the 1930s found only 41 percent of them without tears, small holes or other defects. And, shockingly, from the 1930s through the 1950s, America's most popular birth control method was to apply the household cleaner, Lysol, as a douche after intercourse—which, though accessible and affordable, was dangerous and did not prevent pregnancy. There is no way to know how many college women tried this unhealthy, ineffective—though over the counter—tactic. However, Lysol advertised their product widely in women's magazines with "eminent women physicians" supporting the disinfectant for women's "ritual of personal antisepsis."[20]

Deans of women encouraged sex education in the 1930s as a way to help women negotiate the changing youth culture that the first sexual revolution of the 1910s and 1920s produced. By now, young women commonly participated in "petting," though usually saving intercourse for marriage. At Indiana, Mueller worked directly with the AWS where the student leaders called for counselors more able to advise women on sexuality. Not surprisingly, without dependable birth control, many unmarried women held onto the social codes of conduct against premarital sex, as did parents and university administrators.[21]

In response to these dynamics at Indiana, Mueller and the AWS asked the university for a sexuality education course—and Mueller enlisted future human sexuality expert Alfred Kinsey as a willing instructor to teach it. A zoologist, Kinsey accepted Mueller's charge and created his famous course as an outgrowth of women's deaning. As Mueller explained several decades later: "'In the dean of women's office, we had always been interested in having on the campus a good marriage course, because it was the thing that we were reading about and working on in our national conferences and discussions.'"[22] Mueller "felt frustrated by the old 'Hygiene' course because it failed to meet women students' needs."[23] Like Ohio State's Institute for Social Living, Kinsey's non-credit course required attendance at every session so students could not simply attend sections on sexual mechanics or contraception. The class met two times a week with enrollment open to male and female seniors, graduate students, married or engaged students, and those "peculiarly concerned in still other ways."[24] Involving faculty from various disciplines, Kinsey's course covered menstruation, childbirth, conception, contraception, sterility, loss of romanticism, and the sociology of the family. Unlike at OSU, where administrators hoped to encourage "sex control," Kinsey's course at Indiana fully explored human sexuality.[25]

Despite their collaboration to initiate the course, Kinsey and Mueller disagreed over its administration. Kinsey opposed Mueller's general focus on women's education for future employment, often criticizing her work on campus and telling her in 1941 that "I still hope that we can do more to help our girls look forward to home-making as a career."[26] The most significant difficulty, though, arose as Kinsey tried to secure personal interviews with one hundred percent of his students regarding their sexual experiences. Kinsey and his associates adamantly pursued women to participate in these one-on-one surveys outside the classroom, prompting some women and their parents to complain. Taylor, who worked as Mueller's assistant at the time, remembered Kinsey's work as a "nuisance." "Most of what we talked about was the kind of problems it created for us because of parent concerns," said Taylor.[27] Kinsey's blatant questions about students' sexual history offended some young women and made many more uncomfortable—especially in a society so disdainful of women who were known to experiment with sex before marriage. Mueller, committed to sexuality education, worried that the protests over Kinsey's approach would stymie the class altogether. She tried to evolve the class into one without harassing interviews, suggesting involvement of a head campus psychiatrist. Eventually, President Wells insisted Kinsey choose between teaching the marriage course and conducting his research interviews. Kinsey opted for his research, and published his books, *Sexual Behavior in the Human Male* and *Sexual Behavior in the Human Female*, in 1948 and 1953, respectively.[28]

From the beginning of Kinsey's instruction, Mueller shared the course structure with NADW leaders like Hilda Threlkeld (Louisville), Helen Schleman (Purdue), and others at the 1939 NADW convention. Even after their disagreements, Mueller continued to engage NADW with Kinsey's work on human sexuality. For instance, in July of 1956, Taylor (just about to join KU's administration), Purdue's Helen Schleman (who later became NADW president), and deans of women from Vermont, California, Texas, and Wisconsin all visited IU for a seven-day seminar hosted by Mueller that included a tour of Kinsey's laboratory and his library on sex research. Unquestionably, Kinsey's activity at IU provided Taylor and other deans of women with an example of the sex education model of the future. "Where many of the marriage courses stressed the homemaking aspects of marriage after an initial explanation of sexuality only slightly expanded from the old hygiene days, the course at Indiana University went into explicit detail about sexual anatomy, how to perform intercourse...and how to prevent pregnancy."[29] Kinsey's effort followed the structure that the Sexuality Information and Education Council of the United States (SIECUS) would later define as the nationally accepted sex education model, offering the class to men and women together. His work also opened discussion of homosexuality, something poorly understood by most Americans at the time.[30]

The openness that deans of women showed for sex education likely arose from their interactions with unwed pregnant students, always a reality in their offices, even at the turn of the twentieth century. At Berkeley, Lucy Sprague encountered at least two pregnancies. In one situation, the University of California president forced the young man responsible to marry the student, though the man abandoned the marriage and Sprague helped the young woman find odd jobs so she could complete her degree. In the other, a student at a YWCA meeting induced an abortion and tried to flush the fetus in the water closet. Since trustees and presidents hired deans of women to function as a university's panopticon in order to prevent sexual behavior between male and female students, faculty and staff regularly referred pregnant students to the dean of women. Deans, witnessing students' desperation when a pregnancy occurred out of wedlock, responded in several ways. Some continually tightened parietals in the hopes of student compliance with regulations. Others looked to sex education to help women make informed choices about petting. Still others became quiet advocates of birth control as Sprague did by 1915, just a few years after she left her dean of women position.[31]

Taylor took this third road that supported contraception, agreeing with most Depression-era Americans. "By the time I got to college, I was really committed to things that were way beyond what most women were thinking about...I thought it should be that you determined your own sexuality," said Taylor, recalling that her small town, De Graff, Ohio, had an abortionist in town and that married women went there during the Depression if they became pregnant and could not afford to support the child. Taylor believed that she had markedly progressive views compared to her peers.[32] While at OSU, Taylor read about contraception in Ben Lindsey's *Companionate Marriage* (1927), a book listed in the sexuality education bibliography by the Ohio deans association, and her support for contraception was personal. Her close friend in high school lost the chance to attend college because she married early due to pregnancy. While her friend found fulfillment in marriage, Taylor always felt it unfair society blocked her from higher education because of marriage and motherhood. When Mueller talked about "life phase" planning, Taylor instinctively embraced the concepts—as they would have allowed her friend a college degree through the emerging model of continuing education that deans of women promoted in the 1950s.

Taylor herself never married—though she was asked several times. She seriously considered marrying her college boyfriend whom she met at Urbana College. The two transferred to Ohio State together, avidly wrapped up in young love and sparring intellectually as equals. As a conscientious objector in World War II, however, he was found dead at the bottom of an elevator shaft in a military hospital where he had been assigned to work. Taylor never seriously considered marriage again. Her sister, Genevieve McMahon, believed Taylor could not imagine herself playing a secondary role in a relationship "which was what you really had to do in those days."[33] When people asked Taylor why she never married, she always quipped: "I never thought the last one to ask would be the last one to ask." Once she decided not to marry, however, she sunk herself into the work of feminist deaning. This caused some to say Taylor revealed little about her personal life. Those close to her, though, knew that her work *was* her personal life. And though her KU students and staff often thought her stoicism left her far removed from romantic interests, her sister recalled Taylor once pursuing young love with her college boyfriend at Ohio State as passionately as the young women she eventually oversaw as a dean of women.

Once she arrived as dean of women at Northern Montana College in 1946, Taylor encountered unwed pregnancy among her own students. There, "one woman came in and I went through the set of options. One, she could get married. Two, she could go to a home where she could have the baby. Three, tell her parents and have the baby." Taylor suggested she start with the boyfriend. "She came back and said the boyfriend would marry her if she could prove it was his. In other words, he wasn't going to marry her."[34] Taylor remembered this instance ended well as the woman's parents kept the twins that she delivered and raised them. But not all instances ended so happily. In another Montana case, a pregnant student parked her car on the railroad tracks and committed suicide rather than risk the shame and lack of options as a single mother in that era.

The vantage point from a dean of women's office left few of these women administrators wondering about the very real consequences that unmarried women faced when caught in the double standard with a pregnancy. From her desk as a dean of women, Taylor witnessed the results of women attempting to abort a fetus on their own, botched back-alley abortions, and suicides. Over time, the reality of these women's desperate choices defined her counseling approach, heightening her commitment to educating women about sexuality and contraception so they had information to make proactive decisions that could prevent pregnancy before marriage. Pragmatically, Taylor bridged her commitment to women fulfilling their personal potential in higher education with her "errors least damaging" philosophy. Foremost, she sought to decrease unplanned pregnancies, and, later as the sexual revolution of the 1960s evolved, she educated women on contraceptives, hoping to provide women with choices regarding combining marriage and career.

KU AND SEXUALITY EDUCATION

As Taylor's office deliberately dismantled parietals in the 1950s and early 1960s, she and her staff slowly increased the amount of information they provided on sexuality and contraception as a natural extension of student personnel counseling. To do so, she drew on the knowledge deans of women had already produced about how to educate college women about sexuality. At the same time, she employed the tactics deans of women had long used to convince university administrations to adjust to women students' needs. Taylor followed Mueller's advice for fostering change through incremental steps by both acquiring data on the situation, and using AWS as a voice representing all women students. These strategies pushed the KU administration to adopt provisions for women's sexual health. With this approach, Taylor built a counseling system that helped young women reconcile respectability, dating, sexual curiosity, and the double standard. She employed the concept of self-governance as a means to help young women develop their own standards and beliefs on sexuality, and actively counseled young women as they made decisions about their dating relationships. Shavlik even recalled that as Taylor's assistant, she once naively followed a student couple to a hotel to try to convince the woman to change her mind about premarital sex. Clearly, Taylor and her staff were not on a mission for sexual permissiveness, but they understood that not all unmarried female students would choose abstinence. They wanted women to have the information to make the safest choices possible.[35]

* * *

In the 1950s, when Taylor began deaning at KU, society provided little in the way of role models for educating women about how to balance dating, academics, and sexuality. The baby boom and popular focus on domesticity reversed the pre-war trends in sex education, and marriage courses began to focus more on personal problems and emotions rather than sexuality and physiology—leaving many college students with less education regarding sexuality than in previous years. Public conversation ignored sex, and the Federal Communications Commission even outlawed the word "pregnant" on television. Nationally, students saw narrowly defined imagery of college women with only three manifestations in mainstream popular media. First, the spinster academic in glasses stood as a personification of the unrelenting media message that serious study and future marriage were an either-or proposition. Mid-century dating manuals warned women against too much study with one 1952 book listing academics as a "dating handicap."[36] The second image, promoted in movies like *Where the Boys Are* (1960), pictured college women as sex kittens, sexually available now that they lived away from parents. One brand of condoms actually played on this stereotype; "Co-ed Prophylactics" pictured a university campus and a sports pennant on the package. Aside from these two opposing images of asexuality and hypersexuality, popular culture presented a third iteration of the "college girl"—a smartly dressed, beautiful young white woman ready to attract a husband. This coed exuded youthful charm without a hint of sexuality, idealizing the respectability required to achieve the so-called "MRS. Degree." These images—like those fronting the magazine *Mademoiselle* in its annual "College" issue—all depicted white women, completely overlooking the reality of women of color who also sought higher educations.[37]

In truth, white college women found attractiveness, respectability, and dating a difficult balance to achieve. As Wini Breines noted: "white, middle-class girls had to walk a tightrope of respectability, never going (or never appearing) to go too far sexually, but giving just enough of their bodies to keep boys interested and to receive, they hoped, affection and admiration" that would lead to marriage.[38] This left women in the post-war era in charge of stopping a man's advances. In the 1959 article, "How to Handle a College Man" the author noted, "Your college man may well control the arrangements for the date, but the necking bit requires your holding the reins with a light but very firm touch. Try a velvet glove approach—with an iron hand underneath the glove. And, do try to keep everything good natured."[39]

Interestingly, most midcentury college men held inverse attitudes about sex to those of women. Reflecting the double standard, a 1950s survey found that, as a couple fell in love, men believed it less appropriate to have sex with their partners, while women, conversely, thought sexual activity more acceptable as the relationship increased in seriousness. Mainstream values—reflected in the survey of men—preferred women to be sexually "pure" until marriage. Largely, college women understood that female promiscuity was proscribed by the double standard, and that pregnancy outside of marriage resulted in social rejection. Popular psychology of the era presented unmarried pregnant white women as "problem girls" to be "treated" for mental instability. For black women, however, US society exhibited racism by designating their pregnancies before marriage as a sign of racial promiscuity, or hypersexuality, using them as "proof" of white racial superiority.[40] These factors combined to cause most college women to reign in their sexual experimentation to avoid pregnancy. Author Wini Breines noted, "Girls' recollections are often of real panic they might get pregnant, one of the deciding reasons they did not engage in intercourse."[41]

In this post–World War II milieu, Taylor, like her mentor Mueller, utilized the AWS structure to educate women on—and arm them for—the world of dating and sexuality. Aside from introducing adult role models who illustrated that academic achievement did not preclude women from marriage, Taylor stocked her resource library with books on sex education just as NADW had recommended since the 1930s. Not only did Taylor provide personal advising, her staff also informally counseled women through women's residence halls, and organizations. "We knew a lot about the women students due to the single-sex residence arrangements," said Stroup. "We didn't sit in our offices and wait for women to come and see us. We were in the halls and we knew what was happening."[42] When a pregnancy did occur, Taylor counseled women through making their own decisions about what was right for them, and how she counseled them changed over time.

> In the 1940s, if a woman got pregnant, she probably withdrew from school—and didn't tell anyone. In the forties, I told them about all the legal possibilities. It wasn't until I got to Miami that I really ran into the problem, and I can't think of a specific instance then. This was in the early fifties. They often came and told me they were pregnant, but they had a plan usually. One came and asked if she could have a leave of absence. No one discussed abortion until the sixties.[43]

Sometimes Taylor's staff identified the women experiencing an unplanned pregnancy, other times women sought them out for advice. Women frequently accessed the dean of women and her staff at all hours, often at their homes where they knew it would be private. Taylor, well-known for helping students out of difficult situations, had plenty of couples arrive together at her house seeking advice at night.

While Taylor's staff regularly counseled unmarried pregnant women, in a large school like KU not all women accessed the dean's counseling network for help and some sought abortions on their own. By 1960, the American Medical Association estimated over a million illegal abortions occurred in the United States annually. Taylor, whose one regret was that her life path prevented her from bearing and raising her own child, never supported abortion as a first resort. She had been aware of abortion as an option for unplanned pregnancy from her childhood, though, as her small town, like many towns, housed an abortion provider in the 1920s and 1930s. Through deaning, she realized that women who felt desperate made radical choices. Taylor remembered two specific cases that particularly pushed her to make changes in her programming to support sex education and contraceptive information at KU. One woman tried to abort a pregnancy on her own in the Gertrude Sellards Pearson residence hall, which resulted in uncontrolled bleeding and the hall director rushing her to the Lawrence hospital. Another staff member discovered a student in her dormitory bleeding to death. She had obtained an abortifacient from a medically unlicensed man in Topeka, Kansas, who sent her home to experience the abortion alone. Taylor's staff took her to the hospital to recover, and later Taylor inquired how the women knew where to find the unlicensed service. The woman had learned about the illegal provider through gossip among students.[44]

While no women at KU died from abortion attempts, the close calls caused Taylor to move from quiet, individual sexuality counseling to a full-fledged operation during the 1960s. The changing mores of the sexual revolution opened a new space for Taylor to implement this work, and also increased the amount of counseling needed as more as more women experimented with sex before marriage.[45]

Taylor immediately investigated the gossip surrounding the illegal Topeka abortionist. Her staff network discovered that students went to the man because he had hired a woman who worked at the KU Union to "bird-dog" business for him. Taylor quickly put a stop to this, requesting that student union director Frank Burge fire the woman. Later, Taylor received a call from the woman's legislator, who had been told that Taylor had dismissed the woman without cause. Taylor explained the woman's activities, and the legislator quickly dropped the matter. Despite the removal of the man's representative on campus, gossip continued to refer women to him throughout the 1960s. Taylor recalled, "I can think of a good many who went to the butcher in Topeka. His office, instruments, etc. were dirty. It's a miracle they weren't infected."[46]

The nature of Taylor's counseling at KU changed rapidly with the introduction of the birth control pill in 1960—the same year that Taylor instituted senior keys. The pill provided women with a reliable form of contraception, and the nation quickly adopted it. Between 1960 and 1962, one brand of contraceptive pills increased prescriptions from 191,000 to 1,981,000 as women took advantage of controlling their reproductive and sexual lives. While the nation largely considered the pill as a solution for married couples and relied on physicians to determine whether it should be prescribed, it was not until 1965 that the Supreme Court established the right of married couples to practice contraception. And, it would not be until 1972 that the *Eisenstadt v. Baird* decision claimed the same access to birth control for unmarried couples.

To discuss contraception in AWS venues, Taylor fostered conversation about an emerging policy concern over the exponential growth of the world's population, which many believed would outpace food resources. Nationally, the bi-partisan Zero Population Growth (ZPG) agenda contributed greatly to the increasing acceptance of contraception by providing a reason to support birth control outside the moral debate. Taylor brought ZPG questions to KU women's attention as a new way to discuss contraception, family size, and balancing marriage and career.[47]

The pill ushered in significant changes in youth culture regarding dating and sexuality, and NADW quickly responded at the 1961 national meeting, devoting a general session to "changing sex standards" and creating a national task force of NADW members in state and regional deans' associations to evaluate the shifting sexual norms. By 1962, women deans joined a summit of 23 university leaders including presidents, physicians, and faculty to discuss college women's sexuality. Sponsored by the Sunnen Foundation and Planned Parenthood, the conference called for the combination of sex education with "wholesome, responsible and realistic attitudes." The conference participants decided what Taylor and some deans of women had always believed—they needed to avoid "rigid and unenforceable social restrictions...[and instead] make the values and ideals of the institution more meaningful to the student body as a group."[48]

Reinvigorating the original concepts that underlay self-governance, the conference participants recommended that a university define moral standards and distribute sexuality information to help women with their own private judgments. For sex education programs, they suggested large public forums followed by small group sessions led by mature adults where students could ask questions. Recognizing that student understanding of sex ranged from naïve to sophisticated, they recommended sex questionnaires to gauge the type of sex education needed, which could be combined with the YWCA sex education materials already endorsed by some churches. In no way did these academics desire to enable a culture of sexual permissiveness. However, they recognized that youth had always—and would always—experiment with sexuality before marriage, and that the pill had fundamentally changed youth culture.[49]

Mueller, as NADW journal editor, gathered the profession's thinking on the topic in 1963 with an issue devoted to sexuality. In that volume, she featured a report on the Sunnen Conference and an overview on sex education, premarital pregnancy, and abortion. The following year, the NADW focused a portion of their annual conference on the topic, featuring a noted sociologist and long-term NADW-IAWS colleague who accepted premarital sex, Lester Kirkendall. Taylor attended this 1964 NADW convention where deans listened to Kirkendall discuss "The Challenges Posed for Deans by Changing Sexual Standards," among other presentations on youth attitudes toward sexuality. With many deans of women thinking about how to address the rapidly changing youth culture, the IAWS facilitated a discussion on offering sex education through AWS chapters at the their 1967 biannual convention featuring Mary Calderone, who had co-founded the Sexuality Information and Education Council of the United States (SIECUS) with Kirkendall. In addition, the 1967 IAWS newsletter offered AWS chapters guidance on providing sex education workshops that followed the Sunnen Conference recommendations.[50]

While some deans implemented the new practices, the issue remained contentious into the 1970s, and NADW did not formally recommend sex education until 1971. Campuses changed slowly as most administrations found the Sunnen Conference recommendations fell too far outside local attitudes. In 1971, an AAUW survey found only 43 percent of the schools provided birth control information and counseling at their university health services. KU's Watkins Memorial Hospital was among those that had not embraced contraceptive counseling, and instead provided only scant contraceptive information. What little support existed for contraceptive advising at KU's student health center resulted from Taylor's hard-fought administrative wrangling.[51]

The Pill and Sex Education at KU

At KU, Taylor found the introduction of the pill in 1960 created a more focused need for sex education. While most physicians in Lawrence followed the national practice of refusing to provide the pill to unmarried women, Taylor recalled that "word got around which doctors would prescribe the pill."[52] Not surprisingly, as the pill became available, KU women asked more and more questions regarding sexuality and contraception. Initial requests for information came from women living in the residence halls, and Shavlik responded by mimeographing information sheets to provide answers to student queries. Since some students accessed birth control pills on their own, Taylor and her staff wanted to be certain women understood that pills could not be shared, and that borrowing a single pill did not prevent pregnancy.[53]

In the early 1960s, the women's student body still clung to the parietals for all but senior women. With the pill arriving on campus, Taylor guided the AWS to research topics regarding sexual morality. She strove to show the campus that despite the availability of contraception, most KU women still conformed—or at least said they conformed—to society's prescription for abstinence before marriage. In 1964, AWS surveyed seniors and freshmen with results showing that 91 percent of women disapproved of premarital sex if the couple was not engaged to be married. Even then, only 17 percent of seniors agreed that intercourse between an engaged couple was at all acceptable.[54] Taylor focused AWS women on positive peer norms, distributing the 1964 AWS survey to illustrate that the majority of KU women rejected premarital sex unless engaged to be married, and most disapproved of that as well. The AWS survey set a standard that KU women could reference as an ethical and moral framework for making their own personal decisions, encouraging students to abstain from premarital sex. This approach not only aligned with the deaning tradition of self-governance, but also fit the 1962 Sunnen Foundation conference recommendations as well as Taylor's own long-term thinking about fostering autonomous decision-making through the dyad of self-governance and student government.

Meanwhile, as Taylor and her staff implemented new approaches to answer students' growing questions about sexuality and contraception, Lawrence became one of the few cities in the country where the pill became easy to access. In Kansas, ZPG advocates passed legislation allowing public agencies to distribute contraceptive pills to low-income married women. Nationally less than 20 percent of local health departments participated in such a program. However, by the mid-1960s in Lawrence, the public health department director and ZPG advocate, Dr. Dale Clinton, began to distribute pills liberally and without regard for marital status—bent on stopping population growth—especially among poor women whom mainstream middle and upper class society preferred not reproduce. Some said he handed pills out "like bubble gum," and, to Taylor's dismay, he did not perform the recommended physical examination before prescribing them. Not surprisingly, since youth had been weighing the decision over premarital sex according to risk of pregnancy since the 1930s, university women quickly formed the core of Clinton's clientele rather than the poor married women that the legislation intended to support.[55]

Taylor later recalled that "Clinton didn't have a very good reputation with us" as she and her staff strongly believed that a woman should receive a medical examination before taking a controlled drug.[56] Given the easy access KU women had to the pill through Dr. Clinton, Taylor increased her office's staff support to provide contraception information so that women taking it could make safe choices. To combat Clinton's practice of prescribing pills without a physical examination, Taylor also tried to establish the KU Watkins Memorial Hospital as an alternative place for women to obtain the pill so they would receive a proper medical exam.

To achieve this goal, Taylor would implement all the strategies deans of women developed to facilitate change on a university campus where women were still regarded as "incidental students." She would work through administrative channels, provide statistical data in support of her position, and use the power of AWS to speak for the entire women's student body in asking for change in student health center policy. She started by asking Watkins Hospital for help educating women about sexuality, but received little support from the medical personnel at the health center. She and her staff quickly discovered "that it didn't matter what their background...the nurses, medical doctors, knew very little about human sexuality."[57] In this, KU reflected a national trend. Despite the late-1930s marriage classes, US medical schools did little to educate physicians on sexuality. Shavlik recalled having a dawning recognition that some of the Watkins physicians' reluctance to counsel male or female students on sexuality arose from the fact that they felt unprepared to provide information. In response, Taylor and her staff worked with AWS leaders to collect more materials on women's health for the library in her office, hoping to then share this information with Watkins.[58]

However, the pill still faced the challenge of moralists. Watkins director Dr. Raymond Schwegler, refused to cooperate. Despite the Sunnen Conference recommendations for a partnership between deans of women and student health centers, he rejected Taylor's requests for sexuality education, and contraceptive or pregnancy counseling assistance, believing such work with unmarried women was immoral. To combat Schwegler's resistance, Taylor borrowed Mueller's strategy of surveying women's opinions to provide campus administration with data in support of her position. Where Mueller had used this tactic to manage noise complaints and dance policies, Taylor employed it in her effort to change male administrators' minds. Knowing that the KU administration opposed sex education based on moral grounds, Taylor wielded the 1964 AWS survey to combat morality arguments at the administrative level. With this data in hand, she could show male administrators that by serving women's contraceptive needs, they largely served couples engaged to be married. Despite the survey results, Schwegler refused to assist, so Taylor decided to begin negotiating change through administrative channels that could force change at the hospital.

Taylor believed that if KU women could access birth control pills at the student health center, they would stop using Clinton's practice, which she considered dangerous.

Armed with the AWS research results, the Sunnen Foundation conference recommendations, and NADW discussion on the topic, Taylor formally placed the issue of contraception access on the agenda of the KU Council on Student Affairs (COSA) in 1965. COSA provided the KU chancellor with direction on student affairs policies and included Schwegler, along with the dean of students, dean of men, and student union director, among others. Here, Schwegler's refusal would become a university policy matter, and Taylor believed she had a preponderance of evidence to convince the administration to change its policies. Taylor argued that KU would have less reason to worry about women trying to abort pregnancies if they had university access to contraception to avoid unplanned pregnancy altogether.[59]

Within COSA, a plot-line familiar to women's health advocates took place as Schwegler, a male physician, asserted his medical authority by limiting women's access to contraception. Taylor, on the other hand, advocated for the practice of medicine to include women's needs and health. Repeatedly in COSA meetings, Schwegler rebuffed Taylor's request for Watkins to prescribe or disseminate information on the birth control pill or to change his policy of requiring women to pay for gynecological exams. This particularly frustrated Taylor as KU students already paid required fees to support Watkins, and university policy stated that the health center would provide free physical examinations for all students. Schwegler allowed free comprehensive health examinations for men, yet insisted on charging women for gynecological services, considering them an "extra" service since men did not require them. Taylor and her staff argued vehemently that the male body should not be considered the norm for a full physical examination.[60]

Taylor tried several times through administrative channels to convince university leaders that Watkins Hospital should provide sex education, prescribe contraception, and conduct free gynecological examinations. She advocated her position with Provost James Surface and Woodruff. Surface, though, chose not to intervene, noting that he believed the university preferred to be guided by the convention against sex outside of wedlock. Surface's opinion reflected that of most early-to-mid-1960s state university administrators. He recognized that the services were controversial among the public citizens who paid tax dollars to support the university. Taylor, though not successful, reminded Surface that administering higher education according to popular opinion was not "commensurate with educational processes."[61]

Next, to strengthen her case, Taylor brought Schwegler's refusal to address women's health into the campus-wide discourse at KU. In 1966—the same year that AWS voted to expand senior keys to underclasswomen—Taylor's staff supported students in organizing a forum on birth control at the union. They invited two religious leaders so that the panelists could directly address morality questions: a KU campus minister and a priest from Saint Louis University, both of whom supported the ZPG agenda. Schwegler, an obstetrics physician himself, participated as the third panelist. During the discussion, students asked Schwegler whether a rogue KU student health doctor, might provide pills to the women without his knowledge. While Schwegler answered that his staff supported his position completely, he remained unaware that one of his staff routinely (and covertly) worked with the dean of women's office on reproductive issues, an "underground" option.[62]

The forum brought Schwegler's refusal to offer contraception into the public conversation, with the student newspaper quoting him as saying he would not "contribute to the recreational activities of the campus."[63] As Taylor's office intended, the panel produced campus dialogue on accessing the pill. Letters flowed into the editor of *The University Daily Kansan* regarding morality, student maturity, and student responsibility. Schwegler, though, stood firm in refusing to support sex education or contraception, and COSA again declined to change his health center policies in 1967 when Taylor put the issue on the agenda once more.[64]

With little success in changing Schwegler's approach, Taylor employed another long-time strategy of deans of women—using AWS as the voice for the entire women's student body to force administrative attention to a matter. By 1966, the sexual revolution was well on its way, and New Left groups had begun to agitate on campus. In this environment, AWS leaders and the student governments of the women's dormitories began to provide sex education and contraceptive information seminars themselves with the aid of Taylor's staff. This aligned with IAWS practice, and by doing so, Taylor side-stepped Schwegler, providing information to the student body without involving Watkins Memorial Hospital at all. While Schwegler obviously disagreed with the effort, Taylor recalled no administrative pressure to stop the seminars. "No one complained to me about it. No internal problems about it. Not a word," said Taylor. "I don't have any idea why—maybe they didn't want to oppose me. Maybe they didn't think it was wise to oppose something that popular. I didn't ask before I did it either."[65] Since Taylor had moved on without him, Schwegler finally announced to COSA in March of 1968 that a physician with more liberal views on contraception than his would participate in an educational forum at a women's dormitory. Not surprisingly, Schwegler continued to refuse to have his staff take ownership of the sex education program, or to provide contraception.[66]

At this point, after almost a decade of work by Taylor and her staff, the dean of women's office brought their informal AWS efforts and quiet counseling into a formal operation. During 1968–1969, the AWS and the dean's office hosted a public forum to answer questions regarding birth control. These well-advertised forums hosted speakers and distributed booklets listing where women could obtain birth control information and services. In her sex education agenda, Taylor followed the 1962 Sunnen Foundation and NADW conference recommendations closely. She brought in a doctor affiliated with SIECUS to train the employees in the dean of women's and the dean of men's offices, including residence hall staff members, so they would be prepared to conduct informal, small group sessions with students after

Figure 4.1 Emily Taylor at her desk, Strong Hall, University of Kansas, 1960s

a large lecture. As the forums grew, they featured SIECUS keynote speakers Rita Costick and Don Ward, who addressed KU audiences of 700 to 1,000 students. In order to facilitate questions, the staff passed out cards for attendees to anonymously submit their queries, and Shavlik and the committee of AWS students organizing the events urged women to bring their boyfriends to the presentations in an effort to educate male students as well. Taylor even adopted the Sunnen Foundation summit recommendation to have students produce films about sexuality, featuring a Planned Parenthood–financed film, *Less Than Human* created by Chuck Berg.[67]

By 1969, the changes wrought by the sexual revolution allowed Taylor to voice her long-held belief in contraception. The *University Daily Kansan* quoted her saying that the pill provided women with "personal control over reproduction."[68] With effective contraception, she believed women could combine profession, marriage, and family, and she encouraged AWS to take the office's sex education efforts to a more comprehensive level. In fact, New Left student leader Sarah Scott recalled being incredulous that Taylor insisted she include in sex education programming emerging technological ideas like artificial insemination and test-tube babies. In 1970 Taylor's sex education program extended throughout the dean of women's operation, and she and her staff had transformed the informal sexuality seminar previously offered in a residence hall or at an AWS meeting into a week-long AWS-sponsored "Partners in Humanity" series. Along with training on respectful, healthy relationships, they covered topics such as venereal disease, female and male sexual response, alternatives in unplanned pregnancy, pornography, homosexuality, law and sexual deviancy, birth control, courtship, and sex stereotypes. Taylor's office also produced a "Birth Control Handbook"—with information ranging from the pill to abortion—and even included a panel on human sexuality during its high school leadership day conference to educate high school senior women about campus resources on sexuality.[69]

Though Schwegler continued to resist the program, Watkins Hospital finally agreed to participate regularly in this sexuality series and to provide birth control information there. And, at a 1970 COSA meeting, Schwegler finally promised that the next two physicians Watkins Hospital hired would agree to provide contraceptive options to women regardless of marital status. However, in 1972, Janet Sears, a staff member of Taylor's who ran the sex education agenda, expressed her frustration with Schwegler in the campus newspaper, saying, "I have been counseling about one unwanted pregnancy case a day since Thanksgiving...It's too much. It's counseling which Watkins should be doing."[70] Sears reflected the general attitude in the dean's office, where most employees thought Schwegler's refusal to provide contraception was a refusal to care for women's medical and mental health needs. Schwegler, however, continued to drag his feet on hiring the new physicians he had promised, and no action occurred until after the February Sisters feminist protest in 1972.[71]

Unplanned Pregnancy Counseling

Throughout all of this activity, Taylor promoted self-governance and personal decision-making based on an ethical framework, believing contraception allowed women who chose premarital sex to avoid unplanned pregnancy and the untimely end of their education that typically followed. When unplanned pregnancies occurred, though, Taylor wanted women to have safe options and crisis counseling available to them. Knowing that women continued to access illegal, dangerous abortions, especially in Topeka, Taylor tried to quietly move pregnant students into her counseling network for assistance.

When Taylor had arrived at KU in 1956, abortion rarely entered the public discourse, though that began to change in 1962 when national news reports covered the case of Sherri Finkbine, a married mother of four seeking an abortion because she had ingested the sleeping pill Thalidomide, a pharmaceutical discovered as a teratogenic, during her fifth pregnancy.[72] Despite these compelling circumstances, her hospital refused her the procedure. She eventually underwent the surgery abroad where doctors confirmed the Thalidomide severely deformed her fetus.

While the Finkbine case broke the taboo against discussing abortion in the media, academic discourse had covered it earlier—especially in Alfred Kinsey's work at IU. Through Kinsey's research, Taylor and Mueller learned that four-fifths of non-incarcerated white women to receive abortions in the 1930s and 1940s were college-educated. By 1963, Mueller placed the topic in the NADW journal so that deans and counselors of women like Taylor, clearly understood that at least seven percent of abortions were self-induced, and that almost 20 percent of non-medically provided surgeries resulted in physical damage to the woman. For Taylor, these factors, along with the near-deaths of KU students seeking abortions outside of a physician's care, motivated her to set up a pregnancy counseling program to dissuade young women from choosing illegal and dangerous options. During the 1960s, Taylor's work counseling unplanned pregnancy occurred quietly—if not silently—in the interest of protecting young women's privacy and safety. The dean's office made sure "the word got around they could come in and talk to us with confidentiality" about unplanned pregnancy, and students largely knew the dean's office would provide non-judgmental help.[73]

By the late 1960s, attitudes in Kansas and across the nation had rapidly shifted in support of the type of counseling Taylor's office discreetly provided. In 1967 only 21 percent of Americans approved of abortion if a woman did not plan to keep the child; however, by 1969 40 percent approved abortion in the first trimester of a pregnancy regardless of the circumstances. Youth particularly espoused this new position, according to an American Council on Education survey that showed 83 percent of 180,000 incoming freshmen at 275 colleges supported complete legalization of abortion during the 1969–1970 school year.[74]

Acceptance of abortion was not a new phenomenon in the United States. Before World War II, the medical community had made abortion widely available because physicians lacked technologies to mediate pregnancy complications like gestational diabetes and preeclampsia. However, by the mid-1940s, advances in obstetrics removed physical challenges for some of the conditions once considered dangerous to the health of mothers during pregnancy. This divided the medical community regarding when a woman needed an abortion to protect her health, and some physicians worried about their legal liability if another physician disagreed with their recommendation for the procedure. As a result, physicians increasingly relied upon a woman's psychological condition as an indication for abortion—with suicidal tendencies factoring heavily into physicians' considerations.[75]

By the 1950s, the medical profession managed these liability concerns by creating a board of physicians to make a joint recommendation on each woman's case. Most non-Catholic hospitals established these boards, which included the heads of obstetrics and surgery along with a psychiatrist. (Catholic hospitals did not routinely perform these procedures.) Many boards approved abortions for the medical necessity of the mother. However, some boards also prescribed sterilization for the woman receiving the procedure, reflecting societal beliefs that a woman who did not desire motherhood (or a woman perceived as sexually promiscuous) would not be a fit mother later in life. Hospitals applied sterilization more often in cases of poor or non-white women, and not surprisingly the board process drastically reduced the number of women pursuing an abortion in a hospital. Few wanted to publicly request the procedure in a committee meeting, and the threat of sterilization further limited the number of women, applying to hospitals.[76]

Even with the board procedure, the American Medical Association (AMA) found most state abortion laws difficult to enforce and suggested a new approach that added women's mental health as an express reason to legally access abortions. To implement this, the American Law Institute (ALI) included abortion in its efforts to modernize state penal codes into a uniform format. In their recommended statutes, ALI issued new guidelines for abortion in Article 207, Sexual Offenses and Offenses Against the Family, leaving abortion as a crime except in certain instances. Here, the ALI wording added a specific mental health exemption for medically necessary abortions. Article 207's author hoped that this would open abortions to some of the hardship cases that had traditionally been outside the law. The model penal code required two physicians to approve the procedure, and classified all girls who were victims of statutory rape as qualifying for the surgery. Despite most ALI members doubting that Article 207 would meet with approval by state legislatures, some legislatures did begin to adopt it by the late 1960s.[77]

In 1969, Kansas was one of them. That year, the Kansas legislature came very close to repealing abortion from the criminal code altogether, ending with a compromise to place the ALI standards into law. With this, Kansas adopted mental health as a specific reason for legal abortion. The ALI language passed easily in Kansas, likely because mental health considerations already factored into Kansas medical practice, with one Kansas physician contending that psychiatric referrals formed the basis for the majority of legal abortions in the state. Aborting a fetus for other reasons remained under the Kansas criminal code, and it continued to be illegal after the ALI provisions went into effect in 1970. The national AMA and ALI efforts to change abortion law impacted KU women locally just as the ZPG efforts played a role in women's access to contraception on that campus.[78]

Before the ALI standards passed the Kansas legislature, the early counseling in this area by Taylor and her staff left no trace outside the memories of those who worked in her office or went there for help. In a society that upheld the double standard and pathologized an unmarried pregnant woman, Taylor's counseling operation guarded a woman's privacy. Taylor never recorded any aspect of pregnancy counseling—even when a committed couple married. Given the lack of early written records on the topic, the structure and culture of the office after the ALI standards passed the Kansas legislature provides the best window into this part of Taylor's work.

When Janet Sears began work in the dean of women's office in 1971, she oversaw the office's sex education seminars, providing the sexuality curriculum to residence halls, conducting pregnancy counseling, and serving as staff liaison to the women's liberation groups on campus. She recalled stepping into a well-organized pregnancy counseling effort. Secretaries regularly provided privacy to women seeking appointments. They did not ask students about the purpose of their visit, for their last names, or for phone numbers. Sometimes, Sears remembered, students did not make appointments at all. Instead, they came to the dean of women's suite of offices and sat quietly waiting for her to arrive, often as a referral from the dean of women's network of dormitory staff. Even in 1971, when abortion for mental and physical health of the mother was expressly legal, Sears recalled a strong silence surrounding pregnancy counseling and the women involved. Taylor never asked Sears for a report on her work at a staff meeting as she did the other employees, and Professor Marilyn Stokstad recalled being aware that the dean of women's office provided such help to women, though she and Taylor never discussed it.[79] Clearly, the Kansas locale resisted these initiatives, as Casey Eike commented in the *University Daily Kansan*: "'There are still people out there who are very much against us thinking that people have sexual lives at all,' she said. 'And we hear from them.'"[80]

Once a student arrived for counseling, Taylor and her staff always began by suggesting a session with both the woman and her boyfriend. Some who chose marriage or adoption of the baby opted for this. However, in the few cases where women decided to seek abortion in the early 1960s, none were accompanied by the men involved as they wrestled with their choices. If, after discussing her individual situation, a woman still wanted to terminate the pregnancy, staff sent the woman to meet with Taylor, who then referred the student to a medical professional. Before the ALI law passed, Taylor referred this small group of women to either a Kansas City psychiatrist, or to a clinician at Watkins Hospital who worked with Taylor, unbeknownst to Schwegler. After the ALI standard language went into effect in 1970, the entire counseling operation formalized in Taylor's office.[81]

Taylor and Shavlik both recalled this counseling as a very difficult part of their work, with everyone preferring to stop unplanned pregnancies rather than counsel women making such difficult decisions. However, with some students feeling desperate enough to attempt suicide or to try to abort the fetus themselves, Taylor's office felt an urgency to help women access safe options or a means to carry the pregnancy to term. Neither Taylor nor her staff made any determination regarding the women's mental condition and referred such assessments to the medical community; however, their involvement allowed women students to seek advice where their mental health could be considered as a factor in obtaining a safe, legal abortion. Taylor and her staff knew that a woman's reputation and options for continuing her education rested on privacy in these situations, whether she chose marriage, placed her infant with an adoptive family, or received an abortion. Clearly, Taylor wanted KU women to have facts about sexuality and contraception so they could make their own decisions about how to blend dating, marriage, and career with motherhood. Through this, she hoped more women would avoid unplanned pregnancy. For those who did not, she wanted safe options and comprehensive counseling so the women could make the best decisions for themselves.

Gay and Lesbian Student Advocacy

Since deans of women counseled sexuality issues, they also advised gay and lesbian students. The student affairs profession, increasingly led by male deans of students since the 1940s, left behind the student governance methods developed by women deans in favor of mental health methods. This psychological approach pathologized homosexuality, treating gay and lesbian students as ill. Taylor, however, remained committed to self-governance, and she took a different approach at KU more reminiscent of the self-actualization goals within early deans of women's philosophy. KU's dean of men relied heavily on psychology for handling non-normative behavior, handling homosexuality as a pathology to be treated, often expelling young men whom psychiatrists felt were "dangerous" to the student body.[82]

Taylor's office, however, rarely involved the psychologists in "treating" homosexuality or addressing lesbian activity on campus. Still relying on self-governance as her model, Taylor treated homosexuality as a normal part of human relationships. Again, Taylor's early training at IU made a difference in her approach, as Kinsey's *Sexual Behavior in the Human Female* had outlined lesbian activity as a normal sexual outlet for some women. As with pregnancy counseling, she kept no notes about students' sexual lives, and she did not consider lesbian students a "danger" to the campus community. She allowed at least one woman she knew who had experimented with homosexual activity to enroll at KU, and she disapproved of the dean of men's practice of recording sexuality information in student files, knowing the student would have a difficult time enrolling in another institution of higher learning with such records. She did, however, expect all female students—lesbian or straight—to keep their sexual activities private and out of the public sphere. In fact, Shavlik recalled that in the early 1970s gay and lesbian students staged displays of same-sex sexuality at a dormitory to raise awareness about homosexuality. Taylor's office intervened and asked the students to find other ways to promote their agenda. Despite limiting public displays of sexuality, Taylor facilitated one-on-one counseling of gay and lesbian students within her office and included the topic in her sex education series.[83] Former IAWS National President Louise Douce recalled Taylor as a significant source of strength as Douce came out as a lesbian. When Douce told Taylor she was upset with her parents for lack of support, she recalled that Taylor said, "Louise, how long did it take you to understand and accept you were gay?" When Douce answered "years," Taylor responded, "Maybe you should give your parents at least six months to adjust."[84]

Taylor soon provided administrative support to gay and lesbian students as well when in 1970 the Gay Liberation Front (GLF) applied to be a recognized student group at KU. Shavlik and her husband, Frank, who worked in the more conservative dean of men's office, took the most prominent step to support gay and lesbian students at KU, and Taylor backed them. Frank Shavlik received a visit from a male student who lived in a scholarship hall. The student, representing a group of male and female students, asked Frank if he and Donna would become the advisors to their new student group, the KU GLF. Frank agreed, sending the student to talk with Donna in the dean of women's office. Rather than asking permission, Frank processed the club request in the same manner as he would have for any student organization applying to be a campus-sanctioned group.

This was the first formal recognition of alternative sexuality at KU, and the administration quickly reacted. Within half an hour of notifying the dean of men about the new group, Frank received a summons to attend a meeting with Dean of Students Bill Balfour. Even though Balfour and Taylor would back the KU GLF, Chancellor Chalmers flatly rejected it. Chalmers, though few knew it, was already under significant scrutiny by the Kansas Board of Regents for the accelerating racial and anti-war protests at KU. With Chalmers refusing to recognize the KU GLF, the club filed a lawsuit so contentious it went to the Supreme Court which refused it. Meanwhile, Balfour, Taylor and others quietly made room for the GLF at KU as the case wound its way through courts.

Although KU's GLF labeled Taylor as "most generally helpful," she walked a very fine line in her support of lesbian and gay students. As a heterosexual, middle-aged woman, her unmarried status left her vulnerable to "lesbian-baiting," a strategy of using gossip to attempt to taint activist women. In the late 1960s, an age when the public was still uncomfortable about homosexuality, labeling a woman a lesbian discredited her as a moral authority, which had always been an assumed role for women deans. Despite this risk, Taylor supported the Shavliks' efforts with the KU GLF even though, as Donna Shavlik recalled, the couple's support of the group "didn't make her [Taylor's] life pleasant."[85] The *Lawrence Journal World* sanctioned KU for both the sexuality education series and the GLF, publishing a scathing editorial that read:

> [These] are just the kinds of things that parents want to hear about when they help their youngsters select a school. Because of the unrest and violence of recent months, parents and students are apprehensive about enrolling at KU, or coming back. Now we have two more excellent examples of why there is understandable concern ... [the university] is going to need all the greatness it can muster to weather the current storm without irreparable damage.[86]

Clearly, the sexuality series and support for GLF put Taylor in the midst of the public turmoil, something every dean of women traditionally tried to avoid. With Chalmers opposing the GLF, Taylor's approach toward educating students about same-sex sexuality must have also come under criticism, though Taylor never mentioned it. She did, however, say that she expected Chalmers would have been happy if "a whole bunch of us had dropped dead."[87] Chalmers would not last as chancellor, though, and by 1973 KU recruited Archie Dykes to take over the role. Dykes supported the existence of the GLF on campus, only drawing the line at hosting a regional gay liberation conference during the Kansas legislature's session—knowing that would catapult the GLF into the news. With Dykes on board, Taylor advocated for change in a new arena—sexual assault prevention.

Deaning, Sexual Harassment, and Rape

Deans of women—responsible for the safety of women students—always counseled sexually harassed or assaulted students.[88] There has been little written on the role of deans of women and sexual assault prevention. The

NADW archives hold no formal materials regarding rape, likely because the language and concepts surrounding sexual assault and sexual harassment only arose in the late 1960s and early 1970s. Before that, deans of women thought of these issues as general women's safety. Colleges considered parietals as a means to protect women against assault and unwanted sexual overtures, with administrations contending that women who followed the regulations stayed safe. Rules, however, never truly prevented sexual harassment or rape any more than laws have prevented these crimes today. This parietal fiction, though, stymied discussion and made it difficult to educate women on how to protect themselves from unwanted sexual advances. At KU, with parietals dissolving by the mid-1960s, Taylor, her staff, and AWS brought the topic of sexual assault into public discussion, educating women to protect themselves and enlightening society that these assaults were not brought on by a woman's promiscuous behavior.[89]

Taylor fashioned her own approach to these issues. As a model, she drew on the 1940s example Mueller had provided at Indiana when Kinsey pushed women to participate in his sexual history interviews. Mueller, clearly a supporter of sexual education, took seriously the young women upset by and uncomfortable with the content of Kinsey's questionnaires and worked with administrators to stop Kinsey's interviews. At KU, Taylor took the same approach. When a harassing incident occurred between a student and faculty member, Taylor believed it necessary for the provost or an academic dean to sanction the professor; the shame of the sanction, she believed, would lead the faculty member to consider more seriously the directive to stop the behavior. Through most of her career at KU, she involved Provost James Surface who personally addressed sexual harassment problems. After Surface's retirement in 1970, Taylor found these incidents more difficult to solve and often coordinated meetings of various administrators including a department chair from the faculty member's discipline. In one instance of a professor fondling students, she elected to call a meeting of the provost, the dean of the arts and sciences college, and another administrator to request that they take care of the situation. When one of the men thought Taylor should handle it, she recalled becoming angry. "I said no. I don't hire or pay the faculty member—you do. You take care of it." Taylor always called such work "educating male administrators," and she often used these types of meetings to help male colleagues understand women's issues.[90]

Taylor's campus-wide network played a role in these efforts as well. She often learned of sexual harassment complaints via staff in the residence halls, and secretaries regularly called her office to report incidents that occurred in departments. By the end of her tenure at KU, students clearly understood Taylor's role in stopping sexual harassment, as a radical feminist group noted: "If you know of a classroom situation where the professor discriminates against women in any way, tell Dean Taylor about it. She keeps a record of these incidents, and if more than three women have complaints about a professor, Dean Taylor will investigate the situation and do what she can to change it."[91] This student comment illustrates the broad recognition of

Taylor's advocacy regarding discriminating attitudes about women and the sexual harassment that sometimes accompanied it. Until KU created an office of affirmative action in 1972, the dean of women's office functioned as the location for reporting women's harassment and for pressuring the administration to respond to it.

In the late 1960s, Taylor added rape prevention to her agenda. Like unplanned pregnancies, rape had always factored into deaning. In fact, under the doctrines of *in loco parentis*, a university could be held legally responsible for the protection of a student, and Taylor recalled one university sued by parents for not protecting their daughter from rape. Deans of women's offices across the country regularly counseled sexual assault victims as a part of their work. When Taylor joined KU in 1956, residence hall staff and Watkins hospital already referred any known rape to her office so that she and her staff could engage in one-on-one crisis counseling. When dissolving parietals she also kept safety in mind, frequently reminding women not to walk alone late at night. Taylor initiated a formal program on women's safety, though, when a series of assaults began that she could not solve administratively. With no help to educate male students about what constituted a woman's consent for sex, Taylor created a program for women.

The effort began in the mid-to-late 1960s when Stroup counseled multiple women—some from the same sorority—who had been violently date-raped by the same student athlete.[92] Astoundingly, the "blame the victim" ideology was so strong that the women in the same sorority did not even warn each other not to accept a date with the man. The dean's office reported the incidents to the athletics department, though they received no support to investigate or punish the athlete. With no help from university administration and no way to publicize the problem without revealing victims' identities, Taylor initiated a new AWS program, inviting a national speaker to train women regarding self-defense. She wanted women students to be prepared to physically fight back if violently assaulted. Taylor also amassed informational material in her office library on rape, and these resources brought the emerging national conversation regarding sexual assault prevention into her office, all before Susan Brownmiller published her groundbreaking best-seller *Against Our Will* that labeled rape a violent crime in 1975.[93]

Taylor's work foregrounded this emerging feminist issue as early as 1968. Historians often attribute early sexual assault counseling and assistance to radical feminist groups such as the Bay Area Women Against Rape organizing in Oakland, California, in 1971, and one of the first rape crisis telephone lines in Washington DC in 1972. Taylor's campus work preceded them, and she provided the same services—counseling, creating self-defense courses, and training health care workers likely to encounter rape victims. As the women's movement grew, Taylor fused her staff's rape awareness and counseling efforts with those initiated by campus women's liberation groups as a natural extension of her office's service. Eventually, her staff and AWS worked with police and hospital employees—on campus and off—to educate them on rape and counseling methods, trying to destigmatize the rape victim and stop the "blame the victim" mentality.[94] For these Lawrence-area emergency service personnel, Taylor's staff assembled "rape examination kits," provided workshops on evidence requirements for the prosecution of rapes, and recommended counselors who had expertise working with victims of sexual assault.[95]

These efforts expanded when a series of stranger rapes began at KU in 1972. In 1970, Lawrence police recorded only four rapes in Lawrence, but two years later the number shot up to 26, with another 26 again in 1973. The increase resulted both from enhanced efforts to encourage women to report the crime, and from one man, Al Byron Johnson, a student at nearby Ottawa University, who allegedly committed between eleven and sixteen rapes on the KU campus by February of 1974.[96] Continuing sexual assault prevention training, Taylor put the AWS-dean's office network in motion to address rape as these reports escalated. First, she supported rape victim Pat Henry in establishing the Rape Victim Support Service (RVSS) in 1972 as a joint project between the KU Information Center and the Office of the Dean of Women. This rape crisis center would be one of the first such university efforts in the nation, if not the very first. She also appointed Assistant to the Dean of Women Casey Eike (the former national IAWS president) as director of programs for women's security, with Eike responsible for providing sexual assault prevention materials to women on campus.[97]

However, with Johnson still at large in early 1974, Taylor, Eike, and her staff organized a public awareness campaign designed to engage the community in stopping assaults—especially the string of stranger rapes. First, Taylor called together city officials, state legislators, university administrators, leaders of area and campus women's organizations, and KU rape counselors in a "Women's Security Meeting" in the student union. The group discussed "ways to make Lawrence the safest city in the nation." The agenda, distributed on the dean of women's letterhead, included a proposal for "Whistlestop," a possible initiative for KU women to wear a whistle as a symbol of solidarity and to use as a distress signal if attacked.[98]

The Women's Security Meeting provided Taylor with a preview of the community's divided response to rape, as it drew both support and criticism. On one hand, supporters recommended options for safety. Commending Taylor for trying to help, a circulation librarian suggested an escort service for women working at the library, and a mother of a sophomore daughter suggested changing the campus policy of dimming parking lot lights to save energy.[99] By the 1980s and 1990s, many colleges nationwide implemented similar services to escort women home from campus buildings late at night; today they are standard on most campuses.

On the other hand, the attention to safety and rapes also meant some labeled KU's campus as dangerous, which many KU administrators thought created a public perception problem. As Bill Balfour, vice chancellor for student affairs, stated to the new chancellor, Archie Dykes, "One negative aspect of our work to make the community safer has been the impression given that it is a less safe place than other communities."[100] Within a week of the Women's Security Meeting, the university received at least one parent complaint questioning KU's safety for women students.[101] While Dykes disliked publicity indicating KU was dangerous, he also wanted action to stop the rapes.[102]

The divided response to the safety meeting foreshadowed what occurred when the AWS, now renamed the KU Commission on the Status of Women, rolled out the Whistlestop campaign. This awareness campaign launched with $0.75 whistle sales in the student union. Taylor convinced many area stores to sell whistles at cost and AWS leaders hung 250 eye-popping posters of a woman fleeing from an attacker. In residence halls, sororities, campus buildings, apartment complexes, laundromats, nearby Haskell University, and grocery stores, the posters prompted the community to consider women's safety. Eike also assembled a speaker's bureau on the topic, dispersed news releases and purchased advertisements in the *University Daily Kansan* and the *Lawrence Journal World*. Although the campaign only targeted local media, it quickly gained statewide media attention.[103] In Kansas City, a radio broadcast by WDAF read:

> The rape of a young co-ed inside a residence hall at the University of Kansas is another shocking example of just how ineffective security has become at the Lawrence campus. The rape is another of more than twenty reported attacks on young women at KU within the past year. Who knows how many more incidents have gone unreported for all of the usual reasons. Imagine the anger and disbelief of the fathers of these daughters who have become victims of criminals, doing such a simple and American thing as acquiring a higher education at KU. Campus security? I suspect it is a farce! Why else would a co-ed begin the sale of 5,000 whistles to other co-eds to ward off campus attackers? What defense is a whistle when campus security is such that allows a young girl to be raped inside a residence hall? I might suggest it is time that parents of youngsters at KU back the administration to the wall. Demand that the University come down from its Ivory Tower and stop trifling with this very serious campus problem. That is the way I see it.[104]

Eike and AWS achieved their goal of attracting public attention to the issue of women's safety. However, the effort also tarnished the university's public image as adequate protectors of students.

Whistlestop became one of Taylor's most contentious administrative fights. Taylor recognized that her position as dean of women existed to protect women's safety. University chancellors and presidents had historically given feminist deans of women freedom to act in women students' interests as long as the activities avoided negative public relations. With Whistlestop, however, Taylor tipped the balance, instigating a public image campaign she knew would create negative publicity because she saw no other effective options. The day following the WDAF broadcast, the KU Alumni Association Associate Director Vincent Bilotta wrote to Taylor (carbon copying the chancellor, the Executive Vice Chancellor Del Shankel and the director of public relations), to communicate his anger at Taylor and her staff. Upset over the statewide publicity, Bilotta accused Taylor of significantly damaging the university's reputation and the next year's enrollment of first year women, suggesting her program labeled KU as a "Rape Campus."[105] In fact, Stroup said that the response to Whistlestop was so strong that she recalled it as "the first time I was afraid of losing my job."[106] The AWS posters only increased opponents' ire as Eike had staged the photo of a woman fleeing a rapist in Strong Hall near the chancellor's office—allowing viewers to interpret it as indicating that the KU administration building also failed to be safe.[107] Years later, even Taylor recalled the posters as overly dramatic.

With violent antiwar student protests only recently behind the KU campus, administrators were particularly sensitive about the university's public profile in 1974. Complaints like Bilotta's gained ground within the administration.[108] In a not-so-subtle sanction of Taylor, Shankel distributed the text of the radio editorial to all vice chancellors and deans, noting the damaging effects of the publicity on the university's reputation and asking for suggestions in correcting the perception of the media. Although Taylor recalled that Dykes told her he supported her efforts and thought the criticisms overblown, the new chancellor had reason for concern. He followed two chancellors who had left KU over publicity problems during student protests, riots, and race relations struggles.

Although some in the KU administration opposed Whistlestop, the AWS and Taylor also received queries regarding replicating the program from campuses across the country, including Bethune-Cookman University, Grambling College, New Mexico State University, Louisiana State University, and the University of Missouri among others.[109] The new KU affirmative action director, Shirley Gilham, also supported Taylor, writing "I understand that there is some heated criticism of the Whistlestop program and that you are bearing the brunt of it. My feeling is that the whole controversy is missing the real point. If there's anything I can do to help, just let me know."[110] What Gilham recognized—and what Bilotta and others had missed in their concern over public image—was that to end rape, the topic needed to be brought into the open for discussion and action. Women, long afraid of the double standard that regularly accused rape victims for inducing the crime themselves through promiscuous or suggestive behavior, rarely spoke out about violent assaults. Even in the late 1960s, social conventions regarding women's respectability continued to keep many women from reporting or acknowledging a rape—especially date rape. This allowed society to ignore both the issue and the need for sexual assault prevention.

To de-stigmatize victims, rape prevention advocates recognized that the public needed to understand rape as a violent crime—something that could not occur without public discussion of sexual assault. At KU, the string of stranger rapes created a context that allowed Taylor to publicly address the problem by involving local and state officials, women's organizations, and the campus community. Taylor, who noted that she gave "fair warning" to everyone that they planned to distribute the whistles, believed that the threat of publicity like that from the Kansas City radio editorial kept many universities from addressing the problem of rape and rape education.[111] Traditionally, universities followed Bilotta's logic, preferring that incidents of sexual violence be handled privately and as quietly as possible to protect the university's reputation. Taylor felt this sometimes protected rapists as it had with the KU student athlete, and it left other women students unaware of rapist activity and therefore more vulnerable to sexual assault. These issues continue to challenge universities today, though administrations are much more aware of the importance of protecting a victim's anonymity and far more cases are referred to the local police rather than handled internally.

It is not coincidence that the radio report Shankel circulated sounded remarkably like the complaints against the removal of parietal curfews and closing hours that Taylor had instigated in the late 1950s. The rules and regulations governing women student's lives relied on the fiction that female students who followed the rules would be protected from unwanted pregnancy or sexual violence. For Taylor, it was clear that no set of regulations could produce security for every woman. Even Bilotta noted in his vitriolic letter that the rape of a student inside a residence hall "could not have been prevented by any campus administrator."[112] In a milieu where the KU athletics department felt free to ignore violent assaults by one of its student athletes, the university preference for privately handling disciplinary matters harmed women who became victims of sexual assault. Private handling, in effect, typically translated into inaction at best; victim-blaming at worst, and sometimes little or no punishment for the perpetrator. Taylor, unable to quietly address sexual assault through private administrative channels, took the issue public. Her administrative support for rape prevention still stands, as the Rape Victim Support Service still exists under the name GaDuGi Safe Center in Lawrence, Kansas, now a community-wide effort.

By the time Taylor left KU at the end of 1974, she had instituted a support system for women's health, sexuality education, and sexual assault that rested on the knowledge and strategies of early deans of women. She retained the dean of women's responsibility for protecting women's safety by shunning rote rules and investing in three facets of deaning—university policy change, self-governance through AWS, and one-on-one student-staff counseling. Administratively, she achieved free student gynecological examinations, contraceptive and sexuality education programming, rape crisis services, university support in cases of sexual harassment, and some endorsement of lesbian and gay student needs. She wrought these policy changes using the long-time deaning strategy of harnessing the AWS—which represented the women's student body—to call for university change. With careful guidance by Taylor and her staff, the AWS enacted the sexuality seminars, provided information on contraception and how to obtain it, initiated sexual assault prevention as well as rape crisis support, and included homosexuality in AWS sexuality education forums so that gay and lesbian students had access to knowledge about same-sex relationships. And, she asked AWS to study moral attitudes toward sexuality, and used the data they produced as a leverage point for implementing university policy changes.

At the heart of Taylor's approach to AWS and student government rested her belief that each female student needed to make her own autonomous decisions about her personal life. She used AWS to create a framework for women to see community norms about premarital sex and to consider what was right for each woman, on issues ranging from abstinence to early marriage, adoption, abortion, or, in some cases, a lesbian lifestyle. All of this programming balanced on a teeter-totter, with privacy seated on one end and publicity on the other. Taylor remained steadfastly committed to protecting the privacy of women who would be caught in society's double standard, wanting to provide them with a path to move forward with their lives and educations. However, she pushed the university to move the general topics of sexuality—and rape prevention—into the public sphere for discussion in order to better solve and prevent unplanned premarital pregnancy and rape assaults. Her activity in the late 1960s and early 1970s stretched the bargain feminist deans had always kept with their university leaders—that they would foster change while keeping the university out of the news. With the exceptions of Whistlestop and the GLF, Taylor usually managed to present her efforts as an uncontroversial, middle-ground solution during the university struggles with New Left anti-war protest, civil rights agitation, and radical feminist activism. This made Taylor's advocacy appear to be a compromise position, and she astutely and purposely employed this approach to achieve lasting change—especially for women's health and rape crisis response at KU.

CHAPTER 5

The Dean of Women in the Age of Protest

On a March day in 1965, Emily Taylor sat at her wide wooden desk reading a thank you note from two KU students, Linda Cook and Carol Borg. Notes of appreciation frequently crossed her desk as a matter of etiquette, an expected courtesy reflective of the formality of the time. Most letters expressed gratitude for a speech by Taylor or for her help arranging classes. This note, though, was different. The two women thanked the dean of women for not suspending them—despite Chancellor W. Clarke Wescoe's directive to do so.[1]

Less than a week before, the two women joined over 150 students who held a sit-in in Wescoe's office to protest racial discrimination at KU. Borg and Cook must have been nervous sitting on the floor in Strong Hall as Chancellor Wescoe politely told the group that anyone remaining when the building closed at 5 p.m. would be taken into police custody for trespassing. Some students, fearing arrest, left. Acting under Wescoe's direction, the Douglas County sheriff jailed over 100 protestors. The chancellor offered to bail them out, but also directed the dean of men and dean of women to suspend each activist. Don Alderson complied, immediately issuing telegrams to male students' parents announcing their suspensions. Taylor waited—stalling because she believed the chancellor would change his mind once he had time to put the events into perspective. Her instinct proved correct, and within a week Wescoe rescinded the suspensions and agreed to significant change in how KU operated regarding black students, removing housing and career placement discriminatory practices, along with banning racial segregation in student organizations, or in campus newspaper job advertisements. Borg and Cook thanked Taylor for her prescience, noting "this saved many long distance calls, explanations, visits, tension, and conflict [with parents]." Eventually the dean of men's office "unsuspended" the male protestors.[2]

The sit-in became one of the most effective racial protests ever on the KU campus. As KU civil rights historian Rusty Monhollon noted, "[W]ith a rush of student government resolutions, administrative orders, and a stroke of Wescoe's pen, racial exclusion had been banned from the campus of the University of Kansas."[3] Within that "rush" of activity, however, sat the interwoven links between the dean of women's office, student activism, and civil rights at KU. These links allowed Taylor and her staff to use the feminist activist features long established in her office to benefit black students, and New Left activists as well. She relied on her close relationships with students and staff, her astute understanding of maneuvering within the university setting—skills she learned from her mentors Grace S. M. Zorbaugh and Kate Hevner Mueller—and her own force of personality.

Few liked to challenge Taylor. She was well informed, quick with responses, and had few qualms about embarrassing someone if it served her ends. While other administrators may not have liked Taylor, she cultivated a strong relationship with each chancellor, and by the mid 1960s she amassed a large, loyal staff and significant student support from her position on the margin of the university. By 1964 when the federal Civil Rights Act passed, Taylor had expanded her network to over thirty employees connected to her office, and she had several long-time staffers invested in her approach—Kala Stroup and Donna Shavlik among them. The staff was diverse and included lesbian women, and both black and Hispanic women. Taylor implemented Mueller's practice of staffing each woman's group with an advisor, bringing the staff into close connection with students at the KU YWCA, the African American sororities, and even radical feminist groups. The office ran well, the Associated Women Students (AWS) operation tied women together as a single interest group, and Taylor used these organizational elements to wield significant influence. While sex discrimination sat at the top of Taylor's priority list, she and her staff also supported the inclusion of other marginalized students as well. This caused both male and female students active in racial equality efforts, the New Left, and even the gay and lesbian students of the last chapter to frequent her office for advice on their initiatives.

With a large, loyal staff connected to all women's groups across campus, Taylor was well positioned to advocate for change as the student protests for civil rights, antiwar sentiments, and feminism escalated during the 1960s on the KU campus. Her office assisted civil rights advocates and defused violence during student protests while also fostering radical feminists. These efforts to support racial equity and student autonomy were not new in deans of women's offices. Taylor belonged to a tradition of feminist deans of women who used their influence to broaden racial equality and student autonomy. Taylor drew on this legacy in "deaning" during the challenging times of student protest and violence that rocked the KU campus.

In the 1960s, KU experienced the same protests and tensions reverberating nationwide in the post-World War II United States. Kansas germinated the well-known 1954 Supreme Court decision, *Brown v. Topeka Board of Education*, which mandated the desegregation of public schools, and the state also generated desegregation protest sit-ins at a Wichita, Kansas drug store that predated those in Greensboro, North Carolina. Located on Interstate 70 in the middle of the nation, KU functioned as a stopping point for New Left activists traveling between the east and west coasts, infusing radical student ideas into the KU community. By 1971, KU had experienced bombings, arson and two shooting deaths—one an African American young man involved in Black Power initiatives, the other a white KU student—placing the campus in the midst of the turmoil facing more commonly referenced schools like Berkeley, Columbia, and Kent State University.[4]

Campus activism at KU over racial civil rights and the Vietnam War occurred in a community that accommodated both ends of the political spectrum. While the state had populist roots and the university housed a number of liberal thinkers, the city of Lawrence itself was bifurcated, home also to many who held Barry Goldwater-style beliefs even before his rise to political prominence. Such Lawrencians worked with the Daughters of the American Revolution and likely the John Birch Society. This division meant that the state experienced significant tension over the evolving protests for social change. Reading news accounts of the time, KU events fit into common narratives regarding the sixties. KU saw non-violent racial civil rights protests in the early and mid-1960s give way to drug culture, Vietnam War protests, and increasingly militant black power initiatives, all as the sexual revolution unfolded around it. Reporters portrayed student protestors pushing KU administrators to change, presenting youth convinced older adults would refuse to revise convention and tradition into a modern context. While some KU administrators reacted in opposition to women's and racial civil rights, the New Left, and gay liberation, Taylor listened to student concerns and often looked for administrative solutions. Her belief in self-governance and teaching students to become autonomous decision-makers translated into a commitment to enabling each individual student to access the same educational opportunity as white men—the primary student population at coeducational schools. As a white, middle-class, heterosexual woman, though, Taylor was by no means perfect on these issues. She did, however, put the power of her office and the AWS behind some aspects of racial equality, radical feminism, and student antiwar protest, in addition to the gay rights discussed in the last chapter.[5]

In the mid-1960s, Taylor and her staff worked in the only sanctioned arm of the university administration designed for a marginalized population of students. Until affirmative action and urban affairs offices arose on the nation's campuses in the 1970s, only the dean of women's office existed to represent marginalized students. Some feminist deans exercised their offices on behalf of minority students—a tradition that developed out of the early twentieth century links between deans of women and labor organizing for economic and political citizenship. Fundamentally, the student protests of the mid-to-late 1960s and early 1970s centered on students who insisted on accessing free speech and full citizenship, either for people of color, women, gays and lesbians, or for young white men angry that they were susceptible to the military draft while lacking the right to vote on the leadership of the country. As different student groups protested against the discrimination that blocked each from full and equal citizenship, they called for universities to change, bringing the assumptions of *in loco parentis*, white privilege, and male privilege into stark relief. For some deans of women, their commitment to self-governance and economic and political citizenship spilled over into other minority issues where students lacked these civil rights for reasons other than sex. Taylor belonged to this tradition in deaning, and used her office to benefit both racial civil rights, radical feminists, and New Left anti-war protestors, intertwining her staff intimately with these student efforts.

Deaning toward Racial Inclusion

The early tradition of deaning emanated from the Progressive social reform efforts at the University of Chicago and Hull House where women such as Sophonisba Breckinridge supported the National Association for the Advancement of Colored People (NAACP). The strongest thread tying deans of women to racial activism rested in their cooperation with the Young Women's Christian Association (YWCA) that developed the protest tactics upon which civil rights activism eventually relied in the 1960s. The earliest deans of women worked closely with local YWCAs, even before 1892 when the University of Chicago appointed Alice Freeman Palmer as the first dean of women. In the late 1800s before the advent of deans of women, local YWCA members often found housing for women students and counseled them as they attended coeducational schools. Eventually, when university administrations funded a dean of women for their campus, the YWCA stayed involved and deans of women found the organization "quite useful" for influencing female students—especially when they had small staffs and underdeveloped methods for deaning. At KU, the YWCA filled this role, cooperating with women faculty until 1913–1914 when the chancellor appointed the first official Advisor of Women. These ties continued and when campuses developed a YWCA student chapter, the dean of women commonly advised it. By the 1930s, YWCA coordination ranked as the third largest effort in deans of women's offices.[6] A reciprocity developed, and some deans of women volunteered with the YWCA as well. These connections resulted in the YWCA becoming a regular partner in deans of women's offices, and at the national level throughout the life-span of deaning.[7]

The YWCA has a long, well-researched history of supporting racial integration. At colleges nationwide, the YWCA provided a venue for black women's campus involvement in the early twentieth century when campus organizations often excluded them. At some schools, such as the University of Chicago, the YWCA successfully organized interracial picnics and lunches during the Progressive Era. And, at the University of Pittsburgh, only the YWCA allowed black women students to participate in extra curricular activities. Some deans of women adopted the YWCA mission of racial equality in their own work. For instance, at Berea College in Kentucky, Dean of Women Julia Allen brought her YWCA activism into Berea with interracial conferences in the 1930s and 1940s, and facilitated the college's integration of black students in 1950. At Oberlin, Florence Fitch, one of the early deans who established vocational guidance and women's self-governance, served as president of Oberlin's YWCA when she was a student, and later worked to create interracial cooperation at the university as its dean of women. Future NADW president, Irma Voigt (Ohio), also worked with the national YWCA leadership, and adopted an ethic of racial equity. This YWCA influence meant some deans of women championed black student rights on their own campuses, particularly with regard to substandard housing. At IU, both Agnes Wells and Mueller worked to provide better campus housing for black women, as would Thrysa Amos at the University of Pittsburgh and Ruth McCarn at Northwestern. Over time, this long-term partnership between deaning and the YWCA produced NADW discussion panels at national meetings like the one in 1948 "Education for Intercultural Understanding" organized by Elsie Smithies (Occidental), Sarah Blanding (formerly dean at Kentucky before joining Vassar as president in 1946), Ruth O. McCarn (Northwestern), and Wilma Rothenberger (YWCA secretary at Northwestern).[8]

However, just as only some deans of women carried forward the feminist principles embedded in early deaning, the partnership between deans of women, the YWCA, and racial equality was similarly limited. Plenty of white deans of women carried out exclusion of black women in university housing, as did Cornell University's R. Louise Fitch who denied black women the opportunity to live in campus residence halls in the 1930s. The NADW struggled with racial inclusion too, regularly meeting at the locations selected by its parent organization the National Education Association, which often chose hotels that did not house or serve meals to blacks. Regional or state-located deans associations followed segregation customs common to their own areas, making racist segregation even more likely at the local level—with some African American deans being invited to attend deans meetings, and then un-invited once association leaders learned their race.[9]

All of the earliest deans of women were white, until 1922 when Howard University hired the first black dean of women, Lucy Diggs Slowe. A graduate of Columbia University's Teachers College, Slowe studied with the preeminent scholars in the profession, and adopted the practices early white deans of women developed. With Howard's influence, the dean of women position spread through black colleges, especially since most African American schools had adopted coeducation because the cost of separating women's education proved too expensive. Slowe set the standard for black women deans, establishing the Association of Deans of Women and Advisers to Girls in Negro Schools (ADWAGNS) as the African American counterpart to the NADW. ADWAGNS brought deaning practices into black institutions, especially the focus on self-governance and autonomy which Slowe thought particularly important for black women. Most, like Slowe, incorporated the YWCA into their offices too. And, just as at predominantly white coeducational institutions, substandard housing for black female students topped the list of priorities at institutions such as Howard.[10]

While Slowe built a community of African American women administrators around the professional role of deaning, she also maintained her connection with the Teachers College network that traditionally flowed into the

NADW. She joined the NADW early in her career and brought her former student, Talladega College Dean of Women Hilda Davis, into the NADW network as well. Both believed NADW provided them with the best access to evolving practices in professional deaning. NADW, like most largely white professional groups, had an inconsistent history with racial prejudice. Slowe and Davis worked together, sometimes with NADW executive director Kathryn Heath, to fully open NADW meetings to black women. The process took twenty years. Davis began by calling attention to segregationist practices by boycotting the 1937 NADW meeting in New Orleans where the customs of the segregationist South required blacks to use hotel service elevators, back doors, and refused black women meal service. In 1940, Irma Voigt of the University of Ohio, marched through St. Louis' segregated Hotel Statler with several black women, insistent they would participate in all NADW meetings despite the hotel's policies. Several African American deans noted that along with Voigt, Kate Hevner Mueller and Hilda Threlkeld, welcomed them at NADW.[11]

By the early 1950s, the preponderance of NADW members supported integration, electing civil rights activist Ruth McCarn to their presidency in 1951, and endorsing the *Brown v. Board of Education* desegregation decision for public K–12 schools when it came out in 1954. While NADW was the only higher education guidance organization to support *Brown*, the continued existence of ADWAGNS through 1954 indicated the incomplete partnership between white and black deans of women.[12] However, by 1963, NADW's President Helen Schleman (Purdue) and NADW Executive Secretary Barbara Catton, worked in tandem with the Women's Bureau and the National Women's Committee for Civil Rights to encourage its members to support the legislation which became the Civil Rights Act.[13]

IAWS, by virtue of its connection with deans of women, also had a spotty history regarding racial prejudice. AWS chapters often reflected local attitudes of the community in which the campus resided, which determined whether black women's groups were included under the AWS umbrella. Early photographs of IAWS meetings show a sea of white faces, though Asian women do appear, and light-skinned black women would be difficult to discern in the large groups of women photographed from a distance. Shavlik recalled black women participating in IAWS, and that the regional groups had begun addressing racism in the late 1950s by seeking locations where black women could join the meetings. For instance, Shavlik helped the southern regional IAWS group move its meeting location in the 1950s from Mississippi to Texas in order to accommodate the full participation of black women student leaders.[14]

However, with deans of women always responsible for keeping women students and the school out of public controversy, deans found that at some institutions, outright support for racial or religious civil rights activism could cost a dean her job. At Northwestern University, a private Methodist institution, McCarn lost her position in 1948 because of her public support for both African American and Jewish students. McCarn's story shows the strength of civil rights advocacy that existed among some deans of women and also the risks these deans took when championing racially marginalized students.

When McCarn arrived at Northwestern in 1937, the university did not allow blacks in residence halls or sororities, and only black men could live in the nearby YMCA housing. This forced black women to commute from Chicago or live in substandard housing in the black section of Evanston, Illinois. McCarn advocated for housing arrangements for black women on or near campus, and hosted an interracial conference with Howard University Professor Ralph Bunche in 1938. McCarn, who angered Northwestern administrators with her speeches in support of racial integration, tried to solve the housing problem for African American women by admitting a chapter of Alpha Kappa Alpha (AKA) in 1941. She also pushed for acceptance of Jewish women in sororities—both controversial moves at the time. When McCarn admitted AKA (founded by Slowe at Howard) for black women, the organization had only been accepted into the mainstream sorority governing board, the Panhellenic Council, at one other university, the University of Pittsburgh where Thrysa Amos led the dean of women's office. When McCarn admitted AKA to the Northwestern Panhellenic Council, alumnae complained loudly, particularly worried that the Panhellenic president would eventually be an African American woman. Ultimately, Northwestern President Franklin Bliss Snyder fired McCarn for these efforts.[15]

McCarn's very public dismissal by Northwestern sent a message to other deans of women that racial or non-Protestant civil rights support could endanger the job of even an accomplished administrator like McCarn. Although University of Chicago President Robert Hutchins soon hired McCarn on his campus as an assistant dean of students, her dismissal nonetheless sent a chilling effect through the NADW. For those inclined to work on civil rights for non-majority populations, McCarn's departure from Northwestern and her hiring at the University of Chicago pointed out the importance of the attitude of the university president. A university's chief executive largely determined whether a dean of women could successfully and safely engage in controversial equity issues for non-white or non-Christian students.[16]

* * *

At KU, Taylor found just such a chancellor in Franklin Murphy. Formerly the Dean of the KU School of Medicine located in Kansas City, Murphy desegregated operating rooms and nursing dormitories, employing black technicians in the university medical laboratories before he assumed KU's chancellorship. When he joined the main campus in 1951, he found that despite KU's enrollment of blacks since 1870, both the campus and the city discriminated against African Americans. KU excluded blacks from literary societies, fraternities, sororities, and mainstream social life on the campus. Although KU expanded some access for blacks in the 1940s, the university had not moved past basic access to the cafeteria and campus dances, and participation in varsity athletics. KU did allow blacks to live in university residence halls, though it required racial identification so that blacks would room only with other blacks or with whites who had consented to do so.[17]

This left the KU climate largely discriminatory. Murphy's predecessor, Chancellor Malott, had refused to take further steps or to recognize the local student chapter of the Congress of Racial Equality (CORE), which worked to desegregate local restaurants and theaters. On his arrival in Lawrence in 1951, Murphy began by opening local barbershops, movie theaters, and restaurants to blacks by threatening to initiate competitive businesses on the KU campus at a less-expensive cost than the local fare. The threat of losing such a significant portion of their clientele convinced many business owners to abandon segregationist practices. Coach Phog Allen joined Murphy's efforts when he decided to recruit basketball phenom Wilt Chamberlain who refused to attend a segregated school. Despite these efforts, when Taylor arrived in 1956, she was surprised to see a restaurant with a sign declaring "we reserve the right to refuse service to anyone."[18]

Taylor later recognized that she was "'slower on the uptake'" regarding racial civil rights than she was with her adoption of feminist ideals.[19] She credited her mother with instilling in her a belief in racial acceptance, though she lived a largely segregated life until attending Ohio State, where she joined a group that considered racial equality. After serving on a panel with a black Ohio State law student, Taylor remembered the woman inviting her to attend a movie. "This was not possible without being arrested in those days. I did a lot of soul-searching about the situation, and I decided against it. I've always felt guilty about this. I decided against it because I just could not, in the midst of the Depression, afford to be arrested for anything, and have that on my record."[20] Taylor's adoption of feminist principles, though, gave her a baseline of support for everyone's right to economic and political citizenship.

Initially, Taylor approached racial civil rights with the same strategy that she believed allowed women to move into the workforce—adopting the practices white, male executives used. She thought that women had to adopt a less feminine, no-nonsense approach if they wanted to achieve professional careers. At first, she took the same approach with black students, suggesting they would have to adapt to the norms of white, middle-class culture if they wanted to access economic gain. She recalled preparing a speech in the 1950s for a black sorority which invited her to give a lecture. She proposed to the young African American women that to be successful they needed to model mainstream cultural values. Later in her career, Taylor recognized that this approach simply reaffirmed racist attitudes by asking black women to adopt white culture as their own. In the 1950s, though, Taylor believed minority groups should adopt white, male practices in order to access economic citizenship.[21]

Recognition of the class dynamics of race was still decades away in social and academic circles. Both Taylor and Mueller had deep-seated socioeconomic classism, considering working-class cultural norms to be undesirable at best. Both saw higher education as the road to middle-class financial stability, and assumed women needed to adopt middle-class white values in order to access economic citizenship and middle-class social acceptability. Both Taylor and Mueller spent time educating women—black and white—on etiquette, the norms of appropriate middle-class dress, and even table manners. (Taylor took time to mentor male working-class students as well.) Both women considered adoption of these practices an important part of women's education and advancement. This meant that Taylor and Mueller both disdained non-white cultural practices when they reflected working class values. Although—and perhaps because—Taylor grew up poor in the Depression, she adopted this elitist view, common among deans of women who were well-educated and proud of that unusual accomplishment. Ultimately, this led Taylor to push open doors for economic citizenship for women and minorities, all the while insisting on the cultural practices of wealth as the keys to opening those doors of change. Clearly, Taylor's own understanding of racism grew throughout her career, leading to changes in her own behaviors and beliefs by the end of her life. And while she came to better understand class elitism as a flaw, she never waivered in her belief that success in professional work required the pragmatic adoption of white, male middle-class practices, at least in the workplace.[22]

While Murphy made progress in desegregating Lawrence and KU, he by no means completely addressed inequities between white and black students before he left in 1960 to lead UCLA. When Chancellor Wescoe arrived, the KU YWCA and YMCA, known as the KU-Y, had established the Civil Rights Council (CRC) to advocate against racial discrimination on the campus. The community's active CORE chapter collaborated with the CRC, working to integrate remaining segregated public establishments and to address substandard housing options for black KU students. As at most institutions, the KU student affairs offices oversaw off-campus housing for undergraduate students. Both the dean of women and dean of men maintained a lists of approved rental properties—usually locally owned houses where a family or individual would rent one or more rooms to students.

In 1961, the CRC asked KU to ensure that the landlords rented to both white and black students. Wescoe rejected the request, arguing that KU "will not and cannot interfere in the rights of private citizens to choose the person to whom he wishes to rent his property."[23] While this meant that the chancellor allowed discrimination on the housing lists for male students, Taylor took a different approach, using her control of women's housing to benefit black women. Women students could only live off-campus with Taylor's permission and in rental housing sanctioned by Taylor's office. Early deans established this practice to ensure that women students accessed safe housing at a fair price. This standard process meant Taylor could remove a landlord from her list and the property could not be rented to any KU woman student. Landlords often preferred to rent to women since they had to keep campus hours and were considered more likely to treat the property carefully. Taylor used this preference and her list to encourage acceptance of black women tenants. "'Whenever we knew it, we told the landlady that she couldn't discriminate and be on our list. Now, there was nothing to prevent her choosing renters some other way, and I suspect there was a lot of that,'" said Taylor.[24] However, if a landlord wanted a female student tenant, she had to meet the dean of women's approval. At odds with Chancellor Wescoe's opinion, Taylor quietly integrated her housing list.

Once the Civil Rights Act became federal law in the summer of 1964, Shavlik asked Taylor if she could begin actively desegregating the women's housing list. Taylor agreed, and that fall Shavlik, as advisor to Lewis Hall, organized six young black women to test landlord compliance with the new law. Shavlik trained the young women on how to request a rental in person, and removed from the approved list any who rejected them.[25]

But Taylor did not have an easy solution for housing discrimination in the dormitories or in the sororities. The KU residence halls had been integrated since the university's founding, and by policy during the 1940s. However, the policy allowed any student to request a roommate change for any reason. This meant that white students could refuse to room with black women for any number of stated reasons besides race (even if racism was the real motivation). In addition, Taylor recalled the chancellor refusing to approve the request of a white woman and a black woman who asked to room together in the early 1960s. To combat these attitudes, Taylor worked with residence hall staff to foster inclusive attitudes. For sororities, Taylor had already placed AKA and Delta Sigma Theta black sororities on the overall KU Panhellenic Council, the move that had precipitated McCarn's firing in 1948. Her staffing matrix throughout women's organizations meant she had multiple staff interacting with black women. Shavlik advised the KU-Y, Stroup advised Delta Sigma Theta, and Mumbi (née Helen Kimball) advised the AKA chapter. Despite an integrated Panhellenic Council, the white sororities had not opened rush, the membership selection process. Though none of the white chapters had racial exclusionary clauses in their bylaws, KU sororities' all-white membership rosters displayed the socially sanctioned prejudice that influenced membership decisions. Chapters selected members in private meetings, making it difficult to promote change unless local alumnae supported it. Not surprisingly, anonymous members indicated discrimination existed, and in one known case Chi Omega denied membership to a Jewish student from St. Louis due to a Kansas City alumna objection. Stroup, a member of Chi Omega herself, recalled numerous meetings where she, Taylor, and others worked with sorority members to reject prejudicial exclusion. It was a slow process, with members often blaming racial membership discrimination on their national office.[26]

CRC brought these issues to the forefront in 1960, the same year Taylor issued senior keys. That year the CRC, led by white KU-Y students, protested the prohibitions against blacks joining campus fraternities and sororities. As these non-violent protests grew in the early 1960s, Stroup recalled that rumors became a problem on campus. Each time a national racial civil rights demonstration gained media attention, white fears escalated about racial integration, prompting rumors to spread across KU. As a result, Taylor set up an information phone line that ran into her office so that students—white or black—could call to report a rumor or to verify one. Once Taylor decided to host this line in her office in the early 1960s, she assigned her employees to cover it 24-hours-a-day, with staffers rotating through all-night stays at the office, each taking her turn at calming student and parent fears regarding protests. Taylor's staff answering calls found little of the gossip based on fact. Between the hotline and the employees staffing the campus Y and the two African American sororities, Taylor and her team were well-acquainted with student civil rights activists and their concerns. Often she had advance knowledge that enabled her to open administrative doors on their behalf.[27] In addition, the hotline provided a way for students to express concerns without creating campus agitation. Taylor became committed to this idea of creating a "safety valve" once she talked to Berkeley's Dean of Women Katherine Towle at the 1965 NADW meeting. Towle, who had opposed the University of California's decision to ban students passing out civil rights literature in 1964, believed free speech allowed students a safety valve to express their opinions. By ignoring Towle's advice, the Berkeley administrators prompted the famous Berkeley free speech protests that culminated in Mario Savio speaking to protestors from atop a car in front of Sproul Hall.

At KU, the CRC continued to complain about fraternity discrimination, as some excluded non-whites in their constitutions. Wescoe, a fraternity man himself, responded slowly to the demands for integrated housing, taking modest actions in response to CRC demands. In 1962, he contacted his national fraternity office, Alpha Tau Omega (ATO), to work with the organization to remove its racial restriction. ATO finally removed its discriminatory clause from its constitution in 1964, the year that the Civil Rights Act passed. Even after the new law, the national Sigma Nu (ΣN) office remained staunchly in support of its discriminatory clause, prompting the CRC to focus its attention on picketing that fraternity at KU. In late 1964, Wescoe and Kansas State University President James McCain jointly appealed to the ΣN national office for their campus chapters to receive waivers from the fraternity's ban on non-whites. When ΣN refused to integrate, the KU All Student Council (ASC) passed a resolution giving all university-recognized organizations one year to remove any discriminatory clauses from their organizational charters or lose university backing.[28]

However, by Sunday, March 7, 1965, the ASC bill had not yet arrived on the chancellor's desk for his signature. That evening the nation's television stations broadcast images of police brutally beating non-violent black civil rights marchers in Selma, Alabama. Across the nation, many Americans blanched at the violence known later as Bloody Sunday. At KU, the news spurred the CRC into action. That evening, the black CRC members asked the whites to relinquish their officer roles, and black students assumed the organization's leadership, deciding their first action would be to stage the sit-in at Chancellor Wescoe's office.[29]

Late that Sunday night, CRC black students arrived on Taylor's doorstep, asking to meet with her. Just as her network kept her well informed on women's activities, these students briefed her on their plans, relating that they had asked whites to step aside in the organization.

> They said to the whites who were their officers and the other whites who were there, "Go back to your own people. You can do more to help; you can be of more help to us by going back to your own people and explaining to them what the situation is. Help them to understand. The only thing you have to do is cut your hair and shave and you are one of them again. We could cut our own hair any way we want to, we can shave or not shave and will never be one of them."[30]

Taylor believed the blacks asked the whites to leave the organization because it was more appropriate to have blacks leading blacks. In addition, some of the whites represented the "hippie" crowd, and the black students felt their rag-tag appearance reflected poorly on their cause. Taylor gave the black students specific advice—do not skip class to sit-in because that will give administrators a reason to label the protestors as disciplinary problems; and second, be specific in what you want the KU administration to address. The students asked for six changes to university policy—removal of racial exclusion in student organizations, especially fraternities and sororities; banning the student newspaper from accepting discriminatory advertisements; removing all segregated housing from off-campus room rental lists; stopping preferential treatment for white teacher placement by the KU School of Education; signing assurances for these measures in a broad formal resolution, and a university-sanctioned administrative board for addressing grievances. Taylor, always aware of her role as an administrator responsible for the university's public image, informed Wescoe that the protest would occur.[31]

The day of the sit in, students sat down in the chancellor's office, flowing into the second floor hallway past Taylor and Alderson's office suites and down into the stairs. Students came and went all day, leaving to attend class. Taylor's staff circulated through the students to identify and counsel concerns and help maintain calm. Since some KU administrators claimed the protestors had driven in from Topeka and Kansas City and were not students, Taylor asked her staff to observe all day so that they could verify to Wescoe that the activists were, in fact, students. Stroup recalled checking in with Delta Sigma Theta sorority members throughout the day, "I promised them that the administration would be reasonable and encouraged them to keep going to class."[32]

That night, after the remaining students were jailed, Taylor and Stroup met with Wescoe and other administrators to discuss the demands. While some administrators preferred the law and order approach, Taylor and Stroup convinced Wescoe that arresting students would put the university in a bad light publicly if the complaints turned out to be true. Taylor recommended KU consider investigating the concerns as a means to stop the protests. With the dean of the School of Education assuring Wescoe discrimination did not occur in teacher job placement, Wescoe was not at all certain the student complaints reflected reality. Stroup recalled telling the chancellor, "I promised the students that you will be fair," and recalled he agreed to listen and investigate by creating a board to consider any allegations and address any problems that proved to be true.

The day after the sit-in, once the students had been bailed out of jail, the CRC reconvened and marched across campus to gather outside Wescoe's campus residence. Again, they called for action on their six demands. This time, rather than repeating the arrests from the day before, Wescoe moved forward with the plans he discussed with Taylor and Stroup the evening before. Because Wescoe knew Taylor had established trust with CRC leaders, he asked her to negotiate an end to the protest. "Chancellor Wescoe appointed me to chair a committee, which he called a 'Committee to Deal with These People,'" recalled Taylor.[33] "The chancellor appointed a group of people to get together to form a negotiating committee, but the chancellor didn't want to call it a negotiating committee. He made a big point of it, and he did not want to go rapidly. He wanted us to take our time. It went a lot more rapidly than he wanted."[34]

Taylor found the students willing to accept a grievance board to investigate their complaints, and Wescoe agreed to create a permanent University Human Relations Council (UHRC) to verify and address any charges of racial or religious discrimination. He placed Woodruff, dean of students, as chair of the UHRC, adding Taylor, Alderson, and five students (including CRC representatives) as members. The UHRC then began to investigate the original sit-in demands. Quickly, the council found black student complaints of discrimination to be true. Most egregious, the school of education lied to Wescoe about its nondiscrimination. Upon investigation, it became clear that Shawnee Mission, an affluent suburb in the Kansas City metropolitan area, had asked to review only applications from whites, and that the school of education complied by coding the applications. A former education faculty member explained to Taylor how the system worked.[35]

> Sure enough, it was perfectly plain once it was seen. It was a private arrangement. And even more disgraceful is the fact that the dean of the school denied it to the chancellor, and certainly to us. Applications were coded so that no black student ever ended up there where they were not wanted. It was obvious that something was going on. The school claimed that it just was happenstance, but it wasn't.[36]

After Taylor negotiated the creation of the UHRC in order to end the protests, Wescoe asked her to author a new university policy on discrimination with history professor James Seaver, and sociology department chair Charles Warriner. In Taylor's office, they wrote an "affirmation of principles" articulating that the university would not discriminate on the basis of race or creed.[37] Wescoe retitled it "A Reaffirmation of Principles," though, as Taylor later noted, "obviously it was not a reaffirmation."[38] While writing the statement, Taylor suggested to Seaver and Warriner that they should add the word "sex" to the anti-discrimination policy to be consistent with the 1964 Civil Rights Act. The two faculty members rejected the idea. They felt strongly that the statement should focus on race, believing that adding discrimination against women would dilute the importance of racial equality. "They had a good point, there was no doubt about it," Taylor later recalled. "But, they thought it was going to be simple to get it [the word sex] added and it wasn't. The occasion never arose."[39] Looking back, Taylor often commented that she regretted not insisting on adding sex. "'I stupidly fell for that. And I've always regretted it and resented it...I think the reaffirmation of policy was a good statement; it just wasn't good enough because it left out gender,'" said Taylor.[40] She also believed that throughout US history—especially in the case of suffrage—women had set aside sex discrimination concerns in order to address issues of race, and she thought it better to insist on both race and sex equality together. She knew she had missed the opportunity to have a formal board to address and investigate sex bias which would have provided avenue to address equal employment, sexual harassment, and general sexism complaints occurring on campus. It took until February of 1972 before Taylor and the coalition of women at KU could negotiate "sex" into the policy.

However, the sit-in opened the door for Taylor to expand her office's work on race equity. First, she, Shavlik, and Stroup formalized the housing desegregation efforts for both off-campus rental housing and sorority membership—Shavlik took the lead on housing and Stroup on sorority issues. Two days after the sit-in, Shavlik and the black activists in Lewis Hall escalated their efforts, deciding to ask all landlords to sign a non-discrimination contract. Gaining AWS endorsement through the Inter-Residence Hall Council, the students established a plan to require landlords to agree not to discriminate based on race. Shavlik worked closely with the students, organizing the women into groups of three to make appointments with the landlords. She trained the volunteers to present the landlord with a "letter of identification" from Taylor that endorsed their visit. The women then asked the landlords to sign an agreement that they would comply with the law, as well as the rules of the AWS and dean of women—all of which rejected discrimination in renting. By 1966, the year the majority of KU women received keys to their residences, all approved landlords had agreed to lease to non-white women. At the same time, Stroup addressed sorority rush. Since KU sorority chapters often claimed that their national office did not approve black members, Stroup contacted each national office telling them KU now required a statement of non-discrimination in order for the sorority to be on campus. All signed the statements. However, membership selection remained secret chapter business, which meant that Taylor and her staff continued to address ongoing, at times covert, race and religious discrimination within the chapters. Slowly, though, membership began to open to non-white and non-Christian women.[41]

Beyond housing, Taylor and her staff sought other ways to promote racial equity. She and her staff worked with the AWS senate leaders to consider whether their programming included black women, and in 1967–1968, the AWS decided to integrate its fashion board. The board had a long history at KU, featuring senior women elected by AWS. The models portrayed appropriate clothing for college life, their photos published in an AWS guide to help first year women choose their attire. Considered an honor, fashion board members embodied the ideal KU college women. In 1968, AWS elected the first black woman, Pat Scott, broadening the AWS definition of beauty to include non-white women. That same year, Taylor placed civil rights for racial equity on the AWS Commission on the Status of Women research agenda so that white AWS leaders could begin to understand their own racist attitudes and how the AWS program reflected bias toward white women. At the same time, Taylor's staff worked with AWS to provide a program on "White Racism," followed by a 1969 training entitled "Institutional Racism."[42]

These activities occurred at a time when the broader Lawrence community divided over issues of racial equality as blacks called for access to public facilities such as the local swimming pool. These protests turned more and more contentious as black Lawrence High School students joined efforts with the KU Black Student Union (BSU). As a part of the 1967–1968 BSU

Figure 5.1 Students work and research in Taylor's office library (photograph courtesy of University Archives, Spencer Research Library, University of Kansas Libraries)

agenda, the group demanded the university publicly represent integration by including blacks in all facets of student life. While the addition of Scott started to answer this call within the dean of women's office, the BSU also demanded that black women join the all-white cheerleading squad. In 1968, black football players boycotted drills before the popular spring scrimmage, calling for a black cheerleader to fill a vacancy that opened when a squad member resigned to marry.[43]

The matter went before the UHRC on which Taylor still served. Taylor and Alderson had always judged cheerleading try-outs. Neither had seen discrimination in the selection process, so Taylor hesitated to support a black woman joining the team unless the woman clearly qualified based on her talent. Then, one evening, she had a chance encounter with an incoming freshman regarding the cheer squad.

> I was sitting with a group of high school seniors who had come from Shawnee Mission, and they were telling me what they were going to do when they got here. And one of them said, "I'm going to be a cheerleader." And so I said, "You know, that's a competitive thing; you have to compete for those jobs." And she said, "Oh, that's not the way it's done. The cheerleaders choose the people that they want, and then they teach them the routines, and so of course, when we go before the committee, we're better than the others." So I learned at an orientation dinner from a high school senior how cheerleaders were chosen and how we'd been taken in through all those years.[44]

Taylor was appalled and decided, in her often-used phrase for equalizing inequality, that "two can play at that game." The four white alternate cheerleaders declined to take the opening, and the UHRC decided to hold tryouts among black women. Taylor was determined that the first black cheerleader have the same advantage of preparation before the tryouts and be as qualified as the white women with whom she would cheer. She put Stroup in charge of the effort. Stroup had to find both a KU cheerleader willing to teach the routines to a black student, and a black woman with both the interest and talent to qualify for the squad. Stroup found a former cheerleader who supported civil rights and was willing to help with preparation. Then, she worked through her Delta Sigma Theta network to find a black honors student with dance training who agreed to audition for the role. The two worked together on the routines before the try-outs, the dean of women's office ensuring that the African American woman had the same advantage as did the white women from the wealthy Kansas City suburban cities. She easily qualified. "She didn't have to be chosen, she competed with the best and she was the best," Taylor later said.[45]

Taylor recalled complaints of preferential treatment, especially by the athletic department and the alumni association which both groused that an unqualified black student had been chosen as a capitulation to BSU demands. Stroup handled the complaints, recalling that she spent hours addressing the "concerns" over the addition of a black woman to the squad.

Taylor and Stroup solved the "pre-selection" problem for the future by working with the UHRC to develop a new policy for cheerleader selection that included pre-tryout clinics to teach routines to everyone in advance. Implemented in 1969, the policy also included a recommendation to hire a coach to handle selection operations, eliminating the head cheerleader's role in coordinating tryouts. While adding Scott to the fashion board and integrating the cheerleading squad might seem trivial by today's standards, Taylor and Stroup changed primary public symbols of the university's student body and its standard of female beauty from one of whiteness, to a multicultural image. The intensity of the complaints by the athletics department and alumni association show just how strongly the institution resisted this change.[46]

Antiwar Activism, Student Unrest, and Radical Feminism

Along with racial civil rights protest, campus unrest increased at KU as it did at other colleges nationwide throughout the 1960s. While the early to mid 1960s still reflected the propriety and consensus of the 1950s, small groups of KU students began to protest the Vietnam War in 1963. From this point forward, the New Left generated ever-escalating student protests over the Vietnam War. While Taylor and her staff worked to convince AWS to expand distribution of dormitory keys to juniors and sophomores, antiwar agitators began regular protests. The Student Peace Union (SPU) organized the first anti-war protest at KU in 1963 as a small picket during a Reserve Officers' Training Corps (ROTC) parade. These ROTC reviews became a regular protest event as student activists associated university support of the ROTC with sanctioning the Vietnam War. Just before the Civil Rights Act passed, someone at KU set fire to an ROTC jeep after the May 1964 parade. By fall of 1965, the semester after the CRC sit-in, the small KU branch of Students for a Democratic Society (SDS), SPU and KU-Y jointly hosted a teach-in on the war to protest its purpose. By 1966, as Taylor's office brought the call for contraceptive access at Watkins Hospital into public forums, activist students began weekly silent peace vigils on campus. Eventually, New Left efforts fused with BSU activism as the non-violent CRC protests morphed into a Black Power agenda at KU. Taylor kept her team involved with male and female student leaders, the New Left and with racial equity efforts—believing that all student life should receive the benefit of advice even when it reflected radical ideas. This fundamental philosophy brought her—and her staff—deeply into the student unrest at KU.[47]

As the decade progressed, the work Taylor had pursued quietly was now joined by women discovering women's liberation. Overt feminism became an increasingly important social movement at KU, mirroring its public expansion across the country. Today, historians interested in understanding the various motivations of the women who adopted feminist viewpoints have categorized feminism by the various philosophies resting beneath the activism women produced. Women who worked on legal and economic change tended to adopt the liberal principles associated with early philosophies on women. These women, typically older, professional women, worked within social institutions to create change—often more concerned with economic opportunity and public sphere inclusion. At the same time, women's liberation—often termed radical feminism—burst onto college campuses as young women involved in civil rights and the New Left chafed under the subordinate status that the men in the movements often assigned to women. The radical feminist critiques arose out of the New Left, adopting its strategies of protest, street theater and rejection of American society as fundamentally flawed—though radical feminists saw patriarchy, not capitalism, as the most problematic aspect of US culture. Radical feminists, often invested in the New Left Marxist critiques of capitalism, eschewed the liberal tactic of working within a system, labeling all organizations as tainted by both capitalism and patriarchy, and advocating complete, revolutionary change. Because these philosophical differences often aligned with generations, historians have example after example illustrating older, liberal feminists, at odds with younger radical ones.

In Taylor's office, however, they all mixed—purposely intergenerational—and purposely encouraging women to think through the elements of sex discrimination from various points of view. Taylor swung wide her door to the young women who began to clothe themselves in the various forms of feminism. "The radical women's groups met right in the middle of the office right outside my door," said Janet Sears who recalled that she did not experience the feminism at KU as if they were two separate camps of liberal and radical feminists.[48] In Taylor's office—long the home of progressive, feminist-inspired approaches to women, education and equity—the nascent women's liberation movement of the 1960s, including its radical arm, found a waiting resource.

Using liberal feminist strategies herself, Taylor recognized that to accomplish change, she needed men as part of the solution for women's equity. Early in her years at KU, she included male students and administrators in her network. She believed the dean of women's job was to educate the chancellor on women's issues, but she also believed that to achieve feminist change women needed to "negotiate with men to establish things those men did not really understand."[49] Her office included men on the status of women newsletter mailing list, with men comprising approximately one-third of the five hundred recipients. Eventually, she even hired Associate Dean of Women Caryl Smith's husband, Walter Smith, as an associate dean of women in 1972 as an experiment to include and educate men.

In order to accomplish her goals, she often engaged male student leaders who served with AWS leaders on the Council for Student Affairs (COSA). She found her initiatives met with easier acceptance when she befriended All Student Council leaders and helped them to understand feminist-driven viewpoints. Bill Robinson, a KU student from 1963–1967, met Taylor there when he served as vice-president of the student body. Robinson recalled being in awe of Taylor's style, especially as she confronted Schwegler over gynecological exams as related in chapter 4. Robinson credits Taylor with his education on feminism, remembering that he had a standing invitation to stop by after 11 p.m. to drink coffee and discuss campus issues at Taylor's home. Robinson became a convert. Upon graduation, he took a job in the dean of men's office where he "went commando" and worked on Taylor's sexuality education issues despite Alderson's lack of support for them.[50]

Taylor's adoption of Mueller's deaning structure meant she linked a staff member to each women's organization so that students had a liaison to the dean of women's office. When New Left women's groups began to develop, she assigned Shavlik to work with them—especially since many of the women thought of Taylor as "the system." This paved an open road between her office and emerging radical feminists at KU. Shavlik, still serving on the board of the KU-Y, advised the women's liberation groups, often meeting with them in the dean of women's suite.

Taylor welcomed the thinking of radical feminists, finding that much of the material they produced echoed what she, Mueller, and other feminist deans believed about what is now called the social-construction of gender roles. Taylor put the AWS committees to work collecting radical feminist writings such as Pat Mainardi's 1969 "The Politics of Housework" and what circulated as the 1968 "Florida Paper" by Beverly Jones and Judith Brown, "Toward a Female Liberation Movement." These radical feminist writings—authored in the highly critical tone characteristic of New Left feminism—brought forward many of the same ideas Mueller had politely discussed in the mid-1950s. Taylor once noted in a news article that her ideas and philosophy on women's equality had changed little between 1956 and her later years at KU. "'It's just that more people are listening now so that it makes it seem as though there has been some change.'"[51]

Taylor embraced radical feminist viewpoints in her office, and the university mail carrier must have become accustomed to delivering publications such as *The Bitch Manifesto* and *Vocations for Social Change (Gay Folk)* addressed directly to Taylor in Strong Hall. AWS committees studied these along with Women's Bureau reports, employment manuals, and graduate school guides. Taylor accepted the radical feminist focus on consciousness-raising—developing one's awareness of gender inequity by talking with other women in small groups and noting the continuities in all women's experiences—and sometimes chuckled when people thought of it as a "new" method in women's liberation since she remembered Zorbaugh's mentoring as clarifying her feminist consciousness in the 1930s. Feminist deans had long fostered intergenerational mentoring of students. At KU, 1968–1969 AWS President M. Kay Harris credited Taylor with guiding her understanding of "the personal is political"—one of the radical feminists' rallying cries. "I think Emily Taylor helped me understand that the personal is political and made me think through my personal choices."[52]

Figure 5.2 Taylor with a gift from her students, a poster entitled "Emily Taylor's School of Feminism"

Despite the convergence of radical and liberal feminism in Taylor's office across various generations of women, the fact that her role formed a part of the KU administration always mitigated the connections between radical feminists and the AWS. Taylor and her staff understood that the dean of women's office had to respond to the political realities of existing within a publicly funded institution of higher learning. Thus, some students who advocated for wholesale radical change critiqued Taylor's approach as not strong enough. Patti Spencer, a founder of the radical Women's Coalition (WC) at KU, belonged to the sophomore women's honorary Cwens which had traditionally provided women students a point of entry into the leadership training within Taylor's office. As an upper level student, Spencer remarked, "I remember when we were Cwens—it was one of the few women's organizations on campus, and you had to be a hot shot to get in it. It was just so polite, and repressed. It was just totally tight. Like being somebody's grandmother."[53] While New Left women found Taylor's leadership training constraining, the radical groups like the WC often had difficulty achieving specific results. Their belief that working within the prevailing system to achieve equality was futile meant that many radical groups struggled to develop strategies based on their critiques. Spencer acknowledged this, saying: "'I think a lot of people have created alternatives [to CWENS], like the Coalition [WC], and had those alternatives fall apart or seem to fall apart.'"[54] Barb Krasne, also a WC member, called the AWS too "structured," but also complained that working in the WC was a "waste" by "spinning their wheels" without action.⁵⁵ Both these women eventually left the WC as the group experienced a split between 1972 and 1973.⁵⁶

With Taylor committed to the NADW longtime practice of having initiatives seem to come from the students, many New Left and feminist women did not understand how many administrative doors Taylor opened for women's equal participation in higher education at KU. In fact, some in the women's liberation groups attacked the dean of women's office over the remaining parietal structure. The Women's Liberation Front (WLF) complained loudly about Taylor's office as the arbiter of rules. "Professors treat freshmen women as adults, and so does everyone else except those people in the dean of women's office," said WLF leader Suzanne Atkins in the 1969–1970 school year.⁵⁷ Atkins called for abolition of any remaining parietals so that first and second year women would be allowed to live off-campus without parental approval. Clearly, the WLF had little patience for Taylor's incremental approach that relied on all women students agreeing together on their own regulations. On the other end of the spectrum, even in 1968, Taylor found a large segment of women students continued to resist eliminating the remaining differential rules for women. Harris recalled she worked hard to convince AWS to drop the remaining parietals. In that respect, not much had changed since 1958. As Taylor once quipped, "I viewed the job of the dean of women as to help women become independent. The students themselves didn't particularly want to be independent."⁵⁸

Taylor welcomed the fact that some young women—radical or not—had adopted autonomy. And the radical feminist women made Taylor's ideas look reasonable—a middle-ground consensus between conventional and radical. After the uproar over keys in 1966, Taylor easily accomplished final parietal changes in 1968 and 1969 as anti-war protest and the counterculture significantly changed the stakes as to what counted as controversial. In 1968, Harris achieved COSA's approval for all sophomore women to have keys with less than 30 minutes of discussion—and Wescoe approved the recommendation with no fanfare. The next year he agreed to freshmen women voting dorm by dorm whether each residence would allow freshmen to have keys. Taylor's vision for the elimination of differential rules for women had become reality.⁵⁹

At the same time, Taylor recognized that the AWS, historically organized around governing single-sex residences, would need to shift substantially as women adopted student life without parietals. As she worked to eliminate the remaining curfews and sign outs, she kept her eyes on a new vision for AWS as a fully feminist advocacy project. In 1968, when the AWS chapter at KU began to divest itself of all remaining rule and parietal functions, Harris worked closely with Taylor to formally shift the AWS mission to one of women's leadership—the element feminist deans had always fostered among women students. Taylor focused the women on the work of the AWS Commission on the Status of Women, and the entire group promoted the commission's findings, calling on the university to address areas of inequity.

In 1969, the AWS chose to rename itself the KU Commission on Status of Women (Commission). The entire governing association, now stripped of parietals to coordinate, bore the name of the committee that Taylor had begun in 1958 to study roles of women. The Commission, still advised by Taylor, partnered closely with the Women's Coalition—especially on women's health and contraception access issues.

* * *

While Taylor was working within her office to bring all types of feminism into her network, student protests tore at the relationship between Lawrence citizens and the university. The conservative community, outraged over "hippie" culture, reached a tipping point in 1967 when the *Lawrence Journal-World* carried a photograph of a woman wrapped in a US flag during a campus "be-in." By this time, the 1966 protests Wescoe received about AWS keys paled in comparison to alumni, legislator and community complaints over increasing antiwar protests. Chancellor Wescoe found his days increasingly filled with managing public perception of escalating student activism. The Kansas Board of Regents disapproved of the escalating drug use and antiwar demonstrations, which increased after the Tet Offensive in 1968. At KU, 1,500 students gathered outside Strong Hall to insist on a more powerful student voice in university governance. Wescoe, tiring of the chancellor's role and under pressure from the Board of Regents, announced during the 1968–1969 Opening Convocation that he would resign at the end of the academic year.[60]

Wescoe's announcement foreshadowed a coming year of turmoil unlike anything KU had yet experienced. Isolated instances of violence increased in the Oread neighborhood next to campus where many student activists chose to live. In February, someone hurtled a Molotov cocktail into the ROTC building causing damage, and in April protestors interrupted an ROTC drill by walking among the cadets and taunting them. Tensions rose when Student Body President David Aubrey requested that the university cancel the annual year-end ROTC "Chancellor's Review" parade. Chancellor Wescoe, hemmed in by governor and legislator support for the ROTC, refused to cancel the longtime tradition. Before the event, Wescoe arranged for the Kansas National Guard to wait just outside Lawrence on Highway 40 and US Highway 59 in full battle gear to take over the university should violence break out. Student activists filled a large section of the stadium, chanting and singing "We Shall Overcome" until someone began handing out sticks for the activists to use as pretend rifles. When the protestors charged the cadets on the field, Wescoe feared violence. He called off the event with an announcement over the loudspeaker, dramatically ending his tenure as chancellor.[61]

By July 1969, KU's new leader, E. Laurence Chalmers, began efforts to gain student support. One week after his arrival, he spoke at the prestigious River Club, a male-only venue for select Kansas City business leaders. There, the new chancellor endorsed the students' anti-war attitudes, calling the Vietnam War "unjustifiable."[62] The public comments endeared him to students, but branded him as weak among Kansas legislators, alumni, parents, and the Board of Regents. The choice to side with students would make little difference in Chalmers' leadership at KU. What the new chancellor faced in his first year made the protests Wescoe weathered look like minor incidents.[63]

Escalating Violence and Turbulent Times

As a liaison to race relations and the emerging radical feminist groups on campus, Taylor found her office uniquely situated to act as a facilitator as the campus became an increasingly hostile environment. As September 1969 brought the first military draft lottery since World War II, antiwar attitudes spiked among KU students, bringing KU into a tug-of-war with the Kansas legislature and Board of Regents.[64] To make matters more difficult for the new chancellor, the tension over racial discrimination in Lawrence continued to bleed onto campus. That year, BSU stole thousands of *University Daily Kansan* newspapers and dumped them into Potter Lake, calling Chalmers "Super Pig" in the BSU newspaper. At the same time that New Left and Black Power protests expanded, Taylor announced her support for women's "personal control over reproduction," and took her quiet sex education and counseling efforts public. Despite community complaints, her staff established the formal wide-scale sex-education programs discussed in chapter 4, and she and her staff partnered frequently with the radical feminist Women's Coalition on women's health initiatives.[65]

By April 1970, the community was splitting apart. New Left protestors joined with the BSU in "solidarity," and Lawrence and KU fairly crackled with unease. On April 5, the university discovered a bomb outside Strong Hall. Fifteen days later, arsonists set fire to the KU Union destroying much of the building. Although most thought the arson due to the racial conflict in the city, campus reverberated with tension. State police sat in cars on the outskirts of campus. Gun fire from unknown snipers cracked through the darkness, and student activists opened fire hydrants that poured water onto the campus. The administration watched—uncertain how to handle the escalating violence.[66]

Taylor and her office staff began using their relationships with students to try to defuse the situation. Since Donna and Frank Shavlik advised New Left campus groups, Frank volunteered to walk throughout campus to close the fire hydrants that students had opened. With firefighters and police officers seen by protestors as targets for violence, Frank thought his relationships with students and his long hair would give him cover to turn off the pouring water. Hiding a fire plug wrench inside one leg of his pants, he crisscrossed campus to help diminish the situation. Governor Robert Docking initiated a curfew for the city, though arson and sniper fire continued during the lock-down. Parents overloaded KU telephone circuits calling to confirm their children's safety, and rumors flew across campus. Taylor and her staff re-established the hotline from the early racial equality protests, and it began to ring incessantly. The hotline operated 24-hours a day to allow students and faculty to report incidents and to check the veracity of rumors. The dean of women's staff worked around the clock in Taylor's suite of offices, answering calls and mimeographing informational leaflets to provide accurate information to KU students—both male and female—trying to calm the campus.[67]

Classes continued in the tense situation. Then—only ten days after the union building arson—President Richard Nixon announced the US invasion of Cambodia. KU erupted. Protests exploded across the nation, and the Ohio National Guard at Kent State University killed four unarmed students. Shavlik recalled that the administration seemed to freeze as the Kent State killings occurred. "No one stepped up."[68] Students, on the other hand, organized 500 demonstrators to carry coffins across campus in protest, exchanging blows with ROTC cadets. The situation scared students uninvolved in the protests, and intimidated much of the faculty. From Shavlik's viewpoint, the provost and Taylor entered the void, listening to the student protestors and trying to work with them. Taylor revived Katherine Towle's approach, trying to make sure students had a "safety valve" to communicate their concerns, putting all her resources behind anything she thought would defuse the violence. At the same time, despite over 200 colleges closing after Kent State's killings, the governor announced all Kansas schools would remain open. Chalmers faced an impasse. The active antiwar group, the KU Committee for Alternatives (KUCA), threatened a strike to close the university if Chalmers did not agree to cancel the ROTC review and hold a "teach-in" discussion regarding the Vietnam War.[69]

On May 6, Chalmers finally cancelled the ROTC review when 800 students gathered outside Strong Hall during the day. That night between 200 and 300 students descended upon the Military Science Building, rocks in hand. Notified by the hotline, Taylor's staff immediately responded, counting on their relationships with students to keep them safe from student violence. PhD student Rae Sedgwick, Stroup, both Frank and Donna Shavlik, and others from Taylor's office went to the Military Science Building to defuse the situation. Sedgwick suggested that they calmly ask students to give them their rocks. In and out of the crowd Taylor's staff walked, quietly asking protestors if they could please have his or her rock. Students complied and the women stacked the rocks at Frank's feet. "We ended up with enough for a small dog house," said Donna Shavlik.[70] Sedgwick then publicly spoke to the protestors, encouraging calm, and the group dispersed.[71]

The calm held until Friday, May 8, when Chalmers had scheduled a convocation for the students to vote on how the campus should respond to the situation. Held at the KU football stadium, over 12,000 students attended. Chalmers and student body president Bill Ebert, rose to a microphone to present Chalmers' version of "alternatives" for ending the semester.[72] The KUCA and BSU expected to propose their plans after Ebert finished, with the three platforms then going to a vote of the students. Instead, once Ebert finished explaining the chancellor's plan, he called for a voice vote, declared the motion passed, and closed the meeting. The BSU and KUCA were furious they had not been heard. AWS leader and radical feminist Sarah Scott pursued Chalmers out of the stadium toward his office, frustrated with his actions. KUCA leaders John Sanford and "Butch" Gillespie angrily followed Chalmers as well, cornering him on the hill near Strong Hall. Sanford and Gillespie argued vigorously with Chalmers, calling the "alternatives" he proposed unfair since the students had no clear process to close out their semesters without receiving a poor grade. For male students facing the draft, staying in school and in good standing meant the difference between their current lives and Vietnam service—making Sanford and Gillespie very sensitive to the "workability" of Chalmers' proposal. Chalmers told the two men to fix the problem on their own, suggesting they see Taylor for help. To refer two men to Taylor was odd—but while the chancellor washed his hands of the issue, Taylor agreed to turn her office over to the KUCA under a new name, the KU Coordinating Committee (KUCC).[73] There, in the dean of women's suite, Sanford and Gillespie set up shop, helping a preponderance of male students process their paperwork to complete their semesters and remain in good standing. Since some faculty members resisted Chalmer's options for completing the semester, the KUCC provided each student with a venue to negotiate with a course instructor to reach a satisfactory grade or resolution.

Sanford recalled both Taylor and Dean of Students Bill Balfour intervening with faculty who balked at completing paperwork for a student wanting to exercise one of the options Chalmers recommended. Sanford recalled he and those involved saw their work as a part of the efforts to organize a "revolution," helping students to remain in school where they could continue as a part of the protest movement. Taylor's staff helped maintain the calm by facilitating Sanford and the protestors' concerns, even allowing Sanford regular telephone calls with student protestors at Berkeley and Columbia. While many of the most radical New Left protesters saw Sanford and the KUCC as "sell-outs," diverting student anger from a revolution, Taylor's agreement to serve male students in the dean of women's office tempered the potential for violence by calming men angry about facing the draft.[74] Perhaps a part of the reason she welcomed these young men was her memory of her college beau, killed as a World War II conscientious objector. Whatever the reason for her sympathies, no other KU office stepped up to defuse the anger over the convocation. Taylor turned her office suite over to the men of the KUCC because she thought it would provide the "safety-valve" to calm the threat of more violence and help the young men.

Taylor and her staff played a significant role in negotiating an end to the hostile environment at KU. They mediated with faculty, appeased student concerns, and kept the violence from accelerating at the end of the semester. Taylor provided the channel for the KUCA to find solutions in Chalmers' alternatives, and defused student anger over Chalmers' maneuver. As a result of Taylor's involvement, protests lessened, and Chalmers could fulfill the governor's demand for the campus to remain open without further violence. Chalmers has been widely recognized for avoiding violence at the end of 1970. However, Taylor and her staff's work to lessen tension on campus has never been considered as a reason why student outrage lessened so dramatically and so quickly after the convocation.

Historians have not looked to an office organized for women's affairs in search of the venue that significantly affected New Left activities at KU. Because of this, much of Taylor and her staff's work has disappeared from the historical record. Taylor facilitated both racial equality and New Left ideals from within the organizational structure of the institution, drawing on her belief that all students should be treated as autonomous adult decision-makers. Taylor's efforts on behalf of blacks came from her long-term belief in integration. And her support for antiwar protest arose from her desire to reduce the likelihood of violence on the campus. None of this would have been possible without her network that wound through the women's residences and women's organizations ranging from the KU-Y to the radical feminist groups involved in the New Left. Because she had followed the deaning tradition of placing a staff member in every group that involved women, Taylor and her staffers had close relationships with the KU-Y, black sororities, each of the radical feminist groups, as well as with male student government leaders. This provided a basis for trust and information exchange between student protestors and her office that allowed her to negotiate change and calm.

The office's efforts remained low-profile because they were coordinated through and with students. As Threlkeld advised Taylor in 1948, "Skillfully plant suggestions for changes among your student leaders and let them come apparently, from them."[75] As a result, protestors not individually involved in her office saw Taylor as simply one of many obstacles rather than as the person opening administrative doors that allowed students to communicate their concerns.[76]

For Taylor, the tradition of feminist deaning prepared her to advocate on behalf of civil rights, and to calm the violence of the New Left. Her confidence in self-governance as a tool to help women students embrace autonomy meant she adopted the premise that college should teach students to become adults who were prepared to operate as full citizens of the nation. She believed that students should have an authentic, respected voice in higher education, and she listened to female and male students in order to bring calm to KU during turbulent times. She used the power of AWS, the emerging women's movement, and her links with faculty and students to achieve these changes.

In the increasing mêlée of 1969–1970, Taylor built a new level of credibility with the New Left and with radical feminists. This fashioned a solid platform for the women of KU to stage a radical protest of their own—this time by the February Sisters—an anonymous group of women led by two of Taylor's residence hall AWS activists personally mentored by Donna Shavlik.

CHAPTER 6

From Quiet Activism to Radical Tactics

Casey Eike, University of Kansas student and Intercollegiate Association of Women Students (IAWS) national president, stood in dean of women Emily Taylor's kitchen, peering into the refrigerator. It was Friday, February 4, 1972, and the AWS leader needed food to supply a group of women who were locking themselves into the East Asian Studies building to protest KU's lack of action on women's issues. No one knew how long it would take for Chancellor E. Laurence Chalmers to agree to the women's demands, so Eike loaded enough food to supply 20 women and four children for a week. The anonymous demonstrators, naming themselves the "February Sisters," were inspired a few days prior when AWS leader Sarah Scott and her younger sister, Scottie, hosted radical feminist Robin Morgan on campus as part of a lecture series. After the standing-room-only talk ended, 100 women gathered with Morgan to discuss the KU situation. As the meeting wore on, Sarah Scott stood up and said, "I think we've done enough talking. Let's do something."[1] The group agreed, planning a nonviolent protest to force the university to grant their demands—comprehensive women's health services, campus childcare, an affirmative action office, equal pay for women, hiring women in administrative leadership roles, and creation of a women's studies department. Their list, not surprisingly, looked similar to the agenda Taylor pursued throughout the 1960s. Their tactic of taking over a building, though, reflected the practices of the New Left and racial justice demonstrations that took place at KU a few semesters prior.

Sarah Scott, Eike, Taylor's staffer Janet Sears, and others kept Taylor informed about the Sisters' developing plans to occupy the building. Taylor carefully considered her options. In every other case—the 1964 sit-in, the Black Student Union demands to include African American women on the KU cheerleading squad, and the New Left protests over the Kent State shootings—she had worked behind the scenes to broker negotiations that defused the situation and kept news coverage to a minimum. This time, though, she chose not to act. "We'd tried every other way of getting it done," said Taylor years later, reflecting on her decision to remain silent on the planned protest. Chalmers had regularly refused Taylor's and women faculty members' requests for affirmative action in hiring and salary equity required by Executive Order 11375.[2] "I can't tell you how many times

I informed Chalmers about where we were on setting up an affirmative action office...but Chalmers wouldn't set up the search committee [for the office's director]," recalled Taylor. Without a program director, none of the affirmative action activities could move forward.[3] In addition, her repeated requests for Chalmers to intervene with student health director Raymond Schwegler's anti-contraception policies at Watkins Hospital went unanswered as well. Taylor thought the Sisters' building occupation might produce the results she, the AWS, and women faculty had been unable to achieve. Though not widely known, Chalmers had come close to dismissal by the Kansas Board of Regents during the summer of 1970, and Taylor did not think he could afford more media coverage of student protests. She believed this would give the February Sisters leverage. Taylor, aware that her role as dean of women was to keep KU women out of the news, nonetheless made the difficult decision not to intervene as AWS leaders and her staff assisted the protestors.[4]

Taylor felt an intense loyalty to KU, but her support for Chalmers had waned during the 1969–1970 school year as she and her staff worked hard to calm the campus—sometimes in what seemed like a vacuum—especially after Chalmers left her to sort out the New Left's anger over his 1970 solution to end the school year rather than deal with their demands. She simply could not bring herself to help solve this problem. The February Sisters were not the only women frustrated with the KU leadership, and, in the end, the Sisters' protest achieved success because the demonstration fused radical feminist tactics with the liberal feminist support of Taylor and faculty women. The protest united generations and feminist philosophies, bringing younger and older women together to force KU's institutional change. Often understood as simply radical women's protest, another in the long line of New Left efforts at KU, the Sisters instead represented the apex of the feminist agenda that Taylor and deans of women had long been struggling to achieve. It wove together the emerging women's movement and the various strands within it—radical and liberal—as well as the other forces for social change, notably, the civil rights and New Left movements—employing the gamut of feminist tactics in concert. In the end, the protest not only achieved its stated goals at KU but also ultimately helped solidify the changes that would come with Title IX, the legislation that barred gender discrimination in education. The February Sisters publicly voiced the feminist issues that Taylor and her cohort had begun addressing many years earlier, and their protest led to the creation of a women's studies program that reflected both the knowledge and methods produced by women deans over the previous eight decades.

This fusion of generations to benefit women in higher education was not a new concept. Since the earliest days of women's student government, deans of women harnessed the power of female students' opinions to push administrations to facilitate women's full participation, creating an intergenerational partnership through NADW and IAWS that had fostered a consciousness about women's differential status long before the emergence of an organized, political women's movement in the 1960s and 1970s. By the time overt feminism flooded campuses in the late 1960s, Taylor and her feminist colleagues advised their AWS chapters—and the national IAWS organization—to shift from parietal regulation to feminist advocacy, promoting the Equal Rights Amendment (ERA) and employment equity. The seeds of these efforts took root in the earliest deans' offices as women administrators sought to illustrate the inequities in women's higher education and vocational options.

Commissions on Women's Status and the Engine for Change

From the earliest years—especially at the University of Chicago—deans of women wanted female students to develop a group consciousness about the shared experiences women encountered on campus and in the workplace with its lack of a livable wage and limited vocational options for women beyond teaching. Not only did deans encourage working alumnae to join labor unions in order to develop support for all working women's needs, they also began to teach their students about the economic and political status of women. At the same time, these administrators began to measure and assess women's stature on their campus. They compiled research, and used their data to teach students, male administrators, and university trustees about how women fared in college classrooms. Legal changes in the 1960s and 1970s would add fuel to these efforts as deans, and their long-time Women's Bureau partner joined with the IAWS to advocate for gender equality in higher education.

While deans of women innovated ways to improve women's education, their "colleges within colleges" (the separate spaces women occupied within coeducational institutions) created intergenerational environments where they could mentor students about women's status in US society. Some deans even led classes on how women fared as a group. Marion Talbot and Sophonisba Breckinridge both taught a class entitled "Legal and Economic Position of Women" to their University of Chicago students, and some of Talbot's and Breckinridge's students created their own versions of the class at other institutions, as Chicago PhD Alice Mary Baldwin did at Duke University's coordinate college, where she was dean of women students. Deans' concern over women's legal and economic status became a standard approach in the profession, originally linked to economist Susan Kingsbury and her early Women's Educational and Industrial Union research on women's salaries at the turn of the century. Taylor, herself, absorbed the idea of women as a labor cohort while training at Ohio State University in the 1930s with economist Grace S. M. Zorbaugh.[5]

By the 1930s, aided by deans, AAUW and Kingsbury partnered with the Women's Bureau to study the economic situation of all college-educated women, finding significant discrimination against women in the professions during the Great Depression, particularly for those with husbands. In 1939, when the Women's Bureau released the report, *Economic Status of University*

Women in the U.S.A., deans of women across the country shared the publication with their AWS leaders, placing it in their libraries as a resource for college women. At the same time, the AAUW maintained a Standing Committee on the Economic and Legal Status of Women, institutionalizing the practice of studying women's position in society.[6]

Deans also adopted the practice of tracking women's status within higher education. At the University of Chicago, Talbot charted the institution's treatment of women by identifying deficits in instructional resources, women's facilities, and the number of women faculty. She regularly sent a report of her findings along with suggestions for improvement to the institution's president. Lois Kimball Mathews Rosenberry adopted this same strategy at Wisconsin, and together with Talbot, the women's influence spread university status reporting across coeducational institutions. Lucy Diggs Slowe embraced this tactic at Howard University, making women's status studies an accepted procedure in black higher education as well. The dean of women's report became a vehicle to update the university administration on all aspects of women's participation at an institution—especially regarding areas which shortchanged women.[7]

By the time Taylor arrived at OSU as an undergraduate in the mid-1930s, most deans of women regularly produced reports that briefed the university president and its trustees on challenges facing women on their campuses, cataloguing the need for women's residence halls as well as facilities for dining, physical education and extracurricular activities. These briefings also helped establish the need to hire more women faculty or more dean of women's staff. Often, deans of women dovetailed these report findings with the AAUW accreditation process. Even Howard University's Slowe used the AAUW to help her manage disagreements with her university president. However, since AAUW only offered membership to alumnae of its accredited schools, its connections with black women were limited, only admitting them when they graduated from accredited institutions—and the environments of local branches where the AAUW operated more as social clubs regularly shunned black women.[8]

Despite this racism, higher education sought AAUW certification as a signifier of an institution's rigorous academic standards. AAUW only accredited universities and colleges that offered women the same liberal arts education offered to men, and that integrated women into their mission through appropriate housing, facilities, and staffing. While AAUW left black schools out of its matrix, majority-white coeducational state and private colleges widely sought AAUW accreditation to recruit women (and their tuition dollars) to their campuses. Deans of women regularly included in their university status reports necessary steps to meet and maintain AAUW membership. In this way, deans leveraged the AAUW accreditation to obtain women's campus facilities and to increase the number of women faculty. AAUW even convinced schools without an academically trained dean of women to hire one because the organization's early accreditation standards required a dean of women with a faculty appointment.

Not surprisingly, throughout the twentieth century, deans of women and the AAUW accreditation committee found universities lacked women faculty and paid the ones it had at a lower rate than men. They also sometimes prevented them from advancing through promotion and tenure. Additionally, women's facilities often needed improvements as did women's housing.[9] By the 1940s, deans of women included student opinions in their campus status reports to bolster their arguments. Frequently, they involved the AWS students in surveying women's attitudes. Taylor adopted this method from Kate Hevner Mueller. At KU, Taylor often involved students in measuring coeds' status which raised students' consciousness of how women's educations differed from men's. However, few of these deans' efforts were called "status of women" commissions. Despite AAUW's long-time committee on the political and legal status of women, some found the phrase "status of women" too controversial, a nod toward overt feminism that, in the 1950s Cold War age of anticommunism, indicated nonconformity. In 1958 when Taylor established an early campus Commission on the Status of Women in higher education, Chancellor Franklin Murphy asked Taylor to change the name to a less controversial title and they agreed on "Roles of Women Committee."

Historians have credited the rise of campus commissions on the status of women to the popularity of President John F. Kennedy's President's Commission on the Status of Women (PCSW), tracing the PCSW to the creation of each state's commission, and then to their development on campuses. While some campus commissions did develop this way, many of the schools with a feminist dean of women already had this campus reporting practice in place. And for those that did not, Taylor led an effort in 1969 to establish intergenerational commissions at the 300 IAWS schools across the country. In addition, the PCSW's committee on women's education already reflected the long-term partnership between deans, AAUW, and the Women's Bureau. The PCSW education committee included key leaders from the deans' network. Former American Council on Education (ACE) Commission on the Education of Women (CEW) chairwoman Mary Bunting led the committee, which included former CEW director Opal David and NADW president Helen Schleman (Purdue). Fundamentally, the philosophy the PCSW recommended reflected Mueller's proposal in *Educating Women for a Changing World* that higher education should be used to elevate the status of women's lives. The PCSW extended the deans' and AAUW's historical call for liberal arts education that prepared women for home and work, albeit in the most noncontroversial terms by affirming women's fundamental role as mothers.[10]

* * *

Not surprisingly, feminist deans in the early 1960s actively followed the PCSW as well as the developing civil rights legislation. In 1963, Schleman, as NADW president, worked with the Women's Bureau labor coalition to back the emerging civil rights legislation. When "sex" was added to Title VII of the 1964 Civil Rights Act's list of prohibited reasons for discrimination, the NADW and activist deans increased their political activism, shifting away from the NADW's long-time tradition of "downplaying or disavowing the explicit feminist implications of their activities and interests."[11] Instead, Schleman encouraged NADW members to cultivate relationships with lawmakers and testify on legislation, using their networks across various women's organizations to influence support for fair employment practices.[12]

Taylor, like most feminist deans in 1964, began to watch closely how Title VII would be implemented through the newly formed Equal Employment Opportunity Commission (EEOC). Since "sex" was added as an attempt to kill the racial civil rights bill, no one was certain if or how the EEOC would deal with workplace discrimination against women. And, as many historians have shown, the federal government initially ignored workplace complaints by women. The Justice Department pursued 45 claims of racial bias in court under the provisions of Title VII and its equivalents, but did not prosecute a single discrimination case regarding women until 1970. In fact, when the EEOC first came to the KU campus, Taylor made an appointment with the investigators who informed her that they could only work on racial discrimination matters.[13] The legislation, nonetheless, would provide the first overt intersection of feminist deans of women such as Taylor with the emerging women's movement.

By 1966, some members of the state commissions on the status of women wanted to discuss the EEOC's lack of attention to women. Women's Bureau staff hesitated to allow a conversation that implicitly criticized President Lyndon B. Johnson's administration. This meant the 1966 Washington DC meeting of the Citizens' Advisory Council on the Status of Women promised to be an interesting dialogue about women's issues, so Taylor decided to attend. At the conference, Betty Friedan, Katherine (Kay) Clarenbach, and 26 others met in Friedan's hotel room to discuss their discontent over the EEOC. When Women's Bureau conference organizers Esther Peterson and Mary Keyserling declined to consider the issue during the conference, the women met the next day to establish the National Organization for Women (NOW). While Taylor—friends with Clarenbach—missed the meeting in the hotel room, she quickly connected with the group and joined. Taylor recalled the attitude of the women: "The (State) Commissions are great. But, they are political and there are stands they can't take because it's impolitic for them…What we need is an organization…with the same goal in mind of improving the status of women, but not be handicapped in any way by political appointments."[14] NOW immediately began to push for the EEOC to investigate women's employment discrimination. By late 1966, it called loudly for President Johnson to add "sex" to his 1965 Executive Order 11246 which prohibited racial discrimination among federal government contractors. In 1967, he complied, issuing Executive Order 11375, which extended E.O. 11246 to include sex and mandated preferential action to be taken on behalf of women and minorities.[15]

Kansas, like most states, had to review its labor laws to bring them into compliance with Title VII, and Taylor answered Schleman's call to advocate for women's equity in state political venues. "I can't tell you how many times in those years I went to the legislature," she later recalled. "It seemed like it was everyday...Some bill would come up which would just be inimical to the interest of women."[16] Taylor followed Schleman's recommendation for deans to work across the various organizations which could collaborate on the interests of women. Aside from NADW and AAUW, Taylor belonged to the National Organization for Women (NOW), the board of the Women's Equity Action League (WEAL), the National Women's Political Caucus, and the National Federation of Republican Women. In 1969, the Kansas governor appointed Taylor to the Kansas Commission on the Status of Women and she eventually became the third president of the National Association of Commissions for Women. Between these activities and the WEAL board, Taylor cemented her relationships with such individuals as NOW founder Kay Clarenbach; Marguerite Rawalt, attorney for both NOW and WEAL; Catherine East, a women's activist and government official who became Chief of the Career Services Division of the Bureau of Recruiting and Examining; and "godmother of Title IX" Bernice Sandler. At the same time, Taylor expanded her connections across the Women's Bureau.

Through this network, Taylor had a front seat in the organizing efforts for women's equity in the late 1960s and 1970s—and she brought her students with her. Taylor took AWS leaders to NOW's first national convention, inviting 12 students—including Casey Eike, Sarah Scott, and other AWS leaders. At the conference, NOW pressured the KU women not to speak against the war, so they left the meeting with Taylor and Shavlik. With few young women in attendance, Betty Freidan personally asked them to return, which they did.[17] NOW was not the only conference KU women attended with Taylor. She also brought them to national WEAL conferences, and the National Women's Political Caucus inaugural meeting. By participating in these organizations, KU students became engaged in the national efforts that reflected the feminism of these older, often professionally established women who believed in incremental change through laws, policies, and regulations.[18] At the same time, KU students helped older women see the New Left concerns over the Vietnam War as seen at the NOW conference.

* * *

By 1969, Bernice Sandler, denied tenure by the University of Maryland, realized the newest executive order, E.O. 11375, gave women the leverage they needed to force universities and colleges to diversify their faculties. Since federally funded grants constituted a significant portion of every research university's budget, each qualified as a federal contractor subject to the new order. This meant sex discrimination at any higher education institution accepting federal monies had been outlawed. Finding NOW too controversial for some university women to join, Sandler began working with the smaller, professionally oriented WEAL which wielded significant influence as it attracted older, accomplished women like Taylor. As WEAL president, Sandler used Johnson's order to begin an onslaught against colleges and universities for employment discrimination. By the end of 1970, WEAL had targeted 250 schools with specific charges of sex discrimination using the threat of litigation as a lever to promote changes to salary inequities and hiring practices that excluded women.[19] At KU, the official EEOC complaint filed against the university originated with AWS leader and February Sister Sarah Scott, and was written on a typewriter in Taylor's office. Employed as a typist in the chancellor's office, Scott was given stacks of memos to type—some of which cynically discussed women's salary issues—so she copied the materials, took them to Taylor and, along with IAWS president Casey Eike, used them to file the complaint against KU.[20]

Within the organizational structure, Taylor began working through administrative channels to implement the affirmative action promised by Johnson's order. KU had its share of employment discrimination against women. The university's 1949 nepotism policy allowed only one member of a family to advance as a faculty member, which resulted in academic women married to professors being barred from the classroom. For instance, in the 1950s, Beatrice Wright had authored a text on psychology and disability that KU used in the classroom. However, with her husband a faculty member, KU did not allow her to teach the topic until 1960 when Chancellor W. Clarke Wescoe took the issue to the Kansas Board of Regents. Even after the board approved married couples teaching, Wright remained unable to advance as a faculty member until after Title IX of the Education Amendments Act of 1972 forced KU and universities across the country to change these policies.[21] Before Title IX, though, university administrations across the country stonewalled on E.O. 11375 as the Department of Health, Education and Welfare (HEW) prepared new affirmative action regulations for campuses in response to WEAL and Sandler's efforts. Harvard, Columbia, the University of Michigan, and Cornell began to cooperate when threatened with the loss of federal funding. Other schools stalled—KU, among them.

Once the WEAL onslaught began, Taylor and longtime colleague, noted art historian Marilyn Stokstad, set a strategy to convince KU to comply with E.O. 11375 and the forthcoming HEW guidelines. Stokstad, working with the Committee W of the American Association of University Professors (AAUP), began a review of the KU faculty salary structure. In May 1971, Stokstad's research showed that KU women faculty—as in most universities nationwide—advanced more slowly with lower pay. In addition, KU rarely included women and minorities during the employment search process. Stokstad and four women faculty submitted the findings to Chancellor Chalmers, calling for two actions: an affirmative action plan for women to include specific goals and timetables for rectifying the inequities, and a committee in the University Senate to investigate employment practices to include both a member of Committee W and a student leader from Taylor's AWS/Commission.[22]

Figure 6.1 Emily Taylor leading a group discussion, 1970s

After Committee W submitted its recommendations to Chalmers, the women heard little. In fact, an all-male group of administrators worked with the office of Urban Affairs regarding an affirmative action program focused on minorities that left out women altogether. Committee W continued their efforts, and by July 1971, Chalmers noted to the Urban Affairs Office that he was experiencing "AAUP pressure."[23] Only when HEW formally announced in August 1971 that the affirmative action policy included women did Chalmers begin to involve Taylor. At that time, Taylor and Stokstad counseled Chalmers that he might avoid embarrassment regarding women's agitation for employment equity if he would take two actions: make a statement "asserting your good faith intentions as the leader of an Equal Opportunity Employer institution," and revise the civil rights University Human Relations Council (UHRC) "reaffirmation of principle" to include sex.[24] Neither occurred, though Chalmers did finally select an affirmative action board chair in January 1972. However, progress remained slow as just the month before the KU administration had rejected Committee W's affirmative action plan. While Taylor and women faculty worked to pressure KU to equalize hiring practices, she continued to support the radical activities of women's liberation activists through her office staff. By February 1972, these two flanking feminist agendas would merge to force KU to change.[25]

Women's Governance in an Activist Era

By the mid-1960s, Taylor had a thriving "deaning" operation that incorporated the early dean's mechanisms of self-governance, vocational guidance, and investigations into the status of women. The library in Taylor's office, thick with resources, reflected the diversity of thinking from liberal feminism to radical texts. Women's Bureau materials sat next to graduate school application guides on shelves that also held scrapbooks of news clippings on topics of interest like sex education, and the civil rights act. The AWS Commission on the Status of Women committee researched various topics about KU women and gender roles, raising students' consciousness about discrimination against women. Taylor's work on increasing women's vocational participation expanded from the role model speakers she began inviting to campus in 1956, to a KU Women's Hall of Fame that she founded in 1970 to inspire KU students with examples of successful career alumnae from Kansas. She had a combination of vocational seminars, career days, and even a speakers' bureau of AWS students who could provide lectures on various topics at high schools across the state. This positioned her well for the changing social context that would come with the women's movement of the 1960s and 1970s and the challenges it would bring for women's governance.

Like most schools, KU adopted a joint career services model during the consolidation of student affairs in the 1950s. This established one office to serve both men's and women's needs. Just as Zorbaugh and Zapoleon predicted in the early 1940s, joint career services offices primarily served male student needs. At KU, Taylor decided the career center did not encourage women to consider predominantly male occupations. As a result, Taylor borrowed a page from Zorbaugh's playbook and opened specific career advising in the dean of women's office in the late 1960s. As part of this effort, her staffers Kala Stroup and Walter Smith received a National Science Foundation grant to study women entering science and engineering careers.[26] The two created a handbook on how to interest women in science and math—using the deaning philosophy to create specific sets of exercises to do with young women to increase their interest in science and math careers. The model remains one of the bases for the science, technology, engineering, and math (STEM) activities widely adopted today in organizations ranging from primary and secondary schools to the Girl Scouts.

At schools like KU where women students numbered in the thousands, Taylor relied on a well-trained staff to guide students. She inculcated Mueller's ideas about women's education into her employees, requiring each to read, *Educating Women for a Changing World*. These women—whether in 1956 or in 1969—quickly absorbed the idea that they were preparing women to live in a different type of world where both women and men worked and had families at home. Although Taylor was a single woman with no children, she modeled this new world for KU students through her staff. Stroup worked through two pregnancies, showing KU students it was possible to work while pregnant—and return to work with a small infant at home. Francie Ricks also worked through her pregnancy, and Caryl Smith, Janet Robinson, and Donna Shavlik worked while married. Janet Sears worked as a single mother, and Taylor eventually hired Caryl Smith's husband, Walter Smith, as a male assistant dean of women, to illustrate that women's issues involved men as well. Throughout Taylor's office, KU students saw examples of the types of marriages that Mueller predicted in her 1954 text.[27]

As Taylor's office expanded and parietals declined, New Left women across the country began to question the need for AWS organizations as they called for an end to *in loco parentis*. Taylor agreed with the New Left that parietals should go—though she wanted to maintain the AWS focus on leadership training, vocational guidance, and ability to foster students' understanding of women's political and economic status in society. She knew keeping women students together as a block created a powerful coalition that forced universities to consider women's needs on campuses. By 1967, Taylor could see the approaching end of differential rules for women at KU. As a result, she began to remodel AWS into a new form. Working with KU women—some of whom still held on to parietals—she began to reposition AWS as a women's advocacy group. Taylor's AWS chapter officially shed its name in 1969, and became the KU Commission on the Status of Women. As a result, the commission she established in 1958 took the primary role in the women's governance group, elevating its overall mission toward equity and inclusion for women. Rather than allowing AWS to simply disappear, Taylor set a goal for women students to maintain their sanctioned place in KU's governance, working for change within the university. Donna Shavlik recalled the change:

> AWS was really designed around self-governance. And when self-governance was no longer an issue, because there weren't differential rules for men and women, I think that was really the genius that Emily had was to construct Commission on the Status of Women [out of AWS] so that there was someone still focusing on women's issues. But, it wasn't about self-governance. [It was about] self-esteem and self-realization and self-reflection, but not self-governance.[28]

In short, Taylor angled to retain the feminist aspects of deaning while shedding the disciplinary functions that restricted women's growth as autonomous individuals.

While Taylor's efforts to replace AWS with a Commission on the Status of Women originated at KU, she brought the concept of a remodeled AWS to the national stage in an effort to keep the 56-year-old NADW-IAWS partnership viable. Nationally, in the mid-1960s, IAWS reached an all-time high of over 300 chapters, linking over 200,000 college women. However, two forces began to pressure the organization's existence. Locally, AWS chapters found that student affairs offices—now often consolidated operations run by male deans of students—were trying to subsume AWS chapters into all-campus student government organizations or to abolish them altogether in favor of the male-dominated student government. This would leave these campuses without a block of women to voice their needs as a collective group. Secondly, as young women across the country embraced the sexual revolution, parietal protest, and the youth counterculture, the AWS chapters advised by nonfeminist deans of women began to wither as students rejected their form of control.

In response to the first pressure, IAWS and NADW began to organize to stop deans of students from dissolving women's self-governance. In 1966, KU's region of IAWS suggested that IAWS and NADW remind the men running student affairs operations that women needed their own organization that had autonomy from men's organizations. Despite these efforts, the next year IAWS sought NADW's assistance in crafting a strategy to maintain women's governmental autonomy. The two organizations set up an ad hoc committee to consider the problem. That year, a study found that 50 percent of interested deans of women foresaw a change in AWS' role on campuses, and 79 percent of AWS presidents agreed—all thinking programming should become the focus of the organization for various reasons. However, the survey did not ask about the biggest challenge facing women's self-governance—the elimination of differential parietal rules for women.[29]

While deans and counselors of women remained committed to a women-only organization, the reality of the New Left, the sexual revolution, and women's liberation intruded on the IAWS charter and led some universities to eliminate chapters altogether. In the spring of 1969, both the University of Florida and the University of Washington withdrew from IAWS, replacing their AWS chapters with Women's Commissions focused on women's liberation. Both schools offered programming similar to that at KU, though they rejected the IAWS due to its historical connection to parietal legislation. The combination of these trends sounded a warning to both NADW and the IAWS that the only way to remain viable was to straddle their increasing sublimation into dean of students' offices while also incorporating ideas popular with women's liberation.[30]

Taylor became passionately committed to this project. She identified the ad hoc committee on AWS autonomy as an opportunity to reconsider IAWS' purpose, and to make the changes necessary for the organization to survive into the next decade. One of her strongest KU student leaders at the time was Janice Mendenhall, who served on this national ad hoc committee. Together they strategized to convince NADW and IAWS that AWS chapters should become collegiate Commissions on the Status of Women. At the March 1969 NADW national meeting, Mendenhall pitched the idea at a conference panel, while behind the scenes Taylor recommended the IAWS consider realigning all chapters as Commissions on the Status of Women to accommodate the growing women's movement. By then, with the PCSW legacy and the state commissions active across the nation, the phrase had lost its controversial tinge.[31]

This process moved quickly. The IAWS convention followed just a few weeks later at the University of Alabama, where KU proposed that all AWS chapters establish committees on the status of women, and the IAWS voted in favor of the plan. That year the IAWS hosted its most forthright consideration of feminism yet. The NADW-IAWS liaison Betty Fitzgerald (Michigan State) stewarded the IAWS through a decision to "gear...our programs to the more progressive and advanced school...All of this based on the theory that AWS should be more than a judicial body (might be a big shock to some delegations)."[32] Titling the meeting "Confrontation, Contemplation and Commitment," the 1969 conference program greeted a number of AWS chapters which had not yet seriously considered the workshop topics of racism, drug use, student unrest, access to graduate education, and male chauvinism. Despite some campuses summarizing their year with reports on fashion shows and bridal showers, the IAWS vote in favor of campus status committees meant Taylor had the platform she needed to guide AWS chapters to accept the voices of all women's groups—including radical feminists and countercultural opinions.[33]

However, it would not be an easy adjustment. The 1969 convention illustrated how the radical feminist viewpoint would strain some AWS chapters. Accustomed to a formal voting structure, student leaders wrestled with the informal tactics of women's liberation and the New Left. For instance, AWS officers allowed the preregistered YWCA to set up an information table at the proceedings that year, yet they rejected New Left organizations because they did not register in advance, leaving NOW, the National Student Association, and SDS angry that they could not distribute literature.[34]

With the AWS chapters exhibiting an array of stances regarding the role of women's equity, the national transition Taylor envisioned was not a simple task. Taylor recalled that by watching the arrangement of the chapters during the voting meetings of the IAWS, the divisions between feminist and nonfeminist AWS chapters became obvious:

> ...in the business meetings of IAWS, people were seated by delegations, and there were great big signs, just like in a political convention, saying "University of Kansas" and so forth. You could look around the room and you could see who there was in the room, what schools were represented there, and whether the advisor (who was the dean of women in practically all cases) had a close working relationship with the students—because those people sat with the students. And then there were some others who sat on the sidelines or in the back...It gave all of us a clue as to who was on what side, these [deans on the floor with the students] were always the people who were pushing the boundaries out further.[35]

The developing women's movement exposed the long-time division between feminist deans of women and those deans committed to parietals. Taylor—who missed only one NADW meeting in her career—recalled that NADW members always wrestled with the issue of direct advocacy for women. "We were not the cutting edge for change in the interests of women," said Taylor of the NADW. "I was closest to the edge of our feminist work. We were by no means the majority. There were some on the other side who really did want to control people. They weren't interested in teaching women to be independent. They were interested in keeping them dependent and thinking that was the appropriate role for women."[36] Taylor stayed active on the NADW resolutions committee to push the group toward feminist activism—though many deans of women found her ideas too controversial and her direct style off-putting. Taylor recalled "There were always people who got up and said, 'If we pass that, we'd be out of business; if we pass that we wouldn't be funded to come to the next meeting'...some of them said 'I'd like to.'"[37] However, by 1969, most deans recognized the social changes as permanently altering women's roles, so NADW brought feminist deaning into the center of the profession.[38]

The conference that year featured feminist practices deans could adopt—some implemented at KU in the 1950s—now considered mainstream in the NADW national agenda. Beginning with "Student Activists" (moderated by former KU Dean of Women Martha Peterson, now president of Barnard College), the programs included "Life Span Planning—For the Middle of Now," "Student Participation in University Governance—Sense or Nonsense?" "The Black Student Movement," and "A New Morality." That year, deans considered marriage—motherhood—career planning, free speech and parietal dissolution, race equity, and the sexual revolution. By now, most NADW members recognized the tide had changed on parietals as a flood of requests entered the IAWS clearinghouse asking for information on parietal change and keys for women students. The KU key system was sent out from the IAWS clearinghouse as a recommended model for making the transition since it handled the change incrementally, bridging administrators, parents, and reluctant students into an agreement on the dissolution of parietals.

After the 1969 conventions, the NADW-IAWS ad hoc committee determined that the two organizations needed to have a closer alliance to navigate the changing face of US higher education. The group recommended a new NADW-IAWS Coordinate Committee to replace the NADW-IAWS Liaison Committee, and appointed Taylor to lead it. Under Taylor's watch, the IAWS began to disseminate a model program for changing to Commissions on the Status of Women based on the KU example.[39] As IAWS established campus commissions, it also recommended sex education seminars, high school leadership conferences, and shedding its "tea party" ladylike image. IAWS asked AWS chapters to listen to alternative views expressed by the New Left, NOW, and radical feminists in addition to the longterm AWS partners of women's honorary societies, social sororities, and the YWCA. Clearly, Taylor sought to spread the mixture of generations and ideologies throughout IAWS and AWS chapters, just as she did at KU.[40]

As NADW and IAWS became serious about transitioning women's governance to a post-parietal world, Taylor harked back to the 1950s and reaffirmed IAWS participation with ACE, AAUW, and the Women's Bureau. Under her leadership, the coordinate committee reengaged the historical network that had undergirded the deans-AAUW-IAWS network from its inception, placing IAWS leaders on state commissions, ACE committees, AAUW committees, and involving them in Women's Bureau activities. KU's Mendenhall, now a national IAWS officer, led the effort, asking each chapter to follow the KU research agenda for 1969–1970 so that the IAWS could aggregate each chapter's findings on the discriminatory practices across the nation.

Mendenhall recommended chapters share their commission status reports with university officials and state legislators. IAWS collected the findings, making plans to share the results with Marguerite Gilmore, the director of Women's Bureau Field Offices for use in Bureau advocacy.[41] Consequently, this reinvigorated the outlets for feminism that had been vanishing on college campuses as universities subsumed deans of women into deans of students' offices in the mid-twentieth century. Barbara Cook, NADW University Section Convention Chairman, noted in a letter to Keesling as the two prepared for the 1970 NADW convention:

> The Dean's Organization has long supported attitudes, programs and legislation favorable to women. There are many members of the Association who are actively engaged in some phase of the women's movement, and all of us are searching for ways to be more effective in this area.[42]

By the spring of 1970—two months before the Kent State shootings—the NADW-IAWS adoption of campus commissions was well on its way. That year, amid the student protests flooding campuses across the nation, Taylor worked closely with IAWS President Louise Douce to engineer the IAWS shift toward a vocally feminist mission. Douce recalled Taylor's mentoring as a formative experience as she learned Taylor's practice of dressing and presenting oneself conservatively so she could think and act radically. The practice allowed Douce to bring IAWS into a pro-feminist stance, and became a lifelong strategy she used throughout her career. In 1970, Douce and Taylor overhauled the IAWS into a women's issues forum—calling on the AWS chapter delegations to determine the principles of the organization. Just as Taylor had given the 1958 KU AWS the opportunity to set its own vision, she now recommended the IAWS consider a number of resolutions to determine what they wanted to support as an organization. Taylor always believed the resolutions committee of an organization like IAWS or NADW determined the focus for the work done by the group. "The resolutions represent what the organization stands for, and there were some of us who wanted to make sure that it stood for the right things—namely for economic and political and social justice."[43] Rather than an AWS chapter being a campus interest group solely to pressure its university administration to change, Taylor envisioned the IAWS organization as a larger, national interest group of 200,000 college women pushing legislators and universities to agree to women's equity issues.

Douce and IAWS leaders chose to consider most major issues of the women's movement and New Left platforms, approving a number of new resolutions, as well as an overhaul of the entire IAWS bylaws and constitution so that it matched the new programming. That year, the IAWS voted in favor of the ERA, equal educational opportunities for women and men, repeal of antiabortion laws, an open military draft for men and women under the ERA, birth control and venereal disease educational information, research on birth control health risks, in-depth sex education, preventative health education, adoption by single parents, discontinuation of discriminatory indications of marital status (suggesting Ms. in place of Mrs. and Miss), racial and cultural diversity understanding and representation in its groups, state voting rights at age 18, and environmental awareness programs.[44]

The IAWS proclaimed the ERA its "highest priority" and sent the chapters back to their home campuses to organize pressure on their local congressmen to pass the amendment. In Kansas, the AWS/Commission advocated for the passage of the ERA by attending enrollment and passing out postcards for students to send to elected officials asking for support. In Ohio, the Ohio State University women's self-government association (the AWS chapter) received a commendation from the Ohio State Commission on the Status of Women for their assistance on the ERA effort, and in Wisconsin, the University of Wisconsin, Oshkosh, Associated Women Students chapter joined the Equal Rights Coalition. AWS chapters at schools ranging from New Mexico State University to the University of Nevada, Reno, participated in ERA efforts. As the IAWS rallied around the ERA, many AWS leaders began to see themselves as a part of the women's liberation movement.[45] As a University of Oklahoma AWS woman noted: "'I don't think there would have been any changes on our campus without our organization,' she said. 'We are kind of the ground level for woman's lib in that we are giving women the training and the education.'"[46]

By 1971, the NADW-IAWS featured programming to help reluctant deans of women make the transition to including the New Left. IAWS Executive Director Karen Keesling helped organize a NADW 1971 convention panel entitled "Student Involvement in the Women's Movement—Three Approaches" and invited the IAWS, NOW, and the Women's Liberation Front to present on the topic. That year, NADW finally formally endorsed sex education.[47] By that time, IAWS newsletters advocated listening to New Left points of view—even if the AWS group did not agree, and *IAWS National Notes* sent monthly updates that included information on Executive Order 11375, the ERA, and WEAL's efforts to force change in university hiring practices, even offering Bernice Sandler's contact information for anyone wanting to prepare a complaint against their university. Karen Keesling, IAWS executive director and future White House staffer, relocated to Lawrence and also worked on Taylor's staff—a hire Taylor made to increase communication and to support national efforts with her KU budget. IAWS conventions now met annually, featuring Women's Bureau Director Elizabeth Koontz, and Virginia Allen, Chairwoman of President Nixon's Task Force on Women's Rights and Responsibilities. Taylor's agenda—which she absorbed from feminist deans before her—became overt as she took the helm of IAWS. In 1970, she and Douce featured removal of parietals in favor of personal autonomy, sex education and control of one's body, sexual assault prevention, and advocacy for full political and economic citizenship. They pushed for daycare as a solution to combining marriage and work, and instead of using "contingency planning" as the rationale for women to prepare for occupations, they promoted "life span" planning that showed women how to blend occupation and motherhood—even if they wanted to remain home with their children.[48]

And, just as Susan Kingsbury, AAUW, and the Women's Bureau measured college women's economic status in the 1930s, the AWS commissions implemented campus-by-campus surveys, with the IAWS assembling national statistics to share with the Women's Bureau and other government entities about treatment of women by the nation's universities and colleges. Both IAWS liaisons Betty Fitzgerald (eventually NADW president) and Taylor moved onto the WEAL Board, which also included attorney and future Supreme Court Justice Ruth Bader Ginsburg, civil rights activist Pauli Murray, and NOW legal committee chair Marguerite Rawalt.

By 1970, IAWS actively promoted women's studies courses, following the path of the San Diego State University program, one of the first in the country. KU's first women's studies course began in 1961, six years before the well-recognized course at Cornell.[49] These emerging women's studies programs included topics feminist deans had addressed since the turn of the twentieth century, teaching "The Status of Women," "Human Sexuality," and "Self-Actualization of Women," which all dealt with the familiar topics of marriage, gender roles, percentages of women who worked, and how educated women fared as a class of citizens.[50] The course content looked remarkably similar to what Kate Hevner Mueller developed in the 1940s and 1950s to train future deans of women and student affairs professionals. In fact, Mueller's 1945 comments sound as if they were contemporary with the late 1960s and early 1970s commentary by women educators teaching new women's studies courses:

> The campus marriage is not a marriage of two students. Ninety to ninety-three per cent of campus marriages find the wife working her husband's way through college, or putting him through graduate school. The marriage doesn't start that way, but they end that way, by actual count. Somehow, the present culture has built a tolerance for this kind of exploitation of young women [that] gives the man a self image of the young pioneer, puts a glow of maturity and achievement over a situation which will be eventually a crippling handicap to the able young woman.[51]

For three-quarters of a century, the research, methods, and knowledge produced by deans of women created a philosophy about women that provided ground for Women's Studies as a new field. In fact, many early women's studies courses were taught in the continuing education operations that the NADW and ACE's CEW developed in the 1960s from the life-phases concepts that Mueller and others popularized.

As IAWS students across the country reached out to the variety of student groups interested in women's issues, Schleman's vision of cross-organization cooperation and advocacy among deans of women and women's students had come full circle. By 1973, IAWS recommended that chapters ally with local groups ranging from the traditional partners of AAUW, BPW, YWCA, and the League of Women Voters, to new collaborations with Zero Population

Growth, WEAL, NOW, AAUP, and the State Commission on the Status of Women. IAWS sent chapters checklists on how to support the ERA, and to move the E.O. 11375 forward, and many worked with the local chapters of the aforementioned groups, increasing the intergenerational ties.[52]

By this time, the cross-generational work so long in place between the NADW and IAWS began to be formally recognized as a part of the women's movement. As Taylor and Keesling noted in a letter to NADW members:

> It may truly be said that women deans and women student associations have long been allies, and that this mutually supportive relationship has been and continues to be of utmost importance to both groups. On the divided campuses of today, cross-generational cooperative endeavors have a special significance, as both youth and mature women have much to learn from one another.[53]

As the national IAWS advisor, Taylor specifically sought feminist growth between younger and older women. While IAWS and NADW activism remained anchored in liberal feminist practices, Taylor's reliance on the intergenerational approach meant that some campuses built coalitions across the divide between liberal and radical feminist philosophies as well.

Where "Liberal" and "Radical" Intersect

Historians have relied upon the useful divisions of liberal and radical feminism to help frame the varied approaches to feminism during the social upheaval of the 1960s and 1970s. Because liberal feminists were often older, professional women, and radical ones younger, little attention has been given to how women worked together across generations—something Taylor purposely fostered at KU and in the IAWS. Taylor, by all accounts, adopted a liberal feminist approach. Quoted in 1972, she identified herself as "a conventional feminist" separate from both radical feminists and the broader women's movement.[54] Her position in a university made it impossible to adopt any other label. Clearly, unlike the proponents of radical feminist ideology, she believed in institutions—and in their ability to change. Her tactics, like the ones she employed with the changes to parietals, were gradual. "Incremental change is the only kind of change which was even possible as far as I can see," said Taylor.[55]

Like liberal feminists across the country, she worked for women's equality through legal and policy initiatives. Frequently, she and her staff organized students quietly behind the scenes until a law passed—and then she took her work public. This was clearly the case in desegregating housing in 1964 and her pregnancy counseling operations in 1969 when she waited for the Civil Rights Act and the abortion standards to become law before publicly addressing these controversial areas. Like other feminist deans of women, Taylor used classic liberal strategies: producing data and informational materials about women's issues and inequalities through a Commission on the

Status of Women; educating men and women about women's issues through the AWS/Commission speaker's bureau; and preparing women to enter the public sphere as both political and economic citizens. Radical feminists, on the other hand, critiqued US society as so reliant upon patriarchy that only a wholesale rejection of mainstream US culture could solve ingrained sexism. Unlike Taylor, radical feminists typically rejected men's involvement in their activities and often saw liberal feminists as "bourgeois" and co-opted by patriarchal society. Despite her liberal tactics, Taylor embraced the spectrum of feminist activism and thinking, finding that the radical feminists made her incremental changes seem more palatable to the men in power who actually implemented change. Since many historians have focused on the very real differences between radical and liberal feminists on college campuses, few have considered how they worked together at times in intergenerational, multivaried partnerships.[56]

At KU the February Sisters grew directly out of the cross-generational dialectic Taylor enabled in her office. Historical accounts of women's activism at KU have noted that both radical and liberal feminists existed on the campus—labeling the AWS/Commission as a liberal effort and the Women's Coalition (WC) and Women's Liberation Front (WLF) as the radical arm of the women's movement. While true in some ways, this categorization eclipses the cross-pollination between the groups. As staffer Janet Sears recalled, she experienced the various feminisms of the time as connected within the dean of women's office. The WC and AWS/Commission overlapped inside and outside of Taylor's office intermingling in a tangle of connections between student activists and Taylor's branch of the administration which New Left students sometimes accepted and sometimes rejected. The WC relied on Taylor's office for information on abortion, birth control, and job discrimination, and used the findings by the AWS/Commission to discuss discrimination against women at KU. Women's liberation activists also often used Taylor's library, jobs roster, counseling, and advocacy operation, noting, "They [the dean of women's office] can...help you if you feel you've been discriminated against because of your sex."[57] However, these New Left women cautioned radical feminists that living in dormitories meant, "There are no set penalties for infractions of the rules, so 'punishments' for open or discovered rule-breaking can vary from a 'talk' with your resident assistant to a request that you kindly get the hell out."[58] Clearly, New Left radical women accepted only parts of Taylor's operation.[59]

In turn, Taylor's collaboration with radical feminists remained limited by public attitudes—particularly those of the legislature and Board of Regents. In fact, the cooperation between the AWS/Commission, Taylor's staff, and the WC brought Taylor under intense pressure during the spring of 1970 when the student protests intensified and the union burned. While Chalmers faced increasing displeasure from the governor and Board of Regents about KU student demonstrations, both the AWS/Commission and the WC formally requested funds from the Student Senate to finance the sex education and pregnancy counseling efforts discussed in chapter 4.

Those requests made the news at the same time that journalists covered the Gay Liberation Front student organization that the Shavliks had approved. Not surprisingly, this caused the Board of Regents to demand an explanation for why Taylor's office was furthering radical women's liberation. The AWS/Commission wrote to explain that the KU Commission on the Status of Women was not a new women's liberation group. The letter explained the Commission's long history as AWS, and that the "adult sex education program" only constituted a small part of their overall agenda. While this letter has been used to illustrate that Taylor and the AWS/Commission considered themselves as separate from radical feminists, it was most likely a response to the political challenges Chalmers faced with the regents. The overlapping work between the liberal and radical student groups at KU continued through 1974, with the WC assisting the Dean of Women's office with their seminars on sexuality, and the AWS/Commission calling itself a part of the women's liberation movement.[60]

February Sisters

By February 1972, KU women faculty and a core group of students alike were ready for change. The KU American Association of University Professors (AAUP) Committee W had tired of trying to negotiate an affirmative action plan, and women students remained nonplussed by the Watkins Hospital policies Schwegler kept in place. When Taylor learned of the impending protest influenced by Robin Morgan's lecture, Taylor and the faculty women decided to capitalize on the impending demonstration. AAUP Committee W met on campus on Thursday, February 3, to discuss the administration's stalling tactics on affirmative action planning, drafting a "strong letter" to Chalmers. Meanwhile AWS leader Sarah Scott and sister Scottie planned how to force KU to accommodate their demands, deciding to occupy a building. Calling themselves the "February Sisters," their "nonnegotiable demands" for greater equality on campus echoed the concerns of the WC, Taylor, the AWS/Commission, and Committee W.[61]

By Friday morning, Chalmers learned of the protest brewing and took steps to avert it. Quickly, the KU News Bureau released a statement from the chancellor announcing measures to advance equal opportunity for women and minorities, changing the name of the Office of Urban Affairs to the Office of Minority Affairs, and offering faculty activist Elizabeth Banks, associate professor of classics, a new position reporting to him on hiring equity. Chalmers indicated talks had begun with vice chancellors several weeks before to establish an Advisory Committee on Affirmative Action, though faculty women and Taylor remained skeptical. Stokstad said at the time, "I was very disappointed in the slowness of the administration in developing an affirmative action program...I offered my services to help in any way I could but was never contacted."[62] Several complained that if the administration had indeed been working on the initiative, they left Taylor out of the planning.[63]

Figure 6.2 February Sister Sarah Scott as a University of Kansas student and an Associated Women Students leader (sketch courtesy of artist Kirsten Söderlind)

On Friday afternoon the Sisters swung into action. They called their dean of women staff liaison, Janet Sears, and asked her to take their list of demands to the university administration. Taylor, already informed of both Committee W and the Sisters' plans, agreed to Sears' delivering the document. Ironically, Sears had to secure child care for her daughter before she went to deliver the "statement of action." Meanwhile, Eike provided the food from Taylor's refrigerator as the Sisters locked themselves into the East Asian building.[64]

Chalmers, at a bridge party at his home, reportedly ignored the anonymous telephone call he received informing him of the takeover, thinking it a prank. By 9:15 that night, he recognized the reality of the protest, and summoned Taylor to his office at Strong Hall. Taylor, knowing she planned to help the Sisters achieve their joint goals, assembled a "negotiating team" of five women including Committee W leaders, Stokstad, and Banks. They only brought with them those whom they believed the administration could not later punish; that is, women with tenure. Once in the chancellor's office, Chalmers requested the women convince the February Sisters to leave the building. Taylor and her colleagues refused, knowing Chalmers had no other administrative arm of the university that held relationships with New Left women able to help negotiate them out of the building—especially since AAUP announced its support of the sisters at 10 p.m.[65]

Chalmers tried different tactics to get Taylor, Stokstad, or Banks to help him shut down the demonstration. Chalmers repeatedly threatened to have the police drag the Sisters out of the building, hoping his claim would cause Taylor and the women faculty to intervene. Each time, Taylor met the ultimatum with a reminder to Chalmers that the TV cameras would capture the images for the state—and the regents—to see, eventually telling Chalmers that if he arrested the Sisters, he would have to arrest Taylor too. Chalmers resorted to splitting up the negotiating group to pressure them separately. Stokstad recalled being "plopped" into a secretary's office where she sat stoically while Chalmers "browbeat" her to make a call to the East Asian building, raising his voice and pounding on the desk to emphasize his points.[66]

Once he realized none of the women would carry a desist message to the Sisters, Chalmers accepted their offer to coordinate a negotiation if the SenEx (the university leadership) would agree to talk with the Sisters without reporters or reprisals. After midnight, Banks delivered this message and suggested the Sisters accept the offer. Sarah Scott and several others, with Banks as their advisor, arrived in Strong Hall where Banks told the male administrators that the Sisters consisted of students, staff, and faculty wives. "This ripple of energy went out. You could see every man there deciding whether he knew where his wife was."[67] In the first round of discussions, the SenEx indicated possible police action and provided no assurances of university policy changes. However, Chalmers knew he needed to solve the situation before the next morning when news coverage would begin. At a standstill, Chalmers—who had moved that day to address affirmative action demands—agreed to daycare and the women's health initiatives, signing resolutions. By 9 a.m. the next morning the Sisters left the East Asian building—their peers coming to the building with balloons to surround it so that no one knew who had been inside the building. With very little drama, the radical-liberal intergenerational coalition achieved progress at KU. On one side, the February Sisters approached Chalmers with New Left tactics, on the other side Taylor and Committee W negotiated Chalmers into a position where he would agree to the Sisters' demands.[68]

Looking back from the vantage point of the twenty-first century, the February Sisters achieved the majority of their goals. Here, Taylor provided important assistance to the radicals as it took time and bureaucratic savvy to implement the measures. Taylor supported the Sisters so closely that just a few days after the takeover, the Sisters listed Taylor's office telephone number as one of the three places to call for information on their continuing efforts.[69] Taylor saw to it that the coalition's demands made it through university committees into policy. The efforts stopped and started over the next year. Action on the Sisters' demand for daycare skidded to a halt when the student senate turned down the request for childcare funding, though a petition for child care with over 1,700 signatures eventually led to the Hilltop Child Development Center. Eventually, the chancellor promoted Stokstad to be the first woman Associate Dean of the College of Liberal Arts and Sciences, and a woman served as the head of the Affirmative Action Board. When Chalmers left in 1973, a woman also served as a member of the search committee for the new chancellor.[70]

Chalmers maintained that his administration began significant work on women's Affirmative Action before the Sisters' protest, noting that KU joined many universities in waiting to act on HEW guidelines: "[P]erhaps 12 of the 2,500 or so American colleges and universities have developed affirmative action programs—our 'neglect' is the rule rather than the exception." However, he moved quickly after the Sisters' Friday protest, calling Taylor on Monday morning to have her lead the search committee for an affirmative action director. Taylor moved quickly to capitalize on the Sisters' momentum, and her committee met that afternoon. They soon hired a local woman, Shirley Gilham, who was the group's top choice for the position. Only 12 days after the protest, Chalmers announced the Affirmative Action Board would craft the university's response to the HEW requirements. At the same time, Eike researched affirmative action policies for Taylor, and the two of them wrote the university affirmative action policy that Gilham's office adopted.[71]

Once the chancellor appointed a committee to implement the remaining demands, fractures developed between the coalition of women and the men of color involved in the Office of Urban Affairs. After a committee member, African American Associate Vice Chancellor for Academic Affairs James Rosser, suggested expanding the effort to include race, Sisters declined and Taylor backed them, cognizant that in 1965 she had agreed that sex be excluded from the civil rights arrangements. "I said, 'No. We're not going to broaden it. This is a women's thing. We didn't broaden by sex when it was a racial matter in 1965, and we're not going to do this now.'"[72] The response frustrated Rosser. Taylor later acknowledged that she supported the sole focus on sex because in 1965 "[T]hey talked me into [leaving out the word 'sex'], and I've always resented it and been annoyed at myself for letting them do it." However, at the same time, she noted, "[O]f all the arguments that people get themselves into, I can't think of one that is more unprepossessing than to fight among disadvantaged people as to who's the most disadvantaged."[73]

An implementation committee began meeting in earnest regarding the Sisters' demand for women's health services and sex education counseling. Taylor appointed Janet Sears to the committee to insure that Watkins Hospital no longer defined full physical examinations as based on a male body, with gynecological exams considered an "extra" service.[74] Schwegler continued to suggest that budget constraints made it impossible to hire a gynecologist in order to comply. However, the hospital soon began a process for handling student requests for contraception and discontinued the morality lectures about which women had so often complained. Despite this concession, Schwegler continued to question the changes, asking all doctors to report complaints regarding the new procedures so that he could forward them to Balfour and Taylor. A year after the Sisters' protest, Watkins had not yet adopted the counseling services regarding birth control, sex education, or problem pregnancies that Taylor and the WC continued to provide. Schwegler had, however, retired which cleared the way to chart a new course.[75]

The Sisters also prompted creation of a women's studies program at KU, but not the formal department they requested. While the IAWS had pushed women's studies courses and majors since 1970, Taylor opposed a separate department, believing it would isolate women and feminist perspectives into one small corner of the university, making it easy for the university to ignore them. The dean of women's role gave Taylor a historical perspective on the benefits and costs of separating women in coeducational institutions. Taylor strongly believed a women's studies department would allow administrators and faculty to continue to ignore women and gender issues, just as universities had long relegated women's needs as secondary by separating them from male students. Instead, Taylor wanted a program where other academic departments would be forced to hire women and consider women's perspectives on their disciplines. As a student of early deans, Taylor knew that a few women scholars had always existed in twentieth-century universities— and that they built respect across the university by producing scholarship admired by male colleagues. She wanted that pattern to expand as women's studies hired faculty tenured in other disciplines.[76]

When the February Sisters vacated the East Asian Studies building on the morning of February 5, 1972, the women had little idea they would become symbols of radical feminist action in the American heartland. However, the February Sisters also represented the "longer, quieter road" of feminism in the United States—an intergenerational feminist action that brought the KU chancellor to initiate changes for women on the campus. Together, Taylor, her staff, the AAUP Committee W, AWS, and the radical protestors who barricaded the doors of the East Asian building all contributed to the institutional recognition of women's equity, women's sexuality, and fair hiring practices so that women could advance in the faculty and campus leadership. The radical tactics of taking over a university hall pushed KU administrators to acquiesce to the same requests which had been rebuffed so often when liberal feminists asked for them. While some radical women students felt Taylor never advocated enough, Taylor nonetheless lent her influence to push for change, trying to tip the balance as far toward active feminism as the particular historical context allowed. The executive orders of the late 1960s gave her a legal reason to bring the AWS and her staff into full support for KU women faculty equity, and she fostered the February Sisters to ensure that KU adopted fair practices. These efforts at KU prepared her for the next step in her career, moving to Washington DC to implement a program that fought institutional bias against women's leadership at a national level.

CHAPTER 7

From Deans to Presidents

Late one evening in 1974, Emily Taylor's phone rang at home. When she placed the receiver to her ear, she heard a familiar voice say, "Emily, how would you like to come and be my new boss?" It was Donna Shavlik calling from her desk at the American Council on Education (ACE) in Washington DC. The directorship of the Office of Women in Higher Education (OWHE) had unexpectedly opened, and Shavlik, the assistant director, wanted Taylor—her former boss and mentor—to apply for the job. The ACE Board of Directors established OWHE in 1973 to provide its members—presidents of the nation's universities and colleges—with guidance on identifying women who might become college and university presidents, and with assistance in complying with Title VII of the Civil Rights Act of 1964 and Title IX of the Higher Education Amendments of 1972.

However, while ACE had committed an office to address women's advancement in higher education, it had thought little about how to integrate its first women executives into its organizational structure. ACE leaders frequently left inaugural OWHE director Nancy Schlossberg out of meetings, sometimes holding them at the Cosmos Club, a male-only establishment that required women to enter through the back door. Neither Schlossberg nor Shavlik appreciated the not-so-subtle messages that ACE considered women secondary to its mission of serving the nation's higher education presidents. ACE had conducted a national search to find the first OWHE director, but Scholssberg (a student affairs leader trained by Esther Lloyd-Jones) left after a year, frustrated by ACE's lack of support for the internal steps needed to identify women as potential college and university presidents.

When Shavlik called Taylor to ask her to apply for the position, ACE was planning to appoint Todd Furniss, director of academic affairs, as the OWHE acting director while it searched for a new leader. Shavlik knew that Schlossberg's departure already sent a strong message to women in higher education that ACE was not serious about women's equity, and she feared appointing a male as interim director would be detrimental to securing a new female director for the office. Instead, she suggested to Furniss that ACE leave the directorship open during the search.[1]

As Shavlik pondered the situation one evening, she decided to invite Taylor to apply for the job. After years working with Taylor's blunt manner,

Shavlik had no doubts that Taylor would confront ACE's internal exclusion of women. And, she knew OWHE desperately needed a superb negotiator for women's interests who was already accustomed to working from the margins of an organization. Taylor possessed both a personality that refused to be subordinate and the political savvy to build from without and within simultaneously. Shavlik knew Taylor's close connections with Women's Bureau directors Carmen Rosa Maymi and Elizabeth Koontz would be attractive to ACE, as would her service on the board for the National Association of Commissions for Women. The question was whether ACE would hire a woman with Taylor's no-nonsense, imperious manner, and whether Taylor would accept a role fraught with so many challenges.[2]

Over the phone that night in 1974, Shavlik outlined to Taylor a situation full of both risk and promise. OWHE's dwindling funds threatened its existence and new ACE president Roger Heyns had inherited a sparse, overspent budget so he could not easily fix the problem. In addition, ACE had limited expectations for OWHE: it simply opened the office without clearly defining OWHE's role. However, despite ACE's exclusion of Schlossberg within regular meetings and operations, Shavlik thought Heyns possessed a true desire to address women's equity. If Taylor and Shavlik could craft a vision for women at ACE and find the funding for it, Shavlik believed Taylor could persuade him to take necessary steps for OWHE success.

In all, Shavlik described the same situation that deans of women had long encountered at universities. For much of the twentieth century, women's educational issues sat outside the traditional higher education administrative structure and the men leading these institutions had thought little about how to include women. Deans of women constantly sought financing to support programming for women students, and the role had always required the dean to advocate for women from the institution's margins by swaying (and pressuring) the president to adjust to women's programs and needs. Taylor's tenacity, toughness, and 30 years of "deaning" meant she was well-trained for the organizational change coming at ACE.[3]

The opportunity to permanently cement women into the leadership of the academy interested Taylor as she knew deans of women's days were likely numbered after Title IX passed in 1972. The law was a directive for sex neutrality in higher education institutions that accepted federal funding. Title IX ended the common practice of limiting women's enrollment in graduate and professional schools, and had far-reaching results in college athletics. Taylor correctly predicted that the call for sex equity in higher education spelled the end of segmented, gender-specific student affairs and with it the deans who led these efforts. Without the dean of women role, she wondered where and how women would train for top administrative positions. Deans of women's offices had historically been a route to college presidencies at women's colleges. Ada Comstock, dean of women at the University of Minnesota from 1907 to 1912, became Radcliffe president in 1923; Sarah Blanding, University of Kentucky dean of women from 1929 to 1941, ascended to the Vassar presidency in 1946; and Laura Gill, the early dean and director of the occupational exploration efforts at the Women's Educational and Industrial Union in the early 1900s, became president of Woman's College of Sewanee, Tennessee. Taylor knew her protégé, Kala Stroup, would be ready for a presidency within the next decade. But once the dean of women's offices closed, the training ground they provided would also vanish.[4]

Taylor found the opportunity to extend women's leadership into the top levels of coeducational university administration a compelling mission in the post-Title IX context. With OWHE anchored to the nation's most prestigious association for higher education presidents, she believed OWHE could become the presidency training ground that women were rapidly losing in student affairs offices across the country. After 18 years as the KU dean of women, Taylor retired when ACE offered her the OWHE post—knowing it might last only a year if she and Shavlik could not secure grant funding. To her, the risk was well worth the opportunity to pave women's pathways into presidencies of educational institutions.

Taylor brought to the OWHE eight decades worth of knowledge and strategy developed by feminist deans of women regarding how to move women into a closed employment venue—and she relied on the time-tested tactics the National Association of Deans of Women (NADW) and the Intercollegiate Association of Women Students (IAWS) created to foster women's leadership from a marginal position in the academy. The list of practices Taylor borrowed from deaning is long: collecting data on the areas of greatest importance and using statistics to convince the men in power to act upon the structural barriers keeping women from advancement; developing state-by-state networks and a national venue (similar to IAWS) to both identify and mentor rising leaders; matching lists of qualified women with the universities searching to fill open positions—just as the occupational bureaus had done for early collegiate alumna; one-on-one career advising and mentoring—this time applied so women could move into presidencies; and finally establishing a network of influential women who could advocate for women when it became impossible for an employee to convince an institution to embrace greater equity.

This was not the first time ACE fashioned an office for women through its ties to deans of women and the profession of guidance and counseling. As discussed in chapter 2, in 1952 NADW convinced ACE president Arthur Adams to create the ACE Commission on the Education of Women (CEW). This time, the impetus for OWHE arose in 1971, when former KU and University of Wisconsin dean of women Martha Peterson, then president of Barnard, chaired the ACE board of directors. Only the third woman to lead ACE's board—and the first since 1956—Peterson and other women academic deans worked closely with new ACE president Heyns to conceive a program for women within ACE. Heyns, who inherited a board directive to include women and minorities in the organization despite a membership almost entirely consisting of white men, worked with the few women serving on the ACE board and its coordinating commissions to determine the organization's next steps.

Ultimately, ACE called for universities to move beyond a "compliance mentality" of simply meeting Title VII, Executive Order 11375, and Title IX requirements, and to foster women presidents in the academy. Heyns endorsed Peterson's concept of a roster listing every woman in an academic role who had a PhD so that higher education presidents had a means to find female talent. Creating the OWHE from these discussions, ACE drew heavily on the long-time deans' network to formulate the OWHE and its mission. Not only had Martha Peterson trained in the profession of deaning, its first director, Nancy Schlossberg, studied with Esther Lloyd-Jones at Teachers College in New York, and both Shavlik and Taylor developed their philosophies on women in education through the same tradition.[5]

When she arrived in Washington DC, Taylor had specific goals from Heyns to guide the OWHE's work: determining the factors that barred women from academic administration, setting a program to increase the number of women in top posts, and promoting successful strategies among member institutions and government agencies. During her year at ACE, Schlossberg had determined a number of women were ready and interested in assuming presidencies. This provided a starting point for Taylor and Shavlik's mission in 1975. The two women—one a former dean of women and the other a previous IAWS secretary—fashioned OWHE from the NADW-IAWS model, renovating the career guidance and leadership development practices deans created for college women decades earlier into a pathway to guide professional, academic women into presidencies. Taylor and Shavlik were steeped in the methods NADW and IAWS had refined since the turn of the twentieth century, and the two had a long history of using these practices to produce women leaders.[6]

The move was not simply a transition to a new venue for Taylor; nor did it come easy to her. Accustomed to steering young women and navigating in a familiar administrative culture where she had long-term relationships with key players and a large, loyal staff, at OWHE Taylor found herself in a three-person office (including the secretary). In addition, while she knew a number of women at the Women's Bureau and women's movement operatives such as Bernice Sandler, Director of the Project on the Status and Education of Women at the Association of American Colleges, Taylor found the DC milieu a new terrain and she now had to learn from Shavlik. The role reversal was something to which they both had to adjust. However, Taylor brought with her the knowledge that eight decades of feminist deans had accumulated regarding how to negotiate within the bureaucracy of higher education to create change that benefitted women. As Bernice Sandler said of Taylor's presence in Washington DC, "All of us, we were all babes in the woods...We didn't know what we were doing. Emily mentored us about the politics of higher education and the politics of organizations...She taught us, people like me who had never been involved with politics, and taught us how to change an organization...and she understood women's issues before the rest of us understood there was sex discrimination."[7] Whether everyone liked *the way* she did it was another question entirely. OWHE commission chair, Jean

Fox O'Barr, recalled, "I had never met anyone like Emily." Her strength of presence was legendary among OWHE's National Identification Program for the Advancement of Women in Higher Education Administration (NIP) participants:

> I wasn't sure just how I felt about Emily. She is the only person I've ever known who made me—a branded Yankee from Northern New Jersey—feel truly Southern. In contrast to her blazing style, I felt, for perhaps the first time in my life, like a shrinking violet. Or at least a pale chrysanthemum...I have seen a woman...who can blister a stupid comment with a devastating response, and five minutes later can be all gentle attention; who can tell a joke and sip a drink and dispense academic expertise all in five minutes.[8]

Personalities aside, at OWHE both Taylor and Shavlik felt confident in the deaning strategies, and decided to implement a modified version of the roster idea Martha Peterson had brought to OWHE. Taylor wanted to create opportunities for women who were already prepared to assume the responsibilities of a presidency at the nation's colleges and universities, and she planned to quickly move these women into top roles. As Taylor often remarked, 1975 was a time when many university and college presidential search committees claimed they would like to hire a woman leader; however, they often stated they simply could not locate a qualified one. Taylor wanted to answer that assertion with a list of fully qualified, prepared women that institutions could consider for their top posts. Taylor, who had only missed one NADW meeting in her career, knew that plenty of talented women worked in higher education and possessed the talent and knowledge to lead a college or university. The problem—Taylor and Shavlik agreed—lay in the fact that the all-male networks did not know these women or their qualifications—nor did any venues exist where qualified women regularly interacted with the network of men who recommended newcomers to presidential search committees.

Addressing the lack of women presidents was not a training project—it was a question of how to connect qualified women with males of influence in higher education. "We were trying to get women into other people's networks," said Taylor. "What we wanted to do was identify people who were ready."[9] This meant Taylor needed to develop a way for male higher education leaders to meet and observe the talents of these women so that they could recommend them to open positions. They also needed to convince women they were ready. "Self-selection missed too many [prepared] women because women often have self-doubt and needed encouragement—someone to convince them," recalled Taylor. Together, Taylor and Shavlik set out to create a structure for ACE to introduce talented women to the "old boys' network," and to convince the top women they were prepared for the presidencies. As Judith Prince, vice chancellor at the University of South Carolina Upstate, once stated, "Emily Taylor taught us: it was not a woman's ability that prevented women from being college Presidents; it was access."[10] Before they could launch their program, though, they had to convince funders to invest in their system. And, to apply for funding, they needed to know the current status of women in higher education leadership.[11]

However, when Taylor arrived in Washington DC, ACE did not even know exactly how many women led higher education institutions. Taylor realized that convincing Heyns or grant-makers to invest in OWHE without concrete data would be difficult. Taylor implemented at OWHE the same data-based tracking tactics deans of women employed across the twentieth century (see chapter 6). The data she collected in 1975 revealed the steep mountain left to climb. Only 23 of the nation's 2,656 higher education presidents outside of Catholic women's colleges were female—less than 1 percent. The only place women had made significant headway into presidencies lay in the Catholic institutions for women where 109 nuns had ascended into presidencies via their orders. Overall, with the religious institutions included, only 5 percent of the accredited colleges and universities had women presidents. Strikingly, only five of the large coeducational schools which historically housed deans of women had appointed women to their top post. In fact, even in women's colleges only 49 of the 109 colleges employed women to lead their operations. From this baseline data, OWHE began an annual report on women's progress in achieving presidency appointments. Taylor used these statistics to detail women's top-level placement and how women fit into the different types of college and university leadership roles. The tracking Taylor implemented eventually became the OWHE *Sourcebook* (1988), the *ACE FactBook on Women in Higher Education* (1991) and continues today in the ACE Inclusive Excellence Group. Most importantly, in 1975, it provided the information Taylor and Shavlik needed to convince grant-makers to invest.[12]

Clearly, OWHE had a big task ahead. Just as early deans of women Marion Talbot, Ada Comstock, and Mary Bidwell Breed must have felt overwhelmed by the sheer magnitude of building an infrastructure to support the young women pouring onto their campuses in the early 1900s, Taylor, Shavlik, and their one secretary faced a daunting task with little structure or staff to accomplish it. To achieve their goals, they had to get creative about labor, and they decided to enlist the women they identified for leadership roles, just as student leaders had always provided the peoplepower to accomplish a dean of women's work.

For funding, Taylor turned to the networks she knew best: NADW women and the historic philanthropic partners in women's education efforts. Martha Peterson served on the Exxon Board of Directors beginning in 1975, and the company's foundation made a $6,915 grant to the OWHE. The Carnegie Corporation of New York, which had invested $181,000 between 1959 and 1963 in the continuing education programs spawned by the ACE Commission on the Education of Women (CEW), became OWHE's most substantial supporter. In 1977, Carnegie invested $195,000 in Taylor and Shavlik's initiative to identify women leaders and network them into the "old boys' club." Called NIP (and later the ACE Network), this Carnegie-sponsored initiative became the backbone of OWHE, establishing a system to identify women ready for presidencies and connect them with search committees. Over the life of OWHE, Carnegie provided over $700,000 to NIP's goals—making it possible to increase the number of women presidents from 5 percent in 1975 to 23 percent by 1990. In these early years, Taylor and Shavlik also convinced Mariam Chamberlain at the Ford Foundation, the Johnson Foundation, the National Institute for Education, and the Fund for the Improvement of Post Secondary Education to invest in OWHE.[13]

With the Carnegie Corporation grant, Taylor and Shavlik launched NIP in 12 states, and they focused on six states apiece to begin the network. Though they each employed different strategies in their states, the goal was the same: establishing a national network of women higher education leaders who could become visible to male leaders. With little budget, the two criss-crossed their states, lodging overnight in the homes of women in the network and identifying prospective members and presidents as they went. Taylor recalled she once eliminated a woman from the "immediately ready" list because, while she stayed at her home, she realized the woman did not subscribe to the newspaper, claiming she was too busy to read it. Taylor felt women needed a wide vision for how an institution fit into its community, region, and nation. Overall, though, the work went quickly as women were hungry for the opportunity to advance and improve their skills, and they welcomed Taylor and Shavlik in their homes. By NIP's second year in 1978, 41 states had a program, with all 50 and Puerto Rico on board soon after. From these state networks, Taylor and Shavlik identified the women most prepared to assume presidencies.[14]

Shavlik had the inspiration to develop NIP as a network, not simply another organization on top of an organization. Both Taylor and Shavlik knew NIP needed to be nimble and able to conform to the state and region in which its women worked—successful strategies in Massachusetts would not work in Mississippi and vice versa. Each state had a NIP coordinator whom Taylor and Shavlik chose carefully, selecting women who were already prepared to assume a presidency, whenever possible. Working with OWHE to develop a state's strategy, the coordinator oversaw a state-wide NIP program that provided less advanced women the advantage of growth, networking, and opportunities to strengthen each other's skills. This replicated the networks provided by the state deans associations like the Ohio Association of Deans of Women where Taylor received much of her mentoring and preparation early in her career. Also, just as deans of women with small staffs had historically relied on the work of the AWS and the IAWS leaders to coordinate efforts, OWHE relied on the work of the state coordinators and the team each coordinator assembled to produce the programming. At the same time, OWHE provided the state coordinator with an increased profile in the line of sight of male decision-makers.

Just as deans in the past had used the IAWS to identify women student leaders, the NIP identified a pool of women administrative leaders at the campus level, with the most accomplished singled out for state and regional roles. From the regional networks, Taylor and Shavlik culled the strongest leaders and prepared them to move into a presidency—together they amplified the deaning-IAWS vocational guidance methods into a magnified leadership development strategy. "We made very few mistakes" in our identification of the top women recalled Taylor, who knew OWHE would fail if their identified women proved lacking. "I can almost count on the fingers of one hand in the fifty-six National Forums that I attended, the number of people that I consider to be mistakes. And even then, they weren't mistakes in somebody's opinion because someone had recommended them and said that they were ready for a national forum. But, I didn't find them ready myself."[15] She considered the quality of their candidates paramount; any missteps or failures would damage the prospects of advancement for the women who did possess the skills and talent to become college presidents.

Once they identified women ready to ascend, OWHE invited these women to their national forums held across the country. Each national forum included approximately 30 participants—usually 20 identified women and ten male presidents. These seminars reflected a derivation of the early deans of women's vocational conferences that Taylor helped plan at Ohio State as a student, placing qualified women into venues where they could meet those influential in hiring college presidents. Just as Kate Hevner Mueller positioned Taylor to give a speech in front of NADW President Hilda Threlkeld in 1945, Taylor now placed scores of prepared women in front of male leaders across the country so that men could witness the women's talent. Taylor insisted the topics discussed be central issues facing higher education—not topics about women's advancement or their need for preparation. As ACE women's commission chair Jean O'Barr of Duke University recalled: "People...men...didn't believe that women had the substance [to become presidents] so Emily wanted the men and women in the same room to talk about substantial issues."[16] Taylor knew the men attending NIP events needed to experience the women's expertise in areas that men considered to be most important to higher education—finance, enrollment, and curriculum development.[17]

To do this, O'Barr recalled Taylor had a specific structure for her national forums. First, she relied upon the ACE name to draw male (and the few female) presidents to the event, and always started the events just before lunch. "Emily taught me never to feed people until you tell them what you want them to talk about," quipped O'Barr, noting that Taylor never left her guests to make idle chitchat at the national forums.[18] Instead, she always introduced a substantive, current, topic at the lectern during the forum welcome, so the guests would naturally turn to that subject for discussion at their tables when the meal was served. This insured that the conversation would be directed in a way that allowed men to witness women's leadership and qualifications on serious issues facing higher education. At the same time, the women had an opportunity to recognize that they could "play in these roles," and begin to envision themselves as a college president.[19]

While the national forum structure worked well, OWHE found that racial prejudice needed close attention in order to steward minority women's advancement in higher education. By 1980, OWHE established specialized programming to address the specific challenges women of color faced. The office sought $30,000 of funding from the Donner Foundation which supported the identification of 351 women of color to advance. In addition, OWHE hired Felecia Davis to work with the Focus on Minority Women's Advancement (FMWA), and Davis' presence at OWHE as a minority woman lent credibility to the office among women of color. "The OWHE worked diligently to include women from the historically black colleges as well as the Asian and Hispanic women emerging in leadership roles," recalled O'Barr, who chaired the OWHE's Commission on Women in Higher Education and participated in NIP forums. "The meetings sponsored by the OWHE were the most diverse of my administrative experience and provided a welcome base to explore issues of race, ethnicity and gender."[20]

As the Forums developed, OWHE partnered with other associations interested in women's professional advancement in higher education. These included NADW (which had been renamed the National Association of Women Deans, Administrators and Counselors); American Association of Colleges in conjunction with Bernice Sandler's Project on the Status and Education of Women; the American Association of State Colleges and Universities; the National Association of Land Grant Colleges and Universities; and the National Association of Black Colleges and Universities, to name a few.[21] Both Taylor and Shavlik welcomed other organizations under the tent in order to maximize results for the benefit of women's leaderships through collaborative work. However, ACE sometimes worried its organization lost credit for OWHE's progress.[22]

Grooming Candidates for Success

With the forum structure set, the OWHE began functioning like the women's appointment bureaus that Taylor saw in her earliest training with Grace S. M. Zorbaugh at Ohio State University. Taylor hired Judy Touchton early in OWHE's development after Touchton proved herself during an internship. A long-time career services employee at the University of Maryland, Touchton took the old role of "appointment secretary" and began to handle NIP follow-up and advise women closely as they applied for presidencies, assisting with their applications and preparation. OWHE staff matched candidates with search committees, sending forward women whose strengths fit with needs of a particular institution. At each forum, OWHE produced a book including each forum participant's picture and a one-page vitae so that a listing of these qualified women could circulate among the forum participants—especially the male ACE members. This enabled male forum attendees to share a woman's contact information when they received informal presidential search queries. The old "occupational bureau" model worked well. Within a year of the first National Forum in 1977, three of the attendees attained presidencies. And in the first seven forums, 360 women ranging from assistant vice presidents to provosts to associate deans attended, and 103 of them advanced into higher leadership roles—14 into presidencies,

25 into vice presidencies or provostships, 26 into deanships, and the remainder into other leadership roles.[23]

This success derived from the close personal mentoring Taylor, Shavlik, and Touchton gave each national forum woman, advising them individually on the steps necessary to advance. The OWHE team counseled women on everything from the institutional match between a university and the NIP applicant, to interview strategies and the candidate's appearance. The OWHE always advocated for a conservative presentation, dark suits, serious hairstyles, and moderate cosmetics—even when women preferred otherwise. Shavlik recalled having to tell one woman she needed to wear sensible pumps and to leave her favored cowboy boots at home until she obtained her presidency. OWHE also involved former women presidents in this mentoring effort, creating the Senior Associates program, which included Sister Ann Ida Gannon, past president of Mundelein College; Rosemary Park, past president of Barnard and Connecticut Colleges; Willa Player, past president of Bennett College in Greensboro, North Carolina; and Marjorie Downing Wagner, who led a public four-year institution, Sonoma State University. The senior associates provided the same one-on-one advice for forum participation when the pipeline expanded past the capability of the small staff at OWHE. After women obtained a presidency, the associates and OWHE continued as career coaches available to discuss difficult challenges at their institutions.[24]

While these efforts reflected the informal networks men had established for grooming upcoming male leaders in higher education, Taylor drew her methods from the long-tested career placement and leadership development practices the earliest deans of women began in the 1900s. Since Marion Talbot defined the profession of deaning, the one-on-one casework approach underlay the mentoring methods for women's career advancement and leadership development. Taylor and Shavlik worked hard to keep the NIP nimble and not let "the structure overwhelm the work" of one-on-one mentoring between women. Shavlik recalled that "it was a fight sometimes because the women were very organized and sometimes wanted to create bylaws and things."[25]

However, the real work—as Taylor and Shavlik saw it—was to identify the most intelligent, well-rounded, experienced women and to guide them into presidencies—just as the two had previously done with the IAWS, grooming top women students to move into professional careers. A decade after the OWHE opened, Taylor and Shavlik garnered over 6,000 NIP participants and the office played a significant role in doubling the number of women presidents to 10 percent, increasing women presidencies from 148 to 300 by 1985. By 1987, 24 percent of the nation's women higher education presidents came from OWHE national forums. Today, NIP continues as the ACE Women's Network, still connecting women to help them advance in college administration.[26]

Alongside the NIP, Taylor cultivated OWHE's Commission on Women in Higher Education. ACE had a tradition for each office to have a commission,

Figure 7.1 Kala Stroup, Emily Taylor, and Donna Shavlik attend an American Council on Education National Identification Program event

and Taylor clearly understood the benefit of developing a coalition of dedicated leaders outside of ACE that could pressure the organization to implement needed changes. Deans of women had historically sought influential women to serve on university and college boards, and the AAUW reinforced this by accrediting institutions which had women serving on boards of trustees. Throughout its 38-year history, the OWIIE commission held ACE accountable for funding and supporting the mission of women's leadership in higher education, especially as changing ACE leadership questioned OWHE's purpose and value.[27]

While Taylor and Shavlik worked out plans for funding and implemented the NIP and commission, the office regularly fielded Title IX questions. To answer these, Taylor and Shavlik built a "self-evaluation" tool for institutions and published it as *Institutional Self Evaluation: The Title IX Requirement*. To determine the criteria that mattered in assessing women's equity in higher education, Taylor and Shavlik turned to the old AAUW institutional evaluation model that Marion Talbot and her colleagues developed at the turn of the century. In what some scholars have called an "early form of affirmative action," AAUW measured whether a college or university provided women students with adequate and appropriate living arrangements, dining facilities, and access to the same educational program men studied—the full liberal arts curriculum. It also insisted universities and colleges provide representation for women in administration, and suitable rank for women faculty members based on their educational attainment, along with equal pay based on that rank. Finally, AAUW insisted that women be represented in the faculty, the administration (through a dean of women), and on the institution's board of trustees. Lifelong members of AAUW, both Taylor and Shavlik were well-acquainted with this accreditation system that gauged whether a college or university included women sufficiently. Building these criteria into an updated checklist of sorts, Taylor and Shavlik guided institutions to use the time-tested criteria of AAUW to meet the requirements of Title IX. ACE distributed over 8,000 copies of *Self Evaluation*, embedding the legacy of AAUW's commitment to women's education into the application of Title IX. Today, campuses still use the premises Taylor and Shavlik outlined as guiding principles, carrying out AAUW and early deans' vision for inclusion in today's higher education communities.[28]

While traveling the country addressing the requirements of Title IX on the nation's campuses, Taylor and Shavlik could not help but notice how quickly institutions removed the remaining dean of women positions in favor of male deans of students. Both believed that the elimination of the dean of women's position would lead to the demise of IAWS—and in doing so, remove an important training ground for both women college students and women administrators. In an effort to save the one sanctioned place for women in academic administration, Taylor and Shavlik met with the Health Education and Welfare department Office for Civil Rights, which wrote the regulations on Title IX, to ask the office to consider allowing the dean of women's position to continue. "It was just a bridge too far," said Shavlik, recalling the civil rights office could not reconcile a dean of women with gender neutrality. Instead, as deans of women disappeared in the 1970s, the women's studies programs and women's centers gained stature on campuses and took on the mantle of women's advocacy in higher education.

With higher education eliminating deans of women, the IAWS dwindled quickly as well. By 1978, the organization—once over 300 chapters strong—had only 50 affiliates and no financial resources. Taylor and Shavlik sought to save what they believed was the essence of the IAWS—leadership training for college women. While the two women organized an effort to save IAWS, Taylor's and Shavlik's friends at KU agreed to host two of the last IAWS national conventions in 1979 and 1980 to keep the organization alive so it could evolve. They obtained a grant from the Johnson Foundation to draw together women from AAUW, NADW, and ACE's OWHE to lead the remaining IAWS student officers through an organizational conversion that would maintain young women's leadership development and intergenerational role models. The result was the creation of an annual leadership training meeting for college women, the National Conference for College Women Student Leaders (NCCWSL). In 1984, Taylor and Shavlik convinced leaders in NADW, American University's Women's Institute, AAUW, and the Association of American College's Project on the Status of Education of Women (led by Bernice Sandler) to join OWHE in order to finance the NCCWSL conference. Today, the IAWS legacy continues in NCCWSL, now sponsored by NASPA and the AAUW.[29]

Passing the Torch

When Taylor retired in 1982 and Shavlik took over as OWHE director and Touchton as associate director, the office was ready to address a new chapter in women's higher education administrative advancement. Instead of women changing themselves to fit into leadership roles, the OWHE set an agenda to change higher education to fit women.[30] This became the focus for the next several years and resulted in a 1989 collection of essays edited by Carol S. Pearson, Shavlik, and Touchton: *Educating the Majority: Women Challenge Tradition in Higher Education*. The women published the last chapter of the book to advance what they termed *The New Agenda of Women for Higher Education*. The office worked to change tenure clocks so women did not have to forgo motherhood, to add daycares to campuses, and to address equal pay scales. The ways in which higher education must change to address women's realities remains the fundamental question regarding the advancement of women in higher education today.

In 1992, *The New Agenda* was revisited, addressing many of these issues. However, as women increasingly accessed higher education leadership roles, some individuals began to question the need for a special program for women. Enough female leaders had ascended to the top rung of colleges and universities that some—men and women alike—thought it time to "mainstream" women's leadership and eliminate mentoring programs like the one embedded inside OWHE. When ACE appointed Stanley O. Ikenberry as president in 1996, the organization began to take the approach that women would ascend to presidencies without a system of identification. When Shavlik retired in the fall of 1997, Ikenberry restructured the OWHE from reporting to the president, and subsumed it under the Vice President for Programs and Analysis, Michael Baer. Though Ikenberry thought OWHE fit well among other programs in that division such as the Office of Minorities in Higher Education and the ACE fellowship program, the move created an odd dynamic as the new OWHE Director, Judith Sturnick, had already served two university presidencies and now reported to an ACE vice president who had never worked as a university president himself.[31] This change by Ikenberry in OWHE's organizational status replicated what happened to deans of women in the 1940s and 1950s as universities subsumed deans of women under male deans of students. The change at ACE, while of a different time and nature, created a similar dynamic. Just as midcentury deans of women lost their direct access to the top university decision-maker, OWHE lost the opportunity to voice women's needs in meetings among the institution's key leaders. Sturnick fought successfully for the OWHE to again report directly to ACE's president. However, under Ikenberry's leadership the OWHE's purpose shifted, becoming an office to serve current women presidents. The ACE leadership decided *not* to fund the longtime dean of women strategies that included "a lot of individual, personal executive counseling to presidents and people who were near moving into presidencies." This removed the support for the deans' time-tested strategies of one-on-one mentoring and occupational bureau assistance. Clearly, under Ikenberry's leadership, the OWHE program shifted radically from the premises Heyns supported when Taylor directed the OWHE and those that Robert Atwell endorsed when Shavlik directed the office.[32]

The concept of mainstreaming eventually spelled the end of OWHE at ACE, and it closed its doors in 2011. However, the NIP (now the ACE Women's Network) and the Commission on the Higher Education of Women (now the Commission on Inclusive Excellence) both continue in the newly created ACE Inclusive Excellence Group. The programs still exist because the large, loyal group of women that Taylor, Shavlik, and Touchton assembled in the NIP and the OWHE Commission has continued to insist to ACE that these efforts are valuable to women leaders. And, in 2012, the Inclusive Excellence Group initiated a new effort, "Moving the Needle," to focus on increasing women's presidencies in higher education.

The results of OWHE were substantial when it was a leadership/placement pipeline under Taylor and Shavlik. Together, the former dean of women and IAWS leader adapted 80 years of deans' knowledge about negotiating women's equity within higher education into a system that increased women's presidencies. When Donna Shavlik retired as director of OWHE 23 years after she and Taylor fashioned the NIP out of the cloth of deaning and self-governance, a network participant commented: "I know very few women in higher education whose career path has not been impacted by ACE/NIP...The conferences, workshops and networks they have promoted throughout the country are, in my opinion, responsible for much of the progress women have made removing barriers...in college and university administration."[33]

While the NIP and the OWHE commission continue today as strong champions for women presidents, ACE eliminated significant portions of deans' proven methods as the organization no longer houses an office that functions as a referral service for women seeking presidencies. And though many women and men alike were ready to mainstream women into the normal flow of presidential searches, the change meant a loss of focus on the steps and preparation deans had long used to advance women into closed areas of the public sphere. Today, the percentage of women presidents stands at 26 percent, only 3 percent higher than when ACE "mainstreamed" women in 1997, and a very long way from the 50 percent vision OWHE once strove to achieve.

* * *

When one takes the longest view of deans of women in higher education administration, Marion Talbot and Emily Taylor stand as bookends on either side of the story of women's advancement into higher education—one entering university administration in 1892 because universities hesitated to admit women students, the other leaving it in 1982 after seeing the number of women presidents in higher education double. The feminist deans of women in the eras between these two women crafted a set of knowledge, skills, and practices that Taylor took to Washington DC. There, she and Shavlik finalized women's permanent place in higher education administration—as presidents of the coeducational institutions that once treated them as only incidental students or rule-bent dormitory supervisors. Taylor's no-nonsense personality and her drive for women's equality enabled her to carve a space for women both inside ACE and within higher education institutions themselves.[34]

Throughout her career, Taylor spent her energy, her intellect, and her savvy to teach women autonomy, and to push US higher education to accept and prepare women as full citizens. She carried Marion Talbot's vision from 1892 forward, influencing thousands of women along the way. She wanted the nation to welcome women equally into the public sphere, and for women themselves to develop their full potential while also enjoying motherhood— something she regretted giving up in her choice of career over marriage. Whether addressing women's employment equity, graduate or professional school access, or stemming violence against women, Taylor spent her life advocating for women—always involving men in her efforts. She never forgot the importance of educating male leaders about women's equity, and carefully cultivated buy-in from men such as KU chancellors Franklin Murphy and W. Clarke Wescoe, and ACE president Roger Heyns who all supported her efforts with funding and influence.

Also, among women, Taylor insisted on creating broad coalitions. In IAWS, that meant including a vast array of college women from sororities to scholarship halls to women's liberation groups. At OWHE, this broad coalition stretched across women's and higher education associations. Through these partnerships of influence, the legacy of deans of women advanced feminism into higher education, securing leadership roles for women. And while offices of deans of women are now artifacts—historical structures rarely remembered by the population at large— their influence continues today, in women's centers, status of women committees, rape crisis counseling efforts, Women's Studies programs and—most importantly—by the women now employed in the faculties and administrations of the nation's colleges and universities.

It has been a long road for women to be welcomed into higher education, though our popular memory tends to start this history in the 1960s. Taylor once mentioned, "[M]any times I've read these histories and they've just omitted...they start with NOW and then they go on to the Women's Liberation Movement and they forget that anything happened there before that."[35] Today many women employed in higher education have subscribed to the notion that feminism and women's activism arose in the academy only late in the 1960s. However, at the turn of the twentieth century deans of women began paving a path that institutions have largely forgotten. As men took over student affairs, borrowing the practices deans of women established, they began to think of these methods as their own inventions.[36] Even in 1950, Kate Hevner Mueller chastised a male colleague for cataloguing "new" practices in guidance and counseling, reminding him that the ideas were not introduced by the men's guidance associations. Alluding to the feminist and racial civil rights activism in deans of women's offices, she told him: "Back in 1910...we didn't call the things...'problems' and we didn't call it orientation or morale building...We didn't know about 'minority groups' as such, but there was, and still is...a lot of talk about 'love your neighbor as yourself,' and 'who is my neighbor?' [Women] were doing a lot of talking about the responsibilities of women to their democratic society...[through] the YWCA [and]...the very active and self-conscious [women's] student government associations."[37]

This forgotten system of women's self-government and deaning thrived under higher education's early differential treatment of women. Incredibly, by 1969, the deans and their 300 AWS chapters served over 200,000 college women. And, while women deans recognized that true equity would end the IAWS and the dean of women role, Taylor vigorously supported such legislation as Title IX and the Equal Rights Amendment. In effect, the ERA represented what Taylor spent her career trying to achieve—equal citizenship for women. In fact, when the news reached Taylor in Lawrence, Kansas, on March 21, 1972, that the ERA was slated to pass the US Senate the next day, she immediately hopped an overnight plane with IAWS executive director Karen Keesling so that the two could watch the historic amendment cross the Senate floor.

After a lifetime of pushing for political change, of teaching young women to see their own talents and to make their own decisions for themselves, Taylor watched from the US Senate balcony on March 22, specially seated by Kansas Senator James Pearson so she and Keesling could stay all day to listen to the arguments unfold.[38] Below Taylor on the Senate floor, the visions of citizenship equity that Marion Talbot imagined—and that Taylor glimpsed in the 1930s and 1940s through Grace S. M. Zorbaugh and Kate Hevner Mueller—seemed to be coming to fruition. As the day drew to a close and the Senate neared its vote, Taylor recalled the Senate Gallery filling with women proponents. The director of the Women's Bureau and Washington DC activists even—one of Taylor's former KU students Deanell Reece Tacha, who was in DC working as a White House Fellow—arrived. "The place was pretty filled up," recalled Taylor. "But we were the only ones...except for the press...who sat through the entire day—every argument—Karen Keesling and I," a dean of women and an IAWS leader representing the legacy of deaning that had taught college women citizenship for almost a century.

Although the ERA never met ratification, Title IX quietly passed in a higher education omnibus act, slipped in as a provision to open graduate and professional schools to women. Title IX did for education what Taylor had hoped the ERA would do for US society, completely removing structural barriers against women's participation. And while Taylor finally gave up on the ERA as becoming too laden with negativity to become law, she remained committed to women's economic and political citizenship. "I don't think I ever gave up trying to explain Title IX and the Executive Order 11246 as amended...But I sure did (give up) on the Equal Rights Amendment. It just became an emotional issue."

Even without the ERA, the United States had changed markedly since her years at Ohio State when she chafed under the parietal curfews limiting her own life. Taylor never stopped watching US society debate women's equity, and until her death in Lawrence, Kansas, on May 1, 2004, she continued to advocate for women's issues. As a testament to her influence at KU and among its alumni, the university opened its performing arts center to hold the number of guests who attended her memorial service. More than one of them there remembered sitting in KU's Hoch Auditorium as first year students, listening to the dean of women welcome them to the university. "Many of you will leave school early to marry. It's a tragedy that you will not finish your education—society should be able to benefit from your talents." The echoes of her speech had spurred many of them to pursue both career and marriage.

Notes

Preface

1. Lu Hazelrigg and Pat Lewis, Letter to Dean of Women's Office, June 7, 1956, in Dean of Women's Papers (hereafter RG 53/0), Box 1, Dean of Women Chronological Correspondence, Folder: N.D., University of Kansas Libraries, Kenneth Spencer Research Library, University Archives, Lawrence, KS (hereafter UKL).
2. Ibid.
3. Ibid.
4. Ibid.
5. Emily Taylor, Interview by Author, July 4, 1997 (Lawrence, KS).
6. Elder R. Herring, Letter to Deer Park Superintendent H. H. Bodley, April 26, 1938, in Author's Collection of Emily Taylor's Papers, St. Louis, MO (hereafter Author's Collection); Taylor, Interview by Author, July 7, 1997 (Lawrence, KS); Deer Park High School Alumni Association Inc., Letter to Taylor, September 11, 1995, in Author's Collection.
7. The National Association of Deans of Women (NADW) was founded in 1916 and experienced several name changes before being absorbed in 2000 by the National Association of Student Personnel Administrators (NASPA), which was originally established as the National Association of Deans and Advisors of Men (NADAM). NADW changed its name to the National Association of Women Deans and Counselors (NAWDC) in 1956 as a means to include women who had become senior counselors reporting to deans of students. Again, the organization changed its name in 1973 to the National Association of Women Deans, Administrators and Counselors (NAWDAC) to reflect the growing number of women administrators. Finally, in 1990, the organization became the National Association for Women in Education (NAWE) before it merged with NASPA in 2000. For the purposes of clarity, and to illustrate the 84-year history of the group, I will refer to the organization under the acronym NADW. Taylor, Interview by Donna Shavlik, National Association for Women in Education Records (hereafter MS-218), Bowling Green State University Library, Center for Archival Collections, National Student Affairs Archives, Bowling Green, OH (hereafter BGSUCAC); Taylor, Interview by Author, April 14, 1997 (Lawrence, KS); Mueller, Letter to Taylor, 1944, in Mueller papers 1909–1981, Collection c170 (hereafter c170), Indiana University Archives, Indiana University Bloomington Libraries, Bloomington, IN (hereafter IUA).
8. Hilda Threlkeld, Letter to Taylor, June 7, 1946, in Author's Collection; "Dean Recounts Day," *UDK*, November 9, 1962; Taylor, Interview by

Author, July 19, 1998 (Lawrence, KS); Taylor, Interview by Author, April 7, 1997 (Lawrence, KS); Taylor, Interview by Author, July 7, 1997.
9. American Council on Education (ACE), "Taylor, Senior Associate," 1982, in Author's Collection.
10. Donna Shavlik, Interview by Author, March 4, 2014 (New York); ACE, "Taylor, Senior Associate."
11. ACE, "Taylor, Senior Associate."
12. The National Association of Commissions for Women (NACW) was first formed at the Women's Bureau fiftieth anniversary as the Interstate Association of Commissions for Women. In 1975, the organization changed its name to NACW.
13. Sheila Tobias, *Overcoming Math Anxiety* (New York: Norton, 1978); Tobias, Telephone Interview by Author, May 19, 2013.
14. Gail Short Hanson, "Organizational Transformation: A Case Study of the Intercollegiate Association for Women Students," (PhD diss., George Washington University, 1995); Lynn M. Gangone, "The NAWE: An Enduring Legacy," *NASPA Journal About Women in Higher Education* 1, 1 (2008): 1–22; The Women's Institute, "Herstory," 1998, in Author's Collection; National Conference for College Women Student Leaders (NCCWSL), "History of NCCWSL," http://www.nccwsl.org/about/history/; ACE, "Taylor, Senior Associate;" Tobias, *Overcoming Math Anxiety*.
15. NAWE, in MS-218, Committees, Box 12, Folder: Committee Files Nominations Committee, BGSUCAC.
16. Bernice Sandler, Telephone Interview by Author, March 14, 2014.
17. Shavlik, Interview by Author, September 20, 1997 (Lawrence, KS).
18. Taylor, Interview by Author, July 14, 1998 (Lawrence, KS).
19. Shavlik, Interview by Author, September 20, 1997.
20. Taylor, Interview by Author, June 4, 1998 (Lawrence, KS).
21. Shavlik, Interview by Author, September 20, 1997.
22. Taylor, Interview by Author, August 29, 1998 (Lawrence, KS).
23. Susan S. Comer, Letter to Taylor, December 24, 1996, in Author's Collection.
24. M. Kay Harris, Letter to Taylor, December 10, 1974, in Author's Collection.
25. Carole Suzanne Atkins, Letter to Taylor, Unknown Year, in Author's Collection.

INTRODUCTION

1. Sara M. Evans, *Personal Politics: The Roots of Women's Liberation in the Civil Rights Movement and the New Left* (New York: Alfred A. Knopf, 1979).
2. Leila J. Rupp and Verta Taylor, *Survival in the Doldrums: The American Women's Rights Movement, 1945 to the 1960s* (New York: Oxford University Press, 1987).
3. For discussion of men taking over the profession of student affairs, see Robert Schwartz, "How Deans of Women Became Men," *The Review of Higher Education* 20, 4 (Summer 1997): 419–436; and Schwartz, *Deans of Men and the Shaping of Modern College Culture* (New York: Palgrave Macmillan, 2010).

4. See Dorothy Sue Cobble, *The Other Women's Movement: Workplace Justice and Social Rights in Modern America* (Princeton, NJ: Princeton University Press, 2004); Geraldine Jonçich Clifford, *Lone Voyagers: Academic Women in Coeducational Universities, 1870–1937* (New York: Feminist Press at the City University of New York: Distributed by the Talman Co., 1989); Susan Levine, *Degrees of Equality: The American Association of University Women and the Challenge of Twentieth-Century Feminism* (Philadelphia, PA: Temple University Press, 1995).
5. Jana Nidiffer, "More Than 'a Wise and Pious Matron': The Professionalization of the Position of Dean of Women, 1901–1918" (EdD diss., Harvard University, 1994); Nidiffer, "From Matron to Maven: A New Role and New Professional Identity for Deans of Women, 1892 to 1916," *Mid-Western Educational Researcher* 8, 4 (1995): 17–24; Nidiffer, *Pioneering Deans of Women: More Than Wise and Pious Matrons* (New York: Teachers College Press, 2000); Nidiffer, "The First Deans of Women: What We Can Learn from Them," *About Campus* 6 (2002): 10–16; Linda Eisenmann, *Higher Education for Women in Postwar America, 1945–1965* (Baltimore, MD: Johns Hopkins University Press, 2006); Carolyn Terry Bashaw, *"Stalwart Women": A Historical Analysis of Deans of Women in the South* (New York: Teachers College Press, 1999); Janice J. Gerda, "A History of the Conferences of Deans of Women, 1903–1922" (PhD diss., Bowling Green State University, 2004); Gerda, "Gathering Together: A View of the Earliest Student Affairs Professional Organizations," *NASPA Journal* 43, 4 (2006): 147–163; Schwartz, "How Deans of Women Became Men;" Schwartz, *Deans of Men*; Eisenmann, *Historical Dictionary of Women's Education in the United States* (Westport, CT: Greenwood Press, 1998); Eisenmann, "A Time of Quiet Activism: Research, Practice, and Policy in American Women's Higher Education, 1945–1965," *History of Education Quarterly* 45, 1 (2005): 1–17.
6. Christine Stansell, *The Feminist Promise: 1792 to the Present* (New York: Random House, 2010), 212.
7. Beth L. Bailey, *Sex in the Heartland* (Cambridge, MA: Harvard University Press, 1999), 78–80.
8. Kathryn Nemeth Tuttle, "What Became of the Dean of Women? Changing Roles for Women Administrators in American Higher Education, 1940–1980" (PhD diss., University of Kansas, 1996), 25–27; Renee Nicole Lansley, "College Women or College Girls? Gender, Sexuality and in Loco Parentis on Campus" (PhD diss. Ohio State University, 2004), ii–iii; Bailey, *Sex in the Heartland*, 78–79.
9. For in-depth considerations of early deans and the programming they developed, see Nidiffer, *Pioneering Deans*; and Bashaw, *"Stalwart Women."*
10. Gail Short Hanson, "Organizational Transformation: A Case Study of the Intercollegiate Association for Women Students" (PhD diss., George Washington University, 1995), 82, 85.
11. Schwartz, "How Deans of Women Became Men;" Schwartz, *Deans of Men*.
12. Edmund Griffith Williamson, *The Student Personnel Point of View* (Washington, DC: American Council on Education Committee on Student Personnel Work, 1949).
13. Michel Foucault, *Discipline & Punish* (Canada: Random House, 1977).

14. Nidiffer, *Pioneering Deans*, 46.
15. The concept of women as "incidental students" is used throughout this book and comes from Eisenmann, *Higher Education for Women in Postwar America*.
16. Ruth Barry and Beverly Wolf, *Modern Issues in Guidance–Personnel Work* (New York: Bureau of Publications, Teachers College, Columbia University, 1957); Lynn M. Gangone, "Navigating Turbulence: A Case Study of a Voluntary Higher Education Association" (EdD diss., Teachers College, Columbia University, 1999); Tuttle, "What Became of the Dean of Women?" 345–346.
17. Two books that illustrate this view are Marty Jezer, *The Dark Ages, Life in the United States, 1945–1960* (Boston, MA: South End Press, 1982); and Rupp and Taylor, *Survival in the Doldrums*.
18. Linda Nicholson, "Feminism in 'Waves': Useful Metaphor or Not?" *New Politics* XII, 4 (2010), http://newpol.org/node/173.
19. The argument that the second wave of the women's movement was born from women's participation in racial civil rights activism and the New Left belongs to Evans, *Personal Politics*. Another important text supporting this argument is Alice Echols, *Daring to Be Bad: Radical Feminism in America, 1967–1975* (Minneapolis: University of Minnesota Press, 1989). Also see Rupp and Taylor, *Survival in the Doldrums*. Rusty Monhollon credits the KU women's movement to the same influences, while also noting that Taylor contributed to the growth of liberal feminist views at KU, in *This Is America? The Sixties in Lawrence, Kansas* (New York: Palgrave, 2002).
20. William Henry Chafe, *The Paradox of Change: American Women in the 20th Century* (New York: Oxford University Press, 1991), 202.
21. Nicholson, "Feminism in 'Waves'"; Cobble, *The Other Women's Movement*; Emily Taylor, Interview by Author, July 1, 1997 (Lawrence, KS).
22. Dorothy Truex, "Education of Women, the Student Personnel Profession and the New Feminism," *Journal of the National Association of Women Deans and Counselors* 35 (Fall 1971), 13.
23. Barbara Miller Solomon, *In the Company of Educated Women: A History of Women and Higher Education in America* (New Haven, CT: Yale University Press, 1985), xx.
24. Eisenmann, *Higher Education for Women in Postwar America*; Nidiffer, *Pioneering Deans*.
25. Bailey, *Sex in the Heartland*; Cynthia Ellen Harrison, *On Account of Sex: The Politics of Women's Issues, 1945–1968* (Berkeley: University of California Press, 1988). Bailey's excellent consideration of the sexual revolution at KU notes that Taylor must have been supportive of the students' changes in order to assure their success. However Bailey suggests that the students "co-opted" the administration's philosophy regarding creation of responsible adults to advocate for their own rule changes, and does not reference the work Taylor did in the late 1950s and early 1960s to push women students to release the rules.
26. Taylor, Interview by Author, December 13–14, 2003 (Lawrence, KS).
27. Leigh Schmidt, "Installation Remarks: Mystics, Cranks and William James" (Lecture, Washington University in St. Louis, St. Louis, MO, September 3, 2013).
28. Ibid.

1   VISIONS OF ECONOMIC CITIZENSHIP

1. Emily Taylor, Interviews by Author, April 7 and April 14, 1997 (Lawrence, KS).
2. Ibid.
3. Ibid.
4. At Ohio State University (OSU), the women's student government group was called the Women's Self-Government Association (WSGA). The Intercollegiate Association of Women Students (IAWS), the national umbrella group for women's self-governing associations, though, eventually asked all university campuses to name their groups the Associated Women Students or the Association of Women Students (AWS). For clarity, I refer to all campus chapters of women's self-government as AWS.
5. Taylor, Interview by Author, April 7, 1997.
6. Edith Blizzard, "Highlights of the Vocational Information Conferences (VIC) for Women Students," 1937, in Dean of Women Papers (hereafter RG 9/c-2), Box 20, Folder: Deans of Women—Vocational Information Conferences 1936–1943 Programs, Constitution, Agendas, and all related materials (1), Ohio State University Archives, Columbus, OH (hereafter OSUA); Jana Nidiffer, *Pioneering Deans of Women: More Than Wise and Pious Matrons* (New York: Teachers College Press, 2000); Robert Schwartz, "How Deans of Women Became Men," *The Review of Higher Education* 20, 4 (Summer 1997): 419–436; Schwartz, *Deans of Men and the Shaping of Modern College Culture* (New York: Palgrave Macmillan, 2010); Kathryn Nemeth Tuttle, "What Became of the Dean of Women? Changing Roles for Women Administrators in American Higher Education, 1940–1980" (PhD diss., University of Kansas, 1996), 25–27; Grace S. M. Zorbaugh, "Student Economic Problems and the Counselor—with Special Reference to Women Students," *Yearbook: Proceedings of the Seventeenth Annual Meeting of the National Association of Deans of Women* 11 (1933): 115–120.
7. Taylor, Interviews by Author, April 7 and April 14, 1997.
8. Lulu Haskell Holmes, *A History of the Position of Dean of Women in a Selected Group of Co-Educational Colleges and Universities in the United States* (New York: Teachers College, Columbia University, 1939), 15. For the concept of separate spheres see Nancy F. Cott, *The Bonds of Womanhood: "Woman's Sphere" in New England, 1780–1835* (New Haven, CT: Yale University Press, 1977).
9. The concept of Republican Motherhood belongs to Linda K. Kerber, *Women of the Republic: Intellect & Ideology in Revolutionary America* (Chapel Hill: University of North Carolina Press, 1980).
10. Edward H. Clarke, *Sex in Education: or, a Fair Chance for the Girls* (Boston, MA: James R. Osgood and Company, 1873), 19.
11. Susan Zschoche, "Dr. Clarke Revisited: Science, True Womanhood, and Female Collegiate Education," *History of Education Quarterly* 29 4 (1989): 545–569.
12. The 75 percent figure is drawn from Sharon Hartman Strom, *Beyond the Typewriter: Gender, Class and the Origins of Modern American Office Work, 1900–1930* (Urbana and Chicago, IL: University of Illinois Press, 1992), 326. Barbara Miller Solomon, *In the Company of Educated Women: A History of Women and Higher Education in America* (New Haven, CT: Yale

University Press, 1985), 58–61. Also see Carol Lasser, *Educating Men and Women Together: Coeducation in a Changing World* (Urbana, IL: University of Illinois Press with Oberlin College, 1987).
13. On University of Chicago's dean of women see Nidiffer, *Pioneering Deans*. Also see Carolyn Terry Bashaw, *"Stalwart Women": A Historical Analysis of Deans of Women in the South* (New York: Teachers College Press, 1999); and Schwartz, "How Deans of Women Became Men."
14. The Association of Collegiate Alumnae (ACA) and the American Association of University Women (AAUW) are referred to as AAUW throughout the book. The ACA merged with the Southern Association of College Women in 1921, becoming the AAUW. See Nidiffer, *Pioneering Deans*; Schwartz, "How Deans of Women Became Men"; Marion Talbot and Lois Kimball Mathews Rosenberry, *The History of the American Association of University Women, 1881–1931* (Boston, MA: Houghton Mifflin, 1931); Marion Talbot, *More Than Lore: Reminiscences of Marion Talbot, Dean of Women, the University of Chicago, 1892–1925* (Chicago: University of Chicago Press, 1936); and Tuttle, "What Became of the Dean of Women." The idea of "sanitary science," developed by Ellen Swallow Richards, began the home economics movement. Ellen Richards, *The Cost of Living: As Modified by Sanitary Science* (New York: John Wiley, 1900).
15. "Sophonisba Breckinridge, Ph.D. (Political Science) 1901, J.D. 1904," SSA Centennial Celebration Profiles of Distinction Series, http://ssacentennial.uchicago.edu/features/features-breckinridge.shtml. Also see Talbot and Rosenberry, *The History of the AAUW*; Talbot, *More Than Lore*; and Tuttle, "What Became of the Dean of Women."
16. I grouped the meetings influenced by Talbot under the rubric Deans of Women of the Middle West, as does the Bowling Green State University Center for Archival Collections, Bowling Green, OH (hereafter BGSUCAC) which houses the National Association of Deans of Women (NADW) records. See also Janice J. Gerda, "Gathering Together: A View of the Earliest Student Affairs Professional Organizations," *NASPA Journal* 43, 4 (2006): 147–163; Nidiffer, *Pioneering Deans*; Kathryn Sisson Phillips, "Beginnings," *Journal of NADW* 16 (1953): 143–145; Gerda, "A History of the Conferences of Deans of Women, 1903–1922" (PhD diss., Bowling Green State University, 2004); Holmes, *History of the Position*; Mary Ross Potter, Kathryn Philips, Mina Kerr, and Agnes Wells, "Report of Committee on History of the NADW," 1926, in National Association for Women in Education Records (hereafter MS-218), Box 8, Folder: History Committee, BGSUCAC; Schwartz, *Deans of Men*; Schwartz, "How Deans of Women Became Men."
17. For more discussion, see Tuttle, "What Became of the Dean of Women."
18. At the turn of the century, nursing was considered technical and did not require a higher education degree.
19. As quoted in Joyce Antler, *Lucy Sprague Mitchell: The Making of a Modern Woman* (New Haven, CT: Yale University Press, 1987), 130. Alice Freeman Palmer was instrumental in Sprague's appointment as dean of women at the University of California.
20. Nidiffer, *Pioneering Deans*; Association of Collegiate Alumnae (ACA), *Publications of the ACA Magazine* Series III, No. 18 (December 1908); ACA, *Publications of the ACA Register Supplement* Series III (December 1908); ACA, *Publications of the ACA Magazine* Series III, No. 10 (January

1905), 73; ACA, *Publications of the ACA* Series III, No. 13 (February 1906), 72. For the dangers of vocation, see Antler, *Lucy Sprague Mitchell*, 130; and the ACA proceedings of the 1908 conference.
21. ACA, *Contributions towards a Bibliography of the Higher Education of Women* (Boston, MA: Trustees of the Public Library, 1897); ACA, *Publications of the Magazine* (January 1905), 104; Talbot, "Public and Social Service as Vocations for College Women: Together with a Statement of Preparatory Professional Courses Offered by the Colleges Belonging to the Association of Collegiate Alumnae" in *History of the Chicago Association of Collegiate Alumnae, 1888–1917* (Reprint in public domain: Nabu Press, no date); Margaret C. Dollar, "The Beginnings of Vocational Guidance for College Women: The Women's Educational and Industrial Union, the Association of Collegiate Alumnae, and Women's Colleges" (EdD diss., Harvard University, 1992); ACA, *Contributions Towards a Bibliography of the Higher Education of Women* (Boston, MA: Trustees of the Public Library, 1905), 1547; Kate Holladay Claghorn, "Occupation for the College Graduate," *Publications of the ACA Magazine* Series III, No. 3 (February 1900). Also note that Breckinridge lived at Hull House during summers for over ten years beginning in 1907. See Virginia Kemp Fish, "The Hull House Circle: Women's Friendships and Achievements," in *Gender, Ideology, and Action: Historical Perspectives on Womens Public Lives*, ed. Janet Sharistanian (New York: Greenwood Press, 1986).
22. Talbot and Breckinridge used the casework methodology of social work, employing individual interviews as the basis for student counseling. See Tuttle, "What Became of the Dean of Women," 36–40; Holmes, *History of the Position*, 98–106; Nidiffer, *Pioneering Deans*, 102, 120; Jana Nidiffer and Carolyn Terry Bashaw, *Women Administrators in Higher Education: Historical and Contemporary Perspectives* (Albany: State University of New York Press, 2001), 155.
23. Susan Kingsbury's work has been called the formal start for the growing interest surrounding women's employment by Dollar, though clearly AAUW and deans considered the topic a decade before 1908. Dollar, "Beginnings of Vocational Guidance"; Susan Kingsbury, "Efficiency and Wage of Women in Gainful Occupations," *The Publications of the ACA Magazine* Series III, No. 18 (December 1908); Frederik M. Ohles, Shirley M Ohles, and John G. Ramsay, *Biographical Dictionary of Modern American Educators* (Westport, CT: Greenwood Publishing Group, 1997), 191. Also see Talbot and Rosenberry, *The History of the AAUW*, 229–230; Nidiffer, *Pioneering Deans*; William A. Bryan, "May L. Cheney, First President, 1924–1925," ACPA Presidential Profiles, BGSUCAC, http://www2.bgsu.edu/colleges/library/cac/sahp/pdfs/May%20L.%20Cheney_new.pdf.
24. Antler, *Lucy Sprague Mitchell*, 131; Women's Educational and Industrial Union (WEIU), Appointment Bureau, History, 1909–1932 (inclusive), in WEIU Records, 1877–1980 (hereafter B-8), Folders 65, 66, 67, Radcliffe Institute, Harvard University, Schlesinger Library, Cambridge, MA (hereafter SL).
25. The special committee morphed into the Standing Committee on Vocational Opportunities in 1909, appointing two women deans, Coes and Gill (also serving as AAUW president), along with Cheney. See ACA, *Publications of the Magazine* (December 1908); ACA, *Publications of the ACA Register*

Series III, No. 19 (December 1909); National Association of Social Work Foundation, "NASW Social Work Pioneers, Edith Abbot," http://www.naswfoundation.org/pioneers/a/abbott_e.htm; Talbot and Rosenberry, *The History of the AAUW*, 229–230; WEIU, 1909–1913, in B-8, Folder 65: Early Material Re: Appointment Bureau and A.C.A., 1909–1913, SL; Dollar, "Beginnings of Vocational Guidance," 95–99; Holmes, *History of the Position*, 100, Chapter 8; Nidiffer, *Pioneering Deans*, 120.

26. The practices used at eastern women's colleges were not viable options for the newer Midwest schools, which had younger alumni less advanced in professional work. Influential deans included: Ada Comstock (Minnesota; future president of Radcliffe), Mary Potter (Northwestern), Florence Fitch (Oberlin), Eleanor Lord (Goucher College), and Gertrude Martin (Cornell University). See WEIU historical records in B-8, Folder 65: Early Material Re: Appointment Bureau and A.C.A., 1909–1913, SL.

27. Dollar, "Beginnings of Vocational Guidance," 99; Holmes, *History of the Position*; Nidiffer, *Pioneering Deans*, 103; WEIU, in B-8, Folder 65: Early Material Re: Appointment Bureau and A.C.A., 1909–1913, SL.

28. Holmes, *History of the Position*, 98–100; Lois Kimball Mathews, *The Dean of Women* (Boston, MA: Houghton Mifflin Company, 1915), 105–106, 108–126; Nidiffer, *Pioneering Deans*.

29. As quoted in Nidiffer, *Pioneering Deans*, 121.

30. For an in-depth treatment of the emergence of professional associations, see Hugh Hawkins, *Banding Together: The Rise of National Associations in American Higher Education, 1887–1950* (Baltimore, MD: Johns Hopkins University Press, 1992).

31. Dorothy Sue Cobble, *The Other Women's Movement*. For other information, see Mary Anderson, Letter to Sophonisba Breckinridge, May 14, 1923, in Records of the Women's Bureau in the Department of Labor (hereafter RG 86), Box 10, Folder: University of Chicago, Women's Bureau Records, National Archives at College Park, MD (hereafter NACP); Sophonisba Breckinridge, Letter to Mary Anderson, May 24, 1923, in RG 86, Box 10, Folder: University of Chicago, Women's Bureau Records, NACP; Dollar, "Beginnings of Vocational Guidance," 85–87, 93; Nidiffer, *Pioneering Deans*, 79–106.

32. John M. Brewer, *History of Vocational Guidance: Origins and Early Development* (New York: Harper & Brothers, 1942), 59, 148–149; Bryan, "May L. Cheney, First President, 1924–1925"; Dollar, "Beginnings of Vocational Guidance," 98–99; Holmes, *History of the Position*, 100; Nidiffer, *Pioneering Deans*, 120; Phillips, "Beginnings" (1953). Janice Gerda in "A History of the Conferences of Deans of Women" asserts that NADW expanded to involve outside experts who never met with the deans of women in their Middle Western Deans of Women meetings. This assertion overlooks the fact that the deans worked with these same outside experts in AAUW meetings where they caucused regularly, and that some deans of women involved these outside experts in campus vocational conferences. For instance, the WEIU, Russell Sage Foundation, University Settlement of Chicago, Young Women's Christian Association (YWCA), and the American Council on Education (ACE) were well engaged in the network before 1916 when the NADW was founded. To review the NADW program speakers that Gerda considers to be new additions to NADW's repertoire,

see "Second National Convention of Deans of Women," February 26–28, 1917, in MS-218, Box 9, Folder: National Association of Women Deans, Administrators and Counselors (NAWDAC) Convention Programs 1909–1911, 1913, 1914, 1917–1919; NADW, "Fifth National Conference of Deans of Women," 1919, in MS-218, Box 9, Folder: NAWDAC, Convention Programs 1909–1911, 1913, 1914, 1917–1919; "Third National Conference of Deans of Women," February 25–28, 1918, in MS-218, Box 9; NADW, "Eighth Annual Meeting NADW," February 25–26, 1921, in RG 218, Box 9, all from BGSUCAC. The NADW and the Deans of Women of the Middle West, both met between 1917 and 1921 until the two merged. See Nidiffer, *Pioneering Deans*, 129. The NADW made career education a top priority, calling on the eastern schools to adopt the midwestern practice of providing vocational courses for credit. Kathryn Sisson Phillips, *My Room in the World: A Memoir* (New York: Abingdon Press, 1964), 95–98. For an example of the continued networking between the various associations—the NADW, the National Association of Appointment Secretaries (NAAS), the National Vocational Guidance Association (NVGA) and the AAUW—see conference participants in NADW, *Yearbook: Proceedings of the Eighteenth Annual Meeting of the NADW* (Washington, DC: NADW, 1934), 41–43.

33. Alice Kessler-Harris, *In Pursuit of Equity: Women, Men and Quest for Economic Citizenship in the 20th-Century America* (New York: Oxford University Press, 2001), 78–79, 207; Patrick Selmi and Richard Hunter, "Beyond the Rank and File Movement: Mary van Kleeck and Social Work Radicalism in the Great Depression, 1931–1942," *Journal of Sociology & Social Welfare* 28, 2 (2001), 75–100. The Chicago branch of the National Women's Trade Union League of America, once headquartered at the Hull House, became the nexus for Anderson to connect with Breckinridge. One of many books to consider Anderson's link with the Hull House is Dorothy Sue Cobble, *The Other Women's Movement*, 26–27. For other information on the Women's Bureau and deans of women connections, see Women's Bureau, "The Following Are Some of the Most Important Organizaitons with Which Miss Anderson Has Cooperated..." Unknown date, in RG 86, Office Files of the Director, 1918–1948, Box 1, Folder: Anderson, Mary (Director, 1918—June 30, 1944), NACP; Mary Anderson, "341—Speeches: Paper Written by Mary Anderson and Read by Mrs. Field at the Annual Meeting of the Association of Deans of Women, Chicago, Blackstone Hotel, Feb. 23," in RG 86, Public Information Service, Speeches, 1918–1960, Box 2, Folder: #10 (2-23-1922) Anderson, NACP.
34. Phillips, *My Room in the World*, 95–98. Quotations, 96.
35. Mary Anderson, "341—Speeches: Paper Written by Mary Anderson and Read by Mrs. Field at the Annual Meeting of the Association of Deans of Women, Chicago, Blackstone Hotel, Feb. 23." Phillips, *My Room in the World*, 95–98. The body of work critiquing the women's movement for racism and classism is significant. For a sample of the early critiques by women of color see Cherríe Moraga and Gloria Anzaldúa, *This Bridge Called My Back: Writings by Radical Women of Color* (Watertown, MA: Persephone Press Watertown, 1981); Audre Lorde, *Sister Outsider: Essays and Speeches by Audre Lorde* (Freedom, CA: Crossing: Crossing, 1984); and bell hooks, *Ain't I a Woman: Black Women and Feminism* (Boston, MA: South End Press, 1981).

36. With the exception of Helen Bennett, the women from this group of AAUW and Institute of Women's Professional Relations (IWPR) participants were also members of the NADW. See NADW, *Yearbook: Proceedings of the Fifteenth Regular Meeting (Twelfth Annual Meeting) of the NADW* (Washington, DC: NADW, 1928), 249–250. Chase Going Woodhouse served as director of personnel, Woman's College, at the University of North Carolina and was elected in 1944 to the US House of Representatives. Catherine Filene Shouse was the daughter of A. Lincoln and Therese Filene, and granddaughter of William Filene, who founded Filene's Specialty Store. IWPR published reports on occupational avenues for women. See the papers of Catherine Filene Shouse and the IWPR at SL. In addition, for the involvement of the Filenes in vocational guidance and the NVGA see Brewer, *History of Vocational Guidance*, Chapters 5, 6, and 7 and pages 7, 100, 143, 157–158, 167, 246. The role of AAUW in the IWPR may be found in Talbot and Rosenberry, *The History of the AAUW*, 239–241. For Laura Drake Gill on life phases of women, see: ACA, *Publications of the ACA* (December 1908), 5–6.
37. NADW, *Yearbook: Proceedings of the Seventeenth Annual Meeting of the NADW*, 38. For discussion of the National Association of Deans of Men's lack of involvement in the construction of the student personnel and guidance field, see Schwartz, *Deans of Men*. Also see American Council of Guidance and Personnel Associations (CGPA), "CGPA Program," 1941, in RG 86, Office of the Director General Correspondence of the Women's Bureau, 1919–1948, National I–W, Box 35, Folder: NVGA, NACP; and Williamson, *The Student Personnel Point of View*. For NADW and CGPA annual meeting programs, see MS 218, BGSUCAC.
38. Ohio State University, University of Wisconsin, New Jersey College for Women and Bethany College in West Virginia were cited as offering well established vocational conferences. Frieda S. Miller, Letter to M. Y. Greene, June 13, 1949, in RG 86, Office of the Director General Correspondence of the Women's Bureau, 1948–1963, Box 30, Folder: 3-4-2-1 Universities & Colleges, NACP. In this letter, Miller also cited Zorbaugh, "VICs at Ohio State University," *Occupations, The Vocational Guidance Magazine* 17 (February 1939): 413–417; Zorbaugh, "VICs at Ohio State University," *Occupations: The Vocational Guidance Journal* 21, 5 (January 1943): 376–380. See also Louise Stitt, Division of Minimum Wage, Letter to Zorbaugh, September 17, 1942, in RG 86, Box 87, Office of the Director, General Correspondence of the Women's Bureau, 1919–1948, WO–Z, Folder: Z, NACP.
39. ACA, *ACA Magazine* 20, 2 (1910), 19. Zorbaugh presented to NADW on consumption economics. See programs for 1933 and 1935 in NADW, *Yearbook: Proceedings of the Seventeenth Annual Meeting of the NADW*; NADW, *Yearbook: Proceedings of the Nineteenth Annual Meeting of the NADW* (Washington, DC: NADW, 1935). Zorbaugh's employment history included working as a research specialist for the League of Women Voters. She also belonged to the American Economics Association, National Tax Policy League, Association for Labor Legislation, the National Education Association, the Girl Scouts, and the American Association of University Professors. See Ohio State University Archives, "Zorbaugh," OSUA. Zorbaugh followed Teachers College Professor Ruth Strang as the NADW research committee chairperson.

40. Jessica Foster, Letter to George W. Rightmire, March 31, 1926, in Howard Landis Bevis Papers (hereafter RG 3/f), Box 3, Folder: Women: Dean of: 1926–1927; Esther Allen Gaw, "Annual Report of the Dean of Women to the President of OSU," 1931, in RG 9/c-2, Box 1, Folder: Annual Reports 1931; Zorbaugh, "The Ohio State University VICs for Women Students: A Five-Year Survey 1936–1941," 1941, in RG 9/c-2, Box 19, Folder: VIC—Account of VIC 1920–1940; Zorbaugh, "VICs at Ohio State University: A Brief Account," No Date, in RG 9/c-2, Box 19, Folder: VIC—Account of VIC 1920–1940, all in OSUA. Quotation from Zorbaugh, "VICs at Ohio State University" (February 1939). Also see ACA, "Second Session Held at Trinity College, Washington, D.C.," 1917, in MS-218, State Association Files, Box 2, Folder: NAWDAC Inter-Associational File: ACA 1917, BGSUCAC. Breyfogle served on the ACA credentials committee with both Talbot and Breckinridge. ACA, "Publications of the ACA" (February 1906), 97; Gerda, "A History of the Conferences of Deans of Women, 1903–1922," 243.

41. See Holmes, *History of the Position*, 19–21; Zorbaugh, "Summary Statement," 1937, in RG 3/f, Box 38, Folder: Personnel Activities (Personnel Council 1937–1938), OSUA; Nidiffer, *Pioneering Deans*, 94. Also, Comstock and Talbot created vocational arrangements for students during their university years to help young women finance their educations. Ibid., 94–95. For Zorbaugh's approach to part-time placement and vocational counseling, see Zorbaugh, "Part-Time Placing and Vocational Counseling of Women," *Educational Research Bulletin* 11, 16 (December 1932): 426–432. For discussion of the use of loans in Ohio higher education, see Esther Allen Gaw, "Techniques Used in the Office of a Dean of Women, Educational Research Bulletin," 1930, in RG 9/c-2, Box 5, Folder: Dean of Women Education, College of, 1954–1955 Thru Honoraries–Membership Lists, 1946–1951; "The Fourth Annual Conference of the Ohio Deans of Women," 1928, in RG 9/c-2, Box 9, Folder: Dean of Women: Ohio Association of Women Deans, Administrators and Counselors—Historical Records: 1927–1966, both in OSUA.

42. Zorbaugh, "VICs at Ohio State University: A Brief Account," in RG 9/c-2, Box 19, Folder: VIC—Account of VIC 1920–1940, OSUA.

43. Zorbaugh, "VICs at Ohio State University," *Occupations* 17 (February, 1939). See also Zorbaugh, "Report of the Annual VIC for Women Students of Ohio State University under the Auspices of the Dean of Women's Office," November 7–10, 1932, in RG 9/c-2, Box 19, Folder: VIC Historical File OSU 1932–1938; Zorbaugh, "Ohio State University Dean of Women's Office Progress Report of the Vocational Information Committee Serving the Women Students, 1934–1935," in RG 3/f, Box 7, Folder: Women: Dean of 1935; Zorbaugh, "Progress Report of the VIC Serving the Women Students, 1934–1935," in RG 9/c-2, Box 19, Folder: VIC Historical File OSU 1932–1938; Zorbaugh, "1937–1938 Ohio State University VICs for Women Students," in RG 9/c-2, Box 20, Folder: Deans of Women—VIC 1936–1943 Programs, Constitution, Agendas, and All Related Materials (1); Zorbaugh, "VICs for Women Students, Ohio State University 1937–1938: Progress Report Covering 1937–1938," in RG 9/c-2, Box 20, Folder: Deans of Women—VIC 1936–1943 Programs, Constitution, Agendas, and all related materials (1); Zorbaugh, "VICs at

Ohio State University," in RG 9/c-2, Box 2, Folder: Dean of Women's Office—VIC Historical File 1938–1942; Zorbaugh, "The Ohio State University VICs for Women Students: A Five-Year Survey 1936–1941," in RG 9/c-2, Box 19, Folder: VIC—Account of VIC 1920–1940; Zorbaugh, "Appreciation of the University VICs for Women Students Expressed by Participants & Visitors" September 8, 1941, in RG 3/f, Box 15, Folder: Dean of Women 1941–1942; Zorbaugh, "VICs at Ohio State University: A Brief Account," in RG 9/c-2, Box 19, Folder: VIC—Account of VIC 1920–1940, all in OSUA.

44. Of those who met with their dean of women, only 13 percent said the dean had extensive knowledge of vocational guidance—though 25 percent felt they received good advice. Eunice Mae Acheson, *The Effective Dean of Women: A Study of the Personal and Profesional Characteristics of a Selected Group of Deans of Women* (Chicago: University of Chicago Press, 1932), 39, 46; Zorbaugh, "VICs at Ohio State University" (February 1939).

45. Esther Allen Gaw, "Techniques Used in the Office of a Dean of Women, Educational Research Bulletin," in RG 9/c-2, Box 5, Folder: Dean of Women Education, College of, 1954–1955 Thru Honoraries–Membership Lists, 1946–1951; "Report of the YWCA of the Ohio State University," 1931–1932, in RG 3/f, Box 4, Folder: Annual Report: YWCA (OSU): 1932; Office of the Dean of Women, "1936 VIC for Women Students Conference Program," in RG 9/c-2, Box 19, Folder: VIC Historical File OSU 1932–1938; Office of the Dean of Women, "Highlights of the VICs for Women Students," 1936, in RG 9/c-2, Box 19, Folder: VIC Historical File OSU 1932–1938; Zorbaugh, "The Ohio State University VICs for Women Students: A Five-Year Survey 1936–1941," in RG 9/c-2, Box 19, Folder: VIC—Account of VIC 1920–1940, all in OSUA.

46. "Culture's out; Really Serious," *Cleveland Ohio Plain Dealer*, November 17, 1935.

47. Strom, *Beyond the Typewriter*, 387–389; Zorbaugh, "VICs at Ohio State University" (February 1939); Zorbaugh, "The Ohio State University VICs for Women Students: A Five-Year Survey 1936–1941," in RG 9/c-2, Box 19, Folder: VIC—Account of VIC 1920–1940, OSUA.

48. Quotation from newspaper clippings, "Report of the Publicity Committee for the VICs, 1935," in RG 9/c-2, Box 20, Folder: VIC: Publicity Committee: VICs: 1935, OSUA.

49. Ibid.; Edith Blizzard, "Highlights of the VICs for Women Students," in RG 9/c-2, Box 20, Folder: Deans of Women—VIC 1936–43 Programs, Constitution, Agendas, and all related materials (1); Zorbaugh, "The Ohio State University VICs for Women Students: A Five-Year Survey 1936–1941," in RG 9/c-2, Box 19, Folder: VIC—Account of VIC 1920–1940, both in OSUA.

50. Elaine Tyler May, *Homeward Bound: American Families in the Cold War Era* (New York: Basic Books, 1988), 49.

51. Office of the Dean of Women, "Highlights of the VICs for Women Students," in RG 9/c-2, Box 19, Folder: VIC Historical File OSU 1932–1938, OSUA.

52. Women's Bureau, "Speeches," in RG 86, Office of the Director General Correspondence of the Women's Bureau, 1919–1948, Box 87, Folder: Z,

NACP; Office of the Dean of Women, "VICs for Women Students," 1937, in RG 86, Office of the Director General Correspondence of the Women's Bureau, 1919–1948, V, Box 53, Folder: Vocational Information for College Women, NACP. Also see Zorbaugh, "A Brief of Year by Year Developments," in RG 9/c-2, Box 19, Folder: VIC—Accounting of VIC 1920–1940; Zorbaugh, "Report of the Annual VIC for Women Students of Ohio State University under the Auspices of the Dean of Women's Office," in RG 9/c-2, Box 19, Folder: VIC Historical File OSU 1932–1938; Zorbaugh, "Ohio State University Dean of Women's Office Progress Report of the Vocational Information Committee Serving the Women Students, 1934–1935," in RG 3/f, Box 7, Folder: Women: Dean of 1935; Zorbaugh, "VICs for Women Students, Ohio State University 1937–1938: Progress Report Covering 1937–1938," in RG 9/c-2, Box 20, Folder: Deans of Women—VIC 1936–1943 Programs, Constitution, Agendas, and all related materials (1); Zorbaugh, "Appreciation of the University VICs for Women Students Expressed by Participants & Visitors," in RG 3/f, Box 15, Folder: Dean of Women 1941–1942; Zorbaugh, "The Ohio State University VICs for Women Students: A Five-Year Survey 1936–1941," in RG 9/c-2, Box 19, Folder: VIC—Account of VIC 1920–1940, all in OSUA. Florence Jackson's AAUW service is noted in ACA, *Journal of the ACA* XI, No. 10 (June 1917), 688–691.

53. Bibliographies are found in VIC, "Vocations and Leisure Time Activities: A List of Books, Pamphlets and Periodical Articles," November 16–19, 1937, in RG 9/c-2, Box 20, Folder: Dean of Women—VIC History 1930s–1940s; and VIC for Women Students, "Prepare for What?: A Selected List of Recent Books, Pamphlets and Periodical Articles on Women in Vocations," 1941, in RG 9/c-2, Box 20, Folder: Dean of Women's Office—VIC Historical File 1938–1942, both in OSUA. Zorbaugh included citations such as: Joan Beauchamp, *Women Who Work* (New York: International Publishers, 1937); National Industrial Conference Board, *Women Workers and Labor Supply* (New York: National Industrial Conference Board, 1936); Sophonisba Breckinridge, *Women in the Twentieth Century: A Study of Their Political, Social and Economic Activities* (London: McGraw-Hill Book Company, 1933); Women's Bureau and Mary Veronica Dempsey, *The Occupational Progress of Women, 1910 to 1930* (Washington, DC: US Government Printing Office, 1933); Edith Valet Cook, *The Married Woman and Her Job* (National League of Women Voters, 1936); Charles L. Cooper, "Major Factors Involved in the Vocational Choices of Negro College Students" (PhD diss., Cornell University, 1935); Faye Philip Everett, *The Colored Situation: A Book of Vocational and Civic Guidance for the Negro Youth* (Boston: Meador Publishing Co., 1936); Catherine Filene, *Careers for Women* (Boston, New York: Houghton Mifflin Company, 1920); Doris Elsa Fleischman Bernays, *An Outline of Careers for Women: A Practical Guide to Achievement* (Garden City, NY: Doubleday, Doran and Company, 1931); Helen Christene Hoerle and Eleanor Roosevelt, *The Girl and Her Future* (New York: H. Smith and R. Haas, 1932); IWPR, *Directory of Colleges, Universities and Professional Schools Offering Training in Occupations Concerned with Business and Industry* (New London, CT: IWPR, 1937); Susan Kingsbury, *Economic Status of University Women in the U.S.A.: Report of the Committee on Economic and Legal Status of*

Women, American Association of University Women in Cooperation with the Women's Bureau, United States Department of Labor (Washington, DC: US Government Printing Office, 1939); Human Engineering Laboratory, *Characteristics Common to Professional Women in Law and Other Non-Structural Fields* (Hoboken, NJ: Human Engineering Laboratory, 1938); Catharine Oglesby, *Business Opportunities for Women* (New York, London: Harper, 1932); Adah Peirce, *Vocations for Women* (New York: Macmillan Company, 1933); IWPR, *Proceedings of the Conference on Women's Work and Their Stake in Public Affairs, Mar. 28-29-30, 1935, the Hotel Astor, New York City* (New London, CT: IWPR, 1935); Louis H. Sobel and Joseph Samler, *Group Methods in Vocational Guidance, with Specific Reference to the Economic Adjustment Problems of Jewish Youth* (New York: Furrow Press, 1938); Thomas Wilson Steen, *The Vocational Choices of Students Whose Religious Beliefs Limit Their Occupational Opportunities* (Chicago: University of Chicago Libraries, 1939); Hilda Threlkeld, "The Educational and Vocational Plans of College Seniors: In Relation to the Curricula and the Guidance Programs in Forty-Five Pennsylvania Colleges" (New York: AMS Press, 1935). Other vocational information may be found in Zorbaugh, "Report of the Annual VIC for Women Students of Ohio State University under the Auspices of the Dean of Women's Office," in RG 9/c-2, Box 19, Folder: VIC Historical File OSU 1932-1938; and Zorbaugh, "The Ohio State University VICs for Women Students: A Five-Year Survey 1936-1941," in RG 9/c-2, Box 19, Folder: VIC—Account of VIC 1920-1940, both in OSUA.

54. Esther Allen Gaw, "We the Deans," *The Journal of Higher Education* XI, No. 5 (May 1940): 262-268; Office of the Dean of Women, "VICs for Women Students," 1937, in 9/c-2, Box 19, Folder: VIC Historical File OSU 1932-1938, OSUA; Ohio Association of Deans of Women (OADW), "Speakers Bureau," 1939, in 9/c-2, Box 9, Folder: Dean of Women: Ohio Association of Women Deans, Administrators, and Counselors—Meeting Programs, 1968-1969, OSUA; Zorbaugh, "VICs at Ohio State University" (February 1939), 6-7; Zorbaugh, "The Ohio State University VICs for Women Students: A Five-Year Survey 1936-1941," in RG 9/c-2, Box 19, Folder: VIC—Account of VIC 1920-1940, OSUA; Zorbaugh, "VICs at Ohio State University" (January 1943). Zorbaugh also produced a bibliography in her role as NADW research committee chair: Zorbaugh, "Report of the Committee on Research," *Proceedings of the Twenty-First Annual Meeting of the NADW* 15 (June 1937): 61-77.

55. Zorbaugh, "Progress Report of the VIC Serving the Women Students, 1934-1935," in RG 9/c-2, Box 19, Folder: VIC Historical File OSU 1932-1938, OSUA. The following newspapers published this rationale for the vocational conferences: *Ironton Ohio News, Hudson Ohio Times, Cuyahoga Falls Ohio News, Bucyrus Ohio Democrat, Akron Ohio Democrat, Lebanon Ohio Star* and the *Ohio State Journal*. The *Columbus Dispatch*, the *Columbus Citizen*, the *Ohio State University Lantern*, and the *Cleveland Ohio Plain Dealer* also covered the conference. The Publicity Committee for the VIC that year had over 50 pages of newspaper clippings on the conference. See VIC Publicity Committee, "Selection of Newsclippings," November 1935, in RG 9/c-2, Box 20, Folder: VIC: Publicity Committee: VICs: 1935, OSUA.

56. OADW, "Spring Meeting, 1939, Marietta, Ohio," 1939, in RG 9/c-2, Box 9, Folder: Ohio Assoc. of Women Deans: Board Meeting Minutes: 1931–1954, OSUA.
57. Ibid; OADW, 1939–1959, in RG 9/c-2, Box 9, Folder: Dean of Women: Ohio Association of Women Deans, Administrators and Counselors—Newsletters 1939–1959, OSUA.
58. Taylor perceived OSU Dean Esther Allen Gaw as lacking the feminist activism Zorbaugh possessed. Still, Gaw's willingness to foster Zorbaugh's vocational efforts indicate support for feminist aims. Gaw may have been limited by the university's lack of support for women's education. For instance, the dean of women did not serve on the faculty council on student affairs until 1927, and then only as an ex officio member. Dean of Men Joseph Park served as chairman of the council. The Office of Student Relations, "A Brief History of the Council on Student Affairs, 1920–1958," 1958, in RG 9/c-2/3 Box 3, Folder: Dean of Women—Council on Student Affairs—A Brief History 1920 to 1958, OSUA; Kate Hevner Mueller, Letter to Margaret C. Disert, August 6, 1942, in Dean of Women Records c165, Box 165, Folder: 1942–1943 Mueller—Personal, Indiana University Archives, Bloomington, IN.
59. Zorbaugh, "VICs at Ohio State University" (January 1943). Stitt, who spoke at OSU's vocational conferences, was Ohio's Director of Minimum Wage, and active in the Ohio Consumers' League before taking a job as an industrial economist with the Women's Bureau. See Landon R. Y. Storrs, *Civilizing Capitalism: The National Consumers' League, Women's Activism, and Labor Standards in the New Deal Era* (Chapel Hill: University of North Carolina Press, 2000), 221. Marguerite W. Zapoleon, also from Ohio, attended NADW, CGPA and NVGA meetings regularly, first as an employee of the US Department of Education and later as the Women's Bureau's chief of employment opportunities. Zapoleon would author the 1940s bureau bulletins on employment outlooks for women in various fields of work, and serve on the NVGA executive committee. Though she declined the opportunity, the NVGA invited her to be president in 1948, and she edited the NVGA's journal, then known as *The Vocational Guidance Quarterly*, in 1953 and 1954. Zapoleon graduated from the University of Cincinnati and took summer courses in vocational guidance at Columbia University's Teachers College. See CGPA, "Preliminary Announcement Convention Program CGPA," 1947, in RG 9/c-2, Box 7, Folder: National Association of Deans of Women (NADW) Convention 1947, OSUA; National Career Development Association, "Reclaiming Our History: The NCDA Journal Editors (1911–2011)," *The Career Development Quarterly*, www.ncda.org/aws/NCDA/pt/sp/cd quarterly_history; Brewer, *History of Vocational Guidance*, 117; Zapoleon, Letter to John L. Bergstresser, January 30, 1948, in RG 86, Office of the Director General Correspondence of the Women's Bureau, 1919–1948 Cha–Chau, Box 10, Folder: University of Chicago, NACP; Zapoleon, Letter to Raymond Hatch, June 1, 1949, in RG 86, Office of the Director General Correspondence of the Women's Bureau, 1948–1963 Correspondence File, 1948–1953, Box 30, Folder: 3-4-1-2 Counselors, Guidance, Placement Officers, NACP.
60. Zapoleon, Letter to Gwendolyn S. Crawford, May 19, 1947, in RG 86, Box 1, Division of Research Leaflets, 1938–1948, Folder: Vocational Leaflet,

1947—"Your Job Future after College," NACP. See same box and file for further information on the effort. For the leaflet see Women's Bureau, *Your Job Future after College* (Washington, DC: U.S. Government Printing Office, 1947).
61. Frieda S. Miller, "Series of Letters," in RG 86, Division of Research, Leaflets 1938–1949, Box 1, Folder: Vocational Leaflet, 1947 *Your Job Future After College*, NACP; Zapoleon, Letter to Mueller, March 22, 1948, in RG 86, Office of the Director General Correspondence of the Women's Bureau, 1919–1948, National I–W, Box 35, Folder: NVGA, NACP.
62. Alice J. Archibald, Letter to Miller, April 2, 1951, in RG 86, Office of the Director, General Correspondence of the Women's Bureau, 1948–1953, Box 55, Folder: 4-6-2-1 Vocational Guidance Leaflet for High School Girls & College Girls Correspondence, NACP; Sue Nettel, Letter to Miller, May 26, 1947, in RG 86, Division of Research, Leaflets 1938–1949, Box 1, Folder: Vocational Leaflet, 1947 *Your Job Future After College*, NACP; Helen H. Ringe, Letter to Miller, May 6, 1949, in RG 86, Office of the Director General Correspondence of the Women's Bureau, 1948–1963, Box 55, Folder: 4-6-2-1 Vocational Guidance Leaflet for High School Girls & College Girls Correspondence, NACP.
63. Frances A. Amburser, Letter to Alice K. Leopold, September 26, 1958, in RG 86, Office of the Director General Correspondence of the Women's Bureau, 1948–1963 1958 Publications 4-1 to 4-2, Box 87, Folder: Publications 4-2 Special Distribution—NVGA, NACP; Leopold, Letter to College Deans of Women, June 1958, in RG 86, Office of the Director General Correspondence of the Women's Bureau, 1948–1963, 1958 Publications 4-2 to 5, Box 88, Folder: Publications 5 Projects—NVGA, NACP; Leopold, "Today's Women College Graduates," *The Personnel and Guidance Journal* 38, 4 (1959), 280; Jean Alice Wells, *First Jobs of College Women: Report on Women Graduates, Class of 1957, in Cooperation with NVGA, Women's Section* (Washington, DC: US Government Printing Office, 1959).
64. By 1953 the NADW national convention dates were listed along with six other conferences for Women's Bureau director Miller's planning purposes: Adelia B. Kloak, Letter to Miller, February 10, 1953, in RG 86, Office of the Director General Correspondence of the Women's Bureau, 1948–1963 Correspondence File, 1948–1953, Box 24, Folder: 6-0-3-0 Outside Conferences, NACP. The Women's Bureau considered women deans important enough to include three NADW members: Althea Hottel, University of Pennsylvania's dean of women; Gillie A. Larew, dean of students at Randolph-Macon Women's College; and the YWCA's Thelma Mills, the former University of Missouri dean of women. M. Eunice Hilton, Letter to Women's Bureau, April 17, 1950, in RG 86, Office of the Director General Correspondence of the Women's Bureau, 1948–1963 Correspondence File, 1948–1953, Box 48, Folder: 4-4-3 Listings, Lists and Catalogs, NACP; Hilton, Letter to Women's Bureau, May 31, 1953, in RG 86, Office of the Director General Correspondence of the Women's Bureau, 1948–1963 Correspondence File, 1948–1953, Box 48, Folder: 4-4-3 Listings, Lists and Catalogs, NACP; Adelia B. Kloak, Letter to Director of Information Herbert Little, July 9, 1953, in RG 86, Office of the Director General Correspondence of the Women's Bureau, 1948–1963

Correspondence File, 1948–1953, Box 48, Folder: 4-4-3 Listings, Lists and Catalogs, NACP; Miller, Letter to Hilton, June 4 1953, in RG 86, Office of the Director General Correspondence of the Women's Bureau, 1948–1963 Correspondence File, 1948–1953, Box 48, Folder: 4-4-3 Listings, Lists and Catalogs, NACP; Helen B. Sater, "Women's Bureau Conference," November 10, 1950, in RG 86, Office of the Director General Correspondence of the Women's Bureau, 1948–1963 Correspondence File, 1948–1953, Box 24, Folder: 3-0-3-1-2 WB Conference November 10, 1950, NACP; Zapoleon, Letter to Mary K. Bauman, November 8, 1950, in RG 86, Office of the Director General Correspondence of the Women's Bureau, 1948–1963 Correspondence File, 1948–1953, 3-0-6 to 3-0-8-2, Box 26, Folder: 3-0-6 Surveys, Investigations, NACP.

65. The American College Personnel Association (ACPA), which later joined American Personnel and Guidance Association (APGA), is now the American Counseling Association. Between 1983 and 1992, APGA was also known as the American Association of Counseling and Development. ACPA was founded as NAAS and May L. Cheney served as its first president, representing the women's occupational bureaus across the country.

66. Women's Bureau, "Vocational Counseling and Placement Services in 15 Colleges and Universities in 1951–1952," May, June 1952, in RG 86, Office of the Director General Correspondence of the Women's Bureau, 1948–1963 Correspondence File, 1948–1953, Box 49, Folder: 4-5-2-1 College & University Vocational Train. Counseling & Placement Service Study—Beaven—May 1952, NACP; Leopold, Letter to Selma M. Montasana, in RG 86, Office of the Director General Correspondence of the Women's Bureau, 1948–1963, 1959 Correspondence (N to ST), Box 125, Folder: National Association, NACP. In the 1940s and 1950s, the dean of women's role converted to assistant dean, or advisor of women at some universities when administrations put into place a male dean of students. The women involved in counseling, however, often remained connected with the NADW and the philosophies developed there. The forces that caused the decline in dean of women positions are discussed in Tuttle, "What Became of the Dean of Women."

67. ACA, *Publications of the Magazine* (December 1908), 20–24, 126, 129; ACA, *Magazine* (1910) 12.

68. Women's Bureau staff traveled to the universities of Oklahoma, Texas, Wisconsin, Missouri, Cincinnati, Kentucky, Idaho, Pennsylvania, as well as to Indiana, Purdue, and Arizona State universities and the State College of Washington, Eastern Washington State College, and Northern Idaho Junior College, Heidelberg College, and Peabody College. Leopold, Letter to Arthur A. Hitchcock, February 27, 1959, in RG 86, Office of the Director General Correspondence of the Women's Bureau, 1948–1963, Labor Management to Meetings Conference (3-2) Box 109, Folder: Meetings—Conferences 1 Engagements—Invitations, NACP; Lillian V. Inke, Letter to Kathryn L. Hopwood, August 1, 1952, in RG 86, Office of the Director General Correspondence of the Women's Bureau, 1948–1963, 1948–1953, Box 100, Folder: 6-4-5-1 NVGA, NACP. Further information located in RG 86, Office of the Director General Correspondence of the Women's Bureau, 1948–1963, Correspondence File, 1948–1953, 1-1-7-7-6 to 1-1-7-9-1, Box 12, NACP. Also see Leopold, Letter to Barbara Landy, November 21,

1958, in RG 86, Office of the Director General Correspondence of the Women's Bureau, 1948–1963, 1958, Corresp. Q to Wilson, Box 100, Folder: Universities N–Z; and Mary Lennard, Letter to Leopold, June 12, 1958, in RG 86, Office of the Director General Correspondence of the Women's Bureau, 1948–1963 1958 Correspondence C to Federal, Box 96, Folder: Colleges, both in NACP. Esther Vreeland, Letter to Leopold, October 25, 1958; Leopold, "There Are Only Challenges: Speech at University of Pennsylvania Luncheon," October 1, 1958; and Althea K. Hottel, Letter to Leopold, October 2, 1958, all three in RG 86, Office of the Director General Correspondence of the Women's Bureau, 1948–1963 Correspondence File, 1948–1953, Box 85, Folder: Public Relations 15 Speeches—Lectures—Statements—Skits, NACP. Correspondence regarding the other staff members' travel may be found in RG 86, Office of the Director General Correspondence of the Women's Bureau, 1948–1963, Box 30, Folder: 3-4-2-1 Universities & Colleges, NACP.

2 Practicing Political Citizenship

1. Catharine Evans, Letter to Grace S. M. Zorbaugh, November 5, 1941; and Zorbaugh, Letter to Evans, October 9, 1941, both in Dean of Women Papers (hereafter c165), Folder: Committee on Women's Education 1941–1942; Kate Hevner Mueller, Letter to Margaret Disert, August 6, 1942 c165, Box 165, Folder: 1942–1943 Mueller—Personal; Margaret Wilson, Letter to Mueller, June 22, 1944, in c165, Folder: Committee on Women's Education 1941–1942. For further information, see c165, Folder: Committee on Women's Education 1941–1942; and Folder: 1944, Margaret Wilson Assistant Dean of Women Applicant Hiring File. Also see Mueller, "Memoirs of Mueller," 1937, in Kate Hevner Mueller Papers (hereafter c170), Box 2, Memoirs, 1935–1971; all in Indiana University Archives, Bloomington, IN (hereafter IUA).
2. Taylor, "Handwritten Speech Notes, AAUW," Date Unknown, in Author's Collection of Emily Taylor's Papers (hereafter Author's Collection), St. Louis, MO.
3. Association of Collegiate Alumnae, *ACA Magazine* Series II, No. 14 (February 1907), 44–45.
4. Marion Talbot, *More Than Lore: Reminiscences of Marion Talbot, Dean of Women, the University of Chicago, 1892–1925* (Chicago: University of Chicago Press, 1936), 101.
5. Lynn D. Gordon, *Gender and Higher Education in the Progressive Era* (New Haven: Yale University Press, 1990), 65.
6. Gail Short Hanson, "Organizational Transformation: A Case Study of the Intercollegiate Association for Women Students" (PhD diss., George Washington University, 1995), 83; Jana Nidiffer, *Pioneering Deans of Women: More Than Wise and Pious Matrons* (New York: Teachers College Press, 2000), 99, 112; Talbot, *More Than Lore*, 110, 144.
7. "Resolutions Adopted by the Conference of Deans of Women Held in Chicago and Evanston, Nov. 3–4, 1903," National Association for Women in Education (hereafter NAWE) Records (hereafter MS-218), Bowling Green State University, Center for Archival Collections, Bowling Green, OH (hereafter BGSUCAC).

8. Janice Gerda, "A History of the Conferences of Deans of Women, 1903–1922" (PhD diss., Bowling Green State University, 2004), 97; Nidiffer, *Pioneering Deans*, 74.
9. Gordon, *Gender and Higher Education in the Progressive Era*, 132; Nidiffer, *Pioneering Deans*.
10. Kathryn Sisson Phillips, *My Room in the World: A Memoir* (New York: Abingdon Press, 1964), 71.
11. Christine D. Myers, "Gendering the 'Wisconsin Idea': The Women's Self-Government Association and University Life, c. 1898–1948," in *Gender, Colonialism and Education: The Politics of Experience*, ed. Joyce Goodman and Jane Martin (Portland: Woburn Press, 2002): 148–172.
12. Geraldine Jonçich Clifford, *Lone Voyagers: Academic Women in Coeducational Universities, 1870–1937* (New York: Feminist Press at the City University of New York, 1989), 305. On "social efficiency" versus "citizenship," see Nidiffer, *Pioneering Deans*, 93–94, 99, 118–119.
13. Talbot, *More Than Lore*, 166.
14. Phillips, *My Room in the World*, 46.
15. Helen Lefkowitz Horowitz, *The Power and Passion of M. Carey Thomas* (New York: Alfred A. Knopf, 1994), 246.
16. John Dewey, *Experience and Education* (New York: Macmillan, 1938; reprint, New York: Collier Books, 1963), 67.
17. Talbot, *More Than Lore*, 123–125; Dewey, *The School and Society* (Chicago: University of Chicago Press, 1915); Dewey, *Experience and Education*; Dewey, *Freedom and Culture* (New York: G.P. Putnam's Sons, 1939).
18. Talbot, *More Than Lore*, 162.
19. Nidiffer, *Pioneering Deans*, 55–78; Talbot, *More Than Lore*, 116–155, 162–164.
20. Gordon, *Gender and Higher Education in the Progressive Era*, 59–60, 84.
21. Nidiffer, *Pioneering Deans*, 128, 130; Hanson, "Organizational Transformation," 83. Also see records in MS-218, Folder: Intercollegiate Association of Women Students (IAWS) History, 1935, BGSUCAC.
22. Hanson, "Organizational Transformation," 83–86; MS-218, Folder: IAWS History, 1935, BGSUCAC.
23. Hanson, "Organizational Transformation," 84–86, 95.
24. Hellen Battrick, Letter to Kathryn Heath, February 10, 1939, in MS-218, Folder: Women's Student Government Organizations Covr., BGSUCAC.
25. Hanson, "Organizational Transformation," 38, 93, 95–97, 100. Other bureau employees who spoke to Associated Women Students (AWS) were: Mary Elizabeth Pidgeon, Mildred Dougherty, Jean Wells, Dorothy Frost, and Lillian Inke. See Records of the Women's Bureau in the Department of Labor (hereafter RG 86), Office of the Director General Correspondence of the Women's Bureau, 1948–1963 Correspondence File, 1948–1953, Box 47, Folder: 4-2-4-4 Speeches of Staff Members, National Archives at College Park, MD (hereafter NACP).
26. IAWS, "Manual of the IAWS," 1953, in Associated Women Students Records (hereafter c478), Folder: IAWS Manual 1953–1961, IUA.
27. Eunice Mae Acheson, *The Effective Dean of Women: A Study of the Personal and Professional Characteristics of a Selected Group of Deans of Women* (Chicago: University of Chicago Press, 1932), 38, 51, 76; Hanson, "Organizational Transformation," 39, 84–89. For a discussion of how

deans of women led the development of the student affairs profession, see Robert Schwartz, *Deans of Men and the Shaping of Modern College Culture* (New York: Palgrave Macmillan, 2010); and Robert Schwartz, "How Deans of Women Became Men," *The Review of Higher Education* 20, 4 (Summer, 1997): 419–436.
28. Mueller, "Memoirs of Mueller," p. 22 in c170, Box 2, Memoirs 1937–1949, IUA.
29. Ibid., p. 40.
30. Ibid., 37–49. Mueller and her vocational advisor, Catherine Evans, put this statistical reporting strategy to work in an effort to understand Indiana University (IU) alumnae workforce participation and how former students believed their IU degree helped in "preparation for life via their college experience."
31. Emily Taylor, Interview by Author, December 13–14, 2003 (Lawrence, KS).
32. Mueller, *Educating Women for a Changing World* (Minneapolis: University of Minnesota Press, 1954), 147.
33. Ibid., 152.
34. Ibid., 161–162.
35. Ibid., 160–161.
36. Hilda Threlkeld, Letter to Taylor, June 7, 1946, Author's Collection.
37. Kathryn Nemeth Tuttle, "What Became of the Dean of Women? Changing Roles for Women Administrators in American Higher Education, 1940–1980" (PhD diss., University of Kansas, 1996), 167–213. Also, Mueller; "Memoirs of Mueller," Box 2, Memoirs, 1935–1971; and Mueller, Letter to Mrs. Balz, June 5, 1948, Folder: Women, both in in c170, IUA.
38. Linda Eisenmann, *Higher Education for Women in Postwar America, 1945–1965* (Baltimore, MD: Johns Hopkins University Press, 2006).
39. Tuttle, "What Became of the Dean of Women," 169.
40. Eisenmann, *Higher Education for Women in Postwar America*, 54–55. According to Eisenmann, the GI Bill resulted in the displacement of many non-veteran women. She also includes a discussion of the National Association of Deans of Women (NADW) work to establish the Committee on the Education of Women (CEW) in partnership with the American Council on Education (ACE).
41. Paula S. Fass, *Outside In: Minorities and the Transformation of American Education* (New York: Oxford University Press, 1989), 161–163; Robert G. Foster and Pauline Park Wilson, *Women after College: A Study of the Effectiveness of Their Education* (New York: Columbia University Press, 1942); Ferdinand Lundberg and Marynia F. Farnham, *Modern Woman: The Lost Sex* (New York, London: Harper & Brothers, 1947); Elaine Tyler May, *Homeward Bound: American Families in the Cold War Era* (New York: Basic Books, 1988), 78; Barbara Miller Solomon, *In the Company of Educated Women: A History of Women and Higher Education in America* (New Haven: Yale University Press, 1985), 170; Lynn White Jr., *Educating Our Daughters: A Challenge to the Colleges* (New York: Harper & Brothers, 1950), 164–165. Two of the many books that examine the implications of 1950s culture on women are William Henry Chafe, *The Paradox of Change: American Women in the 20th Century* (New York: Oxford University Press, 1991), Chapter 10; Joanne J. Meyerowitz, ed. *Not June Cleaver: Women and Gender in Postwar America, 1945–1960* (Philadelphia: Temple University Press, 1994).

42. Tuttle, "What Became of the Dean of Women," 170; Mirra Komarovsky, *Women in the Modern World: Their Education and Their Dilemmas* (Boston: Little, Brown, 1953); Mueller, *Educating Women for a Changing World*.
43. Althea Kratz Hottel, *How Fare American Women?* (Washington, DC: Commission on the Education of Women, American Council on Education, 1955), 21–23. According to Donna Shavlik, when ACE dismantled CEW, AAUW took over the CEW publications to continue the conversation regarding women's education. Shavlik, Telephone Interview by Author, May 31, 2014.
44. The "life-phases" concept underpinned the continuing education movement which deans fostered so that women could pursue higher education after marriage. CEW's advocacy of lifelong education for women eventually undergirded the results of President John F. Kennedy's Commission on the Status of Women. Eisenmann, *Higher Education for Women in Postwar America*, 102–105.
45. Ibid., 98–100; IAWS, in c478, Folder: IAWS Manual 1953–1961, IUA; Donna Shavlik, Interview by Author, March 4, 2014 (New York, NY).
46. For background on the "quiet feminism" of NADW, see Eisenmann, *Higher Education for Women in Postwar America*.
47. Mueller, "Memoirs of Mueller," in c170, Box 2, Memoirs, 1935–1971, IUA.
48. Mueller, Letter to Alice K. Leopold, August 3, 1955, in c170, Folder: Women 1949–1959, IUA.
49. Mueller, "The Cultural Pressures on Women," in *The Education of Women— Signs for the Future*, ed. Opal D. David (Washington DC: American Council on Education, 1959), 54.

3 Unlocking Women's Autonomy

1. Sartorius, Kelly C., "Experimental Autonomy: Dean Emily Taylor and the Women's Movement at the University of Kansas," *Kansas History: A Journal of the Central Plains* 33, 1 (Spring 2010), 3–21. Also, the University of Kansas (KU) credits Martha Peterson with establishing a dormitory system for freshmen women at KU. For further information on Peterson see: Todd Cohen, "University Mourns KU Graduate, Former Dean of Women Martha Peterson," Press Release, *University of Kansas, University Relations*, http://www.news.ku.edu/2006/july/19/peterson.shtml; Emily Taylor, Interview by Author, December 13–14, 2003 (Lawrence, KS). Kate Hevner Mueller, Letter to Taylor, March 5, 1955, and Taylor, Letter to Mueller, March 7, 1955, both in Kate Hevner Mueller Papers (hereafter c170), Box 5, Folder: Taylor, Emily, Indiana University Archives, Bloomington, IN (hereafter IUA).
2. Clifford S. Griffin, *The University of Kansas: A History* (Lawrence: University Press of Kansas, 1974), 503, 530, 617.
3. Marilyn Stokstad, Interview by Author, July 28, 2010 (Lawrence, KS).
4. Barbara Miller Solomon, *In the Company of Educated Women: A History of Women and Higher Education in America* (New Haven: Yale University Press, 1985), 189.
5. The exception to this is in institutions with home economics programs, where deans were often women. These programs often resided in land-grant

universities. Linda Eisenmann, *Higher Education for Women in Postwar America, 1945–1965* (Baltimore: Johns Hopkins University Press, 2006), 58–59.
6. KU News Bureau, June 27, 1953, in Chancellor's Papers (hereafter RG 2/11/5), Box 1, Folder: Dean of Students 1953–1954, University of Kansas Libraries, Kenneth Spencer Research Library, University Archives (hereafter UKL). For discussion of demotions of deans of women, see Kathryn Nemeth Tuttle, "What Became of the Dean of Women? Changing Roles for Women Administrators in American Higher Education, 1940–1980" (PhD diss., University of Kansas, 1996).
7. KU News Bureau, in RG 2/11/5, Box 1, Folder: Dean of Students 1953–1954, UKL. In this reorganization of student administrators, Franklin D. Murphy also promoted the assistant dean of men, Donald K. Alderson, to dean of men.
8. Laurence C. Woodruff, Letter to Murphy, March 8, 1956, in RG 2/11/5, Box 3, Folder: Dean of Students 1955–1956, UKL.
9. Taylor, Interview by Author, December 13–14, 2003; Tuttle, "What Became of the Dean of Women," Chapter 7.
10. Murphy wrote to Laurence C. Woodruff to deny Woodruff's request to eliminate the "dean of women" title in favor of an assistant dean or an associate dean title. Murphy noted that it was "desirable to clothe the woman in the office with the additional dignity that goes with the phrase, 'dean of women,'" and also suggested that "our system has worked quite well since 1952." Murphy, Letter to Woodruff, March 16, 1956, in RG 2/11/5, Box 3, Folder: Dean of Students 1955–1956, UKL. Even with tentative increases suggested for the 1958–1959 school year, Woodruff was slated to earn $11,000, Taylor $8,500, and Alderson $7,000. 1957–1958, in RG 2/11/5, Box 1, Folder: Chancellor's Office, 1957–1958, UKL. Peterson's outgoing salary was found in: "Budget for Fiscal Year Ending June 30, 1956," 1955, in Budget Records (hereafter RG 44), UKL.
11. At KU in 1943, students and administrators agreed on a new student government constitution that created an All Student Council (ASC) of 30 members to set the policy for student life. The Kansas Board of Regents approved the program, with the stipulation that all ASC regulations would be subject to the chancellor's veto. Griffin, *The University of Kansas*, 637.
12. Associated Women Students (AWS), "Regulations for University Women, 1955–56," in Dean of Women's Papers (hereafter RG 53/0), Box 1, Folder: Chronological 1957–58–1958–59, UKL; Beth L. Bailey, *Sex in the Heartland* (Cambridge: Harvard University Press, 1999), 78–80.
13. "AWS Grows to Its Present Stature from Small Group," *Lawrence Journal-World* (hereafter *LJW*), September 1958. This clipping is found in AWS 1948–1971, in Associated Women Students Records (hereafter RG 67/12), Folder: 1955–1956, UKL.
14. Taylor, Interview by Author, July 1, 1997 (Lawrence, KS); Simone de Beauvoir, *The Second Sex* (New York: Alfred A. Knopf, 1953); Morton M. Hunt, *The Natural History of Love* (New York: Alfred A. Knopf, 1959); Mirra Komarovsky, *Women in the Modern World: Their Education and Their Dilemmas* (Boston: Little, Brown, 1953); "Reference Data on the Status of Women in America. Part I. Legal Discrimination against Women. Part II. Discrimination in Politics," in RG 67/12, Folder: 1956–1957,

UKL; Sarah Wohlrabe, "Taylor: Committed to Equal Rights for Women," *University Daily Kansan* (*UDK*), October 19, 1973, 8; Office of the Dean of Women, "The Following Information Is on File in the Library of the Dean of Women's Office," Date Unknown, in Commission on the Status of Women Records (hereafter RG 67/48), Box 1, Folder: 1970–1971, UKL.
15. AWS, "AWS," 1956–1957, in RG 67/12, Folder: 1956–1957, UKL.
16. AWS, "Senate Minutes," February 18, 1960, in RG 67/12, Folder: 1959–1960, UKL; Donna Shavlik, Telephone Interview by Author, March 22, 2011; Taylor, Interview by Author, July 3, 1997 (Lawrence, KS); Taylor, Interview by Author, December 13–14, 2003.
17. "Are You a Dedicated, Ambitious, Intelligent Woman?" 1961, in RG 67/12, Folder: July–November 1961, UKL.
18. Mueller, Letter to Sue Frederick, October 22, 1956, in RG 67/12, Folder: 1956–1957, UKL; Shavlik, Interview by Author, September 20, 1997 (Lawrence, KS).
19. Shavlik, Interview by Author, September 20, 1997. Sheila Tobias later credited Taylor with beginning her career by inviting her to speak. "Not least I owe you my first round of talks on sex-role socialization and women's studies. You were the one who recommended me during those first years of the 1970s." Tobias, Letter to Taylor, July 24, 1997, in Author's Collection of Emily Taylor's Papers, St. Louis, MO (hereafter Author's Collection).
20. Dean of Women Thrysa Amos founded Cwens in 1922 at the University of Pittsburgh. For programming information see "Dean Recounts Day," in *UDK*. The changes to the AWS programming are found in: "1957 All Women's Day Materials," 1957, in RG 67/12, UKL; September 28, 1961, in RG 67/12, Folder: July–November 1961, UKL; AWS, "Senate Retreat Minutes," April 26, 1960, in RG 67/12, Folder: 1959–1960, UKL. Also see Taylor, Letter to Mueller, 1956–1957, in RG 67/12, Folder: 1956–1957, UKL. In addition, in preparation for All–Women's Day, Taylor asked the AWS leadership to review documents such as "Reference Data on the Status of Women in America. Part I. Legal Discrimination against Women. Part II. Discrimination in Politics," in RG 67/12, Folder: 1956–1957, UKL.
21. Taylor, Letter to Mueller, October 12, 1954, in c170, Box 5, General Correspondence 1909–1979, Folder: Taylor, Emily—Dean of Women, University of Kansas, Miami University, Oxford, Ohio 1958–1965, IUA.
22. Taylor, Interview by Author, July 1, 1997.
23. Ibid.
24. Ibid.
25. Taylor, Interview by Author, July 5, 1997 (Lawrence, KS).
26. Taylor, Interview by Author, December 13–14, 2003.
27. Taylor, Interview by Author, July 1, 1997.
28. Shavlik, Interview by Author, September 20, 1997.
29. Taylor, Interview by Author, July 1, 1997.
30. Ibid.
31. Anne Hoopingarner Ridder, Interview by Author, February 17, 2009 (Arlington, VA).
32. Ibid.
33. Shavlik continued as Intercollegiate Association of Women Students (IAWS) executive secretary until 1959. The budget statistics may be found in the KU Budget for each fiscal year. RG 44, UKL.

34. Taylor, Interview by Author.
35. Stroup succeeded Taylor as dean of women at KU upon Taylor's retirement. AWS, "University of Kansas Regulations Convention Morning Session," 1959, in RG 67/12, Folder: 1958–1959, UKL.
36. Taylor, "Handwritten Speech Notes, AAUW," in Author's Collection.
37. Ibid.
38. Shavlik, Interview by Author, September 20, 1997.
39. Taylor, Interview by Author, December 13–14, 2003.
40. Ibid.
41. Kala Stroup, Interview by Author, November 14, 2010.
42. Kathie Sarachild, "Consciousness Raising and Intuition: Feminist Consciousness Raising and 'Organizing'" (Paper Presented at the Lake Villa Conference, November 27, 1968); Kala Stroup, Interview by Author, November 14, 2010 (Lawrence, KS).
43. Taylor, Interview by Author, July 1, 1997.
44. M. Kay Harris, Telephone Interview by Author, February 14, 2014.
45. Shavlik, Interview by Author, August 21–22, 2010 (Estes Park, CO).
46. Taylor, "Handwritten Speech Notes," Author's Collection.
47. AWS, "Senate Minutes," May 8, 1956, in RG 67/12, Folder: 1955–1956, UKL.
48. Taylor, "Optimum Use of Students in Faculty Committees," *Journal of the NADW* (March 1953), 126–129. The first higher education institution to provide women with keys was located in Colorado. The author has not been able to determine which school implemented this policy prior to the University of Kansas. Taylor, Interview by Author, December 13–14, 2003; Taylor, Interview by Author, Summer, 1997 (Lawrence, KS). For discussions of the student movements at KU, see Bailey, *Sex in the Heartland*, 75–104. Also see, Rusty L. Monhollon, *This Is America? The Sixties in Lawrence, Kansas* (New York: Palgrave, 2002). Bailey particularly addresses the keys.
49. Taylor, "Optimum Use of Students in Faculty Committees" (March 1953).
50. Taylor, Interview by Author, July 4, 1997 (Lawrence, KS).
51. Taylor, Interview by Author, June 4, 1998 (Lawrence, KS).
52. Taylor, "Employed Women in Recent Periodical Short Fiction: The Fictionalized Portrait of Employed Women Projected against a Background of Factual Data" (EdD diss., Indiana University, 1955), 3.
53. AWS, "Senate Minutes," December 4, 1956, in RG 67/12, Folder: 1956–1957, UKL; AWS, "Senate Minutes," April 5, 1957, in RG 67/12, Folder: 1956–1957, UKL.
54. AWS, "1955–56 Judiciary Board Minutes," 1955–56, in RG 67/12, Folder: 1955–1956, UKL. Assistant Dean Pat Patterson is listed as the advisor to the board of standards. AWS, "Board of Standards 1959–60," 1959–60, in RG 67/12, Folder: 1959–1960, UKL.
55. AWS, "Convention Notes," January 15, 1959, in RG 67/12, Folder: 1958–1959, UKL; AWS, "1959 Regulations Convention Chairman's Report," 1959, in RG 67/12, Folder: 1958–1959, UKL.
56. AWS, "Summary of New Ideas for AWS Regulations," January 15, 1959, in RG 67/12, Folder: 1958–1959, UKL.
57. *UDK*, "AWS Revisions Get Final Ok," 1959, in RG 67/12, Folder: 1958–1959, UKL.

58. The phrase "senior privileges" is from "AWS Seeks Rules Change," *UDK*, February 16, 1959.
59. Clipping, *UDK*, no date. The clipping may be found in AWS 1948–1971 in RG 67/12, Folder: 1958–1959, UKL.
60. AWS, "Senate Minutes," March 3, 1959, in RG 67/12, Folder: 1958–1959, UKL. Also, an article clipping stated that the Chief of the Library Reader Services would consider longer hours permanently but that it was not easily done. *UDK* Clipping, no date, in RG 67/12, Folder: 1958–1959, UKL. The AWS minutes noting final approval of building hours is found in AWS, "Board of Standards Minutes," September 24, 1959, in RG 67/12, Folder: 1959–1960, UKL.
61. "What Experiment," *LJW*, August 15, 1959, 4.
62. Stroup, Telephone Interview by Author, April 16, 2014; Shavlik, Telephone Interview by Author, May 31, 2014.
63. Taylor, Interview by Author, July 4, 1997.
64. The author thanks Ann Gardner, *Lawrence Daily Journal-World* editorial page editor and graduate of KU for providing the information about Mortarboard senior privileges. Lynn Peril, *College Girls: Bluestockings, Sex Kittens, and Co-Eds, Then and Now* (New York, London: Norton, 2006), 150; Ridder, Interview by Author, February 17, 2009.
65. Date rape was not a term used in the 1950s or 1960s, though scholars recognize that the experience later defined as "date rape" existed before the advent of the term itself. I use the term here because it accurately describes the situation women encountered in these time periods.
66. Taylor, Interview by Author, December 13–14, 2003.
67. Edward C. Solomon, "A Condensation of Ideas from a Conference on Educational Needs of College Women for Marriage and Family Planning," *Journal of the National Association of Women Deans and Counselors* 26, 2 (January 1963), 46.
68. Shavlik, Interview by Author, September 20, 1997.
69. Anne Hoopingarner Ridder, Interview by Author, February 17, 2009; AWS, "Senate Minutes," in RG 67/12, Folder: 1958–1959, UKL.
70. AWS, in RG 67/12, Folder: July–November 1961, UKL.
71. Stroup, Letter to Author, June 29, 2014, in Author's Collection.
72. Shavlik, Interview by Author, September 20, 1997.
73. AWS, "Senate Minutes," October 4, 1960, in RG 67/12, Folder: July–November 1961, UKL; "Seniors Hours in Effect Soon," *UDK*, October 14, 1960; "Keys May Be Distributed Monday," *UDK*, September 27, 1961.
74. Taylor, Interview by Author, July 5, 1997.
75. The only evidence of a negative public response was a note in the AWS Senate minutes stating that an article, "Equal Rights Set for KU's Women," was "erroneous and unfavorable." In the article mentioned by the minutes, the journalist implied that senior women would have no oversight at all. "Equal Rights Set for KU's Women," *LJW*, October 6, 1960; AWS, "Senate Minutes," October 25, 1960, in RG 67/12, Folder: July–October 1960, UKL.
76. Taylor, Interview by Author, July 1, 1997.
77. Helen Gibson Throop, Letter to Taylor, January 11, 1961, in RG 53/0, Box 2, Folder: 1966/67–1968/69, UKL.
78. In 1955, an NADW survey of members ranked housing problems as the top issue of concern. Conversely, it ranked student government and

student leaders near the bottom of concerns, with women's education issues last. Raymond C. Kirtland, Letter to Kala Stroup, February 11, 1965; Virginial Lackley, Letter to Taylor, February 4, 1963; Margaret Lahey, Letter to Taylor, November 12, 1960; Patti Teel, Letter to AWS Board, February 11, 1965; Anne Ward, Letter to Taylor, December 3, 1960; Bettie Weaver, Letter to Taylor, March 3, 1964; Dave Haseltine, Letter to Taylor, December 16, 1960; Mary Helen Flentge, Letter to Taylor, January 8, 1964 all in RG 53/0, Box 2, Folder: 1966/67–1968/69, UKL. "Dorm Keys for Senior Women," *The Massachusetts Collegian*, October 31, 1960, 2; Margaret Tietze Senior Privilege Chairman of KU AWS Chapter, "The University of Kansas Senior Privilege Plan 1965–66," Date Unknown, in Intercollegiate Association of Women Students Records, 1922–1980 (hereafter 77-M126-82-M100), Box 4, Folder 17: Hours, Radcliffe Institute, Harvard University, Schlesinger Library, Cambridge, MA (hereafter SL); Eisenmann, *Higher Education for Women in Postwar America*, 135.

79. AWS, "Senate Minutes," November 27, 1960, in RG 67/12, Folder: November 1960–June 1961, UKL.
80. Anne Hoopingarner Ridder, Interview by Author, February 17, 2009.
81. Suzanne Bocell, "Reports of AWS Commission on the Status of Women," 1969–1970, in 77-M126-82-M100, Box 10, Folder 4: Commissions on the Status of Women, 1969–1970, SL; Louise Douce, "IAWS National Office Report: Women's Hours," 1970, in 77-M126-82-M100, Box 4, Folder: 18: Index of Clearinghouse Reports, SL; Gail Short Hanson, "Organizational Transformation: A Case Study of the Intercollegiate Association for Women Students" (PhD diss., George Washington University, 1995), 98; M. Kay Harris, Telephone Interview by Author, February 14, 2014; Tuttle, "What Became of the Dean of Women," 325; AWS Council, "Council/Forum Minutes," April 24, 1969, in RG 53/0, Box 2, Folder: 1968–1969 IV, UKL. By 1969, KU first year women technically had "closing hours" though they could opt out of them. At the same time, sophomore women, with parental permission, could choose to live outside of university housing. This enabled all but first year women to live outside a dormitory or sorority should a woman desire to do so.
82. AWS, "Minutes, Joint Meeting of the House and Senate," January 9, 1962, in RG 67/12; Folder: November 1961–June 1962, UKL.
83. For a discussion of the rules revisions in 1966, see Bailey, *Sex in the Heartland*, 86–104. Bailey examines the changes in parietals at KU, by focusing on how students implemented the changes. She argues that the sexual revolution had roots within student personnel counseling and its support for personal responsibility. She sees students and the SDS as primary agitators to create parietal change at KU. Also see Alderson, "Handwritten Notes from Meeting in Provost Surface's Office Including Woodruff, Alderson and Taylor," March 14, 1966, in Office of Student Affairs Records (RG 76/0 or 76/0/5), Box 10, Folder: 51/0 Student Personnel Council: Council on Student Affairs 1965–4/26/66 I, UKL. Alderson's notes record Taylor advocating for the removal of sign-outs and support of eliminating curfews despite Provost James Surface's preference to keep such regulations.
84. Judy Farrell, "Studied at KU; Hour Reforms," *Topeka Capital-Journal*, March 20, 1966, 1; Todd Gitlin, *The Whole World Is Watching: Mass Media*

in the Making and Unmaking of the New Left (Berkeley: University of California Press, 1980), 26–27.

85. Letters to the chancellor are primarily collected in the following: Chancellor's Papers (Change in Women's Closing Hours) (hereafter RG 2/12/5), Box 11, Folder: Student Correspondence (Change in Women's Closing Hours), 1965–1966, UKL.

86. Mrs. Scott Ashton, Letter to W. Clarke Wescoe, April 28, 1966, in Box 11, RG 2/12/5, Folder: Student Correspondence (Change in Women's Closing Hours), 1965–1966, UKL.

87. Jackie Tietze, Letter to Wescoe, April 12, 1966, in RG 2/12/5, Box 11, Folder: Student Correspondence (Change in Women's Closing Hours), 1965–1966, UKL.

88. Mrs. Perry Fleagle, Letter to Surface, March 15, 1966, in RG 2/12/5, Box 11, Folder: Student Correspondence (Change in Women's Closing Hours), 1965–1966, UKL.

89. Mr. and Mrs. Melford Monsees, Letter to Mrs. John Hughes with carbon copy to Wescoe, April 13, 1966, in RG 2/12/5, Box 11, Folder: Student Correspondence (Change in Women's Closing Hours), 1965–1966, UKL.

90. Mr. and Mrs. Eugene Powers, Letter to Surface, March 16, 1966, in RG 2/12/5, Box 11, Folder: Student Correspondence (Change in Women's Closing Hours), 1965–1966, UKL.

91. Tietze, Letter to Wescoe, April 12, 1966.

92. Taylor, Interview by Author, December 13–14, 2003.

93. Wescoe, Letter to Mr. Roy A. Edwards, Mrs. Harold S. Warwick, Jr. Mrs. Ramon Schumacher, Mr. and Mrs. Robert Goetze, Mr. and Mrs. C. A. Burgardt, Mrs. John H. Tietze, Mrs. Thomas Van Cleave, Mrs. John D. Crouch, Mr. and Mrs. Eugene Powers, and Mrs. Gordon E. Atha, April 12, 1966, in RG 2/12/5, Box 11, Folder: Student Correspondence (Change in Women's Closing Hours), 1965–1966, UKL. Additional letters from Wescoe in response to other citizens contain very similar statements.

94. Taylor, Interview by Author, December 13–14, 2003.

95. Bailey, *Sex in the Heartland*, 100, 102.

96. Taylor, Interview by Author, December 13–14, 2003.

97. Ibid. The author concurs that KU was among the very first of the large public schools to allow first year women to live outside the closing hours. However, there were two other small institutions with no closing hours for any women in 1969, and the author has been unable to date the beginning of those programs. Louise Douce, "IAWS National Office Report: Women's Hours," in 77-M126–82-M100, Box 4, Folder: 18: Index of Clearinghouse Reports, SL.

4 A World without Parietals

1. Associated Women Students (AWS), "Board of Standards Minutes, October 29," 1959; AWS, "Board of Standards Minutes, October 30," 1959; both in Associated Women Students Records (hereafter RG 67/12), Folder: 1959–1960, University of Kansas Libraries, Kenneth Spencer Research Library, University Archives, Lawrence, KS (hereafter UKL).

2. "Dean Cautions Housemothers," 1959, in Dean of Women Chronological Files (hereafter 53/0), Folder: 1957-58–1958-59, UKL; "Disciplinary

Action Should Be Public," *University Daily Kansan (UDK)*, November 11, 1959, 1; Ray Miller, "Probation Raises Policy Quesitons: Authority to Discipline Fraternity Not Defined," *UDK*, November 10, 1959, 1; "The Public Interest," *UDK*, November 13, 1959, 2; "Social Committee Wants No Publicity," *UDK*, 1959; AWS, "Board of Standards Minutes, October 1," 1959, in RG 67/12, Folder: 1959–1960, UKL.

3. Kate Hevner Mueller, "The Role of the Counselor in Sex Behavior and Standards," *Journal of the National Association of Women Deans and Counselors* 26, 2 (January 1963): 3.
4. AWS, "Board of Standards Minutes, October 1," in RG 67/12, Folder: 1959–1960, UKL. Beth L. Bailey uses the phrase "student personnel therapeutic network" to describe how the field of student affairs approached handling student sexual activity. She is correct in this, however the trend came from the profession's mostly male deans of students, not from feminist deaning: Beth L. Bailey, *Sex in the Heartland* (Cambridge: Harvard University Press, 1999).
5. Donna Shavlik, Interview by Author, January 2007 (Kansas City, MO).
6. Kala Stroup, Interview by Author, May 12, 2010 (Lawrence, KS); Stroup, Interview by Author, November 14, 2010 (Lawrence, KS).
7. Caroljean Brune, Interview by Author, February 12, 2011 (Lawrence, KS).
8. Ibid; Marilyn Stokstad, Interview by Author, July 28, 2010 (Lawrence, KS).
9. Joyce Antler, *Lucy Sprague Mitchell: The Making of a Modern Woman* (New Haven: Yale University Press, 1987), 66, 116; *Stanford Mosaic: Reminiscences of the First Seventy Years at Stanford University*, ed. Edith R. Mirrielees and Patricia F. Zelver (Stanford: Stanford University, 1962): 118–124; Kathryn Nemeth Tuttle, "What Became of the Dean of Women? Changing Roles for Women Administrators in American Higher Education, 1940–1980" (PhD diss., University of Kansas, 1996), 25, 27; Sue Zschoche, "Dr. Clarke Revisited: Science, True Womanhood, and Female Collegiate Education," *History of Education Quarterly* 29, 4 (1989): 545–569. For a further discussion of sex education see Jeffrey P. Moran, *Teaching Sex: The Shaping of Adolescence in the 20th Century* (Cambridge: Harvard University Press, 2000). Clelia Duel Mosher promoted her research about women and menstruation, arguing that data proved women would not be incapacitated monthly at work, an important conclusion for those interested in opening vocations to women. Mosher conducted the earliest known research on women's sexuality, predating Alfred Kinsey by 40 years. She traced women's sexual habits from her time as an undergraduate at the University of Wisconsin in the late 1800s throughout her career. However, this research was so controversial that she never published it. See Geraldine Jonçich Clifford, *Lone Voyagers: Academic Women in Coeducational Universities, 1870–1937* (New York: Feminist Press at the City University of New York, 1989), 158–161.
10. National Association of Deans of Women (NADW), "Principles of Social Conduct," 1918, in National Association for Women in Education Records, (hereafter MS-218), Central Office Files, Subject Files Folder, Bowling Green State University Library, Center for Archival Collections, National Student Affairs Archives, Bowling Green, OH (hereafter BGSUCAC).
11. Janice Gerda, "A History of the Conferences of Deans of Women, 1903–1922" (PhD diss., Bowling Green State University, 2004), 91; Tuttle,

"What Became of the Dean of Women," 27; NADW, "Principles of Social Conduct."
12. Lenore Fields, "Student Health," *National Association of Deans of Women (NADW) Twelfth Yearbook*, Cincinnati, OH (1925): 175–178; Women's Foundation for Health, *A Handbook on Positive Health* (Chicago: American Medical Association Press, 1922); Anna E. Pierce, "Report of the Health Committee," *NADW Sixteenth Yearbook*, Cleveland, OH (1929); E. V. McCollum, Mary Swartz Rose, Lillian M. Gilbreth, Jane Bellows, E. C. Lindeman, Era Betzner, Walter B. Cannon, William A. White, and Jessie Taft, *Handbook on Positive Health* (New York: Women's Foundation for Health, 1928), 157–163; NADW *Thirteenth Yearbook*, Washington, DC (1926).
13. Eunice Mae Acheson, *The Effective Dean of Women: A Study of the Personal and Professional Characteristics of a Selected Group of Deans of Women* (Chicago: University of Chicago Press, 1932), 159–160; Alma L. Binzel, "Mental Hygiene One Aspect of Education for Parenthood," *NADW Eleventh Yearbook*, Chicago, IL (1924); Esther Allen Gaw, "Education for Healthy Family Relationships," *Journal of the American Association of University Women* (January 1934), 92–95; Genevieve Taylor McMahon, Telephone Interview by Author, December 31, 2007; LeRoy A. Wilkes, "A Campus Health Program," *NADW Fourteenth Yearbook*, Dallas, TX (1927), 132.
14. Gaw, "Education for Healthy Family Relationships" (1934), 94.
15. Audrey Kenyon Wilder, "Project Committee of the Ohio Deans," in Dean of Women Papers (hereafter RG 9/c-2), Box 9, Folder: Dean of Women—Ohio Assoc. of Women Deans, Administrators & Counselors—Historical Records: 1927–1966, Ohio State University Archives, Columbus, OH (hereafter OSUA).
16. Ibid.
17. Untitled Document, April 23, 1936, in Howard Landis Bevis Papers (hereafter RG 3/f), Box 8, Folder: Personnel Activities (Personnel Council: etc.): 1934–1936, OSUA.
18. Gaw, Howard L. Hamilton, Delbert Oberteuffer, "Report to Personnel Council: Sub-Committee on 'Education for Courtship and Marriage'," June 4, 1936, in RG 3/f, Box 38, Personnel Activities (Personnel Council: etc.): 1934–1936, OSUA.
19. Susan Ware, *Holding Their Own: American Women in the 1930s* (Boston: Twayne Publishers, 1982), 7.
20. Andrea Tone, *Devices and Desires: A History of Contraceptives in America* (New York: Hill & Wang, 2001), 157–161.
21. Carole Joffe, *Doctors of Conscience: The Struggle to Provide Abortion before and after Roe V. Wade* (Boston: Beacon Press, 1995), 35; Mueller, "Notes," in Kate Hevner Mueller Papers, 1909–1981 (hereafter c170), Box 7, Folder: Marriage—College Age Notes, Resources, ca. 1950s, 1945 Research Notes, Indiana University Archives, Bloomington, IN (hereafter IUA); Tone, *Devices and Desires*, 70; Ware, *Holding Their Own*, 7. Conversely, the National Association of College Women [an organization of black collegiate alumnae established as a counterpoint to the racially limited American Association of University Women (AAUW)] added family planning and sex education to their human relations programs in the mid-1950s. For a

discussion of this and AAUW's consideration of contraception, see Susan Levine, *Degrees of Equality: The American Association of University Women and the Challenge of Twentieth-Century Feminism* (Philadelphia: Temple University Press, 1995), 47–52, 167–168. The topic of contraception divided opinions in the white women's groups where deans historically congregated. Those who did not accept contraception in the 1930s strongly opposed it, making it a controversial issue. When the AAUW supported contraception prescriptions by qualified physicians at a 1935 convention, many members protested vehemently. The AAUW reversed course on the position and did not change its stance again until the early 1970s. With the exception of Margaret Sanger's American Birth Control League (later to become the Planned Parenthood Federation of America in 1942), most mainstream women's organizations avoided the issue.

22. Mueller interview quoted in James H. Jones, *Alfred C. Kinsey: A Public/Private Life* (New York: W. W. Norton, 1997), 339.
23. Mueller interview quoted in ibid.
24. "Indiana Unviersity Marriage Course," Fall, 1938, in Kinsey, Box 2, Series V, A.1.a, Folder: 2, The Kinsey Institute for Research in Sex, Gender, and Reproduction, Inc., Bloomington, IN (hereafter: Kinsey Institute).
25. Jones, *Alfred C. Kinsey*, 322, 324; "Indiana Unviersity Marriage Course," in Kinsey, Box 2, Series V, A.1.a, Folder: 2, Kinsey Institute; Herman Wells, Letter to Alfred Kinsey, July 9, 1938, in Kinsey Correspondence, Kinsey Institute.
26. Kinsey, Letter to Mueller, October 30, 1941, in RG c165, Folder: Committee on Women's Education 1941–1942, IUA.
27. Emily Taylor, Interview by Author, December 13–14, 2003 (Lawrence, KS). Mueller came to dislike Kinsey because she felt he inappropriately pressured women students to participate in his surveys. Jones, *Alfred C. Kinsey*, 527.
28. Janice M. Irvine, *Disorders of Desire: Sex and Gender in Modern American Sexology* (Philadelphia: Temple University Press, 1990), 36; Mueller, Letter to Wells, September 27, 1939, in Herman Wells Records (hereafter c213), IUA.
29. Lynn Peril, *College Girls: Bluestockings, Sex Kittens, and Co-Eds, Then and Now* (New York, London: W.W. Norton & Company, Inc., 2006), 281.
30. Mueller, Letter to Kinsey, November 29, 1938; Mueller, Letter to Kinsey, July 17, 1956; and Kinsey, Letter to Wells, May 19, 1939, all in Kinsey Correspondence, Kinsey Institute; "NAWDC—Indiana University Workshop for College Deans," 1956, in c170, Folder: Kinsey, Alfred and the Institute for Sex Research, Correspondence and News Clippings, 1949, IUA; Peril, *College Girls*, 279–281.
31. Tuttle, "What Became of the Dean of Women," 24–25; Antler, *Lucy Sprague Mitchell*, 116, 203.
32. Sherwin L. Davidson, Interview by Author, July 28, 1997 (Portland, OR); Taylor, Interview by Author, December 13–14, 2003. Although the term "free love" has been popularly associated with promiscuity, Taylor meant the historical meaning of the term that love relations should be freely entered without the regulation of the law.
33. Genevieve McMahon, Telephone Interview by Author, May 28, 2014.
34. Taylor, Interview by Author, December 13–14, 2003.

35. Shavlik, Interview by Author, November 18–19, 2006 (Estes Park, CO).
36. Frances Strain, *Love at the Threshold: A Book on Social Dating, Romance, and Marriage* (New York: Appleton-Century-Crofts, 1952), 30–31.
37. Peril, *College Girls*, 278–317; Rickie Solinger, *Pregnancy and Power: A Short History of Reproductive Politics in America* (New York: New York University Press, 2005), 163.
38. Wini Breines, *Young, White, and Miserable: Growing up Female in the Fifties* (Chicago: University of Chicago Press, 2001), 125.
39. "How to Handle a College Man," *DATEbook*, September 1959, 48.
40. Regina G. Kunzel, "White Neurosis, Black Pathology: Constructing Out-of-Wedlock Pregnancy in the Wartime and Postwar United States," in *Not June Cleaver: Women and Gender in Postwar America, 1945–1960*, ed. Joanne Meyerowitz (Philadelphia: Temple University Press, 1994), 305, 312. Kunzel's argument suggests that while American society handled white women's pregnancy as "treatable" at the individual level, it defined unmarried black mothers as reflective of a systemic problem due to sexual promiscuity of the race. Such racist attitudes undergirded constructions like Daniel Patrick Moynihan's *The Negro Family: The Case for National Action* which would underlie national policies on welfare.
41. Quoted from Breines, *Young, White, and Miserable*, 115, 119. Also see Peril, *College Girls*, 303.
42. Stroup, Interview by Author, November 14, 2010.
43. Taylor, Interview by Author, December 13–14, 2003.
44. Ibid.
45. Ibid. For the American Medical Association statistic, see: Rickie Solinger, "Extreme Danger: Women Abortionists and Their Clients before *Roe V. Wade*," in *Not June Cleaver: Women and Gender in Postwar America, 1945–1960*, ed. Joanne Meyerowitz (Philadelphia: Temple University Press, 1994), 335.
46. Taylor, Interview by Author, December 13–14, 2003.
47. On the brand name contraceptive pill prescription increase, see Solinger, *Pregnancy and Power*, 171.
48. Edward C. Solomon, "A Condensation of Ideas from a Conference on Educational Needs of College Women for Marriage and Family Planning" *Journal of the NAWDC* 26, 2 (January 1963), 47.
49. Ibid.
50. Resolution VII in National Association of Women Deans and Counselors (NAWDC), "1971 Resolutions," 1971, in MS-218, Committee Files, Box 12, BGSUCAC; NAWDC, "1964 Convention, Knowledge, Values, Decisions," 1964, in MS-218, Convention Files, Box 4, BGSUCAC; Lynn Bartlett, "IAWS Advisor's Annual Report to NAWDC," March, 1967, in Intercollegiate Association of Women Students Records, 1922–1980 (77-M126–82-M100), Box 17, Folder 196: NAWDC, Radcliffe Institute, Harvard University, Schlesinger Library, Cambridge, MA (hereafter SL). A native Kansan, Kirkendall attended Kansas State University in 1928 where he received his Bachelor of Science degree. He completed his education at Columbia University and was professor of family life at Oregon State University from 1949 through 1969. Calderone was a Republican and a Quaker, and she directed the new organization under the principle that scientific information would ease cultural discomfort and individual anxiety

about sex. Attendance figures are from loose paper inside NAWDC, "1964 Convention, Knowledge, Values, Decisions," in MS-218, Convention Files, Box 4, BGSUCAC.
51. Dorothy Truex, "Education of Women, the Student Personnel Profession and the New Feminism," *Journal of the NAWDC* 35 (Fall 1971), 19.
52. Taylor, Interview by Author, December 13–14, 2003.
53. Shavlik, Interview by Author, August 21–22, 2010 (Estes Park, CO).
54. Bailey, *Sex in the Heartland*, 119.
55. Solinger, *Pregnancy and Power*, 184; Bailey, *Sex in the Heartland*, 105–135; "like bubble gum" is from ibid., 133. Bailey considers the role of the pill in the sexual revolution at KU in detail.
56. Taylor, Interview by Author, December 13–14, 2003.
57. Ibid.
58. R. K. Greenbank, "Are Medical Students Learning Psychiatry?" *Pennsylvania Medical Journal* 64 (1961); H. I. Lief, "Sex Education in Medical Schools," *Journal of Medical Education* 46, 4 (1971); Shavlik, Interview by Author, March 4, 2014 (New York, NY); Isadore Rubin, "Sex and the College Student: A Bibliography of New Findings and Insights," *Journal of the NAWDC* 26, 2 (January 1963), 37.
59. While Bailey suggested that SDS pushed for the first sanctioning of contraception information at KU, Taylor addressed the topic formally in 1965 within the administration. Bailey argues that SDS drove the discussion of removal of parietals when SDS began raising such issues in February of 1966. However, Taylor's efforts to dismantle women's regulations began substantially before the SDS agitation. KU Civil Rights Council and Students for a Democratic Society, "Students Want to Know," March 11, 1966, in Office of Student Affairs Records (Balfour/Alderson) (hereafter RG 76/0 or 76/0/5), Box 4, Folder: COSA 1965–1968, UKL; Donald K. Alderson, "Handwritten Notes from Meeting in Provost Surface's Office Including Woodruff, Alderson and Taylor," March 14, 1966, in RG 76/0, Box 10, Folder: 51/0 Student Personnel Council: Council on Student Affairs 1965–4/26/66 I, UKL; Bailey, *Sex in the Heartland*, 92–94.
60. Janet Sears Robinson, Interview by Author, August 20, 2010 (Kerrville, TX). COSA members included: the dean of students, university registrar, union director, director of the guidance bureau, faculty representatives from the College of Liberal Arts and Sciences and the School of Engineering and two from the university senate as well as the deans of men and women, and six student leaders. See Dean Laurence C. Woodruff, "Council on Student Affairs, Handwritten Notes," no date, in RG 76/0, Box 4, Folder: COSA 1965–1968, UKL. For information on Schwegler's background, see University of Kansas, "Deaths," http://www.oread.ku.edu/Oread96/OreadAug23/page8/deaths.html; Student Personnel Committee, "Agenda 1965–1966," 1965, in RG 76/0, Box 4, Folder: 51/0 COSA 1965–1968, UKL.
61. Alderson, "Handwritten Notes from Meeting in Provost Surface's Office Including Woodruff, Alderson and Taylor," February 28, 1966, in RG 76/0/5, Box 10, Folder: 51/0 Student Personnel Council: Council on Student Affairs 1965–4/26/66 I, UKL.
62. Bailey, *Sex in the Heartland*, 115–118; Shavlik, Interviews by Author, January 2007, August 21–22, 2010, November 18–19, 2006; Stroup,

Interviews by Author, May 12, 2010, November 14, 2010; Taylor, Interview by Author, December 13–14, 2003.
63. *UDK,* November 4, 1966, quoted in Clifford S. Griffin, *The University of Kansas: A History* (Lawrence: University Press of Kansas, 1974), 634.
64. Bailey, *Sex in the Heartland,* 107–112, 115–118, 124.
65. Taylor, Interview by Author, December 13–14, 2003.
66. AWS Forum, "Forum Minutes," January 9, 1969, in Dean of Women's Papers (hereafter RG 53/0), Box 2, Folder: 1968–1969 IV, UKL; Alderson, "Council on Student Affairs Minutes," March 5, 1968, in RG 76/0/5, Box 10, Folder: 51/0 Student Personnel Committee 1966–6/18/69, UKL.
67. AWS Council, "Council Minutes," February 4, 1969, in RG 53/0, Box 2, Folder: 1968–1969 IV, UKL; "Co-Eds Attack Stereotyped Status of Women," *The Wichita Eagle and Beacon,* January 31, 1971, 1; February Sisters, "Addendum II: An Historical Perspective—the Health Concerns of Women Students at the University of Kansas," 1972, in RG 76/0, Box 4, Folder: COSA 1965–1968, UKL; Shavlik, Interview by Author, August 21–22, 2010; Shavlik, "Telephone Interview by Author, March 22, 2011.
68. Julie Thatcher, "Dean Taylor Discusses Sex, the Pill and the New Morality," *UDK,* January 9, 1970. Also quoted in Bailey, *Sex in the Heartland,* 124.
69. Carol Gwinn, "Facing the Abortion Option: KU Information Helps Women Find Counseling and Advice through Three Different Offices," *UDK,* August 23, 1973, 1; Commission on the Status of Women, "Beyond High School," November 7, 1970, in Commission on the Status of Women Chronological Records (hereafter RG 67/48), Box 1, Folder: 1970–1971, UKL; Commission on the Status of Women, "Human Sexuality Series Final Program," April 21, 1971, in RG 67/48, Box 1, Folder: 1970–1971, UKL. The AWS chapter was renamed in 1969 as the Commission on the Status of Women, taking the name of the committee that had existed within AWS since Taylor's earliest years on campus. Commission on the Status of Women, "Comment," November, 1971, in RG 67/48, Box 1, Folder: 1971–1972, UKL; Commission on the Status of Women, "Commission on the Status of Women Calendar 1971–72," in RG 53/0, Box No. 4, Folder: 1971–1972, UKL.
70. Judy Henry, "February Sisters' History Related, Demands Probed," *UDK,* February 17, 1972, 3.
71. February Sisters, "Addendum II: An Historical Perspective—the Health Concerns of Women Students at the University of Kansas," in RG 76/0, Box 4, Folder: COSA 1965–1968, UKL.
72. Solinger, *Pregnancy and Power,* 179–181.
73. Cornelia V. Christenson, "Premarital Pregnancies and Their Outcome," *Journal of the NAWDC* 26, 2 (January 1963), 63; Taylor, Interview by Author, December 13–14, 2003.
74. Lawrence Lader, *Abortion II: Making the Revolution* (Boston: Beacon Press, 1973), 83.
75. The termination of a pregnancy due to medical danger for a mother was legally permitted in the early twentieth century and licensed physicians routinely referred women to clinics for medically approved contraindications like cardiovascular conditions, kidney problems, neurological conditions, toxemia, respiratory disease, blood diseases, diabetes, placental abruption, lupus, and psychiatric disorders. For more on this background see Rickie

Solinger, "'A Complete Disaster': Abortion and the Politics of Hospital Abortion Committees, 1950–1970," *Feminist Studies* 19, 2 (Summer 1993), 243.
76. Boards approved surgical procedures for nonwhite women less often as physicians often perceived them to be promiscuous, an imposition of racist stereotypes. Poor white women, also sometimes perceived as hypersexual, often could not afford hospital operations even if they could convince a board to allow one.
77. Cynthia Gorney, *Articles of Faith* (New York: Simon and Schuster, 1998), 45–48; Joffe, *Doctors of Conscience*, 132. New York, Alaska, Hawaii, and Washington repealed all criminal penalties for abortion provided that the procedure occurred early in the pregnancy by a licensed physician. See Ruth Roemer, "Abortion Law Reform and Repeal: Legislative and Judicial Developments," *American Journal of Public Health* 61, 3 (March 1971), 500.
78. Lader, *Abortion II: Making the Revolution*, 84; Photocopy, "Kansas Abortion Statute," 1970, in Emily Taylor Women's Resource Center Records (hereafter RG 76/3), Box 1, UKL; William R. Roy, "Abortion: A Physician's View," *Washburn Law Journal* 9, 3 (Spring 1970), 404.
79. Robinson, Interview by Author, August 20, 2010; Stokstad, Interview by Author, July 28, 2010. The anonymity practiced in the dean of women's office is also noted in Gwinn, "Facing the Abortion Option," in *UDK*.
80. Peggy Scott, "Participants Traced Women's Groups Past," in *UDK* October 19, 1973.
81. Taylor, Interview by Author, December 13–14, 2003.
82. Bailey, *Sex in the Heartland*, 63–74.
83. Shavlik, Interview by Author, March 4, 2014.
84. Louise Douce, Telephone Interview by Author, February 2, 2014.
85. Shavlik, Interview by Author, November 18–19, 2006.
86. "Two More Extremes," *LJW*, July 24, 1970.
87. Taylor, Interview by Author, July 3, 1997 (Lawrence, KS).
88. Although the term "sexual harassment" did not enter the public parlance until after 1979, I use it here because it is the best way to convey what was actually occurring even before the language for it existed.
89. In 1977, the Equal Employment Opportunity Commission began to address incidents where women faced a hostile work environment, coining the phrase "sexual harassment": Nancy MacLean, *Freedom Is Not Enough: The Opening of the American Work Place* (Cambridge, Mass.: Harvard University Press with Russell Sage Foundation, 2006), 145.
90. Taylor, "Interview by Author, 13–14 December 2003."
91. Women's Coalition, "Women's Stuff," 1971, in RG 67/48, Box 1, Folder: 1971–1972, UKL.
92. Although the term "date rape" did not exist in the 1960s, I use it here because these rapes occurred while women were on a date with their rapist.
93. AWS, 1968–1969, in RG 53/0, Box No. 2, Folder: 1968–1969 IV, UKL; Frederic Storaska, Letter to Taylor, September 20, 1968, in RG 53/0, Box 2, Folder: 1968–1969 II, UKL; Stroup, Interview by Author, November 14, 2010. The organization of the self-defense lecture is also noted in AWS Council, "Council Minutes," in RG 53/0, Box 2, Folder: 1968–1969 IV, UKL.

94. The National Organization for Women established a task force on rape in 1973 and many local chapters followed suit in 1974. Frederika E. Schmitt and Patricia Yancey Martin, "The History of the Anti-Rape and Rape Crisis Center Movements," in *Encyclopedia of Interpersonal Violence*, ed. Clarie M. Renezetti and Jeffery Edleson (Thousand Oaks: Sage Publications, 2006); Susan Schechter, *Women and Male Violence: The Visions and Struggles of the Battered Women's Movement* (Boston,: South End Press, 1982), 35; Sara M. Evans, *Tidal Wave: How Women Changed America at Century's End* (New York: Free Press, 2003), 49.
95. Stroup, Telephone Interview with Author, April 16, 2014.
96. "A. B. Johnson Sentenced, to Face Mental Evaluation," *UDK*, November 11, 1974, 1; Larry Winn Jr, "Time to Act on Rape Bill, Congressional Record," March 7, 1974, in RG 76/3, Box 13, UKL. While rape statistics provide some outline of the scale of the issue, rape was a particularly under-reported crime due to women's reluctance to discuss publicly an attack since society often blamed the victim for causing the assault. Thus, reality may have outpaced the reported number of assaults.
97. Bailey, *Sex in the Heartland*, 197-198; Casey Eike, Telephone Interview by Author, February 27, 2011. Taylor believed it was the first university sanctioned center. Eike recalled that this was the second rape crisis center established in the nation. However, the author has been unable to date such programs independently of Eike and others' memory that this was the case.
98. "Elusive Rapist on K.U. Campus," *Kansas City Times*, March 2, 1974; Office of the Dean of Women, "Women's Security Meeting," February 20, 1974, in RG 53/0, Box 10, Folder: Whistlestop, UKL.
99. Nancy Bingel, Letter to Taylor, May 7, 1974; Joyce Wagley, Letter to Taylor, March 3, 1974, both in RG 53/0, Box 10, Folder: Whistlestop, UKL.
100. William Balfour, Letter to Archie R. Dykes, April 1974; John J. Conard, Letter to Gil Dyck, February 28, 1974; Dorian A. Doherty, Letter to Mr. and Mrs. John Harvey, March 4, 1974; Dykes, Letter to Mr. and Mrs. John Harvey, March 31, 1974, all in RG 53/0, Box 10, Folder: Whistlestop, UKL.
101. John J. Conard, Letter to Dyck, February 28, 1974.
102. Balfour, Letter to Dykes, April 1974; Dykes, Letter to Balfour, 1974, in RG 53/0, Box 10, Folder: Whistlestop, UKL.
103. "Whistlestop Meeting," April 3, 1974, in RG 53/0, Box 10, UKL; Taylor, Letter to Lawrence area stores, 1974; Eike and Kathy Hoggard, Letter to Dykes, April 17, 1974; both in RG 53/0, Box 10, Folder: Whistlestop, UKL.
104. Delbert M. Shankel, Letter to All KU Vice-Chancellors and Deans, April 11 1974, in RG 53/0, Box 10, Folder: Whistlestop, UKL.
105. Vincent J. Bilotta, Letter to Taylor, April 11, 1974, in RG 53/0, Box 10, Folder: Whistlestop, UKL.
106. Stroup, Telephone Interview by Author, April, 16, 2014.
107. Eike, Telephone Interview by Author, February 27, 2011.
108. Taylor, Interview by Author, July 1, 1997 (Lawrence, KS).
109. Faye Dottheim, Letter to Friends of the Commission on the Status of Women, April 25, 1974, in RG 76/0, Box 4, Folder: Commission on the Status of Women April 25, 1974–November 1975, UKL. Other institutions

that requested information were: Phoenix College, Southern Illinois University, University of Arkansas, St. Olaf College and Stephens College.
110. Shirley Gilham, Letter to Taylor, April 20, 1974, in RG 53/0, Box 10, Folder: Whistlestop, UKL.
111. Taylor, Interview by Author, May 20, 1997 (Lawrence, KS); Dykes, Letter to Balfour, 1974, RG 53/0, Box 10, Folder: Whistlestop, UKL.
112. Bilotta, Letter to Taylor, April 11, 1974.

5 The Dean of Women in the Age of Protest

1. Linda Cook and Carol Borg, Letter to Emily Taylor, March 11, 1965.
2. Ibid.
3. Rusty L. Monhollon, *This Is America? The Sixties in Lawrence, Kansas* (New York: Palgrave, 2002), 73.
4. For further discussion of the civil rights movement in Kansas, see Gretchen Cassel Eick, *Dissent in Wichita: The Civil Rights Movement in the Midwest, 1954–72* (Urbana, IL and Chicago: University of Illinois Press, 2001).
5. Monhollon, *This Is America?*, 30–33, 49–50.
6. Eunice Mae Acheson, *The Effective Dean of Women: A Study of the Personal and Professional Characteristics of a Selected Group of Deans of Women* (Chicago: University of Chicago Press, 1932), 31; Janice Gerda, "A History of the Conferences of Deans of Women, 1903–1922" (PhD diss., Bowling Green State University, 2004), 157; Lulu Haskell Holmes, *A History of the Position of Dean of Women in a Selected Group of Co-Educational Colleges and Universities in the United States* (New York: Teachers College, Columbia University, 1939), 13, 18, 57–58, 60; Susan Lynn, "Gender and Progressive Politics," in *Not June Cleaver: Women and Gender in Postwar America, 1945–1960*, ed. Joanne J. Meyerowitz (Philadelphia: Temple University Press, 1994), 121; Jana Nidiffer, *Pioneering Deans of Women: More Than Wise and Pious Matrons* (New York: Teachers College Press, 2000), 73.
7. Gerda, "A History of the Conferences of Deans of Women, 1903–1922," 157.
8. Berea College originally accepted black students and then reversed its policy and denied blacks admission until 1950. See Jacqueline Burnside, "Educated and Organized: Women at the Center of Berea College History, 1850s–2000s," *Hutchins Library, Berea College*, http://libraryguides.berea.edu/genderessay#fn16; Gerda, "A History of the Conferences of Deans of Women, 1903–1922," 157; Lynn D. Gordon, *Gender and Higher Education in the Progressive Era* (New Haven: Yale University Press, 1990), 108; Carolyn Terry Bashaw, *"Stalwart Women": A Historical Analysis of Deans of Women in the South* (New York: Teachers College Press, 1999); Florence Mary Fitch Papers (RG 30/037), Oberlin College Archives, Oberlin, OH; American Council of Guidance and Personnel Associations (hereafter CGPA), "Convention Program," 29 March–1 April, 1948, National Association for Women in Education Records (hereafter MS-218), Bowling Green State University Library, Center for Archival Collections, National Student Affairs Archives, Bowling Green, OH (hereafter BGSUCAC); Office of the Provost University of Pittsburgh, "The History of Women at Pitt: Black Women at Pitt," http://www.provost.pitt.edu/whistory/black/black.html.

9. Cornell University Archives, "Early Black Women at Cornell: Part and Apart, 1890s–1930s," http://rmc.library.cornell.edu/earlyblackwomen/introduction/; Ruth Brett, "Our Living History: Reminiscences of Black Participation in NAWDAC," *Journal of the National Association of Women Deans, Administrators and Counselors* 43, 2 (1980): 3–13. Also, see: Carroll L. L. Miller and Anne S. Pruitt-Logan, *Faithful to the Task at Hand: The Life of Lucy Diggs Slowe* (Albany: SUNY Press, 2012), 240–242.
10. Geraldine Jonçich Clifford, *Lone Voyagers: Academic Women in Coeducational Universities, 1870–1937* (New York: Feminist Press at the City University of New York: Distributed by the Talman Co., 1989), 284, 307.
11. Brett, "Our Living History" (1980), 3–5, 9–11. See also other articles in *Journal of the NAWDAC* 43, 2 (1980).
12. In 1954, the Association of Deans of Women and Advisers to Girls in Negro Schools merged with the National Association of Personnel Deans and Advisers of Men in Negro Institutions.
13. Linda Eisenmann, *Higher Education for Women in Postwar America, 1945–1965* (Baltimore: Johns Hopkins University Press, 2006), 130; "Records of the Women's Bureau, Files of the National Women's Committee for Civil Rights, 1963–1964," in Records of the Women's Bureau in the Department of Labor (RG 86), Box 22, Folder: NAWDC, National Archives at College Park, MD.
14. Donna Shavlik, Interview by Author, March 4, 2014 (New York, NY); Shavlik, Telephone Interview by Author, March 22, 2011.
15. University of Pittsburgh Dean of Women Thrysa Amos worked closely with Lucy Diggs Slowe and Slowe's students. Amos inspired Hilda Davis to become a dean of women while she was a student of Slowe's. Hilda Davis, Interview by Patricia Hill Scott, Video Recording, MS-218, BGSUCAC; Kathryn Nemeth Tuttle, "What Became of the Dean of Women? Changing Roles for Women Administrators in American Higher Education, 1940–1980" (PhD diss., University of Kansas, 1996), 105, 132; Brett, "Our Living History," (1980).
16. For detail regarding Ruth McCarn, see Tuttle, "What Became of the Dean of Women," Chapter Two.
17. Ibid., 210, 626–628.
18. Kristine M. McCusker, "'The Forgotten Years' of America's Civil Rights Movement: The University of Kansas, 1939–1961" (MA thesis, University of Kansas, 1994), 137–144; Tuttle, "What Became of the Dean of Women," 627.
19. Tuttle, "Emily Taylor," in *Reflecting Back, Looking Forward: Civil Rights and Student Affairs,* ed. Lisa E. Wolf-Wendel, Susan B. Twombly, Tuttle, Kelly Ward, and Joy L. Gaston-Gayles (Washington, DC: NASPA, Inc., 2004), 297.
20. Ibid., 297–298.
21. Taylor, Interview by Author, July 3, 1997 (Lawrence, KS).
22. This "elite egalitarianism" was common among American Association of University Women (AAUW) members: Susan Levine, *Degrees of Equality: The American Association of University Women and the Challenge of Twentieth-Century Feminism* (Philadelphia: Temple University Press, 1995), 30.
23. Michael P. Fisher, "The Turbulent Years: The University of Kansas, 1960–1975, a History" (PhD diss., University of Kansas, 1979), 39.

24. Tuttle, "Emily Taylor," 302.
25. Shavlik, Interview by Author, August 21–22, 2010 (Estes Park, CO).
26. "Dean Says Sororities Have No Discriminatory Clauses," *UDK*, October 5, 1960, 6; Monhollon, *This Is America?*, 71; Tuttle, "Emily Taylor," 299. Shavlik recalled that the black sororities were only loosely affiliated with the Panhellenic Council and did not participate in the rush process. Shavlik, Telephone Interview by Author, March 22, 2011.
27. Tuttle, "What Became of the Dean of Women," 271–272.
28. Fisher, "University of Kansas, 1960–1975," 78; W. Clarke Wescoe, "Report to the Board of Regents," March 14, 1965, in Chancellor's Correspondence, Executive Secretary Case Files, 1959–1965 (hereafter RG 2/0/1), Box 9, Folder: Civil Rights Demonstration, March 8–9, 1965, UKL. Fraternities stayed segregated by race until 1968 when the Alpha Kappa Lambda fraternity issued a bid for membership to a black man, Willie R. McDaniel. Donald K. Alderson, "Memorandum for the File of Alpha Kappa Lambda," 1968, in Dean of Men Chronological Records (hereafter RG 52), Box 19, Folder: 1967–1970, UKL.
29. Wescoe, "Report to the Board of Regents."
30. Taylor, Interview by Author.
31. Tuttle, "Emily Taylor," 72; Kala Stroup, Telephone Interview by Author, April 16, 2014; Monhollon, *This Is America?*
32. Stroup, Telephone Interview by Author, April 16, 2014.
33. Tuttle, "Emily Taylor," 300.
34. Ibid., 301. Wescoe, "Report to the Board of Regents."
35. Dean Laurence C. Woodruff, "University Human Relations Committee," No date, in Office of Student Affairs Records (hereafter RG 76/0 or 76/0/5), Box 4, UKL.
36. Tuttle, "Emily Taylor," 301–302.
37. Taylor, Interview by Author.
38. Joy L. Gaston-Gayles, Lisa E. Wolf-Wendel, Kathryn Nemeth Tuttle, Susan B. Twombly, and Kelly Ward, "From Disciplinarian to Change Agent: How the Civil Rights Era Changed the Roles of Student Affairs Professionals," *NASPA Journal* 42, 3 (2005); Taylor, Interview by Author; Tuttle, "Emily Taylor," 302.
39. Taylor, Interview by Author.
40. Taylor, "Handwritten Speech Notes," in Author's Collection of Emily Taylor's Papers, St. Louis, MO (hereafter Author's Collection); As quoted in Tuttle, "Emily Taylor," 302; Taylor, Interview by Author.
41. Ad Hoc Committee of Students from Lewis Hall, "Report to the Inter-Residence Hall Council," 1965, in RG 53/0, Box 6, Folder: Civil Rights March 2, 1965–March 18, 1965, UKL. Drafts of the report may be found in the same location in the archives.
42. Associated Women Students (AWS) Forum, "Forum Minutes," in RG 53/0, Box 2, Folder: 1968–1969 IV, UKL; Lydia Tate, "The Report of the Minutes of the Council Retreat" April 28, 1968, in RG 53/0, Box 2, Folder: 1968–1969 IV, UKL.
43. Unknown, Letter to Wescoe, in RG 52, Box 19, Folder: 1967–1970, UKL; Michael McNally, Letter to Clark E. Bricker, May 16, 1968, in RG 76/0/5, Box 6, Folder: UHRC 1968–1970, UKL.
44. Tuttle, "Emily Taylor," 303.

45. Stroup, Telephone Interview by Author, April 16, 2014. Tuttle, "Emily Taylor." 303.
46. Taylor, Interview by Author, July 4, 1997 (Lawrence, KS); Head Pom Pon Girl Shirley Gossett, Letter to William Balfour, in RG 76/0/5, Box 10, Folder: 51/0 Student Protests 10/26/67–10/3/69, UKL; Michael McNally, Letter to Bricker, May 16, 1968; Tuttle, "Emily Taylor," 295–308.
47. Monhollon, *This Is America?*, 119.
48. Janet Sears Robinson, Interview by Author, August 20, 2010 (Kerrville, TX).
49. Louise A. Douce, "Coming out on the Wave of Feminism, Coming to Age on the Ocean of Multiculturalism," in *Deconstructing Heterosexism in the Counseling Professions: A Narrative Approach*, ed. James M. Croteau, Julianne S. Lark, Melissa A. Lidderdale, and Y. Barry Chung (Thousand Oaks: Sage Publications, 2005), 60.
50. Monhollon, *This Is America?*, 194; William Robinson, Telephone Interview by Author, November 4, 2012.
51. Sarah Wohlrabe, "Taylor: Committed to Equal Rights for Women" in *UDK*; Unknown Author, in RG 53/0, Box 7, Folder: 53/0 "Feminism" October 29, 1969–1971, UKL.
52. "'Feminism' October 29, 1966–1971," in RG 53/0, Box No. 7, UKL; M. Kay Harris, Telephone Interview by Author, February 14, 2014.
53. Caroljean Brune, Interview by Author, February 12, 2011 (Lawrence, KS).
54. Ibid.
55. Peggy Scott, "Participants Traced Women's Groups Past," *UDK*, October 19, 1973.
56. "Co-Eds Attack Stereotyped Status of Women," in *The Wichita Eagle and Beacon*; Caroljean Brune, Interview by Author, February 12, 2011; Scott, "Participants Traced Women's Groups Past," in *UDK*.
57. Gary Murrell, "New K.U. Student Group Seeks End of 'Bias' against Women," in *Kansas City Star*, unknown date, in RG 53/0, Box 1, UKL.
58. Taylor, Interview with Shavlik, Video Recording, MS-218 in BGSUCAC.
59. Hilda Threlkeld, Letter to Taylor, June 7, 1946, Author's Collection.
60. Fisher, "University of Kansas, 1960–1975," 118, 122.
61. Ibid., 128–129; Robbie Lieberman, *Prairie Power: Voices of 1960s Midwestern Student Protest* (Columbia: University of Missouri Press, 2004), 218–219; Monhollon, *This Is America?*, 79–80.
62. Fisher, "University of Kansas, 1960–1975," 153.
63. Ibid., 164–165.
64. Ibid., 155–157.
65. Beth L. Bailey, *Sex in the Heartland* (Cambridge: Harvard University Press, 1999), 124; Fisher, "University of Kansas, 1960–1975," 160.
66. Monhollon, *This Is America?*, 146; Ray Morgan, "Days Are Quiet on K.U. Campus: University Officials Say Class Attendance Normal since Fire, Parents Are Worried, Telephone Circuits Often Overloaded with Calls to Students," *Kansas City Times*, April 24, 1970; Gary Murrell, "Curfew Again at Lawrence: Kansas Governor Acts after Rash of Night Fires," *Kansas City Star*, April 23, 1970.
67. Shavlik, Interview by Author, November 18–19, 2006 (Estes Park, CO); Stroup, Telephone Interview by Author, April 16, 2014.
68. Shavlik, Interview by Author, August 21–22, 2010.

69. Associated Press, "227 Colleges Closed in Wake of Protests," *UDK*, May 8, 1970; Associated Press, "To Plant Trees at K.U.," *Kansas City Times*, May 6, 1970, 1A; Curt Chaudoin, "Committee Seeks Day of Alternatives," *UDK*, May 4, 1970; Ralph Gage, "Protests Center on MS Area," *LJW*, May 5, 1970, 1.
70. Shavlik, Interview by Author, January, 2007 (Kansas City, MO).
71. Casey Eike, Telephone Interview by Author, February 27, 2011; "Decision Time," *LJW*, May 7, 1970; "Two Wanted in Vandalism on Campus," *LJW*, May 7, 1970.
72. Lieberman, *Prairie Power*, 149–150.
73. John Sanford, Telephone Inteview by Author, January 17, 2011; Monhollon, *This Is America?*, 159; Sarah Scott, Telephone Interview by Author, May 26, 2014.
74. John Sanford, Telephone Inteview by Author, January 17.
75. Threlkeld, Letter to Taylor, June 7, 1946, Author's Collection.
76. Taylor, Interview by Author.

6   From Quiet Activism to Radical Tactics

1. Sarah Scott, Telephone Interview by Author, May 26, 2014.
2. Emily Taylor, Interview by Author, December 13–14, 2003 (Lawrence, KS).
3. Ibid.
4. On E. Laurence Chalmers, see Beth L. Bailey, *Sex in the Heartland* (Cambridge: Harvard University Press, 1999), 179; Taylor, Interview by Author, December 13–14, 2003.
5. Geraldine Jonçich Clifford, *Lone Voyagers: Academic Women in Coeducational Universities, 1870–1937* (New York: Feminist Press at the City University of New York, 1989), 94; Margaret A. Lowe, *Looking Good: College Women and Body Image, 1875–1930* (Baltimore, London: Johns Hopkins University Press, 2003), 152.
6. Susan Kingsbury, *Economic Status of University Women in the U.S.A.: Report of the Committee on Economic and Legal Status of Women, American Association of University Women in Cooperation with the Women's Bureau, United States Department of Labor* (Washington, DC: US Government Printing Office, 1939). Also see Susan Levine, *Degrees of Equality: The American Association of University Women and the Challenge of Twentieth-Century Feminism* (Philadelphia: Temple University Press, 1995), 27, 34, 41–42, 59, 60–61, 63–64, 66–67, 90, 96–98, 100–104 162, 164.
7. Clifford, *Lone Voyagers*, 91–92, 302; Jana Nidiffer, *Pioneering Deans of Women: More Than Wise and Pious Matrons* (New York: Teachers College Press, 2000), 119.
8. Carroll L. L. Miller and Anne S. Pruitt-Logan, *Faithful to the Task at Hand: The Life of Lucy Diggs Slowe* (Albany: SUNY Press, 2012), 124–127.
9. For more information about race and the American Association of University Women (AAUW) see Miller and Pruitt-Logan, *Faithful to the Task at Hand*, 70, 124–127, 239, 265, 327; Levine, *Degrees of Equality* 68, 105–135, 154, 159, 175.
10. Also, American Council on Education (ACE) Commission on the Education of Women (CEW) leader, Esther Lloyd-Jones, former Northwestern University student affairs director for women and faculty member at

Teachers College, served on the President's Commission on the Status of Women (PCSW) Committee on Federal Employment. For discussion of the education committee and the PCSW see Linda Eisenmann, *Higher Education for Women in Postwar America, 1945–1965* (Baltimore: Johns Hopkins University Press, 2006), 141–168; and Cynthia Ellen Harrison, *On Account of Sex: The Politics of Women's Issues, 1945–1968* (Berkeley: University of California Press, 1988), 229–236.

11. Eisenmann, "A Time of Quiet Activism: Research, Practice, and Policy in American Women's Higher Education, 1945–1965," *History of Education Quarterly* 45, 1 (2005), 138.
12. "Records of the Women's Bureau, Files of the National Women's Committee for Civil Rights, 1963–1964," in Records of the Women's Bureau in the Department of Labor (hereafter RG 86), Box 22, Folder: NAWDC, National Archives at College Park, MD (hereafter NACP).
13. Alice Kessler-Harris, *In Pursuit of Equity: Women, Men and Quest for Economic Citizenship in the 20th-Century America* (New York: Oxford University Press, 2001), 277; Taylor, Interview by Author, July 7, 1997 (Lawrence, KS).
14. Taylor, Interview by Author, July 14, 1998 (Lawrence, KS).
15. Harrison, *On Account of Sex*, 192–196.
16. Taylor, Interview by Author, July 14, 1998.
17. Scott, Telephone Interview by Author, May 26, 2014.
18. "KU Women to Attend Convention," No date, in Author's Collection of Emily Taylor's Papers, St. Louis, MO (hereafter Author's Collection); Commission on the Status of Women, "Comment," in Commission on the Status of Women Chronological Records (hereafter RG 67/48), Box 1, Folder: 1971–1972, University of Kansas Libraries, Kenneth Spencer Research Library, University Archives, Lawrence, KS (hereafter UKL); Taylor, Interview by Author, July 19, 1998 (Lawrence, KS).
19. Founded by Ohio women in 1968, the Women's Equity Action League (WEAL) avoided the controversial topic of abortion. Sara M. Evans, *Tidal Wave: How Women Changed America at Century's End* (New York: Free Press, 2003), 83; "KU Women to Attend Convention," in Author's Collection.
20. Scott, Telephone Interview by Author, May 26, 2014; Casey Eike, Telephone Interview by Author, February 27, 2011.
21. Margaret W. Rossiter, *Women Scientists in America: Struggles and Strategies to 1940* (Baltimore: The Johns Hopkins University Press, 1982), 35, 141.
22. The group submitting the report consisted of Christine Asch (French), Paul Gilles (Chemistry), Frances Ingemann (Linguistics), Delbert Shankel (Microbiology), and Marilyn Stokstad. Judy Henry, "February Sisters' History Related, Demands Probed," in *UDK*, February 17, 1972; Stokstad, Interview by Author, July 28, 2010 (Lawrence, KS); Stokstad, "AAUP—University of Kansas Chapter Report of the Chapter's Committee (W) on the Status of Women in the Profession," May, 1971, in Marilyn Stokstad Personal Papers (hereafter PP 470), Box 15, Folder 21: Salary Studies, UKL. Also see Nancy MacLean, *Freedom Is Not Enough: The Opening of the American Work Place* (Cambridge: Harvard University Press with Russell Sage Foundation, 2006), 190–191.
23. Chalmers, Letter to Phil Gary, July 9, 1971, in Affirmative Action Artificial Records (hereafter RG 8), Folder: 1971/1972 II, UKL.

24. Taylor and Stokstad, Letter to Chalmers, September 20, 1971, in Office of Academic Affairs, Jim Rosser Records (hereafter RG 10/1/1), Box 1, Folder: Affirmative Action until 1973 Part 3, UKL.
25. Robert E. Duncan, "KU Required to Submit Program Showing Equal Opportunity Plans," *UDK*, February 9, 1972, 1; February Sisters, "Position Paper of the February Sisters," February 4, 1972 (handwritten onto document), 1972, in Student Activities (Judy Browder) Records (hereafter RG 71/18), Box 5, UKL; Philip Gary, Letter to "Gentlemen," May 28, 1971, in RG 8, Folder: 1971/1972 II, UKL; February Sisters, "A History of the Seizure and Occupation of the East Asian Studies Building by the February Sisters, or, What It Takes to Make Men Move," Unknown date, in Emily Taylor Women's Resource Center Records (hereafter RG 76/3), Box 9, Folder: History of Women February Sisters, UKL; Francis H. Heller, Letter to Joan Handley AAUP Committee W Chairwoman, December 6, 1971, in RG 10/1/1, Box 1, Folder: Affirmative Action until 1973 Part 3, UKL.
26. Walter Smith and Kala M. Stroup, *Science Career Exploration for Women* (Washington, DC: National Science Teachers Association, 1978).
27. Stroup, Telephone Interview by Author, April 16, 2014; Kate Hevner Mueller, *Educating Women for a Changing World*.
28. Donna Shavlik, Interview by Author, September 20, 1997 (Lawrence, KS). Shavlik was involved with the Intercollegiate Association of Women Students (IAWS) from 1957 when she served as Executive Secretary until 1982 when she served as national advisor just before the organization shut its doors in 1983.
29. National Association of Women Deans and Counselors (NAWDC), "Inter-Association Files," in National Association for Women in Education Records (hereafter MS-218), Folder: IAWS-NAWDC Liaison Committee 1960–1983, Bowling Green State University Library, Center for Archival Collections, National Student Affairs Archives, Bowling Green, OH (hereafter BGSUCAC).
30. Ibid; Gail Short Hanson, "Organizational Transformation: A Case Study of the Intercollegiate Association for Women Students" (PhD diss., George Washington University, 1995).
31. NAWDC, "Convention Program: Behold! We Are Doing a New Thing," 1969, in Convention Files, MS-218, Box 4, BGSUCAC.
32. Margaret Ingram, Letter to National Executive Board of IAWS, in IAWS Records, 1922–1980 (hereafter 77-M126–82-M100), Box 17, Folder 153: National Conventions, 1969, Radcliffe Institute, Harvard University, Schlesinger Library (hereafter SL).
33. Associated Women Students (AWS) Council, "Council Minutes," in Dean of Women Chronological Files (hereafter 53/0), Box 2, Folder: 1968–1969 IV, UKL; Hanson, "Organizational Transformation," 100; Debbie Vollmer, "Campus NOW News, Clark University," April 24, 1969, in 77-M126–82-M100, Box 7, Folder 16: NOW, SL.
34. Janice Mendenhall, "Memorandum Re: 'How to Establish a Commission on the Status of Women'," 1969, in 77-M126–82-M100, Box 4, Folder 45: Status of Women Commissions, SL; "How to Establish a Collegiate Commission on the Status of Women," in RG 67/48, Box 1, Folder: 1970–71, UKL; Vollmer, "Campus NOW News, Clark University."

35. Taylor, Interview by Author, July 19, 1998.
36. Taylor, Interview with Shavlik, Video Recording in MS-218, BGSUCAC.
37. Ibid.
38. Hanson, "Organizational Transformation," 82.
39. Jacklyn Roberts, Letter to Mendenhall, November 19, 1969, in 77-M126-82-M100, Box 17, Folder: 196, SL.
40. NAWDC, "Inter-Association Files," in MS-218, Folder: IAWS-NAWDC Liaison Committee 1960–1983, BGSUCAC.
41. Suzanne Bocell and Suzanne Kelly, Letter to Kansas Board of Regents, 1970, in RG 67/48, Box 1, Folder: 1970–1971, UKL; Mendenhall, "Memorandum Re: 'How to Establish a Commission on the Status of Women.'"
42. Barbara Cook, Letter to Executive Secretary Karen Keesling, IAWS, March 25, 1970, in 77-M126–82-M100, Box 6, Folder 19: Karen Keesling, Executive Director, 1971–1972, SL.
43. Taylor, Interview by Author, July 19, 1998; Louise A. Douce, Telephone Interview by Author, February 2, 2014; Douce, "Coming out on the Wave of Feminism, Coming to Age on the Ocean of Multiculturalism," in *Deconstructing Heterosexism in the Counseling Professions: A Narrative Approach*, eds James M. Croteau, Julianne S. Lark, Melissa A. Lidderdale, and Y. Barry Chung (Thousand Oaks: Sage Publications, 2005): 59–70.
44. Taylor served her first term from 1970–1971 to 1971–1972. Janet Douglas served for less than a year in the 1972–1973 school year, with Taylor serving out the remainder of the two year term until mid-1974. The abortion resolution produced some debate and the convention changed the resolution from supporting repeal of all laws to "most" laws and also added a statement that birth control was preferable to abortion. IAWS National Convention, "Minutes of Third, Fourth, and Fifth Business Meetings," March 19–20, 1971, in 77-M126–82-M100, Box 13, Folder 156: 1971, SL; "Report of the NAWDC-IAWS Ad Hoc Committee," April 5, 1969, in 77-M126–82-M100, Box 17, Folder: 196, SL; Hanson, "Organizational Transformation," 223; Douce, Telephone Interview by Author.
45. "AWS and WSGA Records," in AWS Records (RG 44/19), Box 6, Folder: Ohio Commission on the Status of Women: Appreciation Certificate, Ohio State University Archives, Columbus, OH; "State Equal Rights Amendment Clarified," *Oshkosh Daily Northwestern*, March 27, 1973, 2; "AWS Calls for Support of ERA," *Round Up: Student Newspaper of New Mexico State University*, April 14, 1975, 1; "Associated Women Students Records—1948–1981," in AWS Records—1949–1981 (RG 197), Box 1, Folder 29, University of Nevada, Reno, University Archives.
46. Hanson, "Organizational Transformation," 115; "Women Promote Rights Amendment," *UDK*, August 31, 1971. The University of Oklahoma AWS member's quote is from Dorothy Oliver, "Women Students Set Humanist Goals: Convention Held at Arlington Towers," April 6, 1972, Author's Collection.
47. NAWDC, "Convention Program: The Educator in an Era of Social Change: Evolutionist or Revolutionist?," 1970, in Convention Files, MS-218, Box 4, BGSUCAC; NAWDC, "1971 Resolutions," in Committee Files, MS-218, Box 12, BGSUCAC.
48. IAWS, *National Notes* (October 1970) in MS-218, BGSUCAC.

49. KU News Bureau, "History of Women and of the WGSS Program at KU," http://wgss.ku.edu/about/history.shtml. The women's studies course at Cornell was started out of a conference organized by Sheila Tobias in 1969.
50. IAWS, *National Notes* (October 1970).
51. Mueller, "Notes," in Kate Hevner Mueller Papers, 1909–1981 (c170), Box 7, Folder: Marriage—College Age Notes, Resources, ca. 1950s, 1945 Research Notes, Indiana University Archives, Bloomington, IN.
52. IAWS, *Feminine Focus* X, No. 1 (September 1973).
53. Taylor and Keesling, Letter to NAWDC Members, February 15, 1971, in 77-M126-82-M100, Box 17, Folder 196: NAWDC, SL.
54. Sarah Wohlrabe, "Taylor: Committed to Equal Rights for Women" in *UDK* October 19, 1973.
55. Taylor, Interview by Author, July 14, 1998.
56. Levine, *Degrees of Equality*, 27–28; Jana Nidiffer and Carolyn Terry Bashaw, *Women Administrators in Higher Education: Historical and Contemporary Perspectives* (Albany, NY: State University of New York Press, 2001), 140–141.
57. Women's Coalition, "Women's Stuff," in RG 67/48, Box 1, Folder: 1971–1972, UKL.
58. Ibid.
59. Rusty L. Monhollon notes that: "From the beginning, women who publicly identified with the women's liberation movement in Lawrence were divided between 'liberal' and 'radical' feminists. These two groups worked together cautiously to achieve common goals but always seemed to eye one another warily." Monhollon, *This Is America? The Sixties in Lawrence, Kansas* (New York: Palgrave, 2002), 188.
60. Bocell and Kelly, Letter to Regents, 1970; Commission on the Status of Women, "Comment," in RG 67/48, Box 1, Folder: 1971–1972, UKL; "Women's Center Asks Student Fee Support," *Lawrence Journal World* (*LJW*), July 16, 1970; Women's Coalition, "Women's Stuff," in RG 67/48, Box 1, Folder: 1971–1972, UKL; Women's Liberation Collective, "Proposal for Women's Center," no date, in RG 67/48, Box 1, Folder: 1971–1972, UKL; "Women's Unit Requests Funds," *LJW*, July 18, 1970.
61. Bailey, *Sex in the Heartland*, 127; Henry, "February Sisters' History Related"; "The February Sisters," in PP 470, Box 15, Folder 21: Salary Studies UKL; February Sisters, "A History of the Seizure and Occupation of the East Asian Studies Building by the February Sisters, or, What It Takes to Make Men Move," in RG 76/3, Box 9, Folder: History of Women February Sisters, UKL; February Sisters, "Press Release, 9:00, February 5, 1972," 1972, in RG 76/3, Box 9, Folder: History of Women February Sisters, UKL.
62. February Sisters, "Statements of Women Faculty Released to February Sisters," February 6, 1972, in RG 71/18, Box 5, UKL.
63. Banks declined the position offered by Chalmers: "Women's Affairs Post Declined, Remains Open," *UDK*, February 10, 1972. See also February Sisters, "Statements of Women Faculty Released to February Sisters," in RG 71/18, Box 5, UKL; KU News Bureau, February 4, 1972, in Office of Student Affairs Records (hereafter RG 76/0), Box 4, Folder: February Sisters 51/0 2/4/1972–2/17/1972, UKL; February Sisters, "A History of the Seizure and Occupation of the East Asian Studies Building by the

February Sisters, or, What It Takes to Make Men Move," in RG 76/3, Box 9, Folder: History of Women February Sisters, UKL.
64. Janet Sears Robinson, Interview by Author, August 20, 2010 (Kerrville, TX); Eike, "Telephone Interview by Author; "The February Sisters," in PP 470, Box 15, Folder 21: Salary Studies UKL.
65. Bailey, *Sex in the Heartland*, 128; February Sisters, "A History of the Seizure and Occupation of the East Asian Studies Building by the February Sisters, or, What It Takes to Make Men Move," in RG 76/3, Box 9, Folder: History of Women February Sisters, UKL; Bob Womack, "Chalmers Concerned over Women's Lib Assertions," *LJW*, February 16, 1972; "The February Sisters," in PP 470, Box 15, Folder 21: Salary Studies UKL; Stokstad, Interview by Author, July 28, 2010. Robbie Lieberman noted that Brune remembered Taylor attending the bridge party at the chancellor's home. However, Brune told me that she did not believe Taylor had attended the bridge party. Taylor did not indicate attending the chancellor's home either. See Lieberman, *Prairie Power: Voices of 1960s Midwestern Student Protest* (Columbia: University of Missouri Press, 2004), 253.
66. Stokstad, Interview by Author, July 28, 2010; Taylor, Interview by Author, December 13–14, 2003; Scott, Telephone Interview by Author, May 26, 2014.
67. Quoted in Monhollon, *This Is America?*, 202.
68. Stokstad, Interview by Author, July 28, 2010; Bonnie Dunham, "Dinner to Commemorate 'February Sisters,'" *LJW*, February 1, 1987, 1; February Sisters, "A History of the Seizure and Occupation of the East Asian Studies Building by the February Sisters, or, What It Takes to Make Men Move," in RG 76/3, Box 9, Folder: History of Women February Sisters, UKL; "The February Sisters," in PP 470, Box 15, Folder 21: Salary Studies UKL.
69. February Sisters, "Do You Need Child Care?," *UDK*, February 17, 1972, 8. The advertisement lists 864-3552 as a telephone number. This is the same number as listed on the Dean of Women's letterhead. For an example of letterhead, see Office of the Dean of Women, "Women's Security Meeting," in RG 53/0, Box 10, Folder: Whistlestop, UKL.
70. February Sisters, "The February Sisters' Demands: A Progress Report," 1973, in RG 76/3, Box 9, Folder: History of Women February Sisters, UKL; Monhollon, *This Is America?*, 206. Stokstad does not associate her appointment as Associate Dean with the February Sisters incident because it happened a year later. Stokstad, Letter to Author, February 23, 2011. The "Progress Report" cited above also notes that these changes were not "a direct result of the demands" made by the February Sisters.
71. Taylor, Interview by Author, July 1, 1997 (Lawrence, KS); February Sisters, "The February Sisters' Demands: A Progress Report," in RG 76/3, Box 9, Folder: History of Women February Sisters, UKL; Eike, Telephone Interview by Author, February 27, 2011.
72. Taylor, Interview by Author.
73. Ibid.
74. Janet Sears Robinson, Interview by Author, August 20, 2010.
75. February Sisters, "The February Sisters' Demands: A Progress Report," in RG 76/3, Box 9, Folder: History of Women February Sisters, UKL; Raymond A. Schwegler, "Memorandum to All Watkins Hospital Doctors," 1972, in RG 76/0, Box 4, Folder: February Sisters 51/0 2/4/1972–2/17/1972,

UKL; Schwegler, Letter to William Balfour, February 9, 1972, in RG 76/0, Box 4, Folder: February Sisters 51/0 2/4/1972–2/17/1972, UKL; University of Kansas, "Deaths" http://www.oread.ku.edu/Oread96/Oread Aug23/page8/deaths.html; Elaine Zimmerman, "Schwegler Views Sisters Demands," 1972, in RG 76/3, Box 9, Folder: History of Women February Sisters, UKL. Eighteen years later, Schwegler stated that he felt the February Sisters did not need to protest to achieve their outcome, noting that he thought the change would have happened without their activism "Six Demands That Never Left Campus," *LJW*, March 2, 1990.
76. The committee meetings regarding the women's studies program met in Taylor's office suite. Taylor, Interview by Author, December 13–14, 2003.

7 From Deans to Presidents

1. Donna Shavlik, Interview by Author, November 18–19, 2006 (Estes Park, CO); Shavlik, Telephone Interview by Author, May 31, 2014.
2. Jacquelyn D. Elliott, "The American Council on Education's Office of Women in Higher Education: A Case Study of Evolution and Decline 1973–2011" (EdD diss., George Washington University, 2014), 218. The National Association of Commissions for Women was known as the Interstate Association of Commissions for Women (IACW) from 1970 until 1975. It was formalized out of the National Conference of Governor's Commission on the Status of Women, and the Women's Bureau Annual National Conference of Commissions, and the IACW was formally created at the fiftieth anniversary conference of the Women's Bureau. "About Us," http://www.nacw.org/about/index.php?page=history.
3. Shavlik, Interview by Author, November 18–19, 2006; Shavlik, Interview by Author, March 4, 2014 (New York, NY); Shavlik, Telephone Interview by Author, May 31, 2014.
4. Janice Gerda, "A History of the Conferences of Deans of Women, 1903–1922" (PhD diss., Bowling Green State University, 2004), 156.
5. Elliott, "The American Council on Education's OWHE," 203–213.
6. Ibid., 235–236.
7. Bernice Sandler, Telephone Interview by Author, March 14, 2014.
8. Judith Gatlin Bainbridge, Letter to Taylor, December 4, 1981, in Author's Collection of Emily Taylor's Papers, St. Louis, MO (hereafter Author's Collection).
9. Taylor, Interview by Author, July 14, 1998 (Lawrence, KS).
10. As quoted in Elliott, "The American Council on Education's OWHE," 298.
11. Taylor, "Pioneering," September 18, 1997, speech delivered at the American Council on Education (ACE) National Network for Women Leaders in Higher Education Kansas/Missouri Annual Meeting.
12. Elliott, "The American Council on Education's OWHE," 226, 237, 240–241, 246, 334.
13. Carnegie Corporation of New York, "Women in Higher Education: It Took Vision, Perseverance and Innovative Strategies to Begin Opening the Doors of Colleges and Universities to Women," *Carnegie Results*, Winter 2012; Shavlik, Interview by Author, March 4, 2014; Shavlik, Telephone Interview by Author, May 31, 2014. In the 1950s and 1960s, Carnegie funded the

"Minnesota Plan" at the University of Minnesota, a continuing education effort that arose out of the National Association of Deans of Women (NADW)-ACE-Women's Bureau coalition that manifested in the ACE Commission on the Education of Women (CEW) and its Rye Conference. For further information, see Linda Eisenmann, *Higher Education for Women in Postwar America, 1945–1965* (Baltimore, MD: Johns Hopkins University Press, 2006); and Helen S. Astin, *Some Action of Her Own: The Adult Woman and Higher Education* (Lexington: Lexington Books, 1976).
14. Shavlik, Interview by Author, November 18–19, 2006; Taylor, "Pioneering;" Taylor, Interview by Author, July 14, 1998; Elliott, "The American Council on Education's OWHE," 251.
15. Taylor, Interview by Author, July 14, 1998.
16. Jean Fox O'Barr, *Feminism in Action: Building Institutions and Community through Women's Studies* (Chapel Hill: The University of North Carolina Press, 1994), 74–76; O'Barr, Telephone Interview by Author, April 14, 2014.
17. Taylor, Interview with Shavlik, Video Recording, National Association for Women in Education (NAWE) Records (hereafter MS-218) in Bowling Green State University Library, Center for Archival Collections, National Student Affairs Archives, Bowling Green, OH (hereafter BGSUCAC).
18. O'Barr, Telephone Interview by Author, April 14, 2014.
19. Ibid.
20. Elliott, "The American Council on Education's OWHE," 271–272. The quotation is drawn from O'Barr, *Feminism in Action*, 75.
21. Shavlik, Telephone Interview by Author, May 31, 2014; NAWE, 1977, Inter-association Files, Folder: American Council on Education 1970–1983, BGSUCAC.
22. For discussion on how ACE wanted OWHE to be more internally focused on ACE's structure and mission, see Elliott, "The American Council on Education's OWHE."
23. Ibid., 267–268.
24. Shavlik, Interview by Author, March 4, 2014.
25. Shavlik, Telephone Interview by Author, May 31, 2014.
26. Elliott, "The American Council on Education's OWHE," 255, 301–302; Shavlik, Telephone Interview by Author, May 31, 2014.
27. Shavlik, Telephone Interview by Author, May 31, 2014; Judy Touchton, Telephone Interview by Author, May 23, 2014.
28. Lulu Haskell Holmes, *A History of the Position of Dean of Women in a Selected Group of Co-Educational Colleges and Universities in the United States* (New York: Teachers College, Columbia University, 1939), 26–27, 38.
29. Gail Short Hanson, "Organizational Transformation: A Case Study of the Intercollegiate Association for Women Students" (PhD diss., George Washington University, 1995), 126–136, 171–172; Shavlik, Interview by Author, January 2007, Kansas City, MO.
30. Elliott, "The American Council on Education's OWHE," 286–287.
31. Ibid., 357–358.
32. Ibid., 350. The quotation is drawn from ibid., 364.
33. As quoted in ibid., 260.
34. Ibid., 301.

35. Taylor, Interview by Author, July 14, 1998.
36. Robert Schwartz, "How Deans of Women Became Men" *The Review of Higher Education* 20, 4 (Summer 1997): 419–436; Schwartz, *Deans of Men and the Shaping of Modern College Culture* (New York: Palgrave Macmillan, 2010).
37. Kate Hevner Mueller, Letter to E. G. Williamson, June 6, 1950, in Kate Hevner Mueller Papers c170, Folder: American Council on Education—Advisory Service on Student Personnel Work, 1947–1950, Indiana University Archives, Bloomington, IN.
38. Taylor, Interview by Author, July 1, 1997.

Archival Records

Alfred C. Kinsey Papers. Series V, The Kinsey Institute for Research in Sex, Gender, and Reproduction, Bloomington, IN.
Associated Women Students Records, (1948–1981), AC 197, University Archives, University Libraries, University of Nevada, Reno.
Association of Women Students, University Archives, RG 44/19, The Ohio State University Libraries, Columbus, OH.
Budget Records, University Archives, RG 44, Kenneth Spencer Research Library, University of Kansas Libraries, Lawrence, KS.
Emily Taylor Collection, University Archives, PP 413, Kenneth Spencer Research Library, University of Kansas Libraries, Lawrence, KS.
Emily Taylor Women's Resource Center Records, University Archives, RG 76/3, Kenneth Spencer Research Library, University of Kansas Libraries, Lawrence, KS.
Florence Mary Fitch Papers (1875–1959), RG 30/037, Oberlin College Archives, Oberlin, OH.
Howard Landis Bevis Papers, University Archives, RG 3/f, The Ohio State University Libraries, Columbus, OH.
Indiana University Association of Women Students Records, Collection c478, Office of University Archives and Records Management, Indiana University Archives, Bloomington, IN.
Indiana University Dean of Women's Office Records, Collection c165, Office of University Archives and Records Management, Indiana University Archives, Bloomington, IN.
Indiana University President's Office records, Collection c213, Office of University Archives and Records Management, Indiana University, Bloomington, IN.
Intercollegiate Association of Women Students Records, 1922–1980, Arthur and Elizabeth Schlesinger Library, 77-M126–82-M100, Radcliffe Institute, Harvard University, Cambridge, MA.
Kate Hevner Mueller Papers, Collection c170, Office of University Archives and Records Management, Indiana University Archives, Bloomington, IN.
Marilyn Stokstad Collection, University Archives, PP 470, Kenneth Spencer Research Library, University of Kansas Libraries, Lawrence, KS.
National Association for Women in Education, Center for Archival Collections, MS 218, National Student Affairs Archives, Bowling Green State University, Bowling Green, OH.
Ohio State University Dean of Women Records, University Archives, RG 9/c2, The Ohio State University Libraries, Columbus, OH.
Records of the Women's Bureau in the Department of Labor, RG 86, National Archives at College Park, MD.

University of Kansas Associated Women Students Records, University Archives, RG 67/12, Kenneth Spencer Research Library, University of Kansas Libraries, Lawrence, KS.

University of Kansas Chancellor's Office Records, University Archives, RG 2, Kenneth Spencer Research Library, University of Kansas Libraries, Lawrence, KS.

University of Kansas Commission on the Status of Women Records, University Archives, RG 67/48, Kenneth Spencer Research Library, University of Kansas Libraries, Lawrence, KS.

University of Kansas Dean of Men Records, University Archives, RG 52, Kenneth Spencer Research Library, University of Kansas Libraries, Lawrence, KS.

University of Kansas Dean of Women Records, University Archives, RG 53/0, Kenneth Spencer Research Library, University of Kansas Libraries, Lawrence, KS.

University of Kansas Equal Opportunity Office Records, University Archives, RG 8, Kenneth Spencer Research Library, University of Kansas Libraries, Lawrence, KS.

University of Kansas Office of Academic Affairs Records, University Archives, RG 10, Kenneth Spencer Research Library, University of Kansas Libraries, Lawrence, KS.

University of Kansas Office of Student Affairs Records, University Archives, RG 76/0, Kenneth Spencer Research Library, University of Kansas Libraries, Lawrence, KS.

University of Kansas Student Activities Records, University Archives, RG 71, Kenneth Spencer Research Library, University of Kansas Libraries, Lawrence, KS.

Women's Educational and Industrial Union Records, Arthur and Elizabeth Schlesinger Library, B-8, Radcliffe Institute, Harvard University, Cambridge, MA.

Index

Abbott, Edith, 26–7
abortion, 13, 88–9, 94–5, 98–100, 106–9, 118, 159, 162–3, 220n77, 227n19, 229n44
Adams, Arthur, 55, 171
Addams, Jane, 5, 24, 26, 30
Advisor of Women role, 122, 203n66
Affirmative Action, 164, 167
African-American women
  AAUW and, 5, 37, 148
  activism and, 121, 129–32, 135, 141, 144–5, 158
  ADWAGNS and, 123–4
  AWS and, 48, 133
  civil rights and, 125–6, 129–30
  CORE and, 126
  CRC and, 129–30
  deans of women and, 5, 41, 122–4
  Guide to Guidance and, 39–40
  historically black colleges and, 5, 46, 48, 123, 148, 177
  IAWS and, 124
  KU and, 119, 125–9
  KU cheerleading squad, 134–5, 145
  Mueller and, 126–7
  NADW and, 123–4
  National Association of College Women and, 39
  Northwestern University and, 125
  pregnancy and, 97
  racism and, 97
  sciences and, 40
  Slowe, Lucy Diggs and, 4, 46, 48, 123–5, 148, 223n15
  socio-economic advancement and, 41, 58
  sororities, 120, 125–8
  student government and, 46
  student housing and, 123, 125, 127–8
  Taylor and, 119–20, 126–9, 144
  UHRC and, 131, 134
  Urban League and, 39
  Wescoe and, 119, 127
  women's studies and, 148
  YWCA and, 120, 122–3
  see also Alpha Kappa Alpha, Black Power; Black Student Union, Delta Sigma Theta, racism, segregation
Against Our Will (Brownmiller), 113
Alderson, Donald, 61–2, 70, 119, 130–1, 134, 137, 208n7, 208n10
  see also deans of men
All Student Council (ASC), 62–3, 87, 129, 136, 208n11
Allen, Julia, 122
Allen, Phog, 126
Allen, Virginia, 160
Alpha Kappa Alpha (AKA) sorority, 125, 128
Alpha Kappa Lambda fraternity, 224n28
Alpha Tau Omega (ATO) fraternity, 129
American Association of University Professors (AAUP), 152–3, 162, 164, 166, 168, 196n39
American Association of University Women (AAUW)
  ACA and, 24, 192n14
  ACE and, 55–8, 158, 179–80
  AWS and, 49–50
  career/vocational assistance and, 27–32
  CEW and, 57–8
  Committee on Economic Efficiency, 27
  Committee on Vocational Opportunities, 36, 193n25
  creation of, 24–5, 27
  Deans of Women of the Middle West and, 25–7

American Association of University
   Women (AAUW)—*Continued*
 deans' network, 38–41
 Education Committee, 57
 feminism and, 10
 IAWS and, 158, 161
 Indiana University and, 54–6
 Kingsbury and, 27, 147, 193n23
 Mueller and, 44, 54
 NVGA and, 30
 OWHE and, 179
 sex education and, 91, 100
 student government and, 44, 50, 54–6
 Talbot and, 24–5
 Taylor and, xvii, 44, 57–8, 64, 147–9, 151, 158
 women of color and, 5
 women's status and, 147–9, 151
 Zorbaugh and, 33–4, 36–8
 see also "College Women Go to Work" report; *News Notes*; Standing Committee on the Economic and Legal Status of Women; Standing Committee on Vocational Opportunities
American Birth Control League, 216n21
American College Personnel Association (ACPA), xvii, 27, 30, 32, 40, 203n65
 see also American Personnel and Guidance Association (APGA)
American Council of Personnel and Guidance Associations (CPGA), 30, 32–3
American Council on Education (ACE)
 AAUW and, 55–8, 158, 179–80
 CEW and, 55–6, 58, 65, 149, 161, 171, 174
 IAWS and, 56, 158
 Inclusive Excellence Group, 174, 182
 NADW and, 55, 58, 149
 OWHE and, xvi–xvii, 169–74, 176–83
 Taylor and, xi, xvi, 1, 13, 15–16, 18, 169–83
 see also *Institutional Self Evaluation: The Title IX Requirement*
American Law Institute (ALI), 108–9
American Medical Association (AMA), 92, 98, 107–8

American Personnel and Guidance Associations (APGA), 40, 203n65
Amos, Thrysa, 123, 125, 209n20, 223n15
Anderson, Mary, 21, 24, 31, 33, 36, 50, 195n33
Antioch College, 37, 91
Associated Women Students (AWS)
 AAUW and, 49–50
 activism, 135–40, 143
 "Bright Woman" committee, 65
 Commission on the Status of Women, 64, 66, 154
 deans of women and, 8
 feminism and, 145–9, 151–64, 168, 175
 IU chapter, 51
 KU chapter, 14, 16, 62–9, 71–85, 87–9, 96–7, 99–105, 112–18, 120–1, 124, 132–40, 144–64, 171–2, 175–6, 178, 180–3
 Mueller and, 51–3, 57–8
 OSU chapter, 34–5, 49
 parietals and, 72–85, 87–9, 92
  see also rules
 race and, 120–1, 124, 132–3
 rules, 8, 14, 62, 81, 87
  see also parietals
 sex education and, 92–3, 96–7, 99–105, 110–18
 student governance and, 5, 7–9, 44, 46, 49–53, 57–8, 184
 Taylor and, 1–5, 16–18, 21, 38, 42, 44, 53, 57, 62–4, 66, 71–2, 135
 UC Berkeley chapter, 48–9
 University of Wisconsin chapter, 46
 Vocational Information Committee, 21
 see also vocational conferences; vocational guidance
Association of American Colleges, 180
Association of Collegiate Alumnae (ACA), 24, 192n14
 see also American Association of University Women (AAUW)
Association of Deans of Women and Advisers to Girls in Negro Schools (ADWAGNS), 123–4
Atkins, Suzanne, xx, 139
Aubrey, David, 140

Baer, Michael, 181
Bailey, Beth, 13, 190n25, 212n83, 214n4, 218n55, 218n59
Baldwin, Alice, 31, 147
Balfour, Bill, 111, 114, 143, 168
Ball, Katherine, 30
Banks, Elizabeth, 164–6, 230n63
Barnard College, 25, 27, 32, 158, 171, 178
Barry, Ruth, 10
Bay Area Women Against Rape, 113
behavioral norms, 7–9, 47, 52, 72, 75
Bennett College, 178
Bennett, Helen, 28, 31–2, 196n36
Berea College, 122
Bethune-Cookman University, 116
Bilotta, Vincent, 115–17
biography, 15–16
birth control
   AWS and, 88, 104
   birth control pill, 65, 99, 101, 103
   condoms, 92
   Eisenstadt v. Baird and, 99
   Great Depression and, 92
   IAWS and, 159
   KU and, 103–6, 163, 168, 229n44
   public support for, 92–3
   sex education and, 91–4, 99–101, 103–6, 159
   ZPG and, 99
   see also contraception; Zero Population Growth (ZPG)
Bishop, Joan, 39
Bitch Manifesto, The (publication), 137
Black Power, 121, 135, 141
   see also African-American women
Black Student Union (BSU), 133–5, 141–3
   see also African-American women
"blame the victim" mentality, 113–14, 117, 221n96
Blanding, Sarah, 123, 170
Bloody Sunday, 129
Bloomfield, Meyer, 30, 33
Board of Regents (Kansas), xvi, xix, 2, 69, 111, 140–1, 146, 152, 163–4, 166, 208n11
Borg, Carol, 119
Boston University, 24
Bowman, Gelene, 35

Bragdon, Helen, 56
Breckinridge, Sophonisba, 5, 24–7, 31, 36, 51, 122, 147
Breed, Mary Bidwell, 45, 72, 174
Breines, Wini, 97
Breyfogle, Caroline, 34, 197n40
"Bright Woman" committee (AWS), 65
Brown, Judith, 137
Brown v. Board of Education (1954), 120, 124
Brownmiller, Susan, 113
Brune, Caroljean, 89, 231n65
Bryn Mawr, 27, 45, 47
Bureau of Occupations, 28, 31–2, 36
   see also vocational conferences; vocational guidance
bureaucracy, 15, 17, 166, 172
Burge, Frank, 99
Business and Professional Women (BPW), 33, 35–6, 39, 91, 161

Calderone, Mary, 100, 217n50
calling hours, 62–3
   see also AWS; parietal rules
careers and contingency planning, 30–3
   see also vocational conferences; vocational guidance
Carruth-O'Leary Hall, 76–7
Catholicism, 107, 174
Chalmers, E. Laurence, 111, 140–6, 152–3, 163–7
Chamberlain, Mariam, 175
Chamberlain, Wilt, 126
chaperones, 6, 23, 87
Cheney, May, 27–8, 31, 90
Chervenik, Emily, 40
Chi Omega sorority, 128
Chicago Collegiate Bureau of Occupations, 28, 32, 36
   see also vocational conferences; vocational guidance
Chimes junior women's honorary, 66
Christianity, 11, 23, 33, 125, 132
citizenship
   see economic citizenship; political citizenship
civil rights, 4–5, 12, 17, 67, 85, 118–22, 124–9, 132–6, 144, 146, 149–50, 153–4, 161–2, 167, 169, 180, 184

Civil Rights Act (1964), xvi, 12, 85,
    120, 124, 128–9, 132, 135,
    150, 162, 169
Civil Rights Council (CRC), 127–31, 135
Clarenbach, Kay, 3, 16, 150–1
Clarke, Edward, 23, 90
Clinton, Dale, 101–3
Class (socioeconomic), 4–5, 8–9,
    11–12, 19, 22–3, 30–2, 36, 41,
    46, 49, 58, 73, 76–7, 97, 101,
    121, 126–7
closing hours, 6, 62–3, 73, 76, 78–83,
    85, 88, 117, 212n81, 213n97
    see also curfews
Cobble, Dorothy Sue, 5, 12, 41
coed, meaning, 8
Coes, Mary, 27, 193n25
Cold War, 3, 85, 14
"College Women Go to Work" report
    (AAUW), 40
    see also American Association of
        University Women (AAUW)
Columbia University, 28, 43, 46, 51,
    121, 123, 143, 152
Columbus Counseling Bureau, 36
Columbus Pan-Hellenic organization, 34
Columbus Scholarship Society, 34
Commission on the Education of
    Women (CEW), 55–8, 64–5, 73,
    84, 149, 161, 171, 174, 206n40,
    207n43–4, 226n10, 233n13
    see also American Council on
        Education (ACE)
Commission on the Status of Women
    (KU), xvi–xvii, 3, 64, 85, 115,
    133, 139, 151, 154–5, 160, 162,
    164, 207n44, 219n69, 227n10
Congress of Racial Equality (CORE),
    126–7
Committee on Economic Efficiency, 27
Committee W (AAUP), 152–3, 164–6,
    168
Commons, John R., 33
communism, 10, 14, 55, 149
Companionate Marriage (Lindsey), 95
Comstock, Ada, 25, 29–30, 32, 34,
    45–6, 91–2, 170, 174, 194n26,
    197n41
consumption economics, 21, 196n39
    see also Zorbaugh, Grace S.M.

contingency planning, 21, 35–6, 39,
    56, 65, 160
contraception, 17–18, 89, 92–6,
    98–109, 117, 135, 140, 146, 167
    see also birth control; Zero
        Population Growth (ZPG)
Cook, Barbara, 119, 159
Cornell University, 91, 123, 152, 161
Costick, Rita, 105
cottage governance, 46
    see also self-governance; student
        government
Council of Guidance and Personnel
    Associations (CGPA), 30
Council on Student Affairs (COSA),
    103–4, 106, 136, 139, 218n60
courtship, 87, 92, 105
Crow, Martha Foote, 25–6, 37
curfews, 6, 47, 62–3, 72–8, 81, 84–5,
    88–9, 117, 139, 141, 185, 212n83
    see also Associated Women Students
        (AWS); closing hours; parietal
        rules; self-governance
curriculum, 22–3, 25, 51, 55, 63–4, 90,
    92, 108, 122, 148, 176, 179

date rape, 78, 113, 116, 211n65, 220n92
    see also rape
dating, 17, 49, 59, 72, 78, 83, 85, 87–9,
    96–9, 109
Davis, Felicia, 177
Davis, Hilda, 4, 124, 223n15
daycare, 57, 160, 166, 181
de Beauvoir, Simone, 64
deans of men, 3, 7, 32, 40, 54
    see also Alderson, Don; National
        Association of Deans of Men
        (NADM)
deans of women
    AAUW and, 25–7, 38–41
    African-American women and, 5, 41,
        122–4
    autonomy and, 3–4, 12, 17–18, 47,
        52–3, 70, 74–6
    AWS and, 8–9, 14–18, 21, 34–5, 38,
        42, 44, 46, 48–53, 56–8
    feminism and, 6–7, 14–18, 24, 43–4,
        95, 123
    student housing and, 45
    Taylor and, 30, 32–5, 38, 53–6, 69–72

women's movement and, 5, 31, 44, 120–1, 124, 132–40, 143, 145–9, 151–2, 155–7, 162–3
Zorbaugh and, 19–21
see also Intercollegiate Association of Women Students (IAWS); National Association of Deans of Women (NADW)
Deans of Women of the Middle West, 25–7, 31, 45, 47, 49, 192n16, 194n32
Delta Sigma Theta sorority, 128, 130, 134
Delta Tau Delta fraternity, 87–9
Department of Health, Education, and Welfare (HEW), 152–3, 167
Department of Labor, 3, 21, 24, 44
see also equal pay/pay equity; Women's Bureau
desegregation, 120, 124–8, 132, 162
see also segregation
Dewey, John, 5, 7, 47, 49, 51, 74
see also self-control; self-governance
discrimination, 32, 58, 63, 71, 113, 119–21, 127–9, 131–2, 134, 136, 141, 146–7, 150–2, 154, 163, 172
Docking, Robert, 141
Dodd, Catherine Filene, 32
Dollar, Margaret C., 193n23
domesticity, 3–4, 9, 11, 22–3, 25, 41, 55, 61, 85, 96
Donner Foundation, 177
door duty, 79
see also curfews; parietal rules
double standard, 52, 78, 87, 91, 95–7, 108, 116, 118
Douce, Louise, 110, 159–60
drug use, 70, 121, 140, 157
Duke University, 32, 147, 176
Dykes, Archie, 111, 114–16

East Asian Studies building (KU), 1, 13, 145, 165–6, 168
East, Catherine, 3, 151
Ebert, Bill, 142
economic citizenship
careers and contingency planning, 30–3
coeducation and, 22–30
overview, 19–22
path toward, 38–42
vocational guidance, 33–8
see also contingency planning; equal pay/pay equity; vocational conferences; vocational guidance
Educating Our Daughters (White), 55
Educating the Majority: Women Challenge Tradition in Higher Education (Pearson, Shavlik, and Touchton), 181
Educating Women for a Changing World (Mueller), 55, 57, 64, 149, 154
Education Amendments Act (1972), 152
Eike, Casey, 109, 114–16, 145, 151–2, 165, 167, 221n97
Eisenstadt v. Baird (1972), 99
Eisenmann, Linda, 190n15, 206n40
see also quiet feminism
elitism, 32, 127
Emily Taylor Center for Women and Gender Equity, 16
Emily Taylor Women's Resource Center, 14
Equal Employment Opportunity Commission (EEOC), 150, 152
equal pay/pay equity, 5, 17, 20, 22, 29, 31, 41, 145, 181
see also Department of Labor; economic citizenship; unions; Women's Bureau
Equal Rights Amendment (ERA), 3, 10, 12, 147, 159–60, 162, 184–5
Equal Suffrage League, 46
errors least damaging, 88, 96
see also double standard
ethnography, 13, 15
Evans, Catherine, 206n30
Evans, Sara, 2, 190n19
Executive Orders, 67, 168
11246, 150, 184
11375, 145, 150–2, 160, 162, 172

family, 7–8, 19–20, 22, 30, 40, 50, 55, 57, 65, 84, 91–3, 99, 105
February Sisters, 13, 106, 144–6, 152, 163–8
see also University of Kansas (KU)
Federal Bureau of Investigation (FBI), 14

Federal Communications Commission, 96
Feminine Mystique, The (Friedan), 3, 71, 85
feminism
  activism and, 30–2, 135–40
  AWS and, 88–9
  beyond "quiet" feminism, 57–8
  CEW and, 55–6
  consciousness-raising, 16, 71, 85
  deans of women and, 6–7, 14–18, 24, 43–4, 95, 123
  divisions within, 162–4
  February Sisters and, 106, 166, 168
  labor and, 5–10, 30, 33, 41–2
  liberal, 9, 11–12, 18, 136, 138, 146, 154, 162
  notes on word, 10–13
  race and, 120–2, 126
  radical, 2, 4, 11, 12, 18, 67, 112, 135–47, 162
  second wave, 9, 11–12, 16, 18, 190n19
  sexual assault and, 112–13, 115, 118
  Taylor and, 1–6, 9, 17–22, 61, 63, 65, 67, 70, 72, 84–5, 126, 190n19
  vocational conferences/guidance, 9, 21, 25–6, 29–42, 63, 71–4, 147
  Women's Coalition (KU), 138–9, 163–4, 168
  Zorbaugh and, 37–8
  see also New Left; quiet feminism; self-governance; women's liberation
Filene family, 196n36
financial loans, 4, 34, 51, 197n41
Finkbine, Sherri, 106
Fisher, Margaret B., 40
Fitch, Florence, 28, 122–3, 194n26
Fitzgerald, Betty, 4, 156, 161
Florida Paper, 137
Florida State College for Women, 77
Focus on Minority Women's Advancement (FMWA), 177
Ford Foundation, 175
Foster, Robert, 55
Foucault, Michel, 8
Freud, Sigmund, 55
Friedan, Betty, 3, 16, 57, 71, 85, 150

Fund for the Improvement of Post Secondary Education, 175
Furniss, Todd, 169

GaDuGi Safe Center, 117
Gannon, Ann Ida, 178
Gaw, Esther Allen, xiv, 33–4, 43, 50–1, 91–3, 201n58
gay and lesbian students, 4, 14, 17, 109–12, 117–18, 120–1
  see also Gay Liberation Front (GLF)
Gay Liberation Front (GLF), 110–11, 118, 164
  see also gay and lesbian students
Gebauer, Dorothy, 39
gender roles, 3, 9, 18, 20, 22, 37, 55, 60–1, 64–6, 68, 74, 78, 85, 137, 154, 161
George Washington University, 56
Gertrude Sellards Pearson Hall, 69, 98
GI Bill, 54, 59, 206n40
Gilham, Shirley, 116, 167, 170
Gill, Laura Drake, 25, 27, 32, 193n25
Gillespie, Butch, 143
Ginsberg, Ruth Bader, 161
Girl Scouts, 154, 196n39
Goldwater, Barry, 121
Grambling College, 116
Great Depression, xiv, 20, 34, 36–7, 66, 92, 94, 126–7, 147
Guide to Guidance (NADW), 37, 39, 64

Habein, Margaret, 56
Handbook on Positive Health (WFH), 91
Harper, William Rainey, 23–4
Harris, M. Kay, xx, 71, 81, 137, 139
Harrison, Cynthia, 13
Harvard University, 24, 152
Hawkes, Anna Rose, 56
Healy, Sarah, 4
Heyns, Roger, 170–2, 174, 182–3
hierarchy, administrative, 2, 54
Higher Education Amendments of 1972, 169
  see also Title IX
Hilltop Child Development Center, 166
Hilton, Eunice, 4, 39, 56
hippie culture, 130, 140
  see also New Left
Hiram College, 37

historically black colleges, 5, 46, 123, 177
Hitt, James, xix
homosexuality
  see gay and lesbian students
Hoopingarner, Anne, 68, 88
Hottel, Althea K., 4, 55–6
housing
  see student housing
How Fare American Women? (CEW), 55–6
Howard University, 4, 46, 48, 123, 125, 148
  see also Slowe, Lucy Diggs
Hull House, 5, 24, 26, 30–1, 41, 47, 122, 193n21, 195n33
Hunt, Morton, 64
Hutchins, Robert, 125
Hyde, Ann Peterson, xxi, 81
hygiene, 23, 90–4

Ikenberry, Stanley O., 181–2
in loco parentis, 6, 52, 62, 113, 121, 155
Independent Woman (periodical), 36
Indiana University, xv, 15, 17, 25, 28, 38–40, 42–3, 45, 49, 51–4, 61, 63, 75, 91
Institute of Women's Professional Relations (IWPR), 32–3, 36, 39, 196n36
institutional racism, 133
Institutional Self Evaluation: The Title IX Requirement (NIP), 179
  see also American Council on Education (ACE); Office of Women in Higher Education (OWHE); Title IX
integration, 11, 48, 54, 71, 122, 124–5, 127–9, 133–5, 144, 148, 169
Inter-Residence Hall Council, 132
Intercollegiate Association of Women Students (IAWS), xvi–xvii, 5, 7, 15–18, 44, 49–50, 56, 58–9, 63–4, 69, 80–1, 100, 104, 110, 114, 124, 145–7, 149, 152, 155–62, 168, 171–2, 175–6, 178, 180, 182–4
  see also Associated Women Students (AWS); deans of women; self-governance; student government

International Women's Year (IWY), xvii, 16
"intimate fireside conferences," 35
  see also vocational conferences; vocational guidance

Jackson, Florence, 28, 36
Jacobsen, Einar, 54
Jefferson, Thomas, 15
Johnson, Al Byron, 114
Johnson Foundation, 175, 180
Johnson, Lyndon B., 150, 152
Jones, Beverly, 137
Journal of the National Association of Deans of Women, 80
judiciary boards, 74, 80
  see also Associated Women Students (AWS); Intercollegiate Association of Women Students (IAWS); parietal rules; self-governance; student government

Kansas LIFE Project, xviii
Kehde, Ned, 14
Kennedy, John F., 3, 64, 85, 149, 207n44
Kent State University, 121, 142, 145, 159
keys, 6, 63, 73, 77–85, 89, 99, 103, 28, 132, 135, 139–40, 158, 210n48
  see also closing hours; curfews
Keyserling, Mary, 3, 150
Kingsbury, Susan, 27, 29, 33, 36–7, 40, 147, 161, 193n22
Kinsey, Alfred, 93–4, 106, 110, 112, 214n9, 216n27
Kirkendall, Lester, 100, 217n50
Komarovsky, Mirra, 55, 64
Koontz, Elizabeth, 3, 160, 170
Krasne, Barb, 138
Kunzel, Regina G., 217n40

Lamba Sigma, 66
  see also Society of Cwens
labor
  see also Department of Labor; equal pay; unions; Women's Bureau

late permission, 63, 84
  see also Associated Women Students (AWS); closing hours; curfew; parietal rules
Lathrop, Julia, 26
Lawrence Caring Communities Council, xvii
Lawrence Journal World (newspaper), 77, 111, 115, 140
League of Women Voters (LWV), 33, 50
  see also National American Woman Suffrage Association
lecturers, 65
Leopold, Alice, 3, 50, 56–7
Lewis Hall, 69, 128, 132
liberal arts, 12, 22, 25, 29, 43, 55–6, 58, 65, 85, 148–9, 167, 179
life-phase model, 56, 65, 95, 161, 207n44
Limbaugh, Rush, 11
Lindsey, Ben, 95
Lloyd-Jones, Esther, 53, 56, 169, 172, 226n10
Louisiana State University, 116
Lysol, 92
  see also contraception

Mademoiselle magazine, 39, 97
Mainardi, Pat, 57, 137
Malott, Deane W., 59, 126
marriage, 3, 7, 11, 17, 19–24, 30, 35, 37–9, 42, 55–6, 58, 63, 65–6, 68, 71, 84–5, 88–9, 91–102, 105, 109, 118, 155, 158, 160–1, 183, 185
Martin, Gertrude S., 91
Marxism, 136
Maryland Commission on the Status of Women, xvi
Massachusetts Institute of Technology (MIT), 24
Maymi, Carmen Rosa, 170
McCain, James, 129
McCarn, Ruth, 123–5, 128
McCarthyism, 10
McMahon, Genevieve Taylor, xxi, 13, 95
Mendenhall, Janice K., 1, 156, 158–9
Michigan State University, 65, 156
Mitchell, Lucy Sprague, 25, 27

Mitchelson, Mary, 1
Monhollon, Rusty, 119, 190n19, 230n59
Moore, Eva Perry, 44
morality, 90, 101–4, 167
Morgan, Robin, 145, 164
Mortar Board program, 66, 77
Mosher, Clelia Duel, 90–1, 214n9
Mosher, Eliza, 90
motherhood, 3–4, 7, 11, 21–2, 32, 35–6, 38, 40–1, 46, 55–7, 63, 65–6, 71, 85, 92, 95, 109, 149, 158, 161, 181, 183
Mount Holyoke College, 36, 39
Mueller, Kate Hevner, 4, 39, 42–4, 50–69, 84, 88, 92–7, 100, 102, 106, 112, 120, 123–4, 126–7, 137, 149, 154–5, 161, 176, 183–4
Mumbi, 128
Mundelein College, 178
Murphy, Franklin, 60–1, 63–4, 69, 73, 76, 80–1, 126–7, 149, 183, 208n7, 208n10
Murray, Pauli, 161
Murray State University, 1

National American Woman Suffrage Association, 5
  see also League of Women Voters
National Association for Women in Education (NAWE), 187n7
National Association of College Women, 39
National Association of Commissions for Women (NACW), xvii, 3, 15, 151, 170, 188n12
  see also President's Commission on the Status of Women
National Association of Deans of Men (NADM), 32
National Association of Deans of Women (NADW), xv–xvii, 4–5, 10, 12, 18, 31–4, 37, 39–40, 44, 47, 187n7, 192n16, 194n32, 196n36–7, 196n39, 200n54, 201n59, 202n64, 203n66, 206n40, 211n78, 233n13
  see also deans of women; National Association for Women in

Education (NAWE); National Association of Women Deans, Administrators and Counselors (NAWDAC); National Association of Women Deans and Counselors (NAWDC)
National Association of Student Personnel Administrators (NASPA), xvii, 40, 54, 81, 180, 187n7
National Association of Women Deans, Administrators and Counselors (NAWDAC), 187n7
National Association of Women Deans and Counselors (NAWDC), 187n7
National Association of Women Educators (NAWE), xvii, 187n7
National Bureau of Occupations, 32
National Conference for College Women Student Leaders (NCCWSL), xvii, 180, 188n14
National Education Association, 123
National Federation of Business and Professional Women's Clubs (BPW), 33, 35–6, 39, 91, 161
National Identification Program for the Advancement of Women in Higher Education (NIP), xvi, 173–9, 182
National Occupations Conference, 32
National Student Association, 157
National Vocational Guidance Association (NVGA), 30–3, 37, 40, 201n59
Natural History of Love, The (Hunt), 64
New Agenda of Women for Higher Education (OWHE), 181
New Left, 1–6, 9, 11, 15, 17–18, 82, 104–5, 118, 120–2, 135–9, 141, 143–6, 151, 155–60, 163, 165–6
New Mexico State University, 116, 160
New York Intercollegiate Bureau of Occupations, 28, 31
   see also van Kleeck, Mary; vocational conferences; vocational guidance
News Notes (AAUW newsletter), 28

Nicholson, Linda, 11
Nixon, Richard, 142, 160
normalization, 7, 9
norms
   behavioral, 7–9, 47, 75
   class, 58, 126–7
   cultural, 4, 89
   gender, 52, 66, 72, 78
   peer groups and, 7–8, 75, 84, 87–9, 101
   sexual, 6, 89, 99, 118
Northern Montana College, 53–4, 95
Northwestern, 22, 25–6, 49, 56, 123–5, 194n26, 226n10

O'Barr, Jean, 3, 173, 176–7
Oberlin College, 23, 25, 28, 122
Occidental College, 39, 123
"occupational bureau" model, 31, 171, 177, 182, 203n65
   see also vocational conferences; vocational guidance
Office of Urban Affairs, 153, 164, 167
Office of Women in Higher Education (OWHE), xvi–xvii, 1, 16, 169–83
   see also American Council on Education (ACE); National Identification Program (NIP); New Agenda of Women for Higher Education
Ohio Association of Deans of Women (OADW), 37, 91
Ohio State University (OSU), 19–21, 33–9, 50–1, 64, 91, 93, 95, 148
Ohio Wesleyan, 37, 56
On Account of Sex (Harrison), 13, 190n25
oral history, 2, 13–14
Other Women's Movement, The (Cobble), 41
Outlook for Women (IWPR), 39–40

Pacific Coast Conference, 49
Palmer, Alice Freeman, 24, 122, 192n19
panopticon, 8–9, 94
   see also Foucault, Michel
Paretsky, Sara, 1

parietal rules, 3, 5, 7, 9, 17–18, 48, 51–2, 58, 63, 72–85, 88–90, 94, 96, 101, 112–13, 117, 139–40, 147, 155–8, 160, 162, 185
 see also Associated Women Students (AWS); closing hours; curfews; door duty; Intercollegiate Association of Women Students (IAWS); keys; late permission; self-governance; student government
Park, Rosemary, 178
Parsons, Frank, 30
Paul, Alice, 10
Pearson, Carol S., 181
Pearson, Gertrude Sellards, 69, 98
Pearson, James, 184
peer groups, 7, 43, 52
personal responsibility, 17, 74, 212n83
Personnel Research Federation, 32
Peters, Iva L., 32
Peterson, Esther, 3, 150
Peterson, Martha, 59–61, 63–4, 69, 84, 158, 171–4
Phillips, Kathryn Sisson, 30–1, 46–7, 56
Pi Beta Phi, 83
Pierce, Adah, 37
Planned Parenthood, 99, 105, 216n21
Player, Willa, 178
political citizenship
 challenges in postwar America, 53–6
 feminism and, 57–8
 Indiana University and, 51–4
 overview, 43–5
 women's self-governance, 45–51
 see also suffrage; voting
Politics of Housework, The (Mainardi), 57, 137
population
 see Zero Population Growth (ZPG)
premarital sex, 6, 88–9, 91–3, 96, 100–1, 106, 118
President's Commission on the Status of Women (PCSW), xvi, 64, 149
 see also National Association of Commissions for Women (NACW)
Prince, Judith, 173
"Principles of Social Conduct" (NADW), 90–1

Progressivism, 4–5, 21, 33
Project on the Status and Education of Women, 172, 177, 180
promiscuity, 87, 92, 97, 107, 112, 116, 216n32, 217n40, 220n76
 see also double standard
protests, 5–6, 17–18, 54, 72–3, 76, 82–4, 87, 93, 106, 111, 116, 118–22, 125, 128–31, 133, 135–6, 139–46, 155, 159, 163–5, 167–8
Purdue University, 9, 37, 94, 124, 149

quiet feminism, 38, 56–7
 see also Einsenmann, Linda; feminism

racism, 4, 32, 58, 97, 123–4, 126–8, 133, 148, 157, 195n35, 217n40, 220n76
 see also African-American women; segregation
Radical Feminism
 see feminism, radical; women's liberation; Women's Liberation Front
Randolph-Macon Women's College, 202n64
rape
 awareness and prevention, 18, 113–18, 221n94
 counseling, 1, 13, 88, 183
 statutory, 108
 student housing and, 78
 see also "blame the victim" mentality; date rape; sexual assault; Whistlestop intiative
Rape Victim Support Service (RVSS), 114
Rawalt, Marguerite, xvii, 151, 161
religion, 64, 103, 124, 131–2, 174
reproductive issues, 104
Republican Motherhood, 22, 191n9
Reserve Officers' Training Corps (ROTC), 135, 140, 142
Richards, Ellen, 27, 192n14
Ricks, Francie, 154
Ridder, Anne Hoopingarner, 58, 77–8, 81, 88
riots, 116
Ritter, Mary Bennett, 48
Robert's Rules of Order, 44, 85

Roberts, Eunice C., 40
Robinson, Bill, 136–7
Robinson, Janet, 154
Rosenberry, Lois Kimball Mathews, 28–9, 46, 49, 148
Rosser, James, 167
Rothenberger, Wilma, 123
rules of conduct, 6

safety, 6, 78–9, 89, 107, 111–15, 117, 129, 142–3
  see also date rape; rape; sexual assault; sexual harrassment
Saint Louis University, 103
San Diego State University, 161
Sandler, Bernice, 3, 15, 151–2, 160, 172, 177, 180
Sanford, John, 143
Savio, Mario, 129
Schleman, Helen, 94, 124, 149–51, 161
Schlesinger Library on the History of Women, 15
Schlossberg, Nancy, 169–70, 172
Schmidt, Leigh, 15–16
scholarships/grants, 4, 51, 66–7, 151
Schwegler, Raymond, 102–4, 106, 109, 137, 146, 164, 167–8
science, technology, engineering, and math (STEM), 154
Scott, Pat, 133–5
Scott, Sarah, 105, 143, 145, 151–2, 164–6
Scott, Scottie, 145, 164
Sears, Janet, 92, 106, 108–9, 136, 145, 154, 163, 165, 167
Seaver, James, 131–2
Second Sex, The (de Beauvoir), 64
second wave feminism, 9, 11–12, 16, 18, 190n19
Sedgwick, Rae, 142
segregation
  gender, 8–9, 18, 40, 62
  housing, 8, 23, 119, 127–30, 132–3, 162
  racial, 119–20, 123–8, 224n28
  see also desegregation
self-control, 4, 47, 52
  see also Associated Women Students (AWS); parietal rules; self-governance

self-evaluation, 179–80
self-governance, 7–9, 17, 44, 46–9, 52–3, 58, 63, 70, 72, 74–5, 84, 90, 96, 100–1, 106, 110, 117, 121–3, 144, 153, 155–6, 160, 182, 184
  see also cottage governance; Associated Women Students (AWS); cottage governance; Intercollegiate Association of Women Students (IAWS); parietal rules; self-control; student government, Women's Self-Government Association
SenEx (KU), 166
Servicemen's Readjustment Act of 1944
  see GI Bill
sex education, 4, 17, 88–9, 141, 154, 158–60, 163–4, 167–8
  birth control pill and, 101–6
  deans of women and, 90–6
  gay and lesbian student advocacy, 109–11
  Kinsey, Alfred/IU courses, 93–4, 106, 110, 112
  KU and, 96–106
  marriage courses, 93–4, 96
  rape and, 111–18
  sexual harassment and, 111–18
  unplanned pregnancy counseling, 106–9
  see also birth control; contraception; Women's Foundation for Health (WFH)
Sex in Education (Clarke), 23
Sex in the Heartland (Bailey), 13
sexual activity, record keeping of, 14
sexual assault, 10, 17, 88–9, 111–14, 116–18, 160, 221n96
  see also "blame the victim" mentality; rape; safety; Whistlestop Inititative
Sexual Behavior in the Human Female (Kinsey), 93, 110
Sexual Behavior in the Human Male (Kinsey), 93
sexual harassment, 111–18, 132, 220n88

Sexuality Information and Education Council of the United States (SIECUS), 94, 100, 104–5
Shankel, Del, 115–17
Shavlik, Donna, xvi, xix, xxi, 16, 66–7, 69–71, 77–9, 89, 96, 101–2, 105, 109–11, 120, 124, 128, 132, 137, 141–2, 144, 151, 154–5, 164, 169–83
Shawnee Mission neighborhood, 131, 134
Shoemaker, Raymond, 54
Sigma Kappa sorority, 79
Sigma Nu fraternity, 129
sit-ins, 119–20, 129–32, 135, 145
Slowe, Lucy Diggs, 4, 46, 48, 123–5, 148, 223n15
Smith, Caryl and Walter, 136, 154
Smith College, 28, 45
Smithies, Elsie May, 39, 123
Snyder, Franklin Bliss, 125
social efficiency, 46, 205n10
social events, 63
Social Security Act, 25, 27
Society of Cwens, 66, 138, 209n20
  see also Labda Sigma
Sonoma State University, 178
sororities, 2, 6, 17–18, 45, 47–8, 51, 68–9, 75, 77–80, 84, 89, 113, 115, 120, 125–6, 128–32, 144, 158, 183, 212n81
Southeast Missouri State University, 1
Southern Women's Educational Alliance, 32
Spencer, Patti, 138
Sprague, Lucy, 25–7, 45, 90, 94, 192n19
Stamp, Adele, 56
Standing Committee on the Economic and Legal Status of Women, 148
  see also American Association of University Women (AAUW)
Standing Committee on Vocational Opportunities, 193n25
  see also American Association of University Women (AAUW)
Stansell, Christine, 5
Stanton, Elizabeth Cady, 15
Steinem, Gloria, 16
Stitt, Louise, 36, 38, 50

Stokstad, Marilyn, 60, 88, 109, 152–3, 164–6
Stroup, Kala Mays, 1, 69–70, 75–6, 89, 98, 113, 116, 120, 128, 130–2, 134–5, 142, 154, 171, 179
student governance, 1, 4–9, 17, 44–53, 58, 62, 72–5, 82, 84, 88, 101, 104, 109, 118–19, 144, 146, 155, 184
  see also Associated Women Students (AWS); cottage governance; Intercollegiate Association of Women Students (IAWS); judiciary boards; self-government; Women's Self-Government Association
student housing
  AAUW and, 148–9
  deans of women and, 45
  parietal rules and, 48
  regulations governing, 62–3
  segregation and, 8, 23, 119, 127–30, 132–3, 148, 162
  shortages, 45, 54
  Taylor and, 61, 73, 89–90
  university-sanctioned, 6
  women's self-governance and, 45, 48, 74–5, 79
  YWCA and, 122–3, 125
  see also closing hours; curfews; keys
Student Peace Union (SPU), 135
Students for a Democratic Society (SDS), 135, 157, 212n83, 218n59
study hours, 72
suffrage, 3–5, 7, 10–11, 17, 33, 46, 61, 132
  see also political citizenship; voting
Sunnen Foundation, 99–105
Supreme Court, 99, 100, 120, 161
Surface, James, 103, 112
Syracuse University, 4, 9, 32, 39, 43, 56

Tacha, Deanelle Reece, 1, 184
Talbot, Marion, 5, 18, 24–8, 30, 33–4, 40–1, 45–50, 70, 72, 90, 147–8, 174, 178–9, 182–4
Task Force on Women's Rights and Responsibilities, 160

INDEX 249

Taylor, Emily
  AAUW and, 44, 57–8, 64, 147–9, 151, 158
  ACE and, 1, 13, 15–16, 18, 169–74
  African-American women and, 119–20, 126–9, 144
  anti-discrimination programs, 125–35
  AWS and, 1–5, 16–18, 21, 38, 42, 44, 53, 57, 62–4, 66, 71–2, 87, 135, 152–3
  belief in teaching autonomy to college women, 59–69
  biography, xi, xiii–xviii, 13–18
  deans of women and, 30, 32–5, 38, 53–6, 69–72
  development in KU role, 69–72
  February Sisters and, 164–8
  feminism and, 1–6, 9–10, 12, 17–22, 61–7, 70, 72, 84–5, 87–9, 126, 162–4, 190n19
  gay and lesbian student advocacy, 110–11
  IAWS and, 59, 63–4, 69, 80–1, 100, 104, 110, 147, 149, 152, 155, 159–62, 171–2, 175–6, 178, 180, 182
  IU and, 38–43, 51–3
  KU and, 1–2, 4, 13–18, 53, 58, 59–69, 125, 171, 180, 184–5
  mentoring, 28, 39, 42–4, 169–83
  Mueller and, 42–4, 57–8
  NACW, xvii, 3, 15, 151, 170, 188n12
  NOW and, 150–1
  OSU and, 19–22, 33–9, 147–9
  OWHE and, 169–83
  parietals and, 50–1, 72–85
  personality, xviii–xx
  sex education and, 90, 92–106
  sexual harassment and rape prevention, 112–18
  Shavlik and, 16, 66–7, 69–71, 77–9, 89, 96, 101–2, 105, 109–11, 120, 124, 128, 132, 137, 141–2, 144, 151, 154–5, 164, 169–83
  student activism and, 135–44, 153–62
  student government and, 1–5, 16–18, 21, 38, 42, 44, 53, 57, 62–4, 66, 71–2, 135
  student housing and, 61, 73, 89–90
  student protests and, 119–22, 145–7
  Title VII and, 150–1
  Title IX, 3, 146, 151–2, 169–72, 179–80, 184
  unplanned pregnancy counseling, 106–9
  WEAL and, 151–2
  Zorbaugh and, 4, 19–21, 28, 44, 63–6, 71, 84, 120, 137, 147, 154, 177, 184
Teachers College network, 123
Teachers College Personnel Association, 32
teaching, as profession, 29, 37
Tet Offensive, 140
  see also Vietnam War
Thalidomide, 106
Thomas, M. Carey, 47
Threlkeld, Hilda, 37, 39, 53, 94, 124, 144, 176
Thurstone, L.L., 51
Title VI, xvi
Title VII, xviii, 12, 150–1, 169, 172
Title IX, xvi–xviii, 1, 3, 10, 18, 40, 146, 151–2, 169–72, 179–80, 184
  see also Higher Education Amendments of 1972
Tobias, Sheila, xvii, 3, 16, 66, 209n19, 230n49
Touchton, Judy, 177–8, 181–2
Towle, Katherine, 129, 142
Truex, Dorothy, 4, 9, 12
tuition assistance, 54

unions, 5, 24, 27, 31, 147, 171
  see also equal pay/pay equity; Women's Bureau
University Daily Kansan (newspaper), 87, 104–5, 109, 115, 141
University Human Relations Council (UHRC), 131, 134–5, 153
University of Alabama, 9, 156
University of California (UC)
  UC Berkeley, 25, 27, 45, 48–9, 82, 90, 94, 121, 129, 143
  UCLA, 81, 127
University of Chicago, 5, 18, 23–9, 31–2, 34, 36, 41, 43, 47, 49, 51, 90, 122, 125, 147–8
University of Cincinnati, 37, 201n59

University of Florida, 156
University of Iowa, 25, 49
University of Kansas (KU)
   All Student Council (ASC), 62–3, 87, 129, 136, 208n11
   AWS and, 14, 16, 62–9, 71–85, 87–9, 96–7, 99–105, 112–18, 120–1, 124, 132–40, 144–64, 171–2, 175–6, 178, 180–3
   CEW and, 56
   Committee for Alternatives (KUCA), 142–3
   Coordinating Committee (KUCC), 143
   CORE and, 126
   Council on Student Affairs (COSA), 103–4, 106, 136, 139, 218n60
   CRC and, 127–31, 135
   February Sisters and, 13, 146, 163–8
   gay and lesbian students, 110–11
   IAWS and, 158–62, 180
   parietals and, 73–85, 88–9
   racial issues and, 125–30, 134
   rape awareness and prevention, 18, 113–18
   sex education and, 90, 94–6, 98–109
   student protests, 119–22, 125–30, 135–44, 146, 149–56
   UHRC, 131, 134
   Whistlestop initiative, 114–18
   see also February Sisters; Taylor, Emily
University of Kentucky, 123, 170, 203n68
University of Louisville, 37, 39, 53–4, 94
University of Maryland, 56, 151, 177
University of Massachusetts, 80
University of Michigan, 24, 28, 90, 152
University of Minnesota, 9, 25, 30, 34, 46, 49, 91, 170
University of Missouri, 25, 28, 49, 116, 202n64, 203n68
University of Nebraska, 25, 28, 49
University of Nevada, Reno, 160
University of North Dakota, 49
University of Oklahoma, 9, 160, 203n68
University of Pennsylvania, 4, 9, 56, 202n64, 203n68
University of Pittsburgh, 122–3, 125, 209n20
University of Rochester, 56
University of South Carolina Upstate, 173
University of Texas, 39, 203n68
University of Washington, 156
University of Wisconsin, 29, 46, 59, 160, 171
unplanned pregnancies, 13, 17–18, 89, 96, 98, 103, 105–9, 113, 118
Urban League, 39
Urbana College, 20, 95

van Kleeck, Mary, 28, 31
   see also WIS, New York Intercollegiate Bureau of Occupations; vocational guidance; vocational conferences
Vassar, 44–5, 123, 170
veterans, 41, 54–5, 59
   see also GI Bill
Vietnam War, 5, 121, 135, 141–3, 151
vocational conferences, 21, 26, 28–9, 31, 33–4, 37–8, 50, 176, 194n32, 196n38, 201n59
   see also Associated Women Students (AWS); careers and contingency planning; economic citizenship; National Vocational Guidance Association (NVGA); "occupational bureau" model; vocational guidance; Women's Bureau
vocational guidance, 9, 17, 27, 29–30, 32–4, 36, 38–9, 41–2, 122, 153, 155, 176
   see also Associated Women Students (AWS); careers and contingency planning; economic citizenship; National Vocational Guidance Association (NVGA); "occupational bureau" model; vocational guidance; Women's Bureau; Women's Educational and Industrial Union (WEIU)
Vocations for Social Change (Gay Folk), 137
Voigt, Irma, 123–4
Voorhees, Helen, 36, 39

voting, 7, 10, 44, 46–7, 50, 75, 78, 82, 121, 139, 142–3, 157, 160, 184
  see also political citizenship; suffrage
Vratil, Kathryn, 1

Wagner, Marjorie Downing, 178
Ward, Don, 105
Warriner, Charles, 131–2
Watkins Memorial Hospital (KU), 100, 102–4, 106, 109, 113, 135, 146, 164, 167–8
Watkins Scholars, 67
WDAF (radio station), 115
Wellesley College, 24, 28, 39
Wells, Agnes, 91, 93, 123
Wescoe, W. Clark, 73, 82–4, 119, 127–31, 139–41, 152, 183
Where the Boys Are (film), 97
Whistlestop intiative, 114–18
  see also feminism, radical; rape; sexual assault
White House Conference on Child Health and Protection, 92
White, Lynn, 55
Wilder, Audrey Kenyon, 91–2
Wilson College, 51
Wilson, Logan, 55
Wilson, Margaret, 43
Wilson, Pauline Park, 55
Wolf, Beverly, 10
Woman in Industry Service (WIS) agency, 31
  see also van Kleeck, Mary; Women's Bureau
Woman's College of Sewanee, Tennessee, 171
Women after College (Wilson), 55
Women in the Modern World (Komarovsky), 55, 64
Women in the Twentieth Century (Breckinridge), 36
Women's Bureau
  AAUW and, 27, 50, 56, 58, 147
  ACE and, 170
  activism and, 154, 158–61
  Anderson, Mary and, 24
  AWS and, 137
  CEW and, 56, 58
  civil rights and, 124, 147, 149–50

Cobble, Dorothy Sue and, 5, 12
  deans of women and, 3, 5, 30–3, 40–2, 50, 56, 58
  EEOC and, 150
  feminism and, 10, 17, 137, 151, 154
  IAWS and, 50, 147, 158–61
  Mueller, Kate Hevner and, 44, 57
  NADW and, 31–2, 39–41, 58, 64, 124
  NOW and, 16
  NWP and, 10
  OSU and, 38–9
  PCSW and, 149
  Taylor and, 3, 12, 15–16, 21, 33, 38, 44, 64, 71, 84–5, 137, 170, 172, 184
  van Kleeck, Mary and, 31
  WIS and, 31
  women's governance and, 154
  Zorbaugh, Marguerite and, 21, 36, 40–2
  see also Department of Labor; equal pay/pay equity; labor; National Vocational Guidance Association (NVGA); unions; vocational conferences; vocational guidance; Woman in Industry Service (WIS) agency; Zapoleon, Marguerite; Zorbaugh, Grace S.M.
Women's Coalition (WC), 138–9, 163–4, 168
  see also feminism, radical
Women's Foundation for Health (WFH), 91
  see also birth control; contraception; sex education
Women's Educational and Industrial Union (WEIU), 27–8, 30, 32, 36
  see also vocational guidance
Women's Equity Action League (WEAL), xvi, 3, 15, 151–2, 160–2, 227n19
women's liberation, 3–4, 9, 11, 15, 17, 43, 58, 71, 108, 113, 135–7, 139, 153, 156–7, 160, 163–4, 183
  see also feminism, radical

Women's Liberation Front (WLF), 139, 163
  see also feminism, radical; New Left
women's movement
  AWS and, 63, 144, 146, 154
  deans of women and, 5, 31, 44
  feminism and, 5–6, 58, 61, 71, 156–7, 159, 162–3, 172
  IAWS, 145–7, 149, 152, 155–62, 168
  NADW and, 162
  sexuality and, 88, 113
  Taylor and, 16, 44, 58, 61, 65, 146, 150
  waves, 4, 10, 18
  see also economic citizenship; Equal Rights Amendment; feminism; New Left; political citizenship; suffrage; women's liberation (see also for each of these and link to radical feminism and liberal feminism)
Women's Security Meeting, 114–15
Women's Self-Government Association, 46, 48–9, 191n4
  see also Associated Women Students (AWS); Intercollegiate Association of Women Students (IAWS); parietal rules; self-governance; student government
Women's studies, 1, 3, 10, 17, 145–6, 161, 168, 180, 183, 209n19, 230n45, 232n76
Women's Trade Union League, 5, 24, 31, 195n33
  see also Department of Labor; Women's Bureau
Woodhouse, Chase Going, 32–3, 36
Woodruff, Laurence C., 59, 61–2, 103, 131, 208n10
World War I, 30–1
World War II, 40–2, 52, 54–5, 59, 65, 88–9, 95, 97, 107, 120, 141, 143

"Young Women of the Year," 40
Young Women's Christian Association (YWCA), 33–5, 39, 51, 90–1, 94, 100, 120, 122–3, 127, 157–8, 161, 184, 194n32, 202n64
"Your Job Future After College" (pamphlet), 38
  see also Women's Bureau; vocational guidance; vocational conferences; economic citizenship; Marguerite Zapoleon

Zapoleon, Marguerite, 38–9, 50, 56, 154, 201n59
Zero Population Growth (ZPG), 99, 101, 103, 108
  see also birth control; contraception
Zorbaugh, Grace S.M.
  AAUW and, 28
  Anderson and, 50
  AWS and, 21
  Bloomfield and, 30
  deans of women and, 19–21
  economic citizenship and, 38–42
  OSU and, 33–8
  political citizenship and, 43–4
  Taylor and, 4, 19–21, 28, 44, 63–6, 71, 84, 120, 137, 147, 154, 177, 184
  vocational counseling and, 21
  Women's Bureau and, 21, 36, 40–2

GPSR Compliance

The European Union's (EU) General Product Safety Regulation (GPSR) is a set of rules that requires consumer products to be safe and our obligations to ensure this.

If you have any concerns about our products, you can contact us on

ProductSafety@springernature.com

In case Publisher is established outside the EU, the EU authorized representative is:

Springer Nature Customer Service Center GmbH
Europaplatz 3
69115 Heidelberg, Germany

www.ingramcontent.com/pod-product-compliance
Lightning Source LLC
LaVergne TN
LVHW051917060526
838200LV00004B/191